As one of the world's longest established and best-known travel brands, Thomas Cook are the experts in travel.

For more than 135 years our guidebooks have unlocked the secrets of destinations around the world, sharing with travellers a wealth of experience and a passion for travel.

Rely on Thomas Cook as your travelling companion on your next trip and benefit from our unique heritage.

G000069182

Thomas Cook **driving** guides

NORTHERN ITALY
& ITALIAN LAKES

Barbara Radcliffe Rogers, Stillman Rogers & Paul Karr

Your travelling companion since 1873

Written by Barbara Radcliffe Rogers, Stillman Rogers and Paul Karr; updated by Barbara Radcliffe Rogers
Original photography by Barbara Radcliffe Rogers and Stillman Rogers

Published by Thomas Cook Publishing
A division of Thomas Cook Tour Operations Limited
Company registration no. 3772199 England
The Thomas Cook Business Park, Unit 9, Coningsby Road,
Peterborough PE3 8SB, United Kingdom
Email: books@thomascook.com, Tel: + 44 (0) 1733 416477
www.thomascookpublishing.com

Produced by Cambridge Publishing Management Limited
Burr Elm Court, Main Street, Caldecote CB23 7NU
www.cambridgepm.co.uk

ISBN: 978-1-84848-379-8

© 2005, 2007, 2009 Thomas Cook Publishing
This fourth edition © 2011
Text © Thomas Cook Publishing
Maps © Thomas Cook Publishing/PCGraphics (UK) Limited

Series Editor: Karen Beaulah
Production/DTP: Steven Collins

Printed and bound in India by Replika Press Pvt Ltd

Cover photography © Angeli Nicola/SIME-4Corners

About the authors

Barbara and **Stillman Rogers** have lived and travelled in northern Italy since post-university days, when they moved to Verona. Their travels have followed their personal interests, which include mountain hikes, medieval villages, local foods, architecture and history. They return to Italy year after year because, although it may seem as though every corner of the country has been catalogued by the 'Grand Tour' writers, many surprises still await the curious traveller. The Rogers are the authors of several other Thomas Cook guides.

Paul Karr has authored, co-authored or edited more than two dozen guidebooks for a variety of publishers, including guides to Rome, Vienna, Montreal, Denmark, and British Columbia.

Acknowledgements

Barbara and Stillman Rogers wish to thank all the people who helped them in their travels and writing: Stephanie Jukes-Amer, Guy Geslin, Randy Stuart, Melissa Parella and Sandra Milani, who operates Bassano del Grappa tourist office, the most helpful we encountered in the whole of northern Italy. Particular thanks go to Marina Tavolato and Chiara Angella for introducing us to some of Italy's finest hotels and restaurants. Also thanks to friends who enriched our travels by sharing their own favourite Italian places: Sara Bergstresser, Juliette Rogers, Erick Castellanos and Christopher Catling, and to Liz and George Bowden for our first introduction to our Italian home. A big *grazie* goes to Rita Cagne, Claudio and Christina Cagne and Roberto Cagne for their advice, friendship and hospitality.

Paul Karr gives very special thanks to Martha Coombs for research assistance and companionship.

The authors would also like to thank Deborah Parker, Edith Summerhayes, Charlotte Christensen, Karen Beaulah and Stuart McLaren for their wise guidance and editing.

Contents

About driving guides

The Anglicised spellings of Florence, Genoa, Mantua, Milan, Padua, Turin and Venice have been used throughout this guide. However, their Italian spellings (Firenze, Genova, Mantova, Milano, Padova, Torino and Venezia) have been added whenever they are mentioned in the gazetteer tour sections. This will make it easier to recognise road signs and also make it possible to ask directions from local residents, who might not recognise the English version.

Thomas Cook's driving guides are designed to provide you with a comprehensive and flexible reference source to guide you as you tour a country or region by car. This guide divides northern Italy's lakes and mountains region into 24 touring areas – one per chapter. Major cities form chapters of their own. Each chapter provides enough attractions for at least a day's activities, usually more.

Ratings

To make it easier for you to plan your time and decide what to see, every area is rated according to its attractions in categories such as Architecture, Scenery and Children.

Chapter contents

Each chapter begins by summing up the area's main attractions and characteristics, including any special travel information, such as road conditions. A ratings box highlights the area's strengths and weaknesses – some areas may be more attractive to families travelling with children, others to wine lovers visiting vineyards and others to people interested in finding castles, churches or beaches. Each chapter is then divided into an alphabetical gazetteer, with a suggested tour. You can decide whether you just want to visit a particular sight or attraction, choosing from those described in the gazetteer, or whether you want to tour the whole area. If the latter, you can construct your own itinerary, or follow the suggested tour at the end of each chapter. In cities, these are walking tours.

The gazetteer

The gazetteer section describes all the major attractions of the area: villages, towns, historic sites, natural areas or parks, and the most interesting museums and sights in a city. Maps of the areas highlight the places described in the text. This comprehensive overview of the area helps you choose which sights to visit. One way to use the guide is simply to find individual sights that interest you, using the index or overview map, and reading what the authors have to say about them. This will help you decide whether to visit the sight. If you do, you will find plenty of practical information, such as the street address and opening times. Alternatively, you can choose a hotel, perhaps with the help of the accommodation suggestions contained in this guide, and decide what to see in its area. Use the 'northern Italy at a glance' map on pages 8–9 to see which chapters in the book describe cities and regions closest to your chosen touring base.

Symbol Key

ℹ Tourist Information Centre

🚭 Advice on arriving or departing

🅿 Parking locations

🅰 Advice on getting around

🠖 Directions

🛈 Sights and attractions

🅲 Accommodation

🅜 Eating

⬤ Shopping

⬤ Entertainment

🆆 Website

Practical information

The practical information in the page margins will help you locate services you need as an independent traveller, including the Tourist Information Centre (TIC), car parks and public transport. Here, too, are opening times and addresses of museums, churches and other attractions, as well as useful tips on parking, shopping, market days and festivals.

Driving tours

The suggested tour is just that – a suggestion, with plenty of optional detours and ideas for making your own discoveries, under the heading 'Also worth exploring'. The routes are designed to link the attractions described in the gazetteer and to cover outstanding buildings, historic sites and scenic coastal, lakeside, mountain and rural landscapes. The total distance is given for each tour, as is the time it will take you to drive the complete route. Bear in mind that this time just covers driving; you will have to add on extra time for visiting attractions along the way. Many of the routes are circular, so you can join them at any point. Sometimes you will use one part of an itinerary as a link route to get from one area of the book to another. Other links are suggested at the beginning of each route, helping you to tie these routes together into your own custom-designed itinerary. As you follow the route descriptions, you will find names picked out in bold capital letters – this means that the place is described fully in the gazetteer. Other names picked out in bold indicate additional villages or attractions worth a brief stop along the route.

Accommodation and food

In each chapter you will find lodging and dining recommendations for individual towns and villages, or for the area as a whole. These cover a range of price brackets, which concentrate on more characterful small hotels and restaurants, while also identifying the best options. In addition, you will find details in the 'Travel facts' chapter on international chain hotels, with a telephone number you can ring for information. The price indications used in this guide are in euros and have the following meanings:

€   budget
€€   typical/average prices
€€€   de luxe

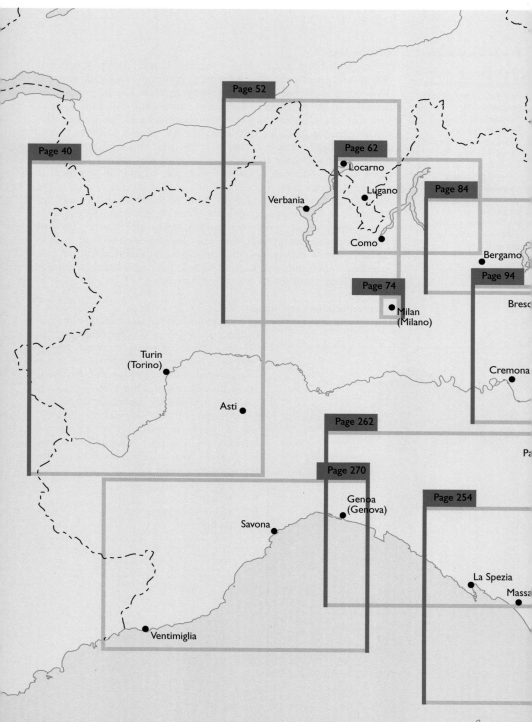

Page 52

Page 40

Page 62

Locarno

Lugano

Page 84

Verbania

Como

Bergamo

Page 74

Page 94

Milan
(Milano)

Bresc

Turin
(Torino)

Cremona

Asti

Page 262

Pa

Page 270

Genoa
(Genova)

Page 254

Savona

La Spezia

Massa

Ventimiglia

Page 134

Page 144

Page 152

Page 186

Bolzano

Page 102

Page 126

Page 160

Belluno

Udine

Page 198

Page 208

Treviso

Trieste

Vicenza

Page 116

Page 220

Page 170

Verona

Padua
(Padova)

Venice
(Venezia)

Mantua
(Mantova)

Page 226

Bologna

Page 246

ucca

Page 234

Prato

Florence
(Firenze)

Introduction

The very name – Italy – brings a dreamy look to the eyes of those who
have travelled or lived there. But a special fraternity exists among
those whose time was spent in the north – for north and south are,
even in the minds of many Italians, two separate Italys.

Northern Italy is a physically beautiful land. Overlooking its dark
blue lakes, candy-coloured villas cluster on lush green hillsides with
white mountain peaks behind them. Deep green vineyards spread
along the valley floors and climb the foothills. Where the land drops
to the sea, it spills into long, white beaches on the Adriatic and falls in
breathtaking cliffs into the Mediterranean. In an easy day, the traveller
can drive from sea level at the Venetian lagoons to mountain passes of
more than 2,000 metres. The Ligurian Coast south of Genoa is hardly
undiscovered, especially the postcard town of Portofino, artfully
arranged about its harbour full of the pleasure craft of the rich and
famous. But other less well-known towns are equally pleasant:
including the five cliff-hung villages of the Cinque Terre, which you
can explore from a walking path that skirts the vertiginous headlands.
Castles guard the Adige Valley from their craggy pinnacles, while a
handful of towns – Castelfranco, Marostica, Soave and others – are
completely encircled by defensive walls. Entire villages and city
centres are filled with buildings whose ages are counted in centuries.
Other sites – from baths and villas built by the Romans to medieval
castles – lie in splendid and romantic ruin, leaving much to the
traveller's imagination. Like a glittering gem in this setting is Venice.
Images of its canals are so familiar that nearly every traveller dreams of
someday standing in Piazza San Marco. But no matter how familiar its
scenes, Venice continues to charm and to offer new secrets to those
who stray from the usual St Mark's-to-Rialto route.

Echoing some of Venice's influence, but overlaid with their own
individual histories and architecture, are the golden trio of Padua,
Verona and Vicenza. These three cities are quite different in
appearance – Vicenza seems a living design book of the great architect
Palladio – but share a warmth and local ambience that is harder to
find in Venice. They also share a wealth of the world's great
Renaissance art. Villas, basilicas, cathedrals and modest parish
churches here and throughout the Veneto have major works by
Giotto, Tintoretto, Titian, Veronese and their contemporaries. At the
southern edge of this guide's scope is Florence, birthplace of the
Renaissance and perhaps the world's greatest repository of its art. Like
Venice, few corners have escaped description, although even here a
traveller can penetrate the veneer of tourism, but not before joining
the throngs to see the unmatched treasures the city displays.

Yet northern Italy offers so much more than castles, canals, art and dramatic scenery. Hidden in its valleys and dotting its lagoons and craggy coast are stunning gardens, prehistoric carvings, Celtic and Lombard sites, medieval villages, fresco-painted buildings, towns devoted to a single variety of wine, and tiny regions with their own unique cultures and even languages. The culture of this region is rich and ancient, benefiting from the many peoples who have invaded or passed through. Many of the latter were so charmed by the land that they settled there, adding their own civilisation to that they found. As you travel you will meet examples of art, architecture, traditions, even languages that reflect everyone from the barbarian hordes to the Habsburgs and Napoleon. The Lombards and the Roman legionnaires who stayed to found the Ladin communities are good examples of those who chose to stay. A unique layer of culture, even history, has also been added by the many foreign visitors – mainly writers and poets – who lived here, including Goethe, Byron, Browning, Joyce and Hemingway. So enchanting are the surroundings that everyone from Shakespeare to Cole Porter has used it for a setting, adding yet another layer to its mystique.

While it may seem that hardly a sight in Italy has escaped the catalogues of centuries of ciceroni, you can still discover delightful places unmentioned in guidebooks or in the memoirs of the Grand Tour's literati. Approach Italy with a sense of discovery. Stray awhile from its well-trod cities, into its soaring mountains, into the 'little Venices' of the Veneto, up Alpine slopes for an unfamiliar perspective on the Matterhorn, into the vineyards of the Cinque Terre and to the eastern-influenced towns of the borderlands. You'll meet an Italy few travellers know.

Below
Venice from the Grand Canal

Travel facts

Accommodation

Italy offers a full range of accommodation, from some of the world's most elegant hotels to places where you'd rather not stay. Fortunately, the latter are few. Lines are blurred between a small *albergo* (hotel) and a *locanda* (inn) or *alloggio* (lodging house), although the latter is usually cheaper. Another alternative, *agriturismo* (agricultural tourism), brings you closer to local life by staying at farmhouses or wine estates. Many serve meals featuring the farm's products, such as their own cheeses. Since each has only a few rooms, always phone ahead or ask a Tourist Information Centre (TIC) to call. Each region has its own listings booklet, often with pictures. You should confirm the rate when reserving and ask for a fax or email confirmation when booking ahead. Always book ahead and get a fax or email confirmation for the month of August, the Easter holidays, in big cities and for your arrival night. Lodgings are inspected regularly and given stars, and although the criteria are often irrelevant to travellers, the stars do give some guidance. Two-star hotel rooms usually have private bathrooms, three-star rooms telephones and television.

Airports

Northern Italy's major international airport is Malpensa, north of Milan. Flights within Europe arrive and depart at Milan's smaller Linate airport and at airports in Bologna, Genoa, Florence, Pisa, Venice and Verona. Malpensa is about halfway between Milan and Lake Maggiore, so motorists bound for it or Lake Como can avoid encountering the city. Buses connect Milan's Centrale railway station to Malpensa every half-hour €€ and Linate every 20 minutes €.

International chain hotels

Best Western:
www.bestwestern.com
Aus 1 800 131 779
Ire 800 709 101
NZ 0 800 237 893
SA 0 800 994 284
UK 0800 393130
USA 1 800 780 7234

Space Hotels:
www.spacehotels.it
Italy 800 813 013
UK 0500 303030
USA/Canada 1 800 843 3311

Ibis:
www.ibishotel.com or contact individual hotels direct.

Labour strikes are very common in Italy and may occur suddenly as you are about to board your plane for Pisa or Milan, cancelling all flights. Alternatively, a rail strike may begin the day you leave, making it difficult to get to your departure city without a car. Try to arrange pick-up and return of cars at the airport, or to allow extra time to reach your departure point. During a rail strike, hire cars are almost impossible to get.

Above
Street car, Milan

Right
Hams and sausages, Bergamo

Children

Although Italians do not travel often with their children, they are most tolerant and quite pleasant about fussy children or crying babies. Don't expect special seats or menus for children in restaurants. It is wise to bring a folding high chair. Bring safety seats for children, too, as many car-hire companies add an extra daily charge for these, if they have them. Lodgings can often supply a baby cot or rollaway bed: ask when booking. Supermarkets supply infant needs, but plan ahead for limited Italian opening times.

Climate

The northern mountains moderate what would otherwise be a hot, dry, Mediterranean climate, but summer is hot nearly everywhere. In the mountains, rain showers are common in spring, summer and autumn, and snow accumulations are high in winter. In the lakes region, sunshine averages 3–4 hours daily in the winter and more than 9 in summer. In the Venetian plain, Milan, Turin and the Po Valley, summers are very hot and sunny, but winters (December–February) are surprisingly cool – colder than London – with snow, fog and rain common. In Tuscany, temperatures are hotter in the summer, more temperate in winter. Tuscany's summer heat can be unremitting in lower and coastal areas.

Currency

Currency-exchange facilities are in all airports, near the arrival gates; those in Malpensa are open 24 hours. Avoid the cash-changing machines; the rates are usurious. Also avoid carrying large amounts of cash, but if you do, hide it well. Safer are traveller's cheques and easier are credit or debit cards. Traveller's cheques are accepted at banks (after much paperwork), large hotels and by some larger stores in cities and major tourist areas, but are difficult to cash elsewhere. If possible, bring at least one major credit card; VISA is the most commonly accepted. Most small hotels, *agriturismo* properties and small restaurants do not accept cards.

ATMs (*bancomat*) offer the best exchange rates, are found everywhere and never close. Check with your bank or card issuer before leaving home to learn which network you can use in Italy. Make sure that your PIN can be used abroad. A credit card is less economical to use for cash advances than one issued by your bank that draws directly on your account, but either assures the best commercial exchange rate. Banks are usually open Monday–Friday 0830–1300 or 1330, often reopening for an hour later in the afternoon. Don't let your supply of euros get low at the weekend, since banks, often even in train stations and airports, will be closed.

ATMs may be out of money or out of order. Try to arrive with euros, especially on a weekend.

Customs and entry formalities

Citizens of the European Union (EU) can enter Italy for an unlimited stay with a valid passport. Citizens of Australia, Canada, New Zealand and the USA can also enter Italy with a passport (valid for at least three months from entry date); no visa is required for a stay of up to 90 days. There are no taxes or duty on articles for personal use that you take into Italy, including reasonable amounts of tobacco and alcoholic drinks.

Eating and drinking

Tip waiters about 5 per cent over the included service charge, unless a waiter has gone to extraordinary measures. Expect a modest *coperto* or cover charge at most restaurants.

Good food is so widely appreciated that dining places abound. Locals eat out frequently, so except in large cities, most restaurants offer good value at moderate prices. A trattoria usually has a more limited menu and lower prices than a *ristorante*. In smaller ones, there may be no menu at all, but the waiter will describe the day's offerings. An *osteria* is a wine bar that serves snacks and sometimes a few dishes, usually changing daily. When a place has a written menu, it will be posted at the door.

Fish and shellfish, except calamari (squid), are pricier than meat. A standard primo (first course) is a large serving of pasta or risotto (rice). A secondo (main course) is typically smaller, containing only the meat and perhaps a garnish. Vegetables and salads are ordered separately. Part of the fun of dining in Italy is sampling the infinite variety of pasta shapes, flavours and textures. Each town seems to have its own special kind, often a variation on the ravioli, filled with anything from cheese or meat to pumpkin. If breakfast is not included in the lodging price, cafés are better value than hotel breakfasts. For plain bread rolls, ask for panini. Coffee with hot milk – cappuccino or caffè latte – is drunk only at breakfast in Italy. Coffee ordered at any other time

Left
Rapallo Castle

Right
Harbour, Vernazza

Electricity
Italy operates at 220 volts. UK appliances will work, but require an adaptor to the European-type plug with two round prongs. American appliances need a transformer and an adaptor.

of day will automatically be espresso. Traditionally, Italians eat their main meal in the middle of the day, although this is changing somewhat in cities. Meal hours are generally lunch 1200–1430 or 1500, dinner 1900–2200, later in summer resort areas and cities. In small towns, hours may be more limited. Italians usually arrive for the evening meal at about 2000, so go earlier if you don't have a reservation on a busy night.

Italy may not be known for as many 'great' wines as France, but it has many very good ones. These itineraries take you through some of Italy's best-known wine regions. You may recognise many of the towns described here as familiar from wine labels: Bardolino, Valpolicella, Soave. Wine areas are scattered, but most are in pockets in the north. From Piedmont try Barbaresco, Barbera d'Alba and Barolo for reds and Gavi or Roero Arneis for whites. In the Veneto the best reds are Valpolicella (fairly light) and the heartier Bardolino from the shores of Lake Garda; for whites taste Soave, Lugana and Bianco di Custoza. The best-known Italian wine, Chianti, comes from Tuscany, around Florence. No matter where you are, the local *vino di tavola* is always worth a try. Ask (*prova?*) for a taste.

Health

Italy is generally a healthy place to travel; drinking water is normally safe (although savvy travellers usually drink bottled varieties). No immunisations are required to enter. For minor medical problems, ask at a chemist's (*farmacia*). These take turns staying open for emergencies; normal hours are Monday–Friday 0830–1230 and 1630–1900. For more serious illness or injury, a Tourist Information Centre (TIC) or hotel can suggest English-speaking doctors. Bring

Right
Balcony with flowers, Belluno

enough prescription medications for the entire trip, with a copy of the prescription in generic form, plus aspirin, available only in chemist's.

Visitors from the EU should carry a European Health Insurance Card, and present it if medical treatment is required. The card is available free from *www.ehic.org.uk*, by phoning *0845 606 2030* or from post offices.

Information

Towns of any size have TICs, usually called APT, IAT or ARPT, and usually found at the main railway station or piazza. Except in large towns, these are normally closed in the midday period. Normal hours are Monday–Saturday 0900–1300 and 1600–1800 or 1900; shorter in winter. Some can make lodging reservations; all can suggest options. They vary greatly in helpfulness and you usually have to request brochures singly rather than being able to gather them from display racks. Some offices offer useful booklets of detailed dining, shopping, lodging and attractions listings, with current opening hours. Remember opening hours in Italy change faster than the phases of the moon!

Information online

Internet
Nearly all large and some small hotels offer Wi-Fi in public areas (often in rooms) or can provide cable connection, with or without a charge for in-room use. Wi-Fi and public Internet is not as widely available as it was a few years ago – Brescia, for example, has very few public Internet points and some towns have none at all; ask at the tourist office or your hotel.

These are a few of the more useful websites:

*   *www.enit.it*   Italian state tourist office
*   *www.regione.umbria.it*   Umbria tourism
*   *www.beniculturali.it*   links to museums
*   *www.aboutflorence.com*   Florence tourism
*   *www.lagodigarda.it*   Lake Garda tourism
*   *www.veniceforvisitors.com*   Venice visitor information
*   *www.aguestinvenice.com*   events and art in Venice
*   *www.turismovenezia.it*   Venice tourism
*   *http://seuropetravel.suite101.com*   northern Italy tourism and culture

Insurance

Experienced travellers carry insurance covering their belongings and holiday investment as well as their health. Travel insurance should include provision for cancelled or delayed flights, as well as immediate

Postal services

Post offices are normally open *Mon–Fri 0830–1400 (often until 1930 in cities) and Sat 0830–1200.* Be sure you go to the right counter for *francobolli* (stamps), or buy them in a *tabacaio* (tobacconist). Mail delivery is unreliable.

Public holidays

The public holidays are:
1 Jan: New Year's Day
6 Jan: Epiphany
Mar/Apr: Easter Monday
25 Apr: Liberation Day
1 May: Labour Day
Jun: Corpus Christi
2 Jun: Anniversary of the Republic
15 Aug: Feast of the Assumption
1 Nov: All Saints' Day
7 Nov: WWI Victory Anniversary Day
8 Dec: Immaculate Conception
25 Dec: Christmas Day
26 Dec: St Stephen's Day
31 Dec: New Year's Eve

Below
The Dolomite Alps near Cortina d'Ampezzo

evacuation home in the case of medical emergency. EU citizens are entitled to free emergency medical care in a public hospital. Showing a passport might be enough but you should carry a European Health Insurance Card; *see Health on pages 16–17.* Non-EU citizens are only covered if they have travel insurance.

Italy's tourism offices

Australia *Italian Consulate, Level 45, Gateway, 1 Macquarie Place, Sydney NSW 2000; tel: 02 9392 7900; fax: 02 9392 7980; email: info.sydney@esteri.it; www.conssydney.esteri.it*
Canada *110 Yonge St, Suite 503, Toronto, Ontario; tel: 416 925 4882; fax: 416 925 4799; brochure hotline: 416 925 3870; www.italiantourism. com or www.ctcpi.ca*
New Zealand *Italian Embassy, 34–38 Grant Rd, Thorndon, Wellington; tel: 04 473 5339; email: ambasciata.wellington@esteri.it; www. ambwellington.esteri.it*
UK *1 Princes St, London W1R 8AY; tel: 020 7408 1254; fax: 020 7399 3567; email: info@italiantouristboard.co.uk; www.italiantouristboard.co.uk*
USA *630 Fifth Avenue, Suite 1565, New York, NY 10111; tel: 212 245 5618; fax: 212 586 9249. 500 North Michigan Avenue, Suite 501, Chicago, IL 60611; tel: 312 644 0996; fax: 312 644 3109. 12400 Wilshire Boulevard, Suite 550, Los Angeles, CA 90025; tel: 310 820 1898; fax: 310 820 6357; www.italiantourism.com*

Language

Italian is one of the easiest languages to learn. There are almost no silent letters, so once you learn the few simple pronunciation rules, you can pronounce a word when you see it. Italian has fewer words than most other Latin-based languages and synonyms are few. Those who read other Romance languages, especially Spanish, will be able to read Italian. Italians are hospitable and quite adept at speaking with their hands, so you will find understanding and being understood quite easy and often entertaining. In the Dolomites, especially in the Sud Tirol (southern Tyrol) and around Lake Garda, German is widely spoken. Always ask, for good manners' sake, if someone speaks English or another language, before launching into it. In heavily travelled areas, those who deal most with travellers speak some English. Italians are good natured about

Senior citizens

Older people are usually treated with respect by young people, especially in smaller towns. You will sometimes find discounts, but may find that Avis is the only car-hire agency that will provide cars for drivers over the age of 75. Leasing a car from Renault Eurodrive is a way of getting around this regressive policy.

Toilets

Petrol stations on the autostrada, museums and bus and train stations will nearly always have toilets (*Uomini* for men and *Donne* for women). Elsewhere, public toilets are a rare surprise. Most cafés don't object if you go in just to use the toilet. Although they are less common with each passing year, be prepared in smaller and rural settings for the 'Turkish toilet' – essentially a hole in the floor flanked by two ceramic footprints.

their language and your inability to speak it, and are very pleased when you try even a smiling *buon giorno*. (*See also page 280*.)

Opening times

Expect all but the largest museums, shops and offices to close during the midday period. Closing times vary at 1200–1300; reopening is most often at 1400 or 1500, but may be even later, especially in the summer. Churches are notoriously irregular and inconsistent in their opening hours, but are usually open 0900–1300 and 1500–1900. These and smaller museums may not even be open during the hours that are clearly listed on their tightly closed doors. Don't blame your guidebook, tourist brochure or the tourist office for not having up-to-date opening hours; these may have changed last Tuesday and will change again next Friday. This is Italy, where time is often secondary to nearly everything else. Many shops are closed on Monday morning. Food stores are usually closed on Wednesday afternoon. Major supermarkets near large cities, department stores in cities and petrol stations on the autostrada stay open during the middle of the day. In tourist places or during the summer, shops may remain open longer. However, many businesses, even restaurants, take a holiday in August. Banks are generally open Monday–Friday 0830–1300 and 1430–1600 (later on Thursday).

Packing

Pack comfortable clothing that you can layer for warmth. The Italians are a bit more formal in the evening than other Europeans, even in beach resort areas, but are not overly dressy otherwise. Even casual clothes are usually smart and stylish. Jeans are acceptable daywear nearly anywhere, but shorts are usually not allowed in churches and frowned on at evening meals. Take a raincoat or umbrella; warm clothes and waterproofs are essential for the mountains year-round. Bring suntan lotion or sunblock for the beach and high altitudes, where the sun is stronger. Essential medications should accompany you, not be packed in checked baggage. A small daypack is handy for carrying picnic lunches, guidebooks and small items, and can double as a spare carry-on for the trip home (travelling to Italy it can fold flat in your suitcase). If you plan to buy Venetian glassware or pottery, bring several sheets of bubble-wrap packing material for the trip home.

Safety and security

Crimes against tourists in Italy are usually from pickpockets, bag-snatchers and car thieves. Be careful, especially in cities and major tourist areas, of your personal possessions. Thieves use motorcycles to approach as close as possible to pedestrians, grab cameras or handbags and speed off into traffic. Florence has a real drug and crime problem, so take special care there. Gypsies can be a problem, especially in the Milan train stations. Some use children, who slip up unnoticed and filch a wallet with deft small fingers. Always carry money and documents in body-wallets, with only enough out for immediate needs. Lock cars and hide any sign of being a tourist, such as maps or guidebooks. Tourists' cars are a target, since they are assumed to have luggage in the boot. If a robbery does occur, report it immediately to the police, to support insurance claims. Carrying identification, such as a passport, is required by law. Although Italian drivers are usually skilful at avoiding pedestrians, they often come perilously close. Before stepping into a street, be sure you're not sharing it with a car.

Below
Arcaded street, Conegliano

Shopping

Shops close during the midday period, usually at 1300. Except in resorts, they close Sunday and often Monday morning. Tourist shops may open longer hours. Local crafts include ceramics and pottery, glass (Venice), lace (be careful, most is imported), leather goods, gilded wooden boxes and trays (Florence), and hand-bound books and marbled papers (Florence and Venice). The last may include beautifully crafted albums or items as small as a bookmark or pocket address book. In Venice, buy carnival masks from a studio where they are made. Italian fashions are very pricey, but even the most expensive shops have sales in July. Street and flea markets are good places to shop, but don't expect to see many real antiques. Be careful shipping goods home; be sure the store is reliable and used to dealing with international shipments. The success rate of Italian mail is about 50 per cent.

Time

Italy is GMT plus I hour in winter and 2 hours ahead from the end of March to the end of September. To many Italians, especially in smaller towns, time is not particularly important, so be prepared for delays and unexpected closures.

Home country direct

To access your own telecom service when placing a call from Italy, use the following direct dial numbers:
Australia: *Optus 172 1161*; *Telstra 172 1061*
Canada: *172 1001*
Ireland: *172 0353*
New Zealand: *172 1064*
UK: *BT 172 0044*;
NTL 172 054
USA: *AT&T 172 1011*; *MCI 172 1022*; *Sprint 172 1877*

Mobile phones

UK, New Zealand and Australian mobiles will work in Italy; those from the USA and Canada will not unless fitted with the GSM European standard. Travellers from the USA and Canada can get a universal mobile from Mobal, a UK firm whose mobiles work worldwide, with a permanent UK number (*UK tel: 1543 426999; fax: 1543 426126; www.mobal.co.uk; USA tel: 888 888 9162 (free call) or 212 785 5800; www.mobalrental.com*). To call a number from a mobile phone with a non-Italian number, dial 0039 before the number.

Sport

While active sports are less generally enjoyed by Italians, those who do cycle, climb, hike or ski are very enthusiastic. In the Dolomites, hiking trails are well marked and generally in good repair, but Italians elsewhere are not avid walkers, so trails in other places are relatively few. One notable exception is the corniche path connecting the towns of the Cinque Terre in Liguria. Italian drivers are usually quite considerate towards cyclists (more so than they are of pedestrians) who share the roads. Tuscany and the Piedmont are favourite venues of packaged cycling tours. Skiing, especially downhill, is popular in the Dolomites and Alps, where there are world-class ski resorts. For watersports, Lake Garda is the best, especially for windsurfing, although their sails are a common sight on northern Lake Como, as well.

Telephones

Telephone numbers are still changing, so if you can't get through, check to see if a digit has been added. Printed materials – even 'official' – often lag far behind reality. Ask a TIC or hotel desk to help if you cannot reach a number. Avoid making international calls from your hotel room; the surcharges can far exceed the price of the call. The easiest way to make a telephone call is to buy a card (*carta telefonica*) from any newsstand. Some of these work only in certain phones, so it is wise to buy them in small denominations. If you find a phone that doesn't use your card, the nearest tobacconist or newsstand will have the right one. You must snap the corner off a phonecard before using it. *A numero verde* (green number) is a free call within Italy. To call or fax Italy from outside the country, dial the international network access code 00, then 39, then the area code, including the initial 0, and then the number. To make an international call from Italy, dial the international network access code 00, then the country code (Australia = 61, Republic of Ireland = 353, New Zealand = 64, UK = 44, USA and Canada = 1), followed by the area code, omitting the first digit, and then the number.

Travellers with disabilities

Except in the cities, where a few more places have wheelchair access, facilities for mobility-impaired travellers are poor. In Venice they are virtually unknown. Airports are mostly wheelchair accessible and major hotels usually have a few rooms adapted, but travel can be very difficult otherwise. Most museums, theatres and public buildings are not ramped. Parking is free in special blue zones for cars with an international disabled sticker. For current information, contact **RADAR**, *12 City Forum, 250 City Rd, London EC1V 8AF; tel: 020 7250 3222* or visit *www.radar.org.uk*

Driver's guide

Accidents

Emergency telephone numbers
Police (*carabinieri*) Tel: 112.

Ambulance (*ambulanza*) Tel: 113.

ACI Breakdown Service (Italian Automobile Association, for road assistance) Tel: 116.

You must stop after any accident. Summon the police, *carabinieri* (*tel: 112*, the EU universal emergency number) or *pronto soccorso* (*tel: 113*) for medical assistance. Place emergency triangles in the road to alert approaching vehicles. Exchange insurance details with other drivers and complete a European Accident Statement form, which you should obtain from your own insurers before leaving home. Remain at the scene until police arrive, stay calm and request an English-speaking interpreter to assist you in making a statement. Notify the police of any injury, however slight.

Automobile associations

Automobile Club d'Italia (ACI) *V. Marsala 8, 00185 Rome; tel: 064 998 234, toll free in Italy 803 116; www.aci.it*

Members of UK automobile associations can extend their services to Italy, which gives them access to the Automobile Club d'Italia (ACI) *Via Marsala 8, 00185 Rome; tel: 064 998 234.* For advance assistance with motoring routes and up-to-date road information, visit *www.theaa.com* (for AA members) or *www.rac.co.uk* (for RAC members).

Autostrade

Most major limited-access motorways in Italy are autostrade (singular: autostrada) toll roads, designated by 'A' in their route number. Rare exceptions are those motorways whose route numbers are prefixed with 'E', which do not charge tolls. On most, you take a ticket as you enter the autostrada and pay according to the distance travelled as you exit. You can pay tolls with euros in cash or by VISA credit card.

Breakdowns

The first thing to do if you have a breakdown is to pull over, if possible; then place a warning triangle 100m behind the vehicle. Then call *116* for assistance. The tow-truck driver will probably not speak English but he will come equipped with a multilingual auto parts manual. You will have to pay for towing and parts. Members of automobile associations in their own country should be able to arrange for coverage. Enquire at your local automobile association about a letter of introduction or ETI booklet. If you are not a member of an automobile association that provides this service, it is wise to

Drinking and driving
Italy has strict limits on the level of blood alcohol a driver can have – 0.05 l per cent. To exceed this is to risk severe penalties.
A driver with a high level who is involved in an accident also risks being automatically held at fault.

Essentials
All vehicles must carry a portable warning triangle to place in the road in case of breakdown or other traffic-blocking situation. This device is called a *triangolo*. A recently passed law requires wearing a reflective safety vest if you are walking on a motorway. While you are not required to carry one, you will be breaking the law if you must walk to an emergency phone without one. These may be obtained by post from *www.rspp.co.uk*. If you drive your own vehicle from the UK, you must have headlight converters to adjust the beam to the right.

take out a continental breakdown insurance policy, so that the details will be handled by a multilingual specialist.

Caravans and camper vans (trailers and RVs)

Camping and caravanning is not so popular among Italians as it is among northern Europeans, and campsites are not as plentiful. But they do exist, especially around popular family tourist areas, such as Lake Garda and the Adriatic Coast east of Venice. To book ahead, and to obtain a camping carnet and list of campsites, contact Centro Internazionale Prenotazioni Campeggio, *Casella Postale 23, 50041 Calenzano, Firenze; tel: 055 882 391; www.federcampeggio.it*. Local and regional tourist offices also offer illustrated directories of campsites or include them in their lodging guides.

The speed limit for caravans in excess of 3.5 tonnes and for camper vans is 100kph on autostrade, 80kph on highways and country roads and 50kph in towns. Remember that engine efficiency decreases by about 10 per cent with each 3,000ft of altitude, so if you are driving in the mountains and towing a trailer, a non-turbo car may not be able to manage the incline.

Documents

Drivers from EU nations and the United States need only their own current driving licence; others should have an International Driving Permit in addition to their original permit. In practice, it is advisable to carry an International Driving Permit even if you are not required to do so, since it translates your own licence into Italian. You must get these in your own country, usually through an automobile association (you usually do not need to be a member). If driving your own car, you must have its registration and insurance documents in the car at all times. It is also important to get a card from your insurer to prove that you have third-party coverage.

Driving in northern Italy and Italian lakes

Touring in Italy is a challenge to even the best driver. Italians drive at outrageous speeds, often whizzing in and out between cars with death-defying abandon. Roads range from state-of-the-art autostrade to winding mountain roads not quite two cars wide. The most nerve-racking problem, apart from Italian drivers, is the number of mountain roads with precipitous drop-offs, some of which have no safety barriers. Avoid these roads in the rain or in winter, and at night. In fact, it is wise to avoid night driving entirely, allowing enough time for daylight arrivals.

Traffic jams lasting several hours are not uncommon when an accident blocks an autostrada (which is a compelling reason to carry both snacks and drinking water with you). Mountain roads can be

Fines

An estimated 15 per cent of drivers in Italy are stopped for speeding, which is a remarkably low number when you consider the disregard most Italian drivers show for speed limits. On-the-spot tickets are issued, and you should be prepared to pay. Although everything in Italy is flexible, the usual fines are €32–125 for speeds under 10kph over the limit (rarely even noticed except in especially hazardous places). Between 11 and 40kph above the limit, the fines are €125–500. Over 40kph in excess means a fine of €500–1,250, plus loss of your driving permit. Drivers are not jailed for speeding in Italy.

narrow and the switchbacks over steep mountain passes will leave you breathless. When choosing a route, be sure to check the map for the tiny chevron marks or inverted brackets that indicate steep grades and passes. Don't be surprised to meet a car rounding a tight corner on a precipitous road with at least half the car in your lane, or to meet motorcycles entirely in your lane. Be alert and defensive at all times and if you want to look at the stunning mountain scenery, pull into a lay-by. The road needs your full attention at every instant.

The most immediate problem will be for those from left-hand drive countries, such as the UK and South Africa, since Italians drive on the right. In normal traffic, it will begin to seem natural as you follow other drivers. But at roundabouts or on dual-lane highways, it becomes more difficult, because your natural instincts give you the wrong signals. Be especially alert and continue to remind yourself of this danger.

The most difficult time for some is in starting out in the morning on a road without other traffic. You can drive for some distance without realising that you are on the wrong side. To solve this, attach a card to your keys, with the words 'Drive Right!' printed in large letters. Whenever you leave the car, and need to pocket your keys, remove it and tape it to your steering wheel. That reminds you as soon as you enter your car, at which time you return the card to your keys.

Driving rules

Traffic drives on the right in Italy. The most important rule of the road is to give way to the right. In the absence of a traffic light (*semaforo*), traffic officer or other indication, the vehicle on the right has the right of way, except at a roundabout, where a vehicle in the circle has right of way over entering traffic. This give-way-to-the-right rule does not apply to vehicles entering from driveways, lay-bys or parking spaces, although you should give way to buses leaving bus stops. It is also important to know that a green arrow indicating a left turn means only that the turn is allowed, not that oncoming traffic is stopped by a red light.

The left lane of an autostrada is only for passing. Slower vehicles are required to keep to the right. If a driver approaching from behind in the same lane flashes his or her high beams, you are expected to move to the right immediately. Do not pass on the right.

Pedestrians have the right of way on marked crossings, but it is not customary to stop for those on the kerb waiting to cross. To do so is to risk a rear-end collision, since other drivers will not anticipate this.

Fuel

Petrol and diesel are sold by the litre, at fairly high prices. Many stations are self-service, and use credit cards at the pump, but

Petrol = *benzina*
Diesel = *gasolio*
Unleaded = *senza piombo*
Full = *pieno*
Oil = *l'olio*
Water = *l'acqua*

Lights

Use headlights at all times in rain, fog or poor visibility conditions. Right-hand drive cars must have their headlight beams modified to prevent blinding oncoming traffic or be fitted with stick-on beam deflectors that make them dip to the right.

Mobile phones

Drivers in Italy are permitted to use only those mobile phones equipped with earpieces for hands-free use. Hand-held phones may only be used by drivers who have pulled off the road and come to a full stop.

the process can be very difficult to follow if you are not fluent in Italian. Some smaller stations take only cash. Many petrol stations, especially those in rural areas, close during the middle of the day, at weekends and on public holidays. It is wise to keep your tank as full as possible, especially at weekends. Be sure to check hire cars carefully when fuelling them yourself, and tell attendants if you are driving a diesel car. The nozzles are not different and attendants may not bother to look at the warning before filling your tank.

Information

The best and most up-to-date road maps are issued by Michelin and Automobile Club d'Italia (ACI). Road maps disagree wildly, so it is best to carry several if you plan to do much exploring. One of your maps should show topography; an attractive-looking shortcut may be straight (or not so straight) over a mountain range.

When asking directions, remember to watch as well as listen: right, left, straight and roundabouts are all described with a wave of the hand. The most common answer is *sempre diritto*, which translates as 'straight ahead' and usually means just that. But it can also mean that the person you asked has no more idea where your destination is than you have, so it's wise to check again before going too far.

Don't expect to always find route numbers on road signs. Instead, know the towns and cities on your route and follow signs from one to the next. Labelling is quite good, especially from major roads. Autostrade are usually labelled not by compass points but by the town or city at each end. This can be quite confusing, since the last point may be a tiny village on the Swiss or Austrian border. Before entering an autostrada, follow it on the map to know the names at each end.

Parking

Many parking areas (and streets where parking is allowed) have meter boxes, which provide tickets when fed coins. These are quite simple to use, even without being able to read the instructions, although they are often not as easy to find. Put the ticket inside the windscreen, visible from the outside. You may find car parks where your stay is free, but limited to an hour or two. You can buy a paper 'clock' at newsstands, or you can write the time you arrive on a piece of paper.

Parking garages usually have a cashier or a machine for payments. Take a time-stamped ticket when you enter. Before leaving, pay for the ticket at the *cassa* (cashier window), drive your vehicle to the exit and insert the ticket to open the gate. Do not expect to find a cashier at the exit (and do expect to find irritated drivers behind you if you get there without the paid ticket).

Seat belts

Seat belts are mandatory for driver and all passengers, in front or back seats. Those under 12 must be in the back seat.

Speed limits

The speed limit on the autostrada is 130kph. Lower speed limits are signposted when the road is dangerous or passes through an urban area (usually 100kph, but they vary between 80kph and 110kph) or when construction is under way (usually 60kph) – and you are required by law to slow down.

In towns, the limit is 50kph, and residential areas often signpost speed limits of 30kph. The maximum speed limit on country roads is 90kph, which may be faster than you would sensibly drive there. Often, they have no verge (shoulder) and you have no margin of error. They go through the centre of villages, where blind turns can hide anything from a parade or street market to a pair of local men discussing politics.

Security

Although Italy has a very high rate of car thefts and break-ins, the rate is not as bad in northern Italy, especially outside cities. But it is still high and precautions are wise. Try to park in a locked or guarded site or at least in a well-lit, busy place. Don't leave anything in the vehicle that you don't want to lose and don't leave anything at all in plain view when you leave your car. Choose vehicles with concealed luggage compartments and empty those when you stop for the night. When stopping for meals at roadside rest areas, try to park where you can watch your car from the table. Above all, don't leave anything visible that marks your car as belonging to a tourist – road maps, travel guides or brochures all lead thieves to believe that there will be luggage in the boot.

If car windows are open, be careful while stopped for a traffic jam or at junctions. Thieves work in teams, one drawing your attention by approaching the car as if to sell you something while another reaches into open windows to snatch bags and cameras – often right out of a passenger's lap. In case of theft, make a report at the nearest *questura* (police station) and ask for a *denuncia*, a stamped form that you must have for making insurance claims.

Road signs

attenzione – watch out
bivio – crossroads
deviazione – detour
divieto di accesso – no entry
gira a destra/sinistra – turn right/left
incrocio – crossroads
limite di velocità – speed limit
parcheggio – parking
pedaggio – toll
pericolo – danger
pronto soccorso – first aid
rallentare – slow down
sempre diritto – straight ahead
senso unico – one-way street
senza uscita – no exit (cul-de-sac, dead-end)
sosta vietata/divieto di sosta – no parking
strada chiusa – road closed
strada senza uscita – dead-end/cul-de-sac
tenere la destra – keep right

traffico limitato – restricted access
uscita veicoli – exit
vietato il sorpasso – no overtaking/passing
vietato il transito – no through traffic
zona rimorchio – tow-away zone

Driving

l'accensione – ignition
l'acqua – water
la benzina/il gasolio – petrol/diesel
il distributore – petrol station
il guasto – breakdown
l'incidente – accident
la macchina – car
il motore – motor
non funziona – does not work
l'olio – oil
pieno – full
la pressione – air pressure
senza piombo – unleaded

ITALIAN ROAD SIGNS

RESTRICTION SIGNS

Maximum speed limit

No Entry,
one way street

No stopping at
any time

No honking

PRECEDENCE SIGNS

Give way

Crossroads with
right of way from
the right

Oncoming traffic
must wait

You have the
right of way

WARNING SIGNS

Roundabout

Signal lights ahead

Double bend,
first curving to
the right

Pedestrian
crossing

GENERAL SIGNS

Snow tyres
required

Stop for
police check

Border between
Italy & other
EU countries

Beginning of motorway
(green background),
or main road
(blue background)

Getting to northern Italy

Airlines in the UK:

Alitalia *Tel: 0871 424 1424; www.alitalia.it*
British Airways *Tel: 0870 850 9850; www.british-airways.com*
Brussels Airlines *Tel: 0902 51 600; www.brusselsairlines.com*
KLM *UK Tel: 0870 507 4074; www.klm.com*
Ryanair *Tel: 0871 246 0000 (Mon–Sat), 0905 566 0000 (Sun – premium rate number); www.ryanair.com*

Airline information in North America:

Air Canada *Tel: (in USA & Canada) 1 888 247 2262; www.aircanada.ca*
Alitalia *Tel: (in USA) 1 800 223 5730; (in Canada) 1 800 361 8336; www.alitalia.com*
American Airlines *Tel: 1 800 433 7300; www.aa.com*
KLM *Tel: (in USA) 1 800 225 2525; (in Canada) 1 800 447 4747; www.klm.com*
United Airlines *Tel: (in USA) 1 800 538 2929; www.ual.com*

The sooner you can begin planning your trip, the better deals you are likely to find. The best of these advance bargains require purchase 21 days ahead of travel, a stay of at least two weeks, return in 90–120 days and are not fully refundable. Conversely, you might also find deals on unsold seats a few days before leaving. On the Internet, visit *www.cheapflights.co.uk, www.lastminute.com* or *www.flightline.co.uk* for last-minute flights.

From the UK by car

The most direct route uses the Dover/Folkestone ferry to Calais, France, and crosses northern France past Reims and Strasbourg before entering Switzerland near Basel. From there it is almost directly south, past Lucerne to the St Gotthard Pass into the Ticino, and between Lake Como and Lake Maggiore, entering Italy near the town of Como. Nearly the entire trip is on motorways.

Allow a minimum of 11 hours' driving time (not counting breaks) to reach Milan from the ferry in Calais, and expect to pay about €50 in tolls and road taxes each way, plus the cost of fuel and the ferry itself.

Although it means hiring a vehicle there, flying on a low-cost airline may be an easier way to reach northern Italy from the UK, and can be a great time-saver. The increasing number of low-cost airlines makes this a competitive route and you can often arrange fly-drive packages that include car hire in Italy. Many of these fly into smaller secondary airports such as those in Turin, Bergamo and Verona.

Right
Taverna al Ponte, Bassano del Grappa

Fly-drive:

Established tour operators offering fly-drive holidays:
Citalia Tel: 0871 200 2004; www.citalia.com
Inghams Short Breaks Tel: 020 8780 8809; www.inghams.co.uk
Italiatour www.italiatours.com
Virgin Vacations Tel: 1 888 937 8474; www.virgin-vacations.com

The English Channel:

Direct Ferries Tel: 08718 900 900; www.directferries.co.uk
Eurotunnel Tel: 08448 79 73 79; www.eurotunnel.com
Norfolkline Tel: 0844 8475 029; www.norfolkline.com/ferry
P&O European Ferries Tel: 0871 664 2121; www.poferries.com
SeaFrance Tel: 0871 423 7119; www.seafrance.com
Stena Line Tel: 08705 707 070; www.stenaline.co.uk

Discount air tickets:

Orbitz Tel: 1 888 656 4546; outside USA 1 312 416 0018; www.orbitz.com
In Canada **Travel CUTS** 187 College St, Toronto M5T 1P7; tel: 866 246 9762; www.travelcuts.com

Low fares and fly-drive:

www.autoeurope.com
www.expedia.com
www.travelocity.com
www.trip.com

For up-to-date details of long-distance bus, ferry and rail services, consult the Thomas Cook *European Rail Timetable*, published monthly.

Rail travel

The train offers no advantage in getting from the UK to Italy. Tickets, added to the cost of lodging and dining en route, are similar to flying and the trip requires at least another day each way. Contact **Eurostar** (*tel: 0990 186186*) for trains to Paris, thence to Milan or other northern cities; **Citalia** (*tel: 0870 909 7555, premium rate line*) for Italian rail tickets and passes; or **Rail Europe** (*tel: 0990 848848; www.raileurope.com*).

Car hire

It is rarely possible to hire a car spontaneously, except in mid winter. By reserving well ahead, you will usually have the best rate and your choice of car. The best rates are often in a package with airfare, booked through the car-hire company, airline or a reliable travel agency.

Major international car-hire companies are represented in Italy, with offices in Milan and Pisa, as well as other airports, for pick-up and delivery. Auto Europe offers some of the most competitive rates and excellent air-auto packages that include mobile phones and other benefits. Contact them in the UK (*tel: 0800 169 9797*), in Ireland (*tel: 1 800 558892*), in Australia and New Zealand (*tel: 0800 169 6414*) and in the USA (*tel: 1 888 223 5555*). Alternatively, visit them on the web at *www.autoeurope.com*. Most companies require a credit card when you claim the vehicle, even if the hire has been prepaid.

One problem with hiring a car in Italy is that you must nearly always purchase the collision damage waiver. Even though credit cards usually cover this, most do not in Italy, adding another expense to car hire. You can avoid this by leasing a car. Renault Eurodrive has a very smooth system for this, and will meet you with a brand new car at Milan airport. The minimum lease period is 17 days, and the rate for additional days is quite inexpensive. Registration, insurance and all details are included and the rate compares very favourably with hire cars (and without added VAT). Drivers over 70 are not banned, as they are by most car-hire agencies. Contact **Renault Eurodrive** (*tel: USA 800 221 1052; www.renaultusa.com; France 0 505 1515*). This plan is not available to residents of Europe.

Before leaving the car park, be sure you have all registration and insurance documents and that you know how to operate the vehicle. Don't plan a long day's driving after a long flight, especially if you are driving on the wrong side of the road.

From North America

Direct flights from several major gateways serve Milan's Malpensa airport. Many airlines fly daily to Bologna, Pisa, Venice and Verona from connecting hub cities in Europe.

Setting the scene

Geography

The Alps and the Dolomites form a tall, wide wall that separates Italy from its European neighbours. Most access from the north is over mountain passes or through highway tunnels that bore through at the base. Nestled at the foot of the mountains is a series of lakes, the largest of which are Como, Garda, Iseo, Lugano and Maggiore. South of the lakes and mountains, a flat plain stretches from Turin on the west to Trieste on the east and continues south to include the lower Adige, Mincio and Po valleys and their deltas on the Adriatic. South of Turin rises the Piedmont, blending into the Apuan Alps and Apennines – 'the spine of Italy' (*lo dosso d'Italia*) – that continues down through Tuscany and into the neighbouring province of Umbria. On the west, these mountains drop precipitously into the Mediterranean, forming the Riviera di Levante between Pisa and Genoa, and the Riviera di Ponente between Genoa and the French border. This steep coastline is punctuated by towns which have managed to find a foothold in the scant spaces between mountains and sea.

Below
Medieval pageantry, Mantua

Timeline

Above
Lion of St Mark, Udine

800–400 BC Etruscan settlements between the Tiber and Arno rivers, including Fiesole.

753 BC Latin and Sabine villages combine, the beginning of Rome.

*c.*600 BC Euganei and Veneti peoples occupy northeast Italy.

350–250 BC Rome conquers the Etruscans and Umbrians.

*c.*300 BC Rome conquers the Euganei and Veneti.

89 BC People of Verona, Padua, Vicenza, Este and Treviso gain full Roman citizenship.

*c.*87 BC Roman poet Catullus born in Verona.

59 BC Roman historian Livy born in Padua.

44 BC Julius Caesar appointed ruler of Rome for life.

AD 13–14 Romans create provinces of Umbria and Tuscia.

313 Christianity recognised by Emperor Constantine I in the Edict of Milan, which recognises freedom of religion.

330 Constantinople supplants Rome as capital of the Roman Empire.

395 Roman Empire divided into eastern and western parts.

410 The Visigoth Alaric invades from the north and sacks Rome.

421 Venice settled.

452 Attila the Hun invades the north but dies in 453.

455 Vandals sack Rome, then leave.

493–552 Ostrogoths under Theodoric seize control.

553 Byzantine Emperor Justinian conquers Italy.

568–71 The Lombards conquer the northern region and are converted to Christianity. The Veneti begin to move to the lagoon islands.

697 Traditional date of founding of the Venetian Republic.

756 Peppin, king of the Franks, seizes Byzantine Umbria, giving it to the Pope and beginning the Papal State.

774 Charlemagne made king of the Lombards, conquers the region and Tuscany and Umbria become provinces of his empire.

800 Charlemagne crowned emperor by Pope Leo III.

828 Body of St Mark taken from Alexandria to Venice.

888 Berengar I crowned king of Italy at Verona.

*c.*1000 Holy Roman Empire breaks up; autonomous city-states in Florence, Lucca, Pisa and elsewhere rise under the influence of the Pope. Guilds and the cloth industry rise; Europe's first banks created.

1028 Venice introduces first street lights.

1095 Venice provides ships and supplies for First Crusade.

1125 Florence destroys Fiesole and fights wars with the Ghibelline cities of Pisa and Siena.

1155 Frederick Barbarossa crowned emperor of Holy Roman Empire, struggle with Popes continues.

Guelphs and Ghibellines

During the Middle Ages, many of Italy's land owning nobility chafed under the political authority of the Popes, which made them subservient to the clergy. It was also a time of rising influence for merchants, bankers and members of the trades guilds, who resented the authority of local lords to interfere in their lives and tax freely. This newly influential group favoured the Pope. The result was a contest between the emperor's (and landed nobility's) authority and the political authority of the Pope. The label 'Guelph' applied to supporters of the Pope, who hoped to achieve greater control over public affairs at the expense of the nobility. 'Ghibellines' supported the emperor and civil authority. For the Ghibellines, it was a matter of preserving feudal rights and authority over the fractious subjects in their city-states. This tension spread throughout the Italian city-states, as faction fought faction and intrigue pitted family members and city-states against one another. Merchant fought nobleman, and rival families fought one another with private armies.

1202 Venice uses the Fourth Crusade to conquer Constantinople, four bronze horses (and other treasure) brought to Venice.

1222 Founding of University of Padua.

1260 Scaligeri rule of Verona begins.

1271–95 Marco Polo journeys to China.

1301 Dante exiled from Florence, welcomed at Verona.

1309 Doge's Palace begun, following year Venetian constitution approved, creating Council of Ten.

1342 English loan default ruins the major banking houses of Florence, starting an economic crisis.

1348 Plague in Tuscany, Umbria and Venice kills half the population.

1380 Battle of Chioggia; Venice defeats Genoa for control of Adriatic.

1453 Constantinople captured by Turks, marking end of high point of Venetian Republic.

1489 Venice gains Kingdom of Cyprus by marriage.

1508 Palladio born at Vicenza.

1518 Birth of Tintoretto in Venice.

1528 Paolo Veronese born.

1559 Spain gains control over Milan region.

1571 Venice loses Cyprus to Turks, whose fleet is then defeated at Battle of Lepanto.

*c.*1595 Shakespeare writes *Romeo and Juliet*.

1630 Second major plague hits Venice, leads to building of Santa Maria Salute as offering.

1669 Venice loses Crete to the Turks.

1678 University of Padua awards doctorate to Elena Piscopia, the first woman in the world ever to receive a degree.

1708 Venetian lagoon freezes solid for the first time.

1718 Venice ceases to be a naval power after defeat by Turks at Morea.

1720 Caffè Florian opens on the Piazza San Marco in Venice.

1789 Dolomite mountains named after geologist Diedonne Dolomieu.

1797 Napoleon Bonaparte conquers the Veneto; last doge resigns; Venetian Republic ends.

1798–9 Napoleon occupies Tuscany and Umbria.

1805 Napoleon crowned king of Italy.

1805–14 Napoleon's sister Elisa rules the Duchy of Lucca.

1814 Napoleon banished to Elba; Papal State restored; Tuscany is ruled by the Austrians.

1831 Giuseppe Mazzini founds Young Italy movement, beginning resistance to Austria.

1848 The first Italian War of Independence. Italians under Mazzini rebel against Austrian rule and the Papal State. Daniele Manin leads Venetian rebels, but the Austrians and Pope prevail.

Above
World War I at Villafranca

Above
Denunciation box, Verona

1859 Second War of Italian Independence; Battle of Solferino leads to founding of Red Cross.

1861 Vittorio Emanuele II crowned king of Italy.

1865–70 Florence capital of Italy.

1866 Austrian rule ends throughout the Veneto.

1870 Completion of Italian unification as the Kingdom of Italy with Rome as its capital.

1902 Campanile of San Marco, Venice falls, reopens in 1912.

1915 Italy joins Allies in World War I against Austria.

1918 Austria invades Italian Dolomites, fierce fighting in the mountains.

1919 Istria/Trentino ceded by Austria, becomes part of Italy.

1922 Benito Mussolini becomes *Il Duce*.

1931 Venice first linked to the mainland by a road.

1937 Italy joins Germany and Japan in Anti-Comintern Pact: the Axis formed.

1939 Italy and Germany sign 'Pact of Steel'.

1940 Italy joins World War II as German ally.

1943 Mussolini deposed, sets up Nazi puppet state at Salò on Lake Garda.

1944–5 Italy joins Allies; Italian partisans battle Nazis in the occupied areas. Livorno, Pisa, San Gimignano and other cities heavily damaged. July 1944 the Nazis blow up all the bridges in Florence, except Ponte Vecchio, and many medieval riverside buildings. All bridges in Verona destroyed.

1946 Vittorio Emanuele III abdicates; Republic of Italy declared.

1954 Trieste incorporated into Italy.

1957 Italy joins the European Economic Community, predecessor of the European Union.

1966 Catastrophic flood sweeps through Florence.

1969 Marxist terrorist group Red Brigade formed. Commit bombings, murder, assassinations and robberies throughout Italy into the mid-1980s.

1978 Aldo Moro, twice prime minister, kidnapped and murdered by the Red Brigade.

1982 Italy wins football World Cup.

1984 Catholicism loses its status as the state religion.

2002 Italy adopts the euro.

2005 Premier Silvio Berlusconi resigns following corruption trial and defeat in regional polls. Romano Prodi succeeds him.

2006 Italy wins its fourth football World Cup.

2008 Silvio Berlusconi wins Italian general election.

2010 Francesco Cossiga, former prime minister and president of Italy and staunch supporter of NATO, dies.

Art and architecture

Roman

While few standing examples remain of the architecture of classical Rome, those few are worth visiting. These structures, or the remnants of them, date mainly from the 1st century BC through to the 2nd century AD and are found primarily in Abano Terme, Aquileia, Brescia, Concordia Sagittaria, Sirmione, Trieste and Verona. In Aquileia are ruins of the riverside port, forum and other important structures (c. 1st centuries BC and AD). Sirmione, on Lake Garda, has the large Grottoes of Catullus and a villa. In Trieste is the well-preserved Roman Theatre. The highest concentration, however, is in Verona and includes the Arena (c. AD 30), Ponte Romano, also known as the Ponte Pietra (1st century AD), Gavi Arch (1st century AD), Scavi Archeologici (c. 1st century BC), Porta Leone and Porta Borsari (c. 1st century BC), and the Roman Theatre (1st century BC).

Romanesque

Romanesque style, while it also applies to art, is best known in architecture. It flourished from the late 11th century until the 13th century, when it was gradually supplanted by Gothic. Romanesque features semicircular Roman-style arches over windows and doors, massive exterior walls and heavy internal columns resting on substantial bases. Ceilings are barrel-vaulted, forming groined junctions where structural segments meet. Sculptural elements were added to buildings, in a less formal and more stylised form than on the classical Greek and Roman buildings. In domestic structures, windows and doorways featured rounded, simple arched tops. The Lombards had the greatest influence on the style, decorating the exteriors of their buildings with bands of colour and detached bell towers, and placing covered porticoes over the elaborately carved doorways. Pisan Romanesque was quite different, with layers of arcades decorating façades, more closely akin to the classical style. Florence had its own variant, using a simpler arched colonnade on the lower level and patterned walls of green and white marble. The best example anywhere of Lombard Romanesque is the church of San Zeno (1123–35), in Verona, closely followed by the city's duomo, or cathedral (1139). In Padua, see the Palazzo della Ragione (1218). Pisan Romanesque is epitomised by Pisa's duomo (1063–1180), with its baptistery (1152) and famous leaning campanile (1173–1350). In nearby Lucca, see San Frediano (1112) and San Michele in Foro (1143). Pistoia has its duomo (1108–1311) and Sant'Andrea (1180). Florentine Romanesque is best seen in the magnificent baptistery (1059–1128) and at the church of San Miniato al Monte (1050), both in Florence.

Gothic

While Gothic supplanted Romanesque, it did not happen overnight and the Gothic style did not reach full maturity until the 14th century. Buildings such as churches took decades to erect and later architects often imposed Gothic elements on to buildings that had started as Romanesque. Gothic structures in Tuscany follow this pattern, so are not pure, most containing Romanesque elements or having Gothic styles built on or around Romanesque buildings. The Gothic architectural style brought a more delicate grace. Rounded arches soared into pointed arches, often with pronounced ribbing. The arches themselves created the strength of the structure and walls became curtains in which great panels of stained glass could be hung. Church interiors reached skyward upon seemingly slender columns. Art and sculpture became more mystical and emotional, dwelling upon themes such as the birth and Passion of Christ. In Italy, it took form in the use of fresco and mosaic. In Venice, Gothic took on a different look. The style was heavily influenced by exposure to eastern styles found in Constantinople and the eastern Mediterranean basin. Domestic architecture shows particularly the use of the pointed arch,

Right
Doge's Palace, Venice

ogee (reverse) curves and delicate tracery. The prime examples of Venetian Gothic are the Basilica San Marco and the Palazzo Ducale in Venice. Gothic is represented in Verona by San Fermo Maggiore (13th century), Sant'Anastasia (late 13th century) and San Fermo (13th century), which shows a mixture of styles. The most outstanding Gothic church in Florence is the duomo (1294) and in Pisa the church of Santa Maria della Spina (1323).

Renaissance

From approximately 1400 until 1600, Europe witnessed a transformation in thinking, which was quickly reflected in all forms of art. Beginning in Italy, it spread across Europe, changing the focus of mankind from the perfection of man to assure redemption to the perfection of man as a civil being. Renaissance man began to see himself as a cognitive being and the real world crept into art. Architecture became appreciated as an art and architects became honoured professionals and not just craftsmen. Classical forms returned and in both art and architecture perspective became important. The rediscovery of *De Architectura* by the Roman architect Vitruvius played a vital role. The sculptor Filippo Brunelleschi turned to architecture between 1412 and 1418, studying classical buildings and their mathematics. In 1418, he completed the dome of the cathedral of Florence, using, for the first time, a drum wall to support the dome. The Renaissance form developed rapidly as studies of classical remnants revealed their secrets. In art and architecture, it

Below
Museo del Cenedese, Vittorio Veneto

became a matter of intellect and human individual endeavour to achieve balance. In architecture, the dome again became important and the familiar church floor plan of a cross with one elongated leg gave way to the Greek cross with equal sides and a domed centre. Stonework took on more sophisticated forms, such as at the Palazzo Medici-Riccardi in Florence, where each level of the building received individual treatment. Classical forms were used in new ways. The orders of the classical world – Corinthian, Doric, Ionic, Tuscan and Composite – became important once again.

The real world began to show in the work of painters such as Piero della Francesca, Paolo Uccello and Masaccio. Perspective and realistic depiction became as important to art as the subject. In sculpture, Donatello and Ghiberti used the new principles to return their art to the classical ideal. Leonardo da Vinci, Michelangelo and Raphael – geniuses all – further developed the theory, creating some of the world's major masterpieces. In Florence, where the Renaissance

gained its prime momentum, look for Spedale degli Innocenti (1419–24), Sagrestia Vecchia in San Lorenzo (1419), Cappella dei Pazzi in Santa Croce (1442), and San Lorenzo (begun in 1425), all by Brunelleschi. Also in Florence, see the Palazzo Medici-Riccardi (1444–59) and San Marco (1437–52), both by Michelozzo, and Sagrestia Nuova in San Lorenzo by Michelangelo (1520).

Mannerism and the Baroque

Towards the end of his life, Michelangelo had already begun to violate the rules of the Renaissance. Those artists that followed him were disparagingly referred to by the Tuscan artist Giorgio Vasari as trying to work 'in the manner of Michelangelo' and the label stuck. The title 'mannerist' refers to those artists who followed Michelangelo's lead, breaking from the rules of the Renaissance. It was their work that led to the Baroque style. From the logical realism of the Renaissance came the emotive world of the Baroque, where the subjects of paintings showed love, anger, fear and penitence in their faces and positions. Classical and mythical subject matter was introduced. Artists such as Bernini, Caravaggio, Tiepolo and Titian brought the form to Italian perfection. In architecture, the classical forms appeared on a monumental scale, with embellished shields and other decorative detail. Classical forms also appeared in statuary, and ceilings were painted with mythological themes. The forms were classical, but the architect and artist had greater freedom of expression. The result was an exuberance of creation. To see these styles in Venice, go to Santa Maria della Salute (mid- to late 17th century), Ca'Pesaro (mid-17th century), both by Longhena, and Santa Maria Assunta, also called Gesuiti (1715–28).

Festivals

With an entire calendar of saints' days, secular holidays, historical anniversaries, arts events and the harvest of locally grown produce, Italians seem never at a loss for something to celebrate. *Carnevale* in Venice (before Lent), Verona's summertime opera festival, Bolzano's Christmas marketplace, Marostica's biennial human chess game, Florence's *Calcio* (a ball game and 16th-century procession) and Cortina's film festival are among the largest (and most crowded) of these. But don't be surprised to enter a small town and find a wine festival in full swing, or a celebration of the cherry or peach harvest, or a procession of the faithful bearing a statue through the streets. The one feature they all have in common is that visitors are welcome to join in the merriment – and sample the food, which is always a part of any festival.

Touring itineraries

While many of the routes described in the following chapters form loops, you can connect several of them into longer itineraries by travelling only one side of each to create larger loops, each a trip that would fill a holiday with a wide variety of sights and experiences. Italy's autostrade system makes it possible to connect even far-apart regions within a few hours of travel.

Venice and the east

Spend at least three days in Venice (*see page 170*), four if you want to explore its islands at leisure. Let it be the centrepiece of your visit if you have not been there before. From Venice, head east to explore a part of Italy that even many Italians have not visited, described in the Borderland route (*see page 168*). The Adriatic Coast between Venice and Trieste is filled with Roman sites and lined with white sandy beaches, and the fascinating area to the north bears visible evidence of the eastern hordes of Goths and Lombards that wrested the region from the Romans. A quick swing into the Dolomites adds another dimension, easy to do by following the eastern Dolomites route (*see page 158*) from Udine through mountain passes to Cortina d'Ampezzo. Return to Venice via some of the Veneto's most fascinating towns: Belluno, Conegliano, Vittorio Veneto and Treviso, described in the eastern Alpine foothills route (*see page 194*).

Below
Market, Bassano del Grappa

The heart of the Veneto

If you have seen Venice, consider concentrating your attention on the trio of cities to its west – Padua, Verona and Vicenza. Each with its own distinct character, these cities (*see pages 220, 116 and 213*) provide focal points for trips into their surrounding regions. South of Padua and Vicenza lie the thermally active Euganean Hills. East of Padua is the Brenta Canal and its magnificent villas. North of Verona is the wine country of Valpolicella, the breathtaking road through the Pasubio Valley and the castellated town of Soave, described in the Valpolicella and Pasubio Valley route (*see page 132*). That route blends easily into the very interesting group of towns in the western Alpine foothills route (*see page 206*). Distances are not great, but the variety is astonishing.

Right
The glorious Dolomite
mountains

Mountains and foothills

For unmatched scenery and towns that capture the heart of the Dolomites and the Veneto's foothills, follow the eastern Alpine foothills route (*see page 194*) north from Venice, visiting the 'little Venice' towns. From Belluno, continue north through the Val di Cadore to Cortina d'Ampezzo, as described in the eastern Dolomites route (*see page 158*). Continue across the mountains, following the Dolomite Road (*see page 150*) to Bolzano. Head south along the Alto Adige route (*see page 142*) to Trento. Here you can head southwest to the northern tip of Lake Garda (*see page 102*), ending at the A4 autostrada, which takes you back to Venice or to Milan.

Highlights of the north

By taking full advantage of Italy's excellent autostrade system, you can combine the landmark cities of Florence, Pisa and Venice with mountain scenery, coastal towns and even a look at Italy's largest lake. Begin in Milan (*see page 74*), heading east past Bergamo (*see page 84*) to Brescia and following the southern part of the Brescia to Mantua (Mantova) route (*see page 100*). Travel south on the A22 to Bologna, following the Bologna to Florence route (*see page 231*) to the Adriatic, then west across the mountains to Florence (*see page 234*). Follow the Florence to Pisa route (*see page 252*) west to the Mediterranean, then the southern Riviera di Levante route (*see page 260*) north, past the Cinque Terre, and the northern Riviera di Levante route (*see page 268*) to Genoa. From there it is a scenic, but straight return to Milan on the A7.

The Valle d'Aosta and Turin

Ratings

Castles	●●●●●
Geology	●●●●●
Mountains	●●●●●
Scenery	●●●●●
Nature	●●●●○
Outdoor activities	●●●●○
Walking	●●●●○
Historical sights	●●●○○

The wall of Alps separating Italy and France includes the range's (and Europe's) highest peak, Mont Blanc – or Monte Bianco, as the Italians call it. The only way through the mountains was over steep passes, and today's roads follow essentially the same routes used by Neolithic travellers and the Celts. Roman legions used the valley carved by the Dora Baltea River to get to their colonies in Gaul, and the way-station they built at Aosta grew to a city so fine that it earnt the nickname 'Rome of the Alps'.

Today the valley is popular with hikers and skiers. Forming its southern wall are Italy's own loftiest peaks, protected in the Gran Paradiso National Park. South of these, Turin flourished as capital of the dukes of Savoy, and although now an important manufacturing centre, it is still easy to see why Italians called it 'Little Paris'.

AOSTA

🛈 *Pza Chanoux 8; tel: 0165 236 627; www.regione.vda.it. Open daily 0900–1230, 1400–1800.*

🏛 **Museo Archeologico** *Pza Roncas 12; tel: 0165 275 902. Open daily 0900–1900. Free.*

Sant'Orso *V. Sant'Orso; tel: 0165 262 026. Call for opening hours. Free.*

An ancient Roman post known originally as Augustus Praetoria, Aosta remains the core market town of the Valle d'Aosta region. Among its preserved Roman ruins are the sturdy stone **Arch of Augustus** built upon the town's founding in 25 BC, a well-preserved **theatre** also constructed by Augustus, **towers** and ancient **catacombs**. The town's good **Museo Archeologico (Archaeological Museum)** makes sense of many artefacts – bronzes, busts, tombstones, chalices, crosses, gemstones, even some bone art – from those heady times and its big piazza is a good place to watch the world go by. As impressive as Aosta's Roman remains is the ecclesiastical complex of **Sant'Orso**, where several centuries of art are packed into a church, bell tower, crypts and cloister. The last is Sant'Orso's highlight, with outstanding intricate stone carving. Almost lost in all this excitement is the fine local **cathedral**, featuring skilled mosaic and stained-glass work and the **Tesoro Museum**, holding icons, sculptures and other religious items of marble, wood and precious metals.

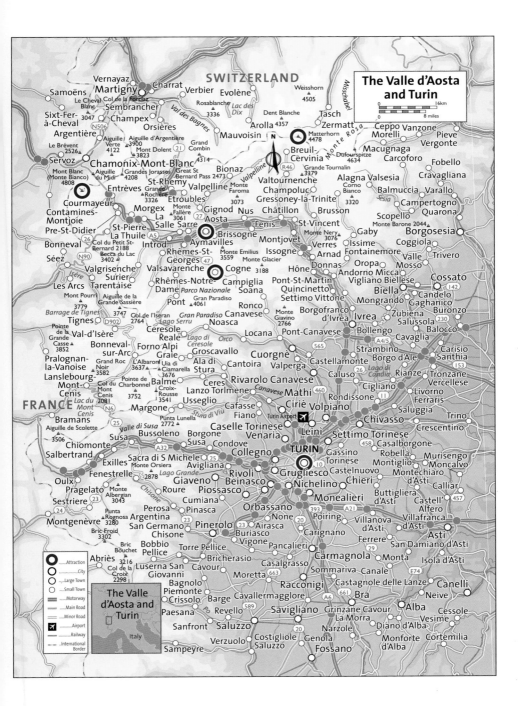

The Valle d'Aosta and Turin

0 _____ 16km
0 _____ 8 miles

The Valle d'Aosta and Turin

Italy

O ....Attraction
O ....City
O ....Large Town
O ....Small Town
▬▬ ....Motorway
▬▬ ....Main Road
── ....Minor Road
✈ ....Airport
▬▬ ....Railway
-·-· ....International Border

Museo del Tesoro della Cattedrale € *Pza Giovanni XXIII; tel: 0165 40 251. Open Sat–Sun 1530–1730 or by appointment.*

Museo dall'Ospizia *Tel: 417 871 236. Open mid-Jun–mid-Oct daily 0800–1930.*

🌣 **Market day:** Tue, on Piazza Cavalieri di Vittorio Veneto.

Strung along the Valle d'Aosta are small castles, each set on its own little hill or crag, many within sight of each other. Overlooking the vineyards of Sarre, 5km west of Aosta, **Castello Reale** was the 'hunting lodge' of Italian King Umberto. To the east is **Fenis Castle**, with a lovely 15th-century courtyard from which a curved stairway rises to wooden balconies. The courtyard and chapel are painted in *freschi*, most in excellent condition. Another noteworthy castle close by is at **Aymavilles**.

From Aosta, it's a 35km trip (longer by the older, slower and more scenic road) north to the scenic top of the Gran San Bernardo Pass. Just over the Swiss border is the **Museo dall'Ospizia**, showing the history of the monk who built the first travellers' hospice and gave his name to the pass and the breed of rescue dogs (some of whom you may meet there).

Accommodation and food in Aosta

La Cave de Tillier Brasserie €–€€ *V. de Tillier 40; tel: 0165 230 133.* Grilled steaks are delectable here, as is the gnocchi with fontina, the local cheese speciality.

Hotel Miage €–€€ *V. Ponte Suaz 252; tel: 0165 238 585; fax: 0165 236 355; www.hotelmiage.it.* Small hotel with views, in-room TVs, parking and a restaurant. Breakfast is served, but extra.

Ristorante Praetoria €–€€ *V. San Anselmo 9; tel: 0165 44 356.* The rabbit and polenta are good choices here, as are the pasta dishes.

Hotel Europe €€–€€€ *Pza Narbonne 8; tel: 0165 236 363; fax: 0165 659 911; www.hoteleuropeaosta.it.* Very attractive hotel in the historic centre with friendly staff, free Internet access and covered parking.

COGNE AND THE GRAN PARADISO

ℹ️ **TIC**, *Fraz Trepont 90; tel: 0165 95 055; www.granparadiso.net. Open daily 0830–1230, 1430–1700.*

Rising abruptly from the Valle d'Aosta are the rugged, snow-capped mountains of **Parco Nazionale Gran Paradiso**. Few roads penetrate this wilderness, following the valleys to end at remote villages. Beyond these are trails to rocky peaks inhabited by ibex and chamois. **Cogne** is one of these villages, overlooking meadows of wild flowers in a panorama backed by craggy mountains. The town is a centre for woodcarving, which is sold in several studios and shops. **Cascata di Lillaz** drops in a series of long falls, a short walk from the village of Lillaz, beyond Cogne. Hiking trails into the park begin here.

Accommodation and food in Cogne

Saint-Pierre €€ *V. Corrado Gex 61; tel: 0165 903 817; www.hotelsaintpierre.it.* Located at the beginning of the road into

Cogne's valley, this attractive modern hotel and restaurant is only 3km from the A5 autostrada, but within easy reach of Cogne and the park.

Bellevue €€€ *Rue Grand Paradis 22; tel: 0165 74 825; www.hotelbellevue.it.* The class act in town, with the best views and restaurant, along with an indoor pool.

MATTERHORN (CERVINO)

ⓘ *V. Carrel 29, Breuil-Cervinia; tel: 0166 944 411; www.cervinia.it*

Few mountains are so universally recognised as the Matterhorn, called Cervino by Italians. But the usual view is from the Swiss town to its north. Much closer, and far more impressive, is the view from its Italian side, an almost sheer wall of rock rising overhead from the cul-de-sac village of **Breuil-Cervinia**. Unusual for mountains, the unique shape that makes this one so recognisable is the same on either side. The town itself is just plain ugly, but the best views of the mountain are from the breathtakingly beautiful foreground of **Lago Bleu**, a few kilometres before town. Its clear Alpine waters mirror the mountain and a frame of dark larch trees complete a stage-set scene. The Alps don't provide a more perfect picnic site. Breuil-Cervinia provides hotels and the starting point for cable cars up the mountain.

Accommodation and food in Breuil-Cervinia

Hotel Bucaneve € *Pza Jumeaux 10; tel: 0464 391 557; fax: 0464 395 352; www.hotel-bucaneve.com.* Small hotel with restaurant and sauna.

Maison de Saussure €€ *V. Gorret 20; tel: 0166 948 259. Open Jul–Aug & Nov–May; closed public holidays.* This friendly restaurant serves the hearty French-influenced cuisine typical of the region.

Hotel Hermitage €€€ *Strada Cristallo; tel: 0166 948 998; fax: 0166 949 032; www.hotelhermitage.com.* Elegant mountain chalet featuring a small gym, sauna, indoor pool and lush garden. There are TVs and Internet connection points in all rooms.

MONT BLANC (MONTE BIANCO)

ⓘ *Pzle Monte Bianco 13, Courmayeur; tel: 0165 842 060.*

ⓜ **Museo Alpina Duca degli Abruzzi** *Pza Henry 2, Courmayeur; tel: 0165 842 357. Open Tue & Thur–Sun 0900–1200, 1530–1830, Wed 1530–1830. Free.*

Mont Blanc (Monte Bianco in Italian) forms a beautiful, but formidable, solid wall 50km long, 13km wide and 4,808m high, separating Italy from France. Its tallest point lies just over the border, in France, and is the highest point in all Europe. It was once nearly impassable, but today can be traversed by car, cable car and even – in places, if you're skilled enough – on foot or skis. The best base from which to visit the Italian side of the mountain is the pricey ski-resort town of **Courmayeur**. The town is rather quaint despite the villas and shops, and there's a good little **Alpine museum** to poke through as

Above
Monte Paradiso, Valle d'Aosta

well as **San Pantaleone**, a parish church dating from the late 14th century. It's only a few kilometres from here to **Entrèves**, the last town before the mountain and the French border, and where you can board a cable car to the dramatic ridge-line dividing the two countries.

To press on into France by car, the 12km-long Mont Blanc Tunnel is the primary way, piercing the mountains to avoid the twisting, minor-road alternative. This was the longest such tunnel in the world when it opened in 1965. Some three-quarters of a million vehicles use it annually.

Accommodation and food in Courmayeur

Hotel Croux €€ *V. Croux 8; tel: 0165 848 735; fax: 0165 845 190; www.hotelcroux.it.* This small hotel with a cordial staff makes a good base for excursions up to Mont Blanc. Opt for rooms with balconies from which you can see the mountain. Parking available.

La Clotze €€€ *Planpincieux Nord; tel: 0165 869 720; www.laclotze.com. Open Jul–mid-Sept & mid-Oct–May Thur–Tue.* Elegant restaurant located above the town and therefore offering splendid views from its outdoor terrace.

Hotel Royale Golf €€€ *V. Roma 87; tel: 0165 831 611; fax: 0165 842 093; www.hotelroyalegolf.com.* This large hotel dominates the townscape and services a loyal – not to mention royal – clientele.

Guests dine at the revered Grill Royale Golf and can take dips in the heated outdoor pool. Parking available.

TURIN

ℹ️ *Pza Salferino 161; tel: 011 535 181.* There are also kiosks at both Porta Nuova Station and the city airport; *tel (for all offices): 011 535 181; www.turismotorino.org*

Below
Palazzo Madama, Turin

Former centre of the Savoy dynasty's power, later a communist hotbed and now Italy's fourth-largest city, Turin (Torino) might not seem a likely candidate for a traveller's attention. But it is. Determined to make their capital a showplace that would gain them respect among the other courts of Europe, the Savoys lavished attention on their capital at Turin. The old Roman street grid provided the base for a well-designed city of broad avenues and spacious piazze. Its modern-day prosperity has allowed the city to maintain and treasure its stately arcaded streets, belle époque cafés, palaces, churches and public gardens. This might be one reason the city was the surprise winner – over Sion, Switzerland – of the right to host the 2006 Winter Olympic

🅘 **Duomo** *Pza San Giovanni; tel: 011 436 1540. Open daily 0700– 1200, 1500–1900. Free.*

Palazzo Madama € *Pza Castello; tel: 011 443 3501; www. palazzomadamatorino. it. Open Sun & Tue–Fri 1000–2000, Sat 1000–2300.*

Palazzo Reale € *Pza Castello; tel: 011 436 1455; www.piemonte.beniculturali.it. Open Tue–Sun 0830–1930; visits by guided tour only (last tour begins 1815).*

Below
Sant'Orso cloister, Valle d'Aosta

Games, or it may be that there are so very many fine ski resorts so near at hand.

Among the city's attractions is its **duomo**, a typical 15th-century structure whose fame rests largely in the Sacra Sindone, the Holy Shroud. Displayed only rarely – the next scheduled time will be in 2025 – it is kept in a plain altar of a side chapel. A replica is displayed, however, and you can learn more about the continuing (and conflicting) tests for its authenticity at the small museum on Via San Domenica, the **Museum of the Holy Shroud** (*tel: 011 436 5832*), which details some of these investigations. Piazza Castello is the largest in a city replete with grand-scale piazze, in which stands **Palazzo Madama**, enlarged in the 1400s from a fortified Roman gate and renovated in the early 1700s to add the façade and a stunning staircase the width of the building itself. Overlooking the piazza is the **Palazzo Reale**, the Savoys' residence until the mid-1800s. The palace of the House of Savoy was the nerve centre of Turin and the entire Savoia, reflecting their grandeur and position in Baroque splendour. The *piano nobile* (main floor) is open only by guided tours in Italian,

Museo Egizio €
Palazzo dell'Accademia delle Scienze 6; tel: 011 561 7776; www. museoegizio.it. Open Tue–Sun 0830–1930 (last admission 1830).

Museo Nazionale del Cinema €
V. Montebello 20; tel: 011 813 8560; www. museonazionaledelcinema.it. Open Tue–Fri & Sun 0900–2000, Sat 09.00–2300.

Borgo Medievale € *Tel: 011 443 1701. Open daily 0900–2000. Free on Fri.*

There's a huge open market each morning in the Piazza della Repubblica of fruit, flowers and other wares. Locals claim it's the largest open market in Europe. There's also a well-attended antiques market known as the Grand Balon on the 2nd Sun of each month behind the Porta Palazzo.

but signs in English offer descriptions. The ballroom is especially grand, with a frescoed ceiling. The series of buildings, connected by arcades, houses the armoury, library (step in to see the magnificent ceiling), archives and theatre. Palazzo Carignano is where the first Italian parliament met and where Risorgimento hero Vittorio Emanuele II (he of many squares throughout Italy) was born. He would later become first king of the newly unified nation. Diagonally opposite this palace is another, the **Science Academy Palace**. This one holds the surprising and excellent **Egizio Museum**, an anthropology museum featuring the starring attraction of loads and loads of Egyptian artefacts from the time of Rameses and other ancient pharaohs. It's one of the world's finest – second only to Cairo's – and its holdings include statues, temples, fabric work, mummies, papyrus, burial items and much more. Best of all, these attractions all lie within perhaps a minute's walk of each other.

There's an active, almost Viennese, café scene in the central city, as well. Tucked under the arcades are some splendid and historic cafés where writers, poets, philosophers and the Savoys lingered and where the leaders of Italy's Risorgimento gathered to drink and plot. The splendid **Caffè San Carlo**, in Piazza San Carlo, serves an excellent buffet at lunch, or cakes any time.

Not far from the arcaded Via Po, is the peculiar **Mole Antonelliana**, which began as a synagogue, but when money ran out was turned into a monument to Vittorio Emanuele II. A glass lift speeds to the top for views to the Alps. Inside is the **Museo Nazionale del Cinema**, filled with screens for viewing classic films and assorted mementos of Turin's flourishing film industry.

Perhaps the city's most offbeat attraction is the faux medieval village, **Borgo Medioevale**, alongside the Po River in the Parco del Valentino. Built for the Italian Exposition of 1884, the village is surprisingly authentic in architecture and decoration.

Accommodation and food in Turin

Brek Ristoranti € *Pza Solferino; tel: 011 545 424; www.brek.com.* At last a serious upmarket, health-conscious, fresh-ingredient cafeteria! This place sparkles with just-picked berries and veggies and prepares them in traditional dishes; you can choose exactly what you want, and pay by plate size. Prices are low, quality high.

Caffè San Carlo €–€€ *Pza San Carlo 156; tel: 011 532 586; http://caffesancarlo.it.* Elegant décor, lots of history, genial service and good lunch dishes and pastries – the carpaccio is outstanding.

La Badessa €€ *Pza Carlo Emanuele II 17; tel: 011 835 940; www.labadessa.net.* Dining rooms are in a palazzo and the menu features specialities of the region's historic convents, such as potato gnocchi with braised guineafowl.

Balbo €€ *V. Asiago 18; tel: 011 772 5829; fax: 011 773 4079; http://hotelbalbo.it.* A comfortable, modern hotel centrally located with Wi-Fi, private underground parking for guests and a café.

Idrovolante €€ *Vle Virgilio, Parco Valentino; tel: 011 668 7602; www.ristoranteidrovolante.com.* Inspired combinations, such as grilled swordfish sauced with limoncello and fresh oregano, served in a waterside setting.

Hotel NH Santo Stefano €€–€€€ *V. Porta Palatina 19; tel: 011 522 3311; fax: 011 522 3313; www.nh-hotels.com.* Smartly decorated modern rooms, multiple mod cons and a location only steps from the Piazza Real make this a top choice.

Victoria Hotel €€€ *V. Nino Costa 4; tel: 011 561 1909; fax: 011 561 1806; www.hotelvictoria-torino.com.* The quiet elegance and atmosphere of a Cotswold country house, set in the midst of the city centre; individually decorated rooms, free Internet access and bicycles. Included breakfasts are exceptional as is the pampering at **Spa Egypt**.

Suggested tour

Total distance: 540km round trip, with detours 600km.

Time: 6 hours, driving one-way from Turin (Torino) to Mont Blanc (Monte Bianco) via the Valle d'Aosta, including the side trip to the Matterhorn (Cervino) and the town of Cogne. Allow 2 to 3 days without detours, 3 days with detours. Those with limited time can use the A5 toll road nearly the entire way. Skipping either the Matterhorn or Cogne saves considerable time as well.

Links: Turin (Torino), the beginning point for this route, is approximately 100km southwest of Arona on the Lake Maggiore route (*see page 59*) via the A4 and A26 toll autostrade.

Route: Leave **TURIN** (Torino) ❶, heading north on the A5 toll autostrada for 80km, exiting at **Châtillon** ❷ and crossing the river, then heading north along the R46 for 27km into the mountains to reach **Breuil-Cervinia** ❸, base camp for cable cars to the **MATTERHORN** (Cervino). Afterwards, backtrack to Châtillon and proceed west on either the fast A5 or the more scenic S26 some 25km to **AOSTA** ❹. From Aosta, turn west on the S26 to Sarre. Cross the valley, following the R47 south, signposted **COGNE** ❺. Backtrack to the valley, turning west along the S26 for 35km to Pré-St-Didier, turning north for **Courmayeur** ❻ and **Entrèves** – the base for cable cars over **MONT BLANC** (Monte Bianco) – and the 12km-long Mont Blanc Tunnel, of which about a third lies in Italian territory.

Detour 1: From Turin (Torino), cross the river going east and follow the S10 through an uneventful, ever-so-slightly rumpled 40km of

Above
Valle d'Aosta landscape

terrain to reach **Asti** ❼. Though the town certainly isn't the most scenic in the Piedmont region, autumn brings an exciting *palio* (horse race) that rivals Siena's much more famous one. Spring brings the Feast of San Secondo, a festival of much parading, costumes, flags and eating, climaxing with, of all things, a bowl of soup. Asti is also the eponymous centre for Italy's Asti Spumante sparkling wine production

ⓘ Alba Tourist Board
*Pza Risorgimento 2,
Alba; tel: 0173 35 833;
fax: 0173 363 878;
www.langheroero.it* or
www.comune.alba.cn.it

**ⓘ Enoteca Regionale
Piemontese
Cavour** *V. Castello 5,
Grinzane Cavour; tel: 0173
262 159; fax: 0173 231
343.*

**ⓘ Restaurant
Combal.Zero €€€**
*Pza Mafalda di Savoia, Rivoli;
tel: 011 956 5225; fax: 011
956 5248; www.combal.org.
Open Tue–Sat.* Perhaps
northern Italy's most
innovative restaurant,
where the food is taken
very seriously, but each
presentation is filled with
happy surprises. Dinner
here is the evening's main
event, and a memorable
one.

**ⓘ Hotel Foresteria
Conti di Roero**
*€€–€€€ Pza San Ponzio
3, Monticello d'Alba; tel:
0173 64 155; fax: 0173
466 928;
www.contiroero.com.*
Set on a hilltop castle, this
hotel has very spacious
rooms; a highpoint of a
stay here is dinner at the
restaurant, Foresteria
Conti Roero. Any menu
choice will be a good one,
but do leave room for the
extraordinary desserts.

– there are plenty of vintners in the surrounding area – and the town's impressive brick **cathedral** is definitely worth a look, as well, for its elegant Gothic facing, trio of rose windows and careful stonework details. Strangely, there's no wine museum here in Asti; for that, head south an additional 30km along the E74 to its rival town of **Alba** ❽ – which holds an interesting horse race each summer – then follow signs south 8km to Diano d'Alba, turning west for **Grinzane Cavour**. The village castle here contains the **Enoteca Regionale Piemontese Cavour** (*tel: 0173 262 159*), an interesting museum with wines for sale and a restaurant. It's perhaps another 5km across rugged little hills to little **La Morra**, with panoramic views from its village square, its own **wine museum** and shops purveying the excellent local Barolo vintages.

Detour 2: Exit Turin (Torino) to the west, using Corso Vittorio Emanuele II (which becomes Corso Francia) for 15km to get to suburban **Rivoli** ❾, where the cutting-edge **Museo d'Arte Contemporanea** is in the partially restored **Castello di Rivoli** (*Pza Mafalda di Savoia; tel: 011 956 5222; www.castellodirivoli.org*), one of the castles that the Savoy family built surrounding Turin. Ignore the A32 autostrada and keep to the secondary S25 for another 15km. Just as you reach the dramatic foothills of the Alps, take the scenic left turn to **Sacra di San Michele** ❿, a climbing road of a few kilometres to a fine little abbey (*tel: 011 939 130; www.sacradisanmichele.com*) that was once a major stopping point for pilgrims coming south across the Alps. Among its spooky charms are a stairway whose walls contain the interred bones of priests, a door decorated with both biblical scenes and signs of the zodiac, and 16th-century fresco work inside the inner church.

Also worth exploring

The southern portion of the **Parco Nazionale Gran Paradiso** does not connect by road to the northern part, explored from the Valle d'Aosta. The region is well worth discovering, for this is one of Italy's best national parks, a sprawling wilderness of remote river valleys, mountains (the peak of Gran Paradiso itself noses above 4,000m) and exotic-seeming creatures like ibex and chamois. Founded in 1922, the park is interlaced throughout with rugged walking tracks; those on the lower slopes wind through Alpine wild flowers in spring, while the upper reaches pass mostly through pine and beech forests before moving above the treeline.

You can reach the park from Turin (Torino) by any number of indirect ways; but it's easiest, perhaps, to head north towards the city airport, then bear left on to the S460 until it gives way to an unnumbered road continuing onwards north and west through **Cuorgnè** ⓫ and beyond. Get a good map before attempting it.

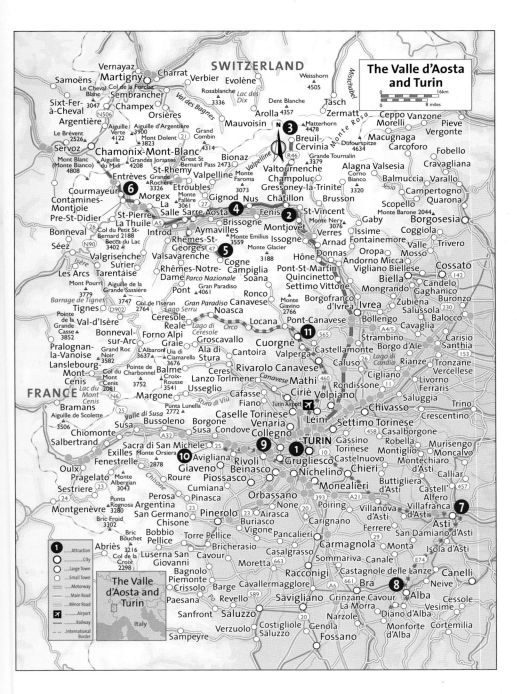

Lake Maggiore

Ratings

Gardens	●●●●●
Villas	●●●●●
Scenery	●●●●○
Architecture	●●●○○
Villages	●●●○○
Walking	●●●○○
Historical sights	●●○○○
Outdoor activities	●●○○○

Lake Maggiore's charms are subtle, rather than overpowering. A circuit of the lake – which juts a bit into Switzerland – soon brings one from the dull holiday villas of the southern shore into much more impressive geology, botany and history, with the lake's characteristic palm trees, colour-washed homes, steamer ferries and harbours to reinforce the sense of gently getting away from the rest of the world. There is a set of small, wonderful islands to explore, along with cutesy resort towns, cable cars and ridges from which to view the expanses of lake and mountains behind. Connecting boats link many of the lake's towns together. The suggested tour traverses the lake's eastern flank first, backtracks, uses a ferry to cross at the midpoint and then finishes with a tour of Maggiore's western shore.

ANGERA

Rocca Borromeo
€ *V. alla Rocca;*
tel: 0331 931 300;
www.roccaborromeo.it. Open
Apr–late Oct 0900–1730.

**Museo dei Transporti
Ogliari** *Off the S629,
Ranco. Open Tue–Sun
1000–1200, 1400–1800.
Free.*

Market day: Thur.

Angera crouches low on the lake's eastern shore under its amazingly well-preserved castle, **Rocca Borromeo**, guarding the strategic southern end of the lake as it has since the 13th century, reached by a steep access road. The Viscontis, bishops from Milan, added frescoes, towers, fortifications and other touches to the crude original structure. There's also a **Museo della Bambola (Doll Museum)** in the main castle, showing more than 1,000 dolls and a courtyard with views of the lake. The small stone palace on the same grounds reveals a further oddity: the **Children's Fashion Museum**, containing tiny examples of luxury children's clothing from the 17th century onwards. Just north, in Ranco, is the thoroughly charming and quirky **Museo dei Transporti Ogliari (Transport Museum)**, an open-air jumble of hundreds of cars, trains, funiculars and other conveyances assembled in a maze of passageways. Some are historically significant – such as Pope Pius IX's railcar chapel – others just interesting. Tracks descend into a coalmine, an escalator into an underground station – all great fun.

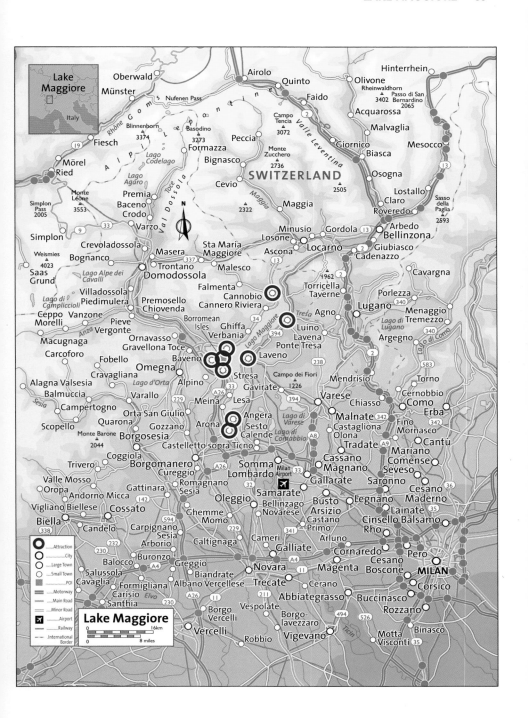

Lake Maggiore
Italy

Oberwald
Münster
Nufenen Pass
Airolo
Quinto
Faido
Olivone
Hinterrhein
Rheinwaldhorn
3402 ▲
Passo di San
Bernardino
2065
Acquarossa
Malvaglia
Mesocco
Giornico
Biasca
Osogna
Lostallo
Claro
Roveredo
Sasso
della
Paglia
2593
Arbedo
Bellinzona
Giubiasco
Cadenazzo
Cavargna
Rhône
Goms
Blinnenhorn
3374
Basodino
3273
Fiesch
Mörel
Ried
Formazza
Peccia
Monte
Zucchero
2736
SWITZERLAND
2505
Lago
Codelago
Bignasco
Cevio
Maggia
Maggia
2322
Minusio
Losone
Ascona
Gordola
Locarno
Lago
Agaro
Premia
Baceno
Crodo
Varzo
Simplon
Pass
2005
Monte
Leone
3553
Simplon
Weismies
4023
Saas
Grund
Crevoladossola
Bognanco
Masera
Trontano
Domodossola
Malesco
Sta Maria
Maggiore
Falmenta
Cannobio
Cannero Riviera
1962
Torricella
Taverne
Porlezza
Lugano
Menaggio
Lago di
Lugano
Tremezzo
Argegno
Val Dossola
Toce
Val Dossola
Villadossola
Piedimulera
Premosello
Chiovenda
Lago Alpe dei
Cavalli
Ceppo
Morelli
Vanzone
Pieve
Vergonte
Borromean
Isles
Ghiffa
Verbania
Agno
Luino
Lavena
Ponte Tresa
Tresa
Lago Maggiore
Macugnaga
Carcoforo
Fobello
Ornavasso
Gravellona Toce
Baveno
Laveno
Lago di Como
Anza
Sesia
Alagna Valsesia
Balmuccia
Campertogno
Scopello
Cravagliana
Omegna
Varallo
Lago d'Orta
Alpino
Stresa
Gavirate
Campo dei Fiori
1226
Mendrisio
Torno
Cernobbio
Como
Erba
583
Meina
Lesa
Varese
Chiasso
Fino
Mornasco
Cantù
Mariano
Comense
Seveso
Quarona
Gozzano
Orta San Giulio
Angera
Sesto
Calende
Lago di
Varese
Malnate
Castagliona
Olona
Tradate
Cassano
Magnano
342
A9
Monte Barone
2044
Borgosesia
Castelletto sopra Ticino
Arona
Lago di
Comabbio
A8
Coggiola
Borgomanero
Cureggio
Somma
Lombardo
Milan
Airport
Gallarate
Saronno
Cesano
Maderno
Trivero
Valle Mosso
Oropa
Andorno Micca
Gattinara
Romagnano
Sesia
Oleggio
Samarate
Bellinzago
Novarese
Busto
Arsizio
Legnano
Lainate
Cinsello Balsamo
Rho
Vigliano
Biella
Biellese
Cossato
Ghemme
Momo
Castano
Primo
338
Candelo
Carpignano
Sesia
Cameri
Arluno
Cornaredo
Pero
Cesano
Boscone
MILAN
Arborio
Caltignaga
Galliate
Magenta
Corsico
Balocco
Buronzo
Greggio
Novara
Salussola
Biandrate
Albano Vercellese
Trecate
Cerano
Abbiategrasso
Buccinasco
Rozzano
Cavaglia
Formigliana
Carisio
Santhia
Elvo
Borgo
Vercelli
Vespolate
Borgo-
lavezzaro
Motta
Visconti
Binasco
Vercelli
Robbio
Vigevano
Ticino

Lake Maggiore
○ Attraction
○ City
○ Large Town
○ Small Town
■ POI
━ Motorway
━ Main Road
━ Minor Road
✈ Airport
┼ Railway
International
Border

0   16km
0   8 miles

Accommodation and food in Angera

Dei Tigli €–€€ *V. Paletta 20; tel: 0331 930 836; fax: 0331 930 911; www.hoteldeitigli.com.* Relatively simple hotel, open spring to autumn; breakfast is served, but there's no restaurant for dinner.

Il Sole di Ranco €€€ *Pza Venezia 5, Ranco; tel: 0331 976 507; fax: 0331 976 620; www.ilsolediranco.it.* One of the best reasons for visiting this part of the lake is to stay in this family-owned villa, whose elegant rooms overlook gardens and Lake Maggiore. Guests get preference for reservations at their highly acclaimed (two-Michelin-starred), extraordinary restaurant.

ARONA

ⓘ Turismo Arona
Largo Vidale 1; tel 0322 243 601. Open Tue–Wed & Sun 0930–1230, Thur–Sat 0930–1230, 1500–1800.

ⓝ San Carlo Borromeo, Belgirate € *Open Mar–Sept daily 0900–1230, 1400–1830; Oct–Nov daily 0930–1700.*

⬤ Market day: Tue.

Arona is the service centre for southern Lake Maggiore, with the shops and amenities that many of the smaller, prettier towns lack. It is neither lovely nor exciting, but it offers a good grocery store, reliable restaurants and plenty of accommodation at affordable prices. Nearby Belgirate strings along the lake shore with good hotels and a more holiday feel to it. The singular monument here that can't be missed – it's 23m tall – is a **statue of San Carlo Borromeo**, which can be ascended via a set of interior stairs and is illuminated at night. The town's **Museum of Archaeology** in Piazza San Graziano (*tel: 0322 48 294*) is worth a look as well.

Accommodation and food in Arona

Hotel Milano €€ *V. Mazzini 4, Belgirate; tel: 0322 76 525; fax: 0322 76 295; www.hotelmilanolagomaggiore.it.* On the lake with its own dock and terrace restaurant; staff couldn't be nicer.

Ristoro Antico €€ *V. Bottelli 46; tel: 0322 246 482. Open mid-Aug–mid-Jul Tue–Sun.* Good-value trattoria.

Villa Carlotta €€ *V. Mazzini 121–125, Belgirate; tel: 0322 76 461; fax: 032 276 705; www.villacarlottalagomaggiore.it.* Villa with terraced gardens, in-room Internet points; favourite of British coach groups.

Taverna del Pittore €€€ *Pza del Popolo 39; tel: 0322 243 366; www.ristorantetavernadelpittore.it. Open mid-Jan–mid-Dec Tue–Sun.* Elaborate fish dishes and lake views make reservations absolutely necessary.

BAVENO

Between busy Verbania and tiny Stresa, the lakeside road circles nearly all the way round to take in the little spur known as Golfo Borromeo.

ℹ *Palazzo Comunale Pza Dante Alighieri 14; tel: 0323 912 311; fax: 0323 924 632; www. comune.baveno.vb.it*

Market day: Mon.

This flat portion of Maggiore is protected as a staging area for songbirds and waterfowl, and is only lightly developed. Round the bend, one emerges at the foot of pinkish Monte Crocino to find Baveno; once rather famous but now a slightly faded resort. It's quite a bit smaller than nearby Stresa, if fairly similar in character. The best church in the village is **Santi Gervasio e Protasio**; its **baptistery** is wonderfully eight-sided and frescoed.

Borromean Isles

ⓩ Ferry information *Tel: 0322 233 200 or 0800 551 801; www. navigazionelaghi.it.* Or use one of the many – and more convenient – water taxis to visit all three on a day ticket.

🅱 Isola Madre € *Tel: 0323 31 261. Open Apr–Oct daily 0900–1730.*

Palazzo Borromeo €€ *Tel: 0323 30 556. Open Apr–Oct daily 0900–1730.*

🄲 Hotel Verbano €€ *V. Ugo Ara 12, Isola dei Pescatori; tel: 0323 30 408; fax: 0323 33 129; www.hotelverbano.it.* Small and serene hotel on the 'fisherman's isle'. Breakfast is included and half-board is available, though the restaurant is only average.

Few sights on Lake Maggiore are as enjoyable as the Borromean Isles, a smattering of villa-covered rocks just off Stresa. Best of all, the three islands are connected to one another – and the lake shore – by frequent ferry runs. Each island's personality is distinct. **Isola Bella**, the most heavily visited of the islands, consists mostly of a palace and its gardens, plus some restaurants and just one simple hotel. The **Palazzo Borromeo** and its associated **gardens** are impressive enough – blooming fruit trees and colourful tropical flowers – but the constructions here pile architectural dazzle upon dazzle, all crests and Murano glass and intricate grottoes; Count Carlo III Borromeo began building the gardens in the 17th century. One ticket admits the traveller into both the palace and its gardens. Smaller **Isola dei Pescatori**, known for its associations with the American novelist Ernest Hemingway, remains a fairly quiet and pleasant place for a stroll – there are alleys, a tiny church and splendid views. The island's fishing industry isn't what it once was, but is still active. **Isola Madre**, the largest, is halfway across the water to Verbania. This island is covered by a **palace**, especially interesting for its puppet theatres, and landscaped **gardens** with terraces, lake views and peacocks.

Right
Boats at Isola dei Pescatori

CANNOBIO

ℹ *V. A Giovanola 25;*
tel: 0323 71 212;
fax: 0323 71 212. Open
Mon–Sat 0900–1200,
1400–1900, Sun
0900–1200.

Market day: Sun.

Very near the Swiss border, Cannobio is a genuine Italian treat, a little lakeside village that has taken full advantage of its position between lake and mountain without having sold its soul to the sprawl of inappropriate development that is encroaching on so many of northern Italy's lakes. There are good walks in town and the environs: walk, drive or cable car into one of the surrounding valleys. Those interested in historic churches should pop into the Renaissance-era **Santuario della Pietà**, an intriguing little structure with a typically Italian history of alleged miracles. Just outside the nearby village of **Cannero Riviera** – itself a fine place to bed down for the night – several ruined castles stand scenically out of the lake water, though closed to the public.

Accommodation and food in Cannobio and Cannero Riviera

Hotel Cannero €€ *Pza Umberto 12, Cannero Riviera; tel: 0323 788 046; fax: 0323 788 048; www.hotelcannero.com.* Serene property with wonderful views of lake and mountains; heated outdoor pool, tennis courts, parking and fine I Castelli restaurant **€€–€€€**.

Hotel Pironi €€ *V. Marconi 35, Cannobio; tel: 0323 70 624; fax: 0323 72 184; www.pironihotel.it.* Former 15th-century palace in the medieval quarter, now comfortably housing guests and serving inclusive breakfasts.

Below
Palace gardens, Isola Bella

Villa Belvedere €€ *V. Casali Cuserina 2, Cannobio; tel: 0323 70 159; fax: 0323 71 991; www. villabelvederehotel.it.* Eighteen rooms in a beautiful setting, plus an attractive heated outdoor pool. Breakfast is included.

Park Hotel Italia €€–€€€ *Lungolago delle Magnolie 19, Cannero Riviera; tel: 0323 788 488; fax: 0323 788 498.* Lovely hotel with splendid views of Maggiore from the garden terrace and pool. Covered car park and on-site restaurant **€€**.

Scalo €€€ *Pza Vittorio Emanuele 32, Cannobio; tel: 0323 71 480; www.loscalo.com. Open Mar–Jul & Sept–Dec.* The outdoor patio heightens the dining experience.

LAVENO

ℹ *Palazzo Municipale, Pza Italia 2; tel: 0332 666 666; www. prolocolavenomombello.com*

⊘ **Ferry information** *Tel: 0800 551 801.*

Laveno sits at the lake's narrowest point. An hourly car-ferry service shortens the driving distance round the lake considerably. Fine ceramics shops sprinkle throughout town and a little cable lift rises to Sasso del Ferro for a good overlook of the lake. Most impressive is the nearby 13th-century hermitage **L'Eremo di Santa Caterina del Sasso** (*open Mar–Oct daily 0900–1200, 1430–1800; Nov–Feb Sat–Sun*), reached by car or small ferry, built into cliffs just outside the town between the villages of Cerro and Reno.

Accommodation and food in Laveno

Il Porticciolo €€ *V. Fortino 40; tel: 0332 667 257; fax: 0332 666 753; www.ilporticciolo.com.* Views of the lake from a classy, ten-room hotel with a restaurant serving regional dishes such as risotto.

LUINO

ℹ *V. Piero Chiara 1; tel: 0332 532 542.*

🏛 **Civico Museo Parisi Valle** € *V. Leopoldo Giampaolo 1, Maccagno; tel: 0332 561 202; www. museoparisivalle.it. Open Jun–Sept Thur–Sun 1000–1200, 1500–1900; Oct–May Fri–Sun & hols 1000–1200, 1500–1800.*

🛒 **Market day:** Wed. This is the biggest market on the entire lake, at Piazza Garibaldi; traffic slows to a snail's pace.

Luino, snuggled on the cosy eastern shore of Lake Maggiore, makes a good stopping point while slowly exploring that shore. Both the **Madonna del Carmine** church (15th century) and the older **San Pietro** (11th century) are worth a look. In nearby Maccagno, the striking **Civico Museo Parisi Valle** art gallery bridges the Giona River, offering an outstanding retrospective of Italian art from the 1930s to the 1980s, as well as works by Picasso. In contrast to its contemporary lines, Maccagno's streets are connected by narrow stone stairways winding through arches beneath a medieval tower.

Accommodation and food in Luino

Hotel Internazionale € *Pza Marconi 24B; tel: 0332 530 193; fax: 0332 537 882. Open Mar–Dec.* Good-value hotel with spacious rooms and amenities such as a lift, in-room TVs and a car park.

Camin Hotel Luino €€ *Vle Dante 35; tel: 0332 530 118; fax: 0332 537 226; www.caminhotelluino.com.* Former villa featuring some rooms with whirlpool baths, a reasonably priced restaurant, a garden and parking.

STRESA

ℹ *V. Canonica 8; tel: 0323 31 308. Open Mar–Nov daily 0900–1800.*

Make no mistake: Stresa is a resort for moneyed holidaymakers and has been since the first of the grand hotels that line its waterfront was built. Its pretty piazze, chic brand-name shops and smart wine bars all cater to this clientele. A well-kept park promenade leads along the

Villa Pallavicino
€€ Tel: 0323 30 235;
www.parcozoopallavicino.it.
Open Mar–Oct daily
0900–1800.

**Monte Mottarone
cable-car service**
€€ Tel: 0323 30 295;
www.stresa-mottarone.it

Stresa Festival
brings world-
renowned classical music
performers and major
symphony orchestras to
beautiful venues along
the lake and islands
each August
(www.stresafestival.eu).

Market day: Fri.

shore from the main steamer dock to the smaller lido station, where boats leave for the Borromean Isles (*see page 55*). Connected to town by a tourist train, **Villa Pallavicino**'s gardens and its expansive parkland, populated with exotic animals from Africa and beyond, make it a good stop for those travelling with children. The villa itself cannot be toured.

A cable car from Lido Station (right on the waterfront) climbs to either **Alpino**, with its wonderful Giardini Alpina (Alpine Gardens), or the last station at **Monte Mottarone** – one of the best places to get a view of the lake and the Alps.

Accommodation and food in Stresa

Triangolo €€ *V. Roma 61; tel: 0323 32 736. Open Jan–Oct Wed–Mon.* Tasty pizza served inside or on an outdoor terrace.

Il Piemontese €€–€€€ *V. Mazzini 25; tel: 0323 30 235. Open Feb–Nov Tue–Sun.* Serving great regional dishes such as *bollito misto*, a boiled meat plate. You can eat outside in the summer.

Grand Hotel des Iles Borromées €€€ *Lungolago Umberto; tel: 0323 938 938; fax: 0323 32 405; www.borromees.it.* One of northern Italy's most renowned luxury hotels; in a lush park, with stunning views.

VERBANIA

Pro Loco Verbania
V. delle Magnolie 1; tel:
0323 557 676.

Villa Táranto € V.
Vittorio Veneto 111,
Verbania Pallanza; tel: 0334
04 555; www.villataranto.it.
Open Apr–Oct daily
0830–1830.

**Lago Maggiore
Jazz Festival**
Summer. Free. Latino-
American, blues, gospel
and Dixieland sounds fill
Verbania piazze, parks and
lake-front promenades.

The western terminus for the cross-lake car ferry, Verbania is really three towns: Intra, Pallanza and Verbania. Pallanza's long waterfront includes gardens, promenades, play parks, cafés and a classic heroic-style monument. South, beyond the Fondo-Toce nature reserve, the town of **Feriolo**, curving around its harbour, is a pleasant low-key base for exploring. The gardens at **Villa Táranto** have thousands of exotic trees, flowers and shrubs in patterned beds. Some come from as far away as the Amazonian rainforest and thrive quite nicely here, in the shadow of the pre-Alps.

Accommodation and food in Verbania

Il Battello del Golfo €€ *Lungolago, Feriolo; tel: 0323 28 122; www.battellodelgolfo.com. Open Jul–Aug daily; Sept–Jun Wed–Sun.* Dine on innovative renditions of local specialities aboard a restored lake steamer.

Il Chiostro €€ *V. Fratelli Cervi 14, Verbania; tel: 0323 404 077; fax: 0323 401 231; www.chiostrovb.it.* Former convent nicely transformed into a large hotel on the lake.

Locanda dei Mai Intees €€–€€€ *V. Nobile Claudio Riva 2, Azzate (Varese); tel: 0332 457 223; fax: 0332 459 339; www.mai-intees.com.* Medieval frescoes decorate walls of this 15th-century manor house above Varese, where guest rooms are filled with antiques. Hospitable owner Carla Promati advises guests on the day's choices from the outstanding kitchen – another reason to stay here.

The area between Lake Maggiore's western shore and Lake Orta is peppered with factory outlets, many of them at the factories themselves and a few in small shopping ventures where several nearby manufacturers have joined to sell their overstocks and seconds. The region is especially known for its metalworking and cookware. At the northern tip of Lake Orta is **Alessi**, whose innovative designs in cooking and tableware are by top international designers. Their dramatic factory showroom sells seconds and current merchandise at discounted prices (*V. Alessi, Crusinallo di Omegna; tel: 0323 868 611. Open Jan–Nov Mon–Sat 0930–1800; Dec daily*). **Lagostina** is known for its everyday cooking utensils and staggering array of pots and pans. At their showroom in Gravellona you can buy these at big discounts (*Parco Commerciale Laghi, V. Stamps 62, Gravellona Toce; tel: 0323 865 058. Open daily 0900–1900*).

L'Osteria €€ *V. Verdi 5, Feriolo; tel: 0323 280 482. Open Wed–Mon.* Behind the rustic wine bar is a stone-vaulted dining room with an acclaimed chef. Pork medallions with porcini mushrooms are delicious.

Serenella €€ *V. Quarantadue Martiri 5, Feriolo; tel: 0323 28 112; www.hotelserenella.net.* Walk from this small, friendly and well-located hotel to several good restaurants or dine in its own – also very good.

Suggested tour

Total distance: 220km, with detours 305km.

Time: 6–7 hours' driving. Allow 2 days without detours, 2–3 days with detours. Those with limited time should choose one shore of the lake on which to concentrate: the eastern shore is generally quieter, the western shore more scenic, historic – and developed.

Links: Milan (Milano) (*see page 74*), the starting point for this route, connects with Lake Como (*see page 62*) via the A2/E35 autostrada. Arona, near the end of this route, can be reached from the Valle d'Aosta and Turin (Torino) route (*see page 48*) via the A5, A4 and A26 autostrade.

Route: From Milan (Milano) ❶, drive the E62 for approximately 55km, exiting for the S33 and Sesto Calende, then continuing west to the lake shore. The road soon turns north along the lake, running for some 50km and becoming progressively more scenic as it passes the magnificent fortress at **ANGERA** ❷, the beaches of **Lido di Montvalle** and **Arolo**, the ferry connection at **LAVENO** ❸ and then lakeside towns such as **LUINO** ❹. After passing a number of attractive side valleys, many worth a short detour, the road eventually reaches the Swiss border. To keep this a purely Italian journey, backtrack 30km to Laveno and catch the car-bearing ferry to **VERBANIA** ❺, then continue north through pretty **Cannero Riveria** and **CANNOBIO** ❻ to the Swiss border once again, this time along the S34, a drive of perhaps 25km to the border post. Backtracking once more, retrace the 25km to Verbania and then drive an additional 35km south along the S33 through winding shore-side scenery and the resort towns of **BAVENO, STRESA** ❼ (jumping-off point for ferries to the **BORROMEAN ISLES**) and finally **ARONA** ❽.

Detour 1: About 50km northwest of Milan (Milano) on the S233 lies **Varese** ❾, the quiet lake of the same name and **Santa Maria del Monte** – one of the region's so-called *sacro monti* (sacred mountains). The walkway climbs past 14 chapels, most dating from the 17th century and each with terracotta statues symbolising the rosary. At the top, the original sanctuary looks out over a park and the lake. Small auberges in Santa Maria include the **Albergo la Samaritana** (*tel: 0332 225 035*) and the **Colonne** (*tel: 0332 244 633; fax: 0332 821 593*).

Giardinetto €€
*V. Provinciale 1,
Pettensasco; tel: 0323 89
118; fax: 0323 89 219;
www.lagodortahotels.com.*
A small hotel overlooking
the island.

Hotel San Rocco
€€–€€€ *V. Gippini 11,
Orta San Giulio; tel: 0322
911 977; fax: 0322 911
964; www.hotelsanrocco.it.*
Set in a former convent
overlooking the lake,
the elegant hotel has a
particularly talented chef.

Villa Crespi €€€
*V. General Fava 8–10; tel:
0322 911 902; fax: 0322
911 919; www.
hotelvillacrespi.it.* Moorish-
style hotel with easy car
access, but somewhat
outside of Orta San Giulio.

Below
The island of San Giulio,
Lake Orta

Detour 2: At Verbania, turn west from the lake shore to find pretty **Lake Orta**, which can be circled via a series of lake-shore roads. (To save time, simply head south on the S229.) The lake's highlights are the well-preserved town of **Orta San Giulio** ❿ and the island of **San Giulio** just across the water, with few tourists, a convent and a surprisingly fine **basilica** (*tel: 0322 90 358. Open summer daily; winter Tue–Sun shorter hours*).

Also worth exploring

To make a complete circuit of the lake, you'll need to bring your passport and continue onwards into Swiss territory for about 20km before re-emerging in Italy; the border post on Maggiore's eastern shore occurs just past little **Pino Lago Maggiore**. Halfway round the Swiss portion is the largest town on the entire lake, **Locarno** ⓫, a combination of tourist services, villas tacked to hillsides and attractions beneath often-sunny skies. You'll almost forget you've crossed a border, what with all the Italian being spoken in the compact streets, piazze and alleyways; summer brings a well-attended, important film festival, further heightening the relaxed sense of Italian cool that prevails here. It's also possible to day trip to Locarno – though you'll have to leave your car behind – via hydrofoil from Arona, Baveno, Cannobio, Luino and Stresa, and other Lake Maggiore towns.

To see some mountains a short distance from the lake, take the E62 autostrada or the slower S33 from Stresa or Verbania to reach **Domodossola** ⓬ and its sacred mountain chapel **Sacro Monte di Domodossola** (*tel: 0324 241 976*), built in 1656. You can continue into Switzerland over the scenic **Simplon Pass** ⓭, over which Napoleon marched his army. Better yet, leave your car in Locarno to board the vintage cars of the Centovalli rail line to Domodossola and back. Among Europe's most scenic train rides, it passes high above the Centovalli (100 Valleys) carved by the Melezza River and its tributaries, crossing 83 bridges in 52km. The route is included on a Eurail Pass.

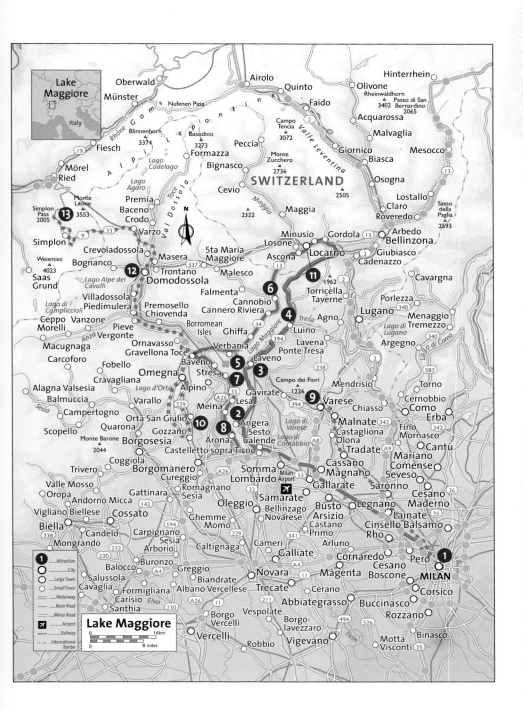

Lake Como

Ratings

Boat trips	●●●●●
Mountains	●●●●●
Scenery	●●●●●
Gardens	●●●●○
Nature	●●●●○
Outdoor activities	●●●●○
Villages	●●●●○
Walking	●●●●○

Como's praises have been sung by centuries of admirers, from the time the Romans built the first villas on its shore. And no wonder. At nearly every point, the narrow lake is enclosed by steep mountainsides, rising to peaks often covered in snow. Pastel villages climb them in picturesque progression, lush foliage painting green all around them. It would be hard to find a prettier place to put a lake, or a more perfect mirror for such mountains. An astonishing array of villas catch these views and although few are open, you can often stroll in their gardens, designed to frame these vistas perfectly. Flowers bloom everywhere, especially in the Tremezzina Riviera, favoured with a mild year-round climate. Explore lakeside villages on foot to find narrow passages hung with flowering vines. Many buildings rise right from the water, often with arcaded watergates and tiny marinas of their own.

BELLAGIO

ℹ IAT *Lungolago Mazzin; tel: 031 950 204; www.bellagiolakecomo.com. Open Mon–Sat 0900–1200, 1500–1800, Sun 0900–1200.*

ℙ Parking, though scarce, may sometimes be found along the shore near the boat landing.

🏛 Villa Melzi d'Eril € *Lungolago Manzoni; tel: 392 214 395; www. giardinidivillamelzi.it. Open Apr–Oct daily 0930–1830.*

In an almost perfect lakeside setting, Bellagio stands at the tip of the peninsula that bisects the lake into a wide inverted Y. The land rises so steeply that the town is built in terraces. Narrow streets climb, lined by balconied yellow buildings with little shops and pleasant cafés at landings between flights of stone stairs. More cafés stretch languidly along an ample waterfront – the lake surrounds Bellagio on all but one side. In the historic town centre sits the 12th-century **Basilica di San Giacamo**, whose bell tower began life as one of Bellagio's defensive towers. Behind the church a long lane leads up to **Villa Serbelloni**, whose outstanding gardens are of 19th-century Italian design, with grottoes and fountains. The villa's interior frescoes are not on view. The surrounding park extends to the very top of the promontory and is landscaped to make the most of the views across the northern arm of the lake to the Alps. Neoclassical **Villa Melzi d'Eril**, with frescoes and stucco work from the early 19th century, sits in splendid isolation

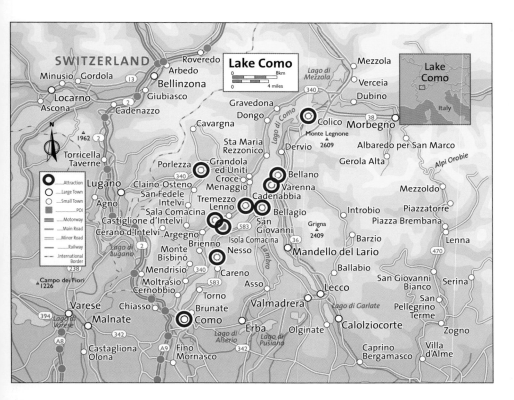

Villa Serbelloni €
Tel: 031 951 555.
Open mid-Apr–mid-Oct
Tue–Sun 1100–1600.

Boutiques, handicraft and antique shops line the streets, but don't expect bargains in this swish little holiday haven.

Tip: Be sure to sample the local cake, *mataloc*, made with nuts and dried fruits.

on the shore south of town, surrounded by its own English-style gardens of exotic plants, azaleas and cypresses.

Walks from Bellagio include down the shore to **Pescallo** (20 mins), a fishing village with waterside cafés, and climbs to the Belvedere at **Mulini del Perlo** (1 hr) or **Makalle** (90 mins) for fine panoramas. Narrow mountain roads climb to the high town of San Primo and to the base of the cable-car ride up **Monte San Primo**, a ski area. At the centre of the lake, Bellagio is a good base for exploring, with boat connections to all three arms and car ferries crossing to either shore.

Accommodation and food in Bellagio

Camping Clarke € *V. Valassina 170c, Località Visgnolà; tel: 031 951 325; www.bellagio-camping.com.* Tent pitches on a small farm with horses, goats and small animals, directly south of Bellagio. You can buy farm-fresh eggs for your breakfast.

Ristorante La Punta €€ *Punta Spartivento 19, Bellagio; tel: 031 951 888; www.ristorantelapunta.it.* The spectacular setting equals the cuisine, such as steak with a green peppercorn sauce or lake-caught whitefish cooked in butter and sage. Garden dining in season.

Opposite
Eastern shore of Lake Como

Grand Hotel Villa Serbelloni €€€ *V. Roma 1; tel: 031 950 216; www.villaserbelloni.it.* Locations don't get any better than this, at the tip of the peninsula, right at the main piazza and boat landing. However grand and palatial the hotel, the staff are as welcoming and hospitable as the smallest country inn.

COMO

ℹ️ **APT** *Pza Cavour 17; tel: 031 330 0128; www.provincia.como.it.* Open Mon–Sat 0900–1300, 1430–1800.

🅝 **Navigazione Lago di Como €–€€€**
Pza Cavour; tel: 800 551 801; www.navigazionelaghi.it. Ferries and hydrofoils run year-round. Day ticket **€€€**.

🅐 **Brunate Funicular**
€ *Pza de Gasperi, on the lake front; tel: 031 303 608; www.funicolarecomo.it.* Open daily 0600–1030.

🅟 **€** Off Via Mazoni, in Piazza Volta, and at the western end of the lake front.

🅜 **Museo Civico (Archeologico) €**
Pza Medaglie d'Oro 1. Open Tue–Sat 0930–1230, 1400–1700, Sun 1000–1300.

Sant'Abbondio *V. Regina, which leads from the train station.* Open daily 0700–1800. Free.

🅾 Como's main product is silk. On the last Sat of each month, Como becomes a giant outdoor antiques market – jammed with people. The market is on *V. Mentana 15, Mon–Sat morning.*

The provincial capital sits at the southern tip, where hills spill into the lake. The palm-lined shore **promenade** past Piazza Cavour is its activity centre, where excursion boats and a regular passenger service leave several times daily. For good views, ride the funicular to **Brunate**, a hilltop resort and good place to begin hikes. Allow about 90 minutes to walk back to Como. The exuberant 14th-century **duomo**, with a Gothic rose window and fine carvings, is considered the best transition in Italy from Gothic to Renaissance. Gothic pinnacles soar and the doorway in the highly decorated marble façade is flanked, not by the usual saints, but the Plinys, both native sons. An odd choice, in the light of Pliny the Younger's correspondence with Emperor Trajan about the reasons for executing Christians. The **Museo Archeologico (Museum of Archaeology)**, part of the Museo Civico, has Neolithic and Roman artefacts discovered in the lake region. **Museo Alessandro Volta**, named after another local boy, whose name we remember in the electric volt, has equipment used in his research. The white 'temple' by the lake front was built to commemorate the centennial of Volta's death. The Romanesque church of **Sant'Abbondio**, created in the 11th century by the *maestri comacini*, Como's own and highly regarded school of architects, has cycles of bright Gothic frescoes in the apse. Its high naves are reminiscent of palaeo-Christian churches. Other sights of architectural interest are **Casa del Fascio**, built 1932–6, behind the duomo, **Porta Vittoria**, the 12th-century gate to the city, and the neoclassical villas, **Villa Geno** and **Villa Olmo**, each surrounded by a public park.

Accommodation and food in Como

Hotel Metropole & Suisse au Lac €€ *Pza Cavour 19; tel: 031 269 444; fax: 031 300 808; www.hotelmetropolesuisse.com.* Right at the lake shore, overlooking the main square and a few steps from sights, restaurants and shopping; look for special weekend rates.

Ristorante Hosterietta €€ *Pza Volta 57; tel: 031 241 516; www.hosterietta.com.* Risotto is the speciality, especially with seafood or truffles.

Terminus €€€ *Lungo Lario Trieste; tel: 031 329 111; fax: 031 302 550; www.hotelterminus-como.it.* The stylish choice in Como is this belle époque grand hotel, recently refurbished to its old polish and right at the centre of the lake front.

ISOLA COMACINA AND SALA COMACINA

🅿 Parking for boats to Isola Comacina is uphill, north of the dock above the S340.

🏛 **Villa Balbianello** *€€ Lenno; tel: 0344 56 110; fax: 0344 55 575. Gardens open to boat arrivals Mar–5 Oct Tue & Thur–Sun 1000–1800. Open to visits on foot same hours Mon–Tue & Sat; guided tours of villa by appointment. Access by boat from Sala Comacina every 30 mins during opening hours.*

⚓ A festival is held at the Oratorio di San Giovanni on Isola Comacina the Sun following St John's Day in late Jun.

Reach the lake's only island, **Isola Comacina**, from **Sala Comacina** by boat €. Fortified and used by both the Romans and Byzantines, the island where the Lombard King Berengar II took refuge in 962 was razed by the citizens of Como in 1169. Only the Baroque **Oratorio di San Giovanni** is intact; the rest are remains of medieval buildings. There are ruins of the pre-1169 **Basilica di Sant'Eufemia**, a palaeo-Christian **baptistery** and eight ruined churches, but the island is short on restaurants. Great for an atmospheric picnic. Between Sala Comacina and Lenno, to the north, is a peninsula ending in the stunningly located Baroque **Villa Balbianello**, reached by boat from Sala. Created by Cardinal Durini in the 1700s, the villa is set in grand gardens at the tip of a wooded point. Statuary and urns filled with bright flowers frame incomparable views. The best view of the villa and its setting is from the water, from a passing lake steamer. **Ospedaletto**, which seems to blend right into Sala, is easy to spot by the unusual late-Gothic campanile that sits below the road. At **Ossuccio**, just off the main road, is the **Santuario della Madonna del Soccorso** and good views of the lake. A processional route leads up to it, past 14 chapels built in the 17th and 18th centuries, each with painted terracotta statues.

Accommodation and food in Isola Comacina and Sala Comacina

Lavedo € *V. Lavedo 1, Lenno; tel: 0344 55 172; fax: 0344 56 115; www.albergolavedo.com.* Small hotel just south of the Tremezzina with a restaurant and patio dining.

Crotto dei Platani €€–€€€ *V. Regina 73, Brienno; tel/fax: 031 814 038.* Dine on creative dishes in a medieval fort, in the winter in its vaulted cellar and in summer on a garden terrace overlooking Como's waters, 8km south of Sala Comacina.

LAKE LUGANO AND PORLEZZA

Opposite
The waterfront at Como

Menaggio, a smart resort town with an attractive historic centre, is more lively than Tremezzo and is the beginning of the road to **Lake Lugano**. Just north, in the shore village of Nobiallo, is the **Santuario della Madonna della Pace**, its setting idyllic in olives and cypresses. After a steep climb from Menaggio to a viewpoint high above Lake Como, the S340 makes its relatively level way west to Porlezza, via **Piano Porlezza**, at the shore of a small lake. **Porlezza** overlooks **Lake Lugano** and although there is a road along part of its shore, the best way to explore the lake towns of **Osteno** and **Valsolda** is by the lake

ℹ️ *Palazzo Civico, Riva Albertoli 5, Lugano; tel: 913 32 32; www.lugano-tourism.ch. Open daily.*

⛵ **Carlo Gilardoni Farm** *V. Roccolo 1, Velzo; tel: 0344 32 671; www.italy-farmholiday.com. Open year-round daily.*

steamer. These boats continue into the Swiss portion of the lake and are the only way from this side to reach the small Italian compound of **Campione d'Italia**, completely surrounded by Switzerland, on the eastern shore of Lugano. It is a lively place, filled with cafés and restaurants. A meandering back-road travels through the hill towns of **Grandola ed Uniti**, roughly paralleling the S340 to Porlezza. The **Carlo Gilardoni Farm** in the little settlement of **Velzo** is a good source of picnic provisions, including farm-produced sausages, ham and cheeses.

Accommodation and food in Lake Lugano and Porlezza

La Vecchia Chioderia €–€€ *V. ai Mulini 3, Grandola; tel: 0344 30 152; fax: 0344 32 937; www.lavecchiachioderia.it.* The rustic dining room specialises in trout, smoked, fresh, sun-dried and in delectable pâtés. Guest rooms, cottages and tent pitches encourage travellers to stay and enjoy riding, walking, cycling and fishing in the Sanagra River.

Villa Principe Leopoldo €€€ *V. Montalbano 5; tel: 91 985 88 55; www.leopoldohotel.com.* The villa's spacious rooms and suites overlook lush gardens and out to Lugano and the distant mountains. The restaurant is exceptional.

Below
Nesso lake front

NESSO

P Parking in Nesso is alongside the S583 below the castle, high above the lake.

Wholly unlike the towns across the lake, Nesso is visited by only a few of the lake steamers and is well hidden from the road high above it. Steep cobbled streets and stone stairs lined with **medieval stone houses** cluster along the sides of a **deep ravine** that cuts the town in two. Through this rocky cleft, which is spanned by a **Roman bridge**, drops a long **waterfall**, as the Nose River reaches Lake Como. It's a steep climb back up to the **ruined castle** and road level, but this is a rare spot on the lake shore where you are likely to be the only visitor in town. It is at its most atmospherically mossy in the morning, but it photographs better when the afternoon sun penetrates the west-facing stone crevices. Just to its south, **Careno** is another tiny moss-covered stone town nearly hidden in the steep lake shore. Like Nesso, it is reached by a path from the road above. At the shore is the Romanesque church of **San Martino**.

Accommodation and food in Nesso

Buy local honey at Locanda Mose.

Locanda Mose € *Località Pian di Nesso; tel: 031 917 909. Open year-round Thur–Tue.* Almost 1,000m above Lake Como, this farm has guest rooms and tent pitches and is a good base for walking and hiking. The restaurant specialises in the produce of the farm itself, filling ravioli with fresh ricotta and baking tarts with fresh-picked berries.

THE NORTHEAST: COLICO, BELLANO AND VARENNA

Abbazia di Piona
Tel: 341 940 331; www.cistercensi.info/piona. Open daily 0830–1230, 1330–1830. Free.

Orrido di Bellano €
Tel: 338 325 7117. Open Apr–Jun daily 1000–1300, 1430–1900; Jul–Sept daily 1000–1300, 1430–1900, 2045–2200; Oct–Mar Sat–Sun & hols 1000–1230, 1430–1700.

Villa Monastero €
V. Statale 22, Pino; tel: 341 814 013. Open mid-Mar–Apr Sat–Sun 1000–1300, 1400–1700; May–Sept Fri 1400–1900, Sat–Sun 1000–1900.

Neither of the small industrial towns of **Colico** or **Bellano** have much charm. Between them, the restored 13th-century abbey, **Abbazia di Piona**, stands at the end of a peninsula that almost encloses the little bay called Laghetto di Piona. The abbey, built by Benedictines, has a very fine **Romanesque cloister** that shows the early transitions into Gothic style. Notice the columns, with their wide variety of carved capitals. Also at the abbey is the 11th-century **San Nicola** church. North of Colico is what Napoleon's army left of **Forte di Fuentes**, a Vauban-style fort. **Orrido di Bellano** is a steep gorge in Bellano, through which cascades a river, seen from walkways above. The cathedral, built in 1348, has a good Gothic façade. A former fishing village, built on its original Roman layout and fortified in the Middle Ages, **Varenna** is connected to both the western and central lake shores by car ferries. **Villa Monastero**, a Cistercian convent abandoned in the 16th century and now a conference centre, has excellent views from the terraces of its formal gardens, less lush than the west shore, but rich in Mediterranean and exotic plants. The ruins of **Castello di Vezio** (€€ *Perledo; tel: 348 824 2504; www.castellodivezio.it; open Mar–Oct daily 1000–1800*), north of town, offer fine views, as well as a ceramics studio, artisanal shops and falconry demonstrations.

Accommodation and food in the northeast

Royal Victoria Hotel €–€€ *Pza San Giorgio 7, Varenna; tel: 0341 815 111; fax: 0341 830 722; www.royalvictoria.com.* Overlooking the boat landing and the flower-lined promenade, the pretty Victoria is also known for its modestly priced grill room, where you can get pizza or full-course meals.

Hosteria del Platano €€–€€€ *V. Statale 29, Fiumelatte; tel: 0341 815 215. Open Wed–Mon 1200–1430, 1900–2130.* The homey and hospitable atmosphere is just right for the dishes based on good local ingredients. Located just south of the town centre, so call first and ask for a free ride there and back.

Below
View from Tremezzo

THE TREMEZZINA RIVIERA

ℹ️ *V. Regina 3, Tremezzo; tel: 0344 40 493; www.tremezzina.com. Open May–Sept Mon–Wed & Fri–Sat 0900–1200, 1530–1830.*

🏛️ **Villa Carlotta €€** *V. del Paradiso, north of Tremezzo; tel: 0344 40 405; www.villacarlotta.it. Open mid-Mar & early Nov daily 1000–1600; Apr–mid-Oct daily 0900–1800; late Oct daily 1000–1700.*

If Lake Como is the garden spot of Italy, then the Tremezzina is the garden spot of Como. The mild climate produces the lushest greenery and flowers, with palms, camellias and blossoming trees in the spring. The Tremezzina begins with Lenno, whose 11th-century **Santo Stefano** has an ancient crypt and octagonal baptistery, also Romanesque. **Mezzegra**, a short distance inland, is where a partisan leader dispatched Mussolini and his mistress in 1945, after their capture at Dongo. Just north of Tremezzo, **Villa Carlotta**, 18th-century palace of Prussian Princess Carlotta, is a museum with sculpture and paintings by masters of the Lombard School. But Villa Carlotta is best known for its **terraced gardens**, built in the 1850s. Camellias, rhododendrons, azaleas and exotic trees frame a never-ending series of lake views. **Cadenabbia** is just past Tremezzo and an easy, pleasant walk along the shore promenade, an alley of plane trees known as Via del Paradiso. Drive up the hill to **Griante** and the little cone-towered church of **San Martino** for a matchless view. This is a good area for those who plan to see the lake by boat, since steamers to all parts of the lake stop here and both car and passenger ferries connect to Bellagio and Varenna across the lake. Lodgings are good, restaurants numerous – if a bit dull – and the atmosphere relaxed and pleasant.

Accommodation and food in the Tremezzina Riviera

Trattoria del Rana €–€€ *V. Monte Grappa 27, Tremezzo; tel: 0344 40 602.* No surprises on the menu, just delicious local favourites, well prepared and served in a pleasant atmosphere.

Grand Hotel Tremezzo Palace €€€ *V. Regina 8, Tremezzo; tel: 0344 42 491; fax: 0344 40 201; www.grandhoteltremezzo.com.* The name says it all; it's both grand and palatial. One of the finest views on the lake and a swimming pool that floats above its waters.

Suggested tour

ℹ️ *V. Regina 23, Cernobbio; tel: 031 343 235; www.comune. cernobbio.co.it. Open Jun–Sept Tue–Sat 1000–1200, 1430–1630, Sun 1000–1300.*

Total distance: 117km, with detours 160km.

Time: 4 hours' driving. Allow 2 days for the main route, 3 days with detours. Those with limited time should concentrate on the Tremezzina and Belaggio, circling the southwestern arm only.

Links: From Milan (Milano) (*see page 74*) Como is a short distance north via the A9. Bergamo (*see page 84*) is east of Como via the S342.

Route: Leave **COMO ❶**, heading north on the S340, following signs to **Cernobbio**. (See *Detour 1 on page 72*.) This is perhaps the most

International approaches From Colico, the S36 heads north for the Swiss border and San Moritz, and the S38 goes east to Tirano, where it connects with the S38A, and to the Bernina Pass, also to St Moritz.

Tip: The road from Bellagio to Como, while scenic, is so narrow and precipitous that it is difficult to focus on the scenery. An option to this tortuous trip is to cross the lake on the car ferry at Bellagio and return to Como along the western shore. Or you can visit this shore from Como by taking the northbound boat.

elegant of all the lakeside resorts, much to the credit of **Villa d'Este**, a late 16th-century villa designed by Pellegrino Tibaldi. Formerly home of the English Queen Caroline, it is now a posh hotel and still hosts royalty, who stroll in its Italianate garden. Not far north of Cernobbio is garden-studded **Moltrasio**, with the 11th-century church dedicated to **St Agatha**. The road borders the lake closely, with excellent views through **Brienno** to **Argegno ❷** (21km). (*See Detour 2 on page 73.*) At the elbow-bend of the lake's western arm are fine views north across the lake to mountains. Even more panoramic are those from the village of **Pigra**, reached by a tramway on the north side of town. Leave Argegno, continuing north on the S340 to **SALA COMACINA ❸** , stopping to take the boats to **ISOLA COMACINA** and **Villa Balbianello**. Continue north along the spectacular coast through **Tremezzo ❹** and **Cadenabbia** to **Menaggio ❺** (14.5km). In Menaggio, follow the S340 to the west, leaving the lake shore and climbing steeply to the viewpoint at **Croce**. A diversion shortly past this leads up the Sanagra Valley to the several small villages of **Grandola ed Uniti**. The S340 continues on its fairly level route to **PORLEZZA ❻** , passing Lago di Piano (Lake Piano) on its way.

From Porlezza, return to Menaggio via the S340, this time turning right before Lake Piano, on a road signposted **Bene Lario**, travelling along the other side of Lake Piano. Rejoin the S340 before the descent into Menaggio (25km). In Menaggio, turn north (left) on to the S340D, following the lake shore through a series of small towns. In **Gravedona ❼**, the 13th-century church of **Santa Maria del Tiglio** is one of the major Romanesque sites in the region, with an octagonal bell tower and outstanding early frescoes of St John the Baptist. Above Rezzonico is the 14th-century **Castello della Torre**, in ruin except for its crenellated tower. The northern end of the lake is flatter, especially in the delta of the Adda and Mera rivers. A sharp right turn after Sorico takes you over these and to the S36, where you turn right, passing **COLICO** and **BELLANO**, before reaching **VARENNA ❽** (54km). At Varenna, take the car ferry to **BELLAGIO ❾**. Follow the S583 southwest along the eastern arm of the lake, following signs to **Lezzeno**. Stop in **San Giovanni** to see the old church, with statuary by Canova. Pass through a succession of towns before reaching **NESSO ❿** and **Careno. Torno** is a medieval village, known for **Villa Pliniana**, built in the 16th century at one of Pliny the Younger's villa sites. The cascade of water there still flows at regular six-hour intervals, just as Pliny described. A path leads 1.5km from the village to the villa's grounds. The road continues along the shore to Como (31km).

Detour 1: Leave Cernobbio, continuing north on the S340, watching for signs to **Monte Bisbino**, a 1,355m mountain whose summit road offers a spectacular panorama. The international boundary with Switzerland runs close to the mountain top. Return to the S340 by the same road (34km).

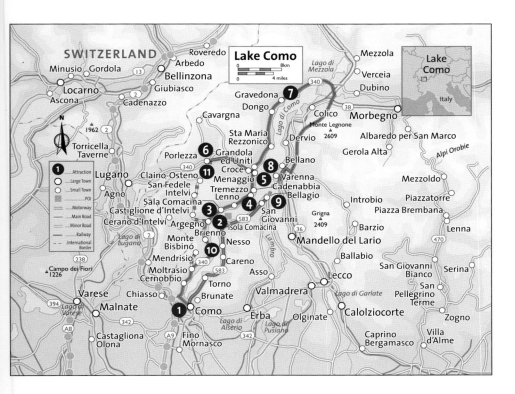

If you choose this inland route over the next lakeside attractions, you can either make a short detour south from Menaggio to see the shore highlights, or you can cross by passenger boat from Bellagio and Lezzeno, later in the itinerary.

Detour 2: For a slower, mountainous ride that leaves the lake's most crowded section, the **TREMEZZINA RIVIERA**, take the unnumbered road from Argegno up the valley of the Telo River. Follow signs to **Cerano d'Intelvi, Castiglione d'Intelvi** and **San Fedele Intelvi**. In Pellio d'Intelvi (10km), turn right to **Laino**. In Laino, bear left to **Claino-Osteno ⑪**, on the shore of **LAKE LUGANO**. Follow the lake shore to the right, to **Porlezza**, where you rejoin the main route, the S340 (12km).

Also worth exploring

The other arm of the lake, known as Lake Lecco, is wilder, with fewer holiday resort towns. The S583 hugs the narrow corniche between the steep mountains and the water. Several roads over the mountainous interior of the triangle connect the lake's two branches.

Milan

Ratings

Shopping	●●●●●
Food and drink	●●●●○
Art	●●●○○
Historical sights	●●●○○
Museums	●●●○○
Architecture	●●○○○
Children	●●○○○
Scenery	●○○○○

Milan is, quite simply, the centre of the New Italia. The nation's most prosperous, important – and self-important – city, Milan remains the home of the catwalk, where the world's fickle fashion decisions are first made. But it is so much more: a teeming manufacturing centre, an arts dynamo and the hub of the Italian sport and publishing industries. It is also an increasingly diverse place, as immigrants rush north to participate in this wealth. Yet visitors will probably do best to avoid the commercial glitter and endless suburbs, focusing rather on historical sights – most of them within a kilometre of the duomo, an over-the-top confection that must be Italy's splashiest cathedral. You can window-shop, sip coffee, view impressive art collections and tour a castle without ever straying terribly far from this unique church.

Getting there

ⓘ *V. Marconi 1; tel: 02 7252 4300; www. milanoinfotourist.com. Open Mon–Fri 0845–1300, 1400–1745, Sat–Sun 0900–1300, 1400–1645.*

Stazione Milano Centrale; tel: 02 7252 4360 or 02 7252 4370. Open Mon–Sat 0900–1900, Sun 0900–1800.

Arriving in Milan is a snap. The city is served by two large airports, nearby Linate (*tel: 02 7485 2200*) and more distant Malpensa (*tel: 02 7485 200*), which is often handier for beginning an excursion to the lakes and mountains. Both are connected to the city centre by regular transport connections: Linate by the No 73 bus to San Babila near the duomo, Malpensa by express trains and buses to Central Station (Stazione Milano Centrale). Once in the city, Milan's railway station is handy enough that one can reach the duomo and the other important sights with a short taxi trip or four-stop Metro ride on the M3 (yellow) line. The railway station neighbourhood and a few others, it should be added, are a bit rough around the edges; crime is on the increase and walking around the city isn't advisable at night except in heavily trafficked shopping or tourist areas. The city's white taxis cruise the key areas day and night; there's a minimum charge of about €3 – more at nights and during holidays, and for luggage.

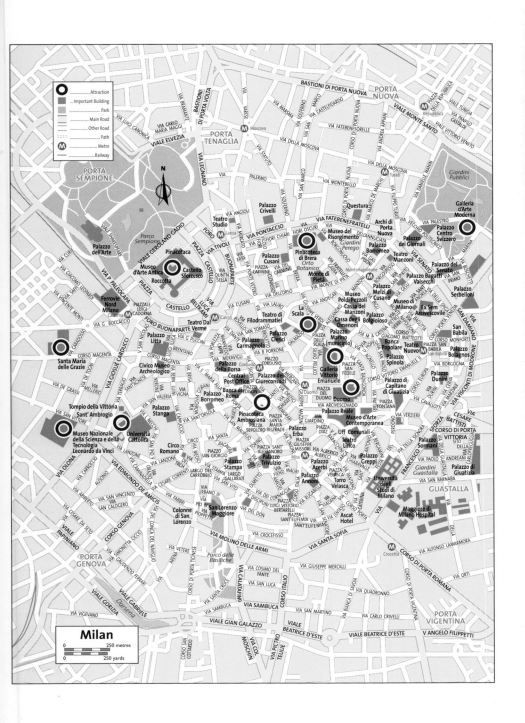

Getting around

The M1 underground line does not run at night; at that time, it is replaced by buses.

Parking is very, very difficult in Milan's city centre and isn't recommended. If it must be done, however, there are car parks on Piazza Diaz (just south of Piazza del Duomo) and near Central Station (on Via Pirelli). Don't challenge the city's traffic patrols, either – you're likely to receive not just a ticket but a free tow to a distant car pound as well.

Milan's shopping is second to none in Italy. For high fashion, explore the Quadilatero district first – bounded by Via Monte Napoleone, Via Sant'Andrea, Via Borgospesso and Via della Spiga – but bring your wallet, things are pricey. For takeaway snacks, produce and budget clothing, find the Saturday morning market at Viale Papiniano, located south of the science museum and near the Porta Genova Metro stop.

Milan is board-flat, making transport easy; but, as Italy's largest commercial centre, there's a good deal of congestion in the central city. Thus, the Metropolitan underground system, which operates along two axes, is the swiftest form of public transport – reliable and inexpensive. Once here, travel to the Duomo Metro station from the central rail station: it's four stops in the direction of San Donato on the yellow M3 line; from San Babila, dropping-off point for the Linate airport bus, it's a one-stop ride on the M1 red line towards Bisceglie or a short walk – as this is where most of the major sights are concentrated.

Driving

Visitors claiming hire cars at the airport can drive into the city centre, but it's not advised – especially during morning and evening rush hours – as traffic is nearly always thick during these times and barely tolerable at others. For those who must, follow signs towards the Centro Historico. Note that Milan's city-centre street system is geared towards pedestrian traffic rather than vehicular traffic, and funnels cars around a ring road and then into congested, narrow one-way streets; you must drive into one of six wedge-shaped sections, so choose carefully using a good map – if you've miscalculated, you'll need to double back out to the ring road to reach the adjacent wedge.

Trams and buses

Buses circulate slowly but regularly through the city; maps can be purchased for approximately €2 at stations and newsstands. Ticket prices are the same for underground or overground transport; purchase them from tobacconists, newsstands or automatic ticket-vending machines on the street. Among the options are single-ride tickets valid for 75 minutes (costing €1), 24-hour tickets (€3) and 48-hour tickets (€5.50). For information, call 800 808181.

Sights

Castello Sforzesco
€ Pza Castello;
tel: 02 8846 3703;
www.milanocastello.it.
Open May–Sept Tue–Sun
0700–1900; Oct–Apr
Tue–Sun 0700–1800.

Castello Sforzesco
Once the exceptionally well-defended stronghold of the dukes of Milan, the city's blockish castle is today better known for the clutch of fine museums behind its walls. There are separate galleries here devoted to artwork, historical artefacts from all over the world, even ancient musical instruments. The sculpture area is probably the best of the lot, but the musical collection gives it a run for its money with an appropriately medieval collection of lute-like instruments.

Duomo € *Pza del Duomo; tel: 02 860 358; www.duomomilano.it.* **Cathedral** *Open daily 0650–1900; roof open daily 0700–1900; crypt open daily 0900–1200, 1430–1800; baptistery open Tue–Sun 1000–1200, 1500–1700.* **Museo del Duomo** *Open Tue–Sun 0930–1230, 1500–1800.*

Below
Duomo, Milan

Duomo

The exterior of Milan's enormous cathedral is the gaudiest, most magnificent example of late-period Gothic architecture in Italy – it is also the nation's largest. Begun in the 14th century by the first duke of Milan, it took some five centuries to get just right. And no wonder! There were more than one hundred intricate (and quite tall) marble spires to contend with, thousands of statues sprinkled throughout its cruciform body, as well as carvings, stained-glass work and the 16th-century tomb of Gian Giacomo Medici. It's free to enter the massive church, though there's a charge to climb the stairs to the roof and gaze out over the piazza and city below. The in-house museum, which also charges a fee, describes the history and contains even more examples of religious artwork. Below is a palaeo-Christian baptistery.

ⓝ Galleria d'Arte Moderna V. Palestro 16; tel: 02 8844 5947; www.gam-milano.com. Open Tue–Sun 0900–1730; € for adjacent PAC complex at No 14.

Galleria Vittorio Emanuele Pza del Duomo. The Galleria's shops open Mon–Sat 0930–1300, 1530–1900.

Museo Nazionale della Scienza e della Tecnologia Leonardo da Vinci € V. San Vittore 21; tel: 02 485 551; www.museoscienza.org. Open Wed–Fri 1000–1700, Sat–Sun & hols 1000–1830.

Pinacoteca Ambrosiana € Pza Pio XI 2; tel: 02 806 921; www.ambrosiana.eu. Open Tue–Sat 1000–1730.

Pinacoteca di Brera € V. Brera 28; tel: 02 722 631; www.brera. beniculturali.it. Open Tue–Sun 0830–1915.

Sant'Ambrogio € Pza Sant'Ambrogio 15; tel: 02 8645 0895; http://santambrogio-basilica.it. Open Mon–Sat 0700–1200, 1400–1900, Sun 0700–1300, 1500–2000.

Galleria d'Arte Moderna

Milan's modern art museum, housed inside an 18th-century palace, is well worth a detour if only for its holdings of paintings by the Impressionists and their kin. You'll find the work of Cézanne, Corot, Gauguin and Van Gogh – all the usual suspects and then some – in the Grassi collection. The PAC next door at No 14 displays revolving exhibits by contemporary artists.

Galleria Vittorio Emanuele

There can't be any doubt what this cruciform, 19th-century complex is all about: it's the city's central shopping centre, meeting place, eating place and agora all in one, domed in magnificent glass ceilings and touched up with mosaic work for good measure. Imagine a beautiful street preserved beneath glass and you've about got the idea. Rarely is a shopping centre such a major attraction. An espresso or cappuccino in one of the cafés can easily cost more than lunch.

Museo Nazionale della Scienza e della Tecnologia Leonardo da Vinci

This sprawling museum just south of the historic centre focuses on Italy's considerable scientific and technical achievements, and while there is much to see here some of the exhibits might be lost on non-Italians. It's best to concentrate on the Leonardo da Vinci Gallery, with drawings, documents and exhibits that chronicle the great inventor's creativity.

Pinacoteca Ambrosiana

This art gallery – originally a palace built for the powerful Cardinal Borromeo – began as a home for his considerable collections. The works include those of Leonardo da Vinci and Caravaggio, as well as non-Italians such as Brueghel the Elder. The attached library contains more drawings by Leonardo da Vinci.

Pinacoteca di Brera

Milan's largest art museum is a sprawling complex on the northerly edge of the historic centre. Its art leans heavily towards Italian masters, both the well known and the lesser known; expect to find paintings by Caravaggio, Piero della Francesca, Raphael or Tintoretto alongside works of Veronese and the Bellinis. The modern rooms are good, though not quite up to the level of the Renaissance holdings. Equally interesting are the streets surrounding the Pinacoteca; they hold numerous smaller galleries, artists' studios and cafés, and convey the same exuberantly artistic feeling as, say, Paris's Left Bank – albeit in trim, elegant Italian clothing.

Sant'Ambrogio

But for the amazing, wedding cake-like duomo, this oft-overlooked church would certainly be Milan's most fascinating. Its foundations were laid under the watch of none other than St Ambrose

Treasury € *Open daily 0930–1200, 1430–1800.*

Chiesa di Santa Maria delle Grazie €–€€
Pza Santa Maria delle Grazie 2; tel: 02 467 6111. Open Mon–Fri 0700–1200, 1500–1900, Sat–Sun & hols 0715–1215, 1530–2100.

Cenacolo €€ *Open Tue–Sun 0815–1900.* Timed Cenacolo tickets must be reserved in advance; obtaining tickets to the Cenacolo is very difficult and there is no guarantee that they will be available at all. Tour companies are allowed to buy up the tickets and package them with city tours. There is no web or telephone access to direct ticketing; it is all done through ticket agencies such as *www.tickitaly.com.* In the off-season in particular it is occasionally possible to get tickets on the spot at the last minute if there are no-shows.

Museo Teatrale alla Scala € *V. Filodrammatici 2; tel: 02 88 791; www.teatroallascala.org. Open daily 0900–1230, 1330–1700.*

(Sant'Ambrogio) himself back in the 4th century and subsequent centuries of work have only rendered it more beautiful. Two bell towers frame the exterior. In its **Treasury (€)** are some splendid bronze doors and a golden altar – both from the 9th century and well preserved – as well as a chapel of exceptional mosaic work and the saint's remains.

Santa Maria delle Grazie

This small 15th-century Dominican friary would normally be drowned in a sea of better attractions, but it just happens to hold Leonardo da Vinci's singular painting *The Last Supper* and thus qualifies as an almost obligatory detour off the beaten Milanese track. The painting doesn't actually reside in the church itself, but rather in the attached **Refectory (Cenacolo)**. Note that all tickets to the Cenacolo must be reserved in advance by telephone; to compensate, however, its opening hours are unusually long by Italian standards.

La Scala

The world's best-known opera house, La Scala's real treasures are within, reserved for those who have landed a precious (and pricey) ticket to an evening's performance. La Scala's theatre season opens annually on 7 December, Milan's patron saint (Sant'Ambrogio) day. To the side of the theatre, the **Museo Teatrale alla Scala** contains stunning costumes worn by the great divas, models of stage sets and touching mementos of Verdi and others; the museum is a must-see for any opera lover and usually offers a visit inside the great opera house itself. An automated ticket sales point lets you choose seats and buy tickets by credit card.

Accommodation and food

Be careful selecting a hotel in Milan; a one- or two-star hotel, normally a sure bet in Italy, is a risky gamble at best here. Pay more for a hotel with at least three stars, especially in neighbourhoods such as that surrounding the railway station. Remember that most of the city's restaurants close on Sunday and in August.

Trattoria Il Carpaccio €–€€ *V. Lazzaro Palazzi 9 (opposite Hotel Sanpi); tel: 02 2940 5982.* Warm, village-style trattoria right in the city, with outstanding carpaccio and *tortelloni*.

First Hotel Malpensa Airport €€ *Case Nuove Somma Lombardo, V. Baracca 34; tel: 0331 717 045; fax: 0331 230 827; www.firsthotel.it.* If you have a morning flight from Malpensa, it is wise to stay as close to the airport as possible, and this is a good choice. Unlike many airport hotels, it is in a nearby village and has a good restaurant, plus there are others close by. Free airport shuttle.

Hotel Ariston €€ *Largo Carrobbio 2; tel: 02 7200 0556; fax: 02 7200 0914; www.aristonhotel.com.* An ecologically friendly place, with all air circulated and ionised, and building materials recycled wherever possible. Bicycles are even available for touring the city once you've left your car in the car park.

Hotel Sanpi Milano €€ *V. Lazzaro Palazzi 18; tel: 02 2951 3341; fax: 02 2940 2451; www.hotelsanpimilano.it.* Stylish and spacious rooms, individually decorated. Quiet courtyard, close to the Stazione Centrale.

Trattoria Casa Fontana €€ *Pza Carbonari 5 (near Metro Sondrio); tel: 02 670 4710; www.23risotti.it.* Risotto Milanese, Milan's speciality, is served here in more than 20 variations, from traditional porcini mushrooms or *zucca* (pumpkin) to some very unexpected combinations.

Trattoria Milanese €€ *V. Santa Marta 11; tel: 02 8645 1991; www.trattoriamilanese.it. Open Sept–Jul Wed–Mon.* Milanese favourites such as osso buco and veal cutlets.

Hotel Ascot €€–€€€ *V. Lentasio 3–5; tel: 02 5830 3300; fax: 02 5830 3203; www.hotelascotmilano.it.* Part of the world wide Best Western group, this is a pleasant hotel with covered parking and includes breakfast.

Below
Pastry shop, Milan

Joia €€–€€€ *V. Panfilo Castaldi 18; tel: 02 2952 2124; www.joia.it. Open Feb–Jul & Sept–Nov Mon–Sat.* Classy, top-quality vegetarian place whose Swiss chef dabbles inventively with aubergine, courgette and ravioli – and also cooks some good fish dishes.

Hotel Mediolanum €€€ *V. Mauro Macchi 1 at V. Napo Torriani; tel: 02 670 5312; fax: 02 6698 1921; www.mediolanumhotel.com.* Contemporary hotel, with a hospitable staff, Wi-Fi and a fitness centre; convenient for the Stazione Centrale.

Shopping

Italy's finest, most expensive shops are located in Milan; besides the **Galleria Vittorio Emanuele** (*see page 78*), the key district is the **Quadilatero**, a region bounded by four streets that contain most of the high fashion houses – of them, Via Sant'Andrea is perhaps the most elegant of the four. Among the local stars are **Giorgio Armani** (*V. Sant'Andrea 9*), **Trussardi** (*V. Sant'Andrea 5*) and **Prada** (*in the Galleria Vittorio Emanuele and also on V. Sant'Andrea*). **Armani Megastore** (*V. Manzoni 31; tel: 02*

7231 8630), a cavernous three-storey shop, is a world unto itself. For more modest prices, look for one of the cut-price designer outlets such as **Il Salvagente**, offering top labels at amazing discounts (*V. Bronzetti 16; tel: 02 7611 0328; www.salvagentemilano.it*). **La Rinascente** (*Pza del Duomo; tel: 02 88 521*) is Milan's most famous department store, featuring well-made yet moderately priced goods; its chief competition is **Coin** (*Pza Cinque Giornate; tel: 02 5519 2083*).

Entertainment

Nightlife tips: Clubbing in Milan requires knowing when to go to which club, as music, clientele and the entire scene changes from one night to the next. Bouncers appear to be there to filter out those who don't look like the sort they think other clients will want to see and be seen with. So dress the part if you want to get into the most popular clubs.

For an interesting neighbourhood with lots of choice, head for the Navigli, south of the city centre. **Le Biciclette** (*V. Torti at Conca del Naviglio; tel: 02 839 4177; www.lebiciclette.com*) has a long happy hour with a buffet, and later shows aimed at the young professional set, while nearby **Scimmie** (*V. Ascanio Sforze 49; tel: 02 8940 2874*) offers eclectic and well-loved jazz. **Propaganda** (*V. Castelbarco 11; tel: 02 5831 0682)* – also in Navigli – is one of the city's most popular nightclubs; sometimes there are live shows and salsa nights. **Hollywood** (*V. Como 15; tel: 02 659 8996*) is the nightclub in the equally chic La Brera neighbourhood. To see top-name international performers at **FilaForum** (*V. G di Vittorio; tel: 02 5300 6501*), get tickets from Ticket One (*www.ticketone.it*) or Easy Tickets (*www.easytickets.it*).

Walking tour

Total distance: 2–3km, with detours 4–5km.

Time: Allow 1 full day with or without detours, perhaps an additional day to explore more fully the duomo and all the churches and museums on this itinerary. If you're pressed for time, you can skip Sant'Ambrogio, Santa Maria delle Grazie and the Leonardo da Vinci Gallery; from the Castello, it's a short (though crowded) walk back down busy Via Dante to the duomo.

Links: Milan is located approximately 50km south of Como (*see page 64*) – the A9 autostrada connects the city to the Como region – and approximately 50km southwest of Bergamo (*see page 84*), reached via the A4 autostrada.

Route: Begin at the always lively Piazza del Duomo, with its tourist information kiosk and awe-inspiring duomo. Jump right in by visiting the elegant, over-the-top **DUOMO ❶**, one of Italy's very finest, making time to take in both the marvellously intricate exterior and the somewhat subdued (but obviously enormous) interior. The piazza's northern side is taken up by the **GALLERIA VITTORIO EMANUELE ❷**, a gorgeous shopping complex that's the nexus point of Milanese society and the perfect place to down an espresso or browse through every manner of wares. Thus fortified, proceed a short distance north to **LA SCALA** ❸, Italy's – indeed, the world's – best-known opera house.

From La Scala, the walking begins in earnest. Head two blocks north along Via Brera to the large **PINACOTECA DI BRERA** ❹, Milan's biggest and most significant museum complex. Also take time to explore the surrounding area, a kind of bohemian Milan. It's a few blocks west – along the direct, busy ring road, Via Pontaccio, or smaller alleys that locals can show you – to the **CASTELLO SFORZESCO** ❺. This imposing edifice once defended the city's dukes from invasion and now holds a good concentration of several galleries in one place, some of them quite intriguing. From the Castello, busy Via Dante brings you smartly back to the city centre and the duomo in a few minutes' time if you so choose. If you've still the energy, however, there are churches and museums in the southern quarter of the city centre remaining to be explored. (*See **Detour 2** below.*)

Detour 1: From La Scala, walk northeast along crowded Via Alessandro Manzoni away from the city centre. Shortly you come to the **Museo Poldi Pezzoli** (€ *www.museopoldipezzoli.it. Open daily 1000–1800*) on the right, an old house containing a good selection of paintings, timepieces and whatnot, and then – again right, past the cross-street called Via Monte Napoleone – is the atmospheric **Palazzo Bagatti Valsecchi** (€ *www.museobagattivalsecchi.org. Open Sept–Jul Tue–Sun 1300–1700*), which is full of rooms interestingly furnished in various themes. Return to Via Manzoni and continue along it past the ring road, until you reach the city's botanic gardens and two museums. Milan's U-shaped **GALLERIA D'ARTE MODERNA** ❻ contains the city's primary collection of modern art; its holdings include work by Cézanne and Van Gogh. Just adjacent and across Via Palestro, the city's **Museo Civico di Storia Naturale (Natural History Museum)** is not exceptional, but makes a child-friendly detour – it's a good idea to send half the family here while others are contemplating the artwork.

Detour 2: A few blocks south along the ring road (named Via Giosuè Carducci at this point), one soon reaches the Corso. Turn right and continue to **CHIESA DI SANTA MARIA DELLE GRAZIE** ❼, a small friary (*see page 79*) with Leonardo da Vinci's great *The Last Supper* concealed within the attached **Refectory (Cenacolo)**. A bit further south along Via Carducci, is the cross-street called Via San Vittore. A left turn brings you to the church of **SANT'AMBROGIO** ❽, a fairly simple yet remarkable Romanesque structure whose origins go all the way back to Saint Ambrose himself in the 4th century. A right turn and you're soon at the entrance to the cavernous (and hard-to-say) **MUSEO NAZIONALE DELLA SCIENZA E DELLA TECNOLOGIA LEONARDO DA VINCI** ❾. As you might expect, it is heavy with exhibits tracing the scientific contributions of Italians, most notably Mr da Vinci.

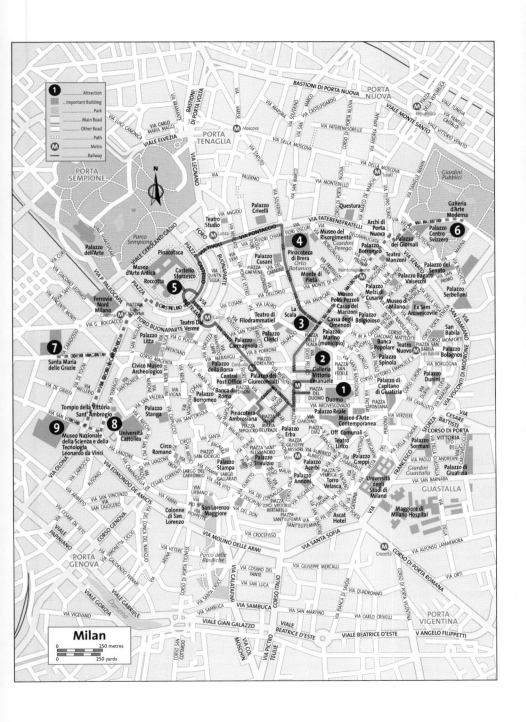

Milan

0 ——— 250 metres

0 ——— 250 yards

Bergamo and Lake Iseo

Ratings

Architecture	●●●●○
Art	●●●●○
Scenery	●●●●○
Boat trips	●●●○○
Food and drink	●●●○○
Historical sights	●●●○○
Mountains	●●●○○
Outdoor activities	●●○○○

High on a rocky promontory, Bergamo's old city is a charming warren of stone buildings that wear their centuries well. Its cobbled streets are lively with cafés and restaurants, and art treasures abound. Yet Bergamo is not on every traveller's list. It ought to be, along with the most overlooked of Italy's larger lakes, Iseo. Sheer limestone cliffs drop straight from tiny medieval villages; a cone-shaped island rises out of the middle, its shores busy with fishermen, its heights crowned by castles. Along the eastern shore are a remarkable string of medieval churches decorated with frescoes that are hardly ever mentioned. To the north is the Valle Camonica, where prehistoric peoples carved hundreds of pictographs on to the valley's rocks. So rich are these finds that a national park surrounds them. It's a part of Italy well worth exploring.

BERGAMO

ⓘ **APT** Città Alta (Upper City) V. Gombito 13; tel: 035 242 226; www. provincia.bergamo.it; Città Bassa (Lower City), Pzle Marconi; Tel: 035 210 204. Open daily 0900–1200, 1400–1730. **Bergamo Airport** Tel: 035 320 402.

Ⓟ Parking € is limited, but available in the Città Alta (Upper City) at Piazza Mercato Fieno, off Via San Lorenzo and along the walls near Porta Sant'Agostino.

High above Bergamo's newer city is the walled **Città Alta**, the old Upper City, where Bergamo's treasures are concentrated. The Venetian Lion of St Mark above the Città Alta's entrance gate, **Porta Sant'Agostino** (1592), on the east, leaves no doubt who built the 5km of walls that surround the old town. To the north is the least pretentious gate, **Porta San Lorenzo**, through whose single passage Garibaldi entered with his troops and liberation in 1859. At the centre of the old city is the beautiful ensemble of **Piazza Vecchia**, bounded by **Palazzo del Podestà**, the tall **Torre del Comune** and the **Palazzo della Ragione**, with its columned staircase, triple-arched loggia, Gothic arches and a definite Venetian flavour complete with lion. In the centre of the piazza is the **Contarini Fountain** with its friendly, looking lions and serpents. Tucked into the corner by the loggia is a café, a prime spot for seeing the piazza at night – a highlight of Bergamo. Through the loggia is **Piazza Duomo**, with the Romanesque

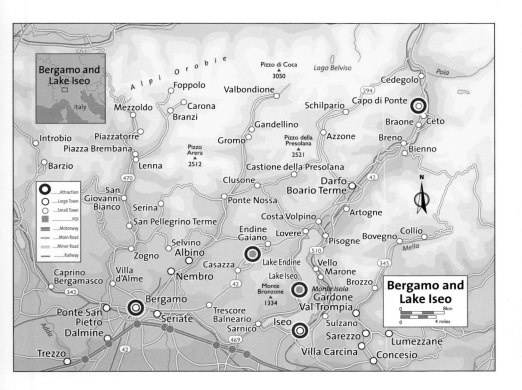

Santa Maria Maggiore *Pza Duomo; tel: 035 222 327.* Open Apr–Oct daily 0900–1200, 1500–1900; Nov–Mar daily 0900–1200, 1500–1800. Hours may vary seasonally. Free.

Colleoni Chapel *Pza del Duomo; tel: 035 210 061.* Open Mar–Oct daily 0900–1230, 1400–1830; Nov–Feb daily 0900–1230, 1400–1630. Free.

Donizetti Birthplace € *V. Borgo Canale 14; tel: 035 242 839.* Open by appointment.

Santa Maria Maggiore and the Renaissance **Colleoni Chapel**, mausoleum of *condottiere* Bartolomeo Colleoni, designed by Giovanni Amadeo. Built on to Santa Maria Maggiore, its Renaissance polychrome marble and embellishment jars with the Gothic simplicity of the church. Inside, however, is some of the finest Lombard art. The centrepiece is the tomb of Colleoni, topped by a gilt equestrian statue. The tomb of Medea, his daughter, is graceful and serene.

Outside, the unusual **baptistery** (*tel: 035 210 311. Open by appointment*) faces the duomo from across the piazza. It was originally inside, removed in 1659 and stored, re-erected in 1856, again torn down and rebuilt. Eight 14th-century statues of virtues surround the roof. **Santa Maria Maggiore** was begun in 1137 and, as the Colleoni Chapel and a vestry, retains its original exterior. Inside, the church has lost its Gothic past to the Baroque, but 13th-century frescoes survive on the left side and by the south door is an exquisite fresco from 1347. The walls are hung with nine 16th-century Tuscan tapestries. Of interest to music lovers are the tombs of Simone Mayer and Gaetano Donizetti. On the backs of the benches in the Presbytery is outstanding marquetry of biblical scenes. Behind Piazza Duomo is the **Tempietto di Santa Croce**, from the 9th and 10th centuries (*tel: 035 237 279. Open by appointment*).

Museo Donizettiano
€–€€ *V. Arena 9; tel: 035 399 269. Open Mon–Fri 1000–1300, Sat–Sun 1000–1300, 1430–1700.*

Rocca Viscontea
V. Rocca; tel: 035 236 284; www.museostoricobg.org. Open Jun–Sept daily 0930–1300, 1400–1730; Oct–May Tue–Sun 0930–1300, 1400–1730. Free.

Accademia Carrara €
Pza G Carrara 82A; tel: 035 399 677; www. accademiacarrara.bergamo.it. Open Jun–Sept Tue–Fri & Sun 1000–2100, Sat 1000–2300; Oct–May Tue–Fri 0930–1730, Sat–Sun 1000–1800.

Galleria d'Arte Moderna e Contemporanea
V. San Tomaso 53; tel: 035 339 527. Times vary with exhibitions. Free.

Torre del Comune
Pza Vecchia; tel: 035 262 565. Open Mar–Apr Tue–Fri 1000–1230, 1400–1800; May–Sept daily 0800–2200; Oct Sat–Sun 1000–1800; Nov–Feb Sat–Sun 1030–1600. Free.

Shopping for gourmet foods is a highlight of Bergamo, especially at Mangili Angelo (*V. Gombito 8; tel: 035 248 774*), where you will find cheeses from local farms, sausage, cured meats, dried pasta and the ingredients for the local polenta.

Leading back to Piazza Duomo is a passage through the **Aula della Curia**, the ancient entry hall to the diocesan offices. Inside are splendid 13th- and 14th-century frescoes, including one of Christ Judging the Damned, showing Christ with a dagger between his teeth. On the same street is the **Museo Donizettiano**, the home where Donizetti wrote many of his operas. The town's castle, **Rocca Viscontea**, dates back to the 11th century. Access it through Remembrance Park. The outstanding **Accademia Carrara**, in the lower city, houses Italian and European art covering several centuries. One of Europe's major collections, it has over 1,600 paintings, plus prints, bronzes and sculptures. Artists include Titian, Tiepolo, Dürer, Velázquez, the Bellinis, Mantegna, Canaletto, Longhi, Carpaccio, Pisano, Botticelli and more. Opposite is the **Galleria d'Arte Moderna e Contemporanea** in a 16th-century monastery.

Right
Castle entrance, Bergamo

Accommodation and food in Bergamo

Caffè del Tasso € *Pza Vecchia 3; tel: 035 237 966; www.caffedeltasso.it.* In a corner of the piazza next to the loggia, a good place for breakfast, coffee or for evening drinks in the piano bar.

Trattoria Tre Torri € *Pza Mercato del Fieno (south end of V. San Lorenzo); tel: 035 244 366.* Try the *gnocchetti* with cream and rocket and don't miss their polenta with porcini and Taleggio cheese.

Da Franco Ristorante €€ *V. Colleoni 8; tel: 035 238 565; www.dafrancoitalianrestaurant.com.* A good choice for dining in the Città Alta, serving beautifully prepared local specialities.

Hotel Agnello d'Oro €€ *V. Gombito 22; tel: 035 249 883; fax: 035 235 612; www.agnellodoro.it.* This comfortable and attractive hotel is in the centre of the Città Alta, only a few steps from Piazza Vecchia and the main attractions. Its restaurant serves local specialities.

San Lorenzo €€ *Pza Lorenzo Mascheroni 9A; tel: 035 237 383; fax: 035 237 958; www.hotelsanlorenzobg.it.* Within an easy walk of Piazza Vecchia, in a historic building with parking available, it is suitable for people with disabilities.

Best Western Premier Cappello D'Oro €€–€€€ *Vle Pappa Giovanni XXIII 12; tel: 035 232 503; fax: 035 242 946; www.bestwestern.it.* Easy to reach by car and with covered parking, in the centre of the Lower City, near the funicular station to the Upper City. Full English breakfast.

CAPO DI PONTE

ⓘ *At Darfo Boario Terme, tel: 0364 531 609; at Edolo, tel: 0364 71 065; at Ponte di Legno, tel: 0364 91 122.*

Ⓟ *Parking for the national park is signposted from the S42, in a large car park in town. A footpath climbs to the park. In quiet seasons, you can drive to a higher point, parking in the few spaces at the entrance.*

ⓘ Parco Nazionale delle Incisioni Rupestri € *Signposted from the S42, tel: 0364 42 140. Open Mar–mid-Oct Tue–Sun 0830–1930.*

History records human settlements in the **Valle Camonica** from the Rhaetians, then the Cenomani tribe of Celts, as early as 400 BC. But even earlier prehistoric peoples provide the valley's highlight, **Parco Nazionale delle Incisioni Rupestri**, at **Capo di Ponte**. Located at several different places, all well signposted, are groups that total hundreds of prehistoric images carved into the rock. Incisions include deer, shovels, labyrinths, hunters and ladders, as well as 'northern Etruscan' alphabets. A descriptive map in English is available. Small museums at two of these locations help set the scene. Close by is the **Monasterio di San Salvatore**, from the 11th and 12th centuries, in Burgundian Romanesque style with beautifully carved capitals. Capo di Ponte's parish church of **San Siro** is of 8th-century Lombard origin, but the present church is 11th-century Romanesque, with good stone carving. Two parks, **Parco dell'Adamello** and the **Parco Nazionale dello Stelvio**, provide opportunities for getting out of the car and hiking.

Accommodation and food in Capo di Ponte

Monasterio di San Salvatore € *Open daily 0900–1200, 1500–1800.*

Bressanelli € *V. Medaglie d'Argento 2, Sellero (just north of Capo di Ponte); tel: 0364 637 307.* Cottages and rooms by reservation in an inviting *agriturismo* inn, hidden in the forest close to hiking trails and the Parco Rupestri. It also has a restaurant **€** that serves good lamb stew or rabbit with polenta.

Iseo

Azienda Promozione Turistica *Lungolago Marconi 2; tel: 030 986 8533. Open Mon–Sat 0900–1230, 1530–1830, Sun 0900–1230.*

Parking is available along the lake front.

Castello Olfredi *V. Mirolte. Open Mon–Fri 0900–1200, 1400–1700.*

San Pietro in Lamas *Amici del Monastero c/o Batista Simonini, Provaglio d'Iseo; tel: 030 983 477. Call for opening hours.*

The long Lake Iseo, at the end of the Camonica Valley, was from prehistoric times an important highway for the products of the entire region and **Iseo** was its major trading post. With the building of a shoreline road and a railway in the 19th century, lake traffic declined, but Iseo remains an important community for the lake's tourism. On Piazza Garibaldi is its **town hall**, built in 1830 at the height of the town's power. On nearby Via Mirolte is the **Castello Olfredi**, dating from the 11th century, burnt by Frederick I of Swabia (The Redbeard) on his campaign to suppress the Guelphs. Rebuilt in the 14th century, it has served as a monastery and today houses the town's library. The church of **Sant'Andrea**, from the 12th century, shows its Lombard Romanesque heritage on the outside, particularly in its notable bell tower, but the interior was 'modernised' in the 19th century in the neoclassical style. On the exterior is the **tomb of Giacomo Olfredi**. **Lungolago Marconi** is a promenade with beautiful views of the lake, towards **Monte Isola** island. At **Provaglio d'Iseo**, on the main road south of Iseo, is the 12th-century monastery of **San Pietro in Lamas**, with fine frescoes dating from the 15th century.

Accommodation and food in Iseo

Hotel Milano € *V. Lungolago G Marconi 4; tel: 030 980 449; fax: 030 982 1903; www.hotelmilano.info.* The hotel looks out across the lake and several of its 15 rooms have lake-front balconies. The restaurant **€–€€**, with a terrace, serves trout, grilled duck and several veal dishes.

L'Albereta €€€ *V. Vittorio Emanuele 11, Erbusco; tel: 030 776 0550; fax: 030 776 0573; www.terramoretti.it.* A 19th-century villa hotel with beautifully decorated guest rooms, sumptuous baths, gardens and an elegant restaurant with a creative chef – delicate pasta may enclose scallops touched with ginger. The villa is south of Iseo, close to the A4 autostrada.

Above
Vello, from upper terrace, Lake Iseo

LAKE ENDINE

P Parking is available
along the lake shore,
in a large lay-by apart from
hotels or other facilities,
whose purpose seems to
be for enjoying the scenery
and picnicking.

Even few Italians choose quiet Lake Endine, one of the prettiest and least developed of the Italian lakes. Long and very narrow, it winds along the base of a mountain to its east. On the valley floor and along the shore are farms. Unlike other lakes, it has almost no development along its shore, despite the fact that a well-travelled road borders it on one side and a smaller one on the other. An ochre-coloured farmhouse is about all you'll see along its tree-lined banks. The town of Endine Gaiano spreads along the western side, providing traveller services, but doesn't quite touch the shore itself.

Accommodation and food in Lake Endine

Hotel Bonanza € *V. per Ranzanico, Valcavallina (near Bianzano); tel: 035 814 161; www.ristorantebonanza.it.* Rooms are not large, but have private baths; the hotel has Wi-Fi access and a restaurant serving regional dishes.

Hostaria la Trisa €€ *V. IV Novembre 2; tel: 035 825 119.* Expect the likes of quail breast or ravioli filled with porcini.

LAKE ISEO

ⓘ APT *V. Lantieri 6,
Sarnico; tel: 035 910
900.*

➋ A ferry service to
Peschiera Maraglio
and Sensole operates from
Sulzano on the east shore
road. Ferries to Carzano
leave from Sale Marasino.
Both ferries are frequent
but hours vary.

**Santuario della
Madonna della Ceriola**
*Monte Isola, on the top of
the mountain outside Cure,
accessible by bus in summer.
Free.*

Rocca Martinengo
*Monte Isola, near Menzino,
north of Sensole.*

Castello Oldofredi
*Monte Isola, west of
Peschiera Maraglio on the
road to Sensole.*

**ⓑ Barcaioli
Monteisola** € *Boat
trips around Monte Isola. By
appointment; tel: 0347 819
9172 Mario or 0335 844
0916 Emanuele; www.
barcaiolimonteisola.it*

**Gestione Navigazione
Lago d'Iseo** €–€€€ *V.
Ariosto 21, Milano; tel: 02
467 6101; fax: 02 4676
1059. Reservations: V.
Nazionale 16, Costa Volpino;
tel: 035 971 483; fax: 035
972 970. Boat tours and
ferries on the lake.*

Santa Maria della Neve
*On the road towards Fraine,
Pisogne; tel: 0364 87 032.
Open daily 0930–1130,
1500–1800. Free. If closed,
enquire at Romanino Bar,
next door.*

Lake Iseo, not far west of Lake Garda, has much of the same beauty, but far fewer visitors. For more than a millennium it has been a place of fishermen, merchants and nobles from Brescia and Bergamo who summered in palaces along its shore. In the middle of the lake is **Monte Isola**, the largest freshwater lake island in Europe. At the top of the lake, **Santuario della Madonna della Ceriola** has a venerated wooden statue of Mary and an Ecce Homo fresco. **Rocca Martinengo**, from the beginning of the 14th century, and **Castello Oldofredi**, outside Peschiera Maraglio, are the island's castles. Fishing and the curing of fish are still important occupations on the island and you can see the curing houses and watch people making or mending fishing nets. **Barcaioli**, a local cooperative, conducts private tours of Monte Isola and two other islands, including visits to a net-making shop and a boatbuilder. While a road encircles Lake Iseo, you can also tour it by boat and by train. **Gestione Navigazione Lago d'Iseo** operates ferries and touring boats with dining facilities.

The region is especially known for its frescoes. From the town of **Marone**, a narrow road winds uphill to **Zone**. On the way, **Santa Maria delle Rota** has several frescoes by Giovanni da Marone and there are more at **San Giorgio di Cislano** in Zone. Along the lake road, at the **Chiesa Cimiterio (Cemetery Church)** on the right just as you enter the village of Vello, are more da Marone works. At the head of the lake on the east shore is **Pisogne**, a small town at the entrance to the Camonica Valley, where **Santa Maria della Neve**, a former monastery, has an outstanding series of frescoes by Girolamo Romani. The parish church of **Santa Maria in Silvis** (1485) also has restored frescoes by Giovanni da Marone. For wild scenery, head uphill to the old centre of **Riva di Solta**, called **Zorzino**, to see the vertical limestone cliffs that drop into the lake. The old town of **Castro**, built on Roman foundations, has another vertical cliff.

Accommodation and food in and around Lake Iseo

Trattoria Cacciatorre €–€€ *V. Molini 28, Sulzano; tel: 030 985 184; www.trattoriacacciatore.it. Open Mon lunch, Wed–Sun.* Traditional dishes, friendly owners and views over the lake to Monte Isola; modest guest rooms share baths.

Albergo/Ristorante La Foresta €€ *Peschiera Maraglio; tel: 030 988 6210; fax: 030 988 6455.* A modest lodging on the lake, with a restaurant and bar.

Trattoria Al Porto €€ *Porto del Pescatori 12, Clusane; tel: 030 989 014; www.alportoclusane.it. Open Thur–Tue.* The restaurant's fame rests on a special way of preparing lake fish – *tinca al forno con polenta* – but everything on the menu is good.

Suggested tour

Total distance: 178km, with detours 188km.

Tim: 6 hours' driving. Allow 3 days for the main route with or without detours. Those with limited time should concentrate on Bergamo.

Links: The A4 connects Milan (Milano) (*see page 74*) to Bergamo from the west and to Brescia (*see page 94*) on the east. From Iseo, it is only a few kilometres to Brescia on the S510.

Route: Leave **BERGAMO** ❶ heading southeast on the A4, exiting at **Palazzolo**. Bear northeast and follow the S469 until you reach **ISEO** ❷. Follow the eastern side of **LAKE ISEO** ❸ on the shore road, avoiding the S510, which does not access the lake as well. Continue through **Sulzano, Marone** and past Vello, bearing right on to the S42 before reaching **Pisogne** (64km). Follow the S42 along the Valle Camonica past **Darfo** and **Breno** to **CAPO DI PONTE** ❹. Backtrack to Darfo, bearing right on to the S42, signposted **Lovere**, bypassing that town (70km). (*See Detour 1 below.*) From Lovere, at the north end of Lake Iseo, the S42 leaves the lake's steep west shore and after passing through a series of tunnels it emerges at the town of **Endine Gaiano** near the head of **LAKE ENDINE** ❺. (*See Detour 2 below.*) From the lake, continue south on the S42, following signs back to Bergamo (44km).

Detour 1: Instead of bypassing Lovere, take the local route through it, following the lake shore and signs to **Castro** and **Riva di Solto**. Follow the scenic shore to the less-than-scenic industrial town of Sarnico. Continue south, following signs to Credaro and Palazzolo, turning west at the A4 and following it back to Bergamo (55km).

Detour 2: For an even more rustic view of Lake Endine, before reaching Endine Gaiano, bear left at the head of the lake, following signs to **Monasterolo del Castello**. The road follows the wooded shore, past a few farms. Stop for views of the castle before rejoining the S42 in **Casazza** (8km).

Getting out of the car

You can reach Lake Iseo from Bergamo via the **Treno Blu** (*tel: 035 424 3937; www.ferrovieturistiche.it*), a tourist railway that runs to Sarnico, where it links with the boats of Navigazione del Lago for a water tour of the lake and Monte Isola. Buy tickets on board or at **Clio Viaggi** (*V. G d'Alanzo, Bergamo; tel: 035 233 031; fax: 035 248 023*). A day excursion includes train, boat to Monte Isola and lunch.

Right
View from Lungolago Marconi,
Iseo

Opposite
Monte Isola, Lake Iseo

Also worth exploring

ℹ️ Ask at any APT office
for a copy of the
Agriturismo booklet for
Lombardy. It will list small
farms that welcome
visitors to buy their
produce, dine or spend
the night.

The **Val Bremabana** is the valley of the Brembo River, as it flows through the mountains on a route that traders have followed for centuries. This rural area is filled with small farms, many of which welcome visitors to buy their cheese, sausage, fresh-baked goods, wines and fruit. Follow the Brembo to the spa town of **San Pellegrino Terme ❻**, whose belle époque grand hotel is sadly closed, but whose Art Deco cafés and spas still thrive.

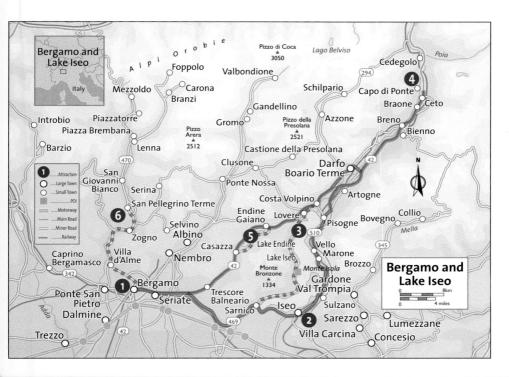

Bergamo and
Lake Iseo

Italy

A l p i   O r o b i e

Pizzo di Coca
▲ 3050

Lago Belviso

Poia

Foppolo

Valbondione

Cedegolo

294

Capo di Ponte

Mezzoldo

Carona
Branzi

Schilpario

Braone
Ceto

Introbio

Piazzatorre

Gandellino

Azzone

Breno

Piazza Brembana

Gromo

Pizzo della
Presolana
▲ 2521

Bienno

Barzio

Lenna

Pizzo
Arera
▲ 2512

Castione della Presolana

42

Clusone

Darfo
Boario Terme

San
Giovanni
Bianco

470

Ponte Nossa

N

Serina

Costa Volpino

Artogne

San Pellegrino Terme

Endine
Gaiano

Lovere

Collio

6

Selvino
Albino

Pisogne

Bovegno

Mella

Zogno

Casazza

Lake Endine

510

Vello
Marone

345

Caprino
Bergamasco

Villa
d'Alme

Nembro

Lake Iseo

Brozzo

342

42

Monte
Bronzone
▲ 1334

Monte Isola

**Bergamo and
Lake Iseo**

1

Bergamo

Gardone
Val Trompia

0   8km
0   4 miles

Ponte San
Pietro
Dalmine

Seriate

Trescore
Balneario
Sarnico

Iseo

Sulzano

Lumezzane

Trezzo

42

469

2

Villa Carcina

Sarezzo

Concesio

3

4

5

- **1**   Attraction
- ○   Large Town
- ○   Small Town
- ▪   POI
- ▬   Motorway
- ▬   Main Road
- ▬   Minor Road
- ▬   Railway

Brescia to Mantua

Ratings

Art	●●●● ○
Food and drink	●●●● ○
Historical sights	●●●● ○
Museums	●●●● ○
Architecture	●●● ○ ○
Nature	●●● ○ ○
Outdoor activities	●●● ○ ○
Castles	●● ○ ○ ○

The hills at the foot of Lake Garda soon melt into the low plain of the Po and the Mincio, rich alluvial farmlands, but flat. What could be a dull landscape is not, because of the lakes and rivers, and because of the green farms and rice fields spreading on all sides. Add little farming villages, the appealing ducal seat of one of the great families of Italian history and a major Roman centre in the first centuries BC and AD, still well preserved. This is a far from boring route, and the driver will appreciate a break from mountain roads. It is prime birdwatching, boating and biking country, and tourist offices offer an excellent cycling guide detailing several routes. As you might expect in a land so filled with farms, abundant *agriturismo* establishments sell fruit, vegetables, honey, farm cheeses and a wide variety of pork sausages and hams.

BRESCIA

ⓘ **Ufficio IAT Brescia**
Palazzo Broletto, Pza Paolo VI 29; tel: 030 374 9916; fax: 030 374 9982; www.provincia.brescia.it/ turismo. Open Mon–Fri 0900–1230, 1430–1730.

Ⓟ Parking € for the Castello is at Via della Rocca and Via del Castello. There is also parking at Piazza Vittoria (close to the TIC) and close to Piazza Mercato.

By the 1st century AD, Romans were building grand, classic buildings in Brixia and a surprising number survive. Today's visitor can stand in the forum, **Piazza del Foro**, and see the **Capitolium** temple with four of its six columns and much of its pediment. Remnants of the 1st-century **basilica** are integrated into a wall on Piazza Labus. To the right of the Capitolium is the 3rd-century **Teatro Romano**, built to hold 15,000 spectators. On the left are remnants of the **Roman East Gate**, while part of the Roman main road, the **Decumanus Maximus**, remains below. On Decumanus Maximus is the **Civici Musei d'Arte e Storia Santa Giulia (Santa Giulia Museum)**, a 14,000sq m museum of art and history that brings together the riches of the city's past in a former Benedictine monastery. In the complex are Roman homes with mosaic floors, an outstanding Winged Victory, stellae, altars and architectural fragments dating from the 1st century BC to the 5th century AD. The Treasury contains exceptional jewellery and gold work, including the

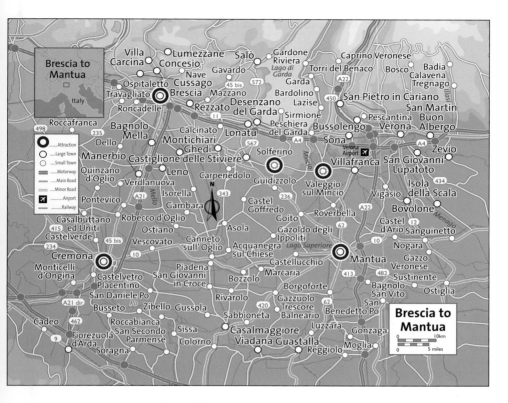

Brescia to Mantua

🖼 **Civici Musei d'Arte e Storia Santa Giulia** €€ V. Musei 81B; tel: 030 240 0640; www.bresciamusei.com. Open Jun–Sept Tue–Sun 1000–1800; Oct–May Tue–Sun 0930–1730. Park at Piazza Tebaldo Bruscato.

jewelled gold **Cross of Desiderio**. The medieval periods, the commune and Venetian era are shown in art and architectural artefacts, providing a complete picture of the late Gothic and Renaissance periods. Few museums have this range so well displayed.

At the **Piazza Paolo VI** (named after native Brescian Pope Paul VI), stands the 13th-century tower and buildings of the **Broletto** and the nearby 11th-century **Duomo Vecchio**, called 'Rotonda' for its unusual round shape. Inside are a carved red marble sarcophagus and carved wooden choir stalls. Shades of Renaissance Venice haunt **Piazza Loggia's** 15th-century colonnades by Sansovino and Palladio. Topping the clock tower are two *Macc de le ure* ('crazy timekeepers') made of metal-covered wood, at work since 1581. **Galleria d'Arte Tosio Martinengo** (*V. M da Barco*) has a collection by 13th- to 18th-century Brescian painters. The **Museo d'Arte Moderno e Contemporario** (*V. Monti 9*) has fine collections, with works by Picasso, Dalí, Chagall and Matisse. The hilltop **Castello**, fortified since the 13th century, is today surrounded by quiet gardens, although its contents recall its defensive past in museums of ancient arms and the Risorgimento.

Accommodation and food in Brescia

Hotel Industria €–€€ *V. Orzinuovi 58; tel: 030 353 1431; fax: 030 334 7904; www.hotelindustria.it.* Just off Tangenziale Ovest, close to the Piazza Repubblica, the hotel has parking and a restaurant €.

Ambasciatori €€ *V. Crocifissa Rosa 92; tel: 030 399 144; fax: 030 381 883; www.ambasciatori.net.* Well-located hotel with parking and a restaurant € serving local specialities.

Gambero Rosso €€ *V. Laura Cereto 8A; tel: 030 43 338. Open Sun–Mon & Wed–Fri 1130–1430, Wed–Mon 1900–2300.* Smart and stylish, superb pasta and meat dishes, good house wine, all at reasonable prices.

Trattoria Al Fontanone €€ *V. Musei 47; tel: 030 40 554.* Near the Santa Giulia Museum (you can leave and return), with good service and excellent house wine.

Trattoria Labirinto €€ *V. Corsica 224; tel: 030 354 1607.* Beautifully prepared local dishes with a contemporary twist.

CREMONA

ⓘ APT *Pza del Comune 5; tel: 0372 21 722 or 0372 23 233; www.provincia.cremona.it or www.cremonaturismo.com. Open daily.*

ⓟ Parking € is around Piazza Cadornaat (near Piazza del Comune), Piazza Marconi or nearby Piazza Sant'Angelo; on the east at Piazza Lodi on Via Amati, at Piazza della Libertà and in the north along Via Dante.

ⓗ Il Torazzo € *Open Tue–Sun 1000–1300, 1430–1700.*

Baptistery € *Open Tue–Sun 1000–1300, 1430–1800.*

Although its name is synonymous with violin-making, Cremona has a lot more. The **duomo** is filled with art: its arches and vaulting painted in detailed fresco, as is the crypt. The high altar and both pulpits are faced in relief-carved marble. In the left transept is a magnificent 15th-century **silver cross** with 160 miniature figures of saints. It is also home to the late 15th-century **Palazzo Fodri**. You can climb **Il Torazzo**, Europe's tallest stone bell tower at 111m, and visit the **Baptistery**, opposite the **Palazzo Comunale**, where there is an exhibit of priceless **violins** €€. Look into workshops as you pass, to see violin-makers at work. Cremona is well known for its restaurants and food emporia; behind the Duomo, visit **Formaggi d'Italia di Losi Pietro** (*V. Boccaccino; tel: 0372 23 270*) for cheese, salami, *torrone* and other local delicacies.

Accommodation and food in Cremona

Hotel Duomo € *V. Gonfalonieri 13; tel: 0372 35 242; fax: 0372 458 392; www.hotelduomocremona.com.* Central, but with quick access to the autostrada, it has a restaurant € and parking.

La Sosta €–€€ *V. Sicardo 9; tel: 0372 456 656; www.osterialasosta.it.* Local dishes with a nod to newer styles, and delectable potato gnocchi.

Continental €€ *Pza della Libertà 26; tel: 0372 434 141; fax: 0372 454 873; www.hotelcontinentalcremona.it.* Hotel in the centre of town, with many extras, a restaurant €–€€ with local specialities, and parking.

**Palazzo Comunale
Collezione di Violini**
€€ Pza del Comune; tel:
0372 22 138.

Hosteria Il 700 €€ *Pza Gallina 1; tel: 0372 36 175. Open Wed–Mon.* Elegant restaurant with local dishes, such as Cremonese *marubini*, ravioli filled with chicken and salami.

MANTUA

**Ufficio
Informazioni** Pza
Mantegna 6; tel: 0376 432
432; fax: 0376 432 433;
www.aptmantova.it.
Open Mon–Sat 0930–1230,
1400–1800, Sun
0900–1230.

Parking € areas are
well marked close to
the centre.

Palazzo Ducale €€
Pza Sordello;
www.mantovaducale.
beniculturali.it. Open
Tue–Sun 0845–1915 (last
entry 1830).

Palazzo Te €€ V. Te;
tel: 0376 323 266. Open
Tue–Sun 0900–1830.

Sant'Andrea Open daily
0800–1200, 1500–1900.
Crypt € Open Tue–Fri
1030–1130, 1530–1800,
Sat 1030–1130,
1530–1730 Sun
1530–1730.

Archaeology Museum
Tel: 0376 329 223. Open
Tue–Sat 0830–1830, Sun &
hols 0830–1330.

Antiques Market
3rd Sun of each month.

Market day: Thur.

Lying between three lakes, Mantua (Mantova) combines the pleasures of a small city with the nature and outdoor pursuits a water-setting provides. Mantua was the town of the Gonzagas, a strong but enlightened and public-spirited family. The **Palazzo Ducale** was their home for centuries. Their palace, a sombre pile of grey-brown stone, houses splendid rooms filled with paintings by Rubens and Tintoretto, among others. The Spouses' Room is decorated in frescoes by Mantegna. In the same piazza is the mid-15th-century **duomo**, its façade neoclassical, its campanile Romanesque. Inside, Corinthian columns support an ornate coffered ceiling. Behind, opera lovers should seek **Casa di Rigoletto**, with a statue of the jester in its walled garden. Opposite, a bakery makes typical local sweets. **Palazzo Te**, built for later Gonzagas, is more Renaissance in flavour. **Sala dei Cavalli** features the family's favourite horse and in the startling **Sala dei Gigantei**, the painted walls give the impression that the world is falling down; an Egyptology museum is tucked into its upper levels. **Basilica di Sant'Andrea** dates from 1472, Baroque, with coffered vaulted ceilings and an 80m dome. Adjacent is **Piazza delle Erbe**, with the market, a splendid **Torre Orologio (Clock Tower)** and **La Rotonda di San Lorenzo**, a small, round church from 1083 that was discovered among later buildings. A small, free **Archaeology Museum** is inside the Mercato Bozzoli building beside the **Palazzo Ducale**, detailing local settlements from Palaeolithic times; ask for descriptive papers in English.

Accommodation and food in Mantua

Sunday is a popular day for food festivals and expositions of local products, which often take place in Piazza delle Erbe.

Il Girasole € *Pza delle Erbe 16.* In the centre of town, a good place for a glass of Prosecco and excellent bruschetta.

Hotel ABC € *Pza Don Leoni 25; tel: 0376 322 329; fax: 0376 310 303; www.hotelabcmantova.it.* A comfortable hotel, breakfast included, dining room, bar/café, parking available.

Casa Margherita €–€€ *V. Broletto 44; tel/fax: 0349 750 6117; www.lacasadimargherita.it.* A B&B a few steps from the Palazzo Ducale.

Antica Fiera dei Mangiari *End May–mid-Jun Sat–Sun 1100–2000.* A colourful celebration of local produce, with medieval dress and flag-throwing.

Above
Cafés on the Piazza Sordello, Mantua

Osteria delle Erbe €–€€ *Pza delle Erbe 15; tel/fax: 0376 225 880.* Tables in the market square, with pizza and light meals.

Ristorante Cortaccia Biocucina €–€€ *Corte dei Sogliari 6; tel: 0376 368 760; www.cortaccia.com. Closed Tue lunch & Mon.* Specialises in Mantovese dishes: pumpkin tortellini with local sausage, *bigoli* (pasta) with porcini, also vegetarian dishes.

Osteria delle Vecchia Mantova €€ *Pza Sordello 26; tel: 0376 329 720.* Its location opposite the Palazzo Ducale has not turned this local favourite into a typical tourist stop; the gnocchi with porcini is divine.

SOLFERINO

ⓘ Associazione Turistica Colline Moreniche del Garda
Pza Torelli 1;
tel: 0376 893 160;
www.collinemoreniche.it

ⓗ La Capella Ossaria and Museo Storico
€ Pza Ossaria; tel: 0376 854 019. Open 0830–1230, 1400–1830 Tue–Sun.

⬤ Antiques Market
Mar–Nov 2nd Sun of each month.

In 1859, as Italians fought for independence from Austria, this was the scene of some of the heaviest losses on both sides. A Swiss, Henry Dunant, was so moved by the aftermath of the Battle of Solferino – more than 40,000 troops dead or injured and without medical care or burial – that he began a campaign that resulted in the Geneva Convention and later, the International Red Cross. Today the hill town is marked by the solemn **Capella Ossaria**, its walls lined row-on-row with skulls of the dead from that battle. Below, the **Museo Storico** contains artefacts from the battle, including cannon and uniforms. Further up the hill is the lovely enclosure of the **castle** that was the seat of the Gonzaga family. Houses line two sides; a church stands in the middle next to a tiny walled garden. Below spreads a view of mountain-framed Lake Garda. Above, the **Rocca di Solferino** tower (1022) was used by Italian forces as an observation point for its wide views. On the lane to the tower is a memorial to Henry Dunant, the **Red Cross Monument**.

Accommodation and food in Solferino

Albergo Ristorante Vittoria € *V. Ossario 37; tel/fax: 0376 854 051; www.darenato.it*. A friendly hotel with a restaurant featuring surprisingly creative cooking, opposite the Museo Storico.

La Barche € *V. Barche 6; tel: 0376 854 113 or 0376 854 5262. Open Feb–Dec Wed–Mon.* Regional dishes include *bigoli* (a wide, fresh pasta), pigeon, mixed grill meats and braised beef. Rooms and cottages available, and they sell their own produce and wines.

Ristorante/Pizzeria al Castello € *Pza Castello; tel: 0376 855 366.* Local specialities, such as *i capunsei*, made of bread, egg, cheese and parsley. Fantastic views of Lake Garda from the terrace dining area.

Ristorante/Pizzeria Vecchia Fontana € *Pza Marconi 3; tel: 0376 855 000.* In the middle of the old town.

VALEGGIO SUL MINCIO

ⓘ Turismo
Pro Loco Valeggio;
tel: 045 795 1880;
email: tourist@valeggio.com;
www.valeggio.com

Snatching success from adversity when the local silk industry failed, local women did what they knew – they made the best pasta in the valley. Little restaurants opened, word spread and Valeggio sul Mincio put tortellini on the map. Now the once-abandoned mill village on the river, **Borghetto**, is devoted entirely to tourists, with cafés and craft studios in the picturesque restored buildings, sitting over the water. Crossing the Mincio above Borghetto is a long, heavily fortified bridge, **Ponte Visconteo**, which has guarded the town since 1393.

Castello Scaligeri
€ Open daily; tower
Sun & hols 0900–1200,
1430–1900.

Parco Giardino Sigurta
€€ Valeggio sul Mincio,
signposted; tel: 045 637
1033; email:
sigurta@sigurta.it;
www.sigurta.it.
Open daily 0900–1800.

Antiques Market
4th Sun of each month.

Market day: Sat.

Overlooking it is the restored **Castello Scaligeri** with outstanding views to the Dolomites. In the valley, **Parco Giardino Sigurta**, a beautifully landscaped flower garden, stretches over 455.3ha.

Accommodation and food in Valeggio sul Mincio

Ristorante Albergo San Giorgio € V. Cavour 12; tel: 045 795 0125; fax: 045 737 0555. Comfortable rooms above a centrally located restaurant €, with parking.

Ristorante Lepre € V. Marsala 5; tel: 045 637 0735. Closed Wed & Thur evenings. One of the original restaurants; a third generation is now enjoying their tortellini in brodo.

Ristorante San Marco €€ Borghetto; tel: 045 795 0018. Open Wed–Sun. Lots of jovial Italian families on Sun, quieter during the week.

Suggested tour

Tour Mantua's three lakes with
Motonaves Andes €€
Pza Sordello 8; tel: 0376
322 875; www.
motonaviandes.it

Total distance: 182km, with detours 185km.

Time: 4–5 hours' driving. Allow 3 days with or without detours. Those with limited time should concentrate on Brescia and Mantua (Mantova).

Links: From Bergamo (see page 84), the A4 leads directly to Brescia. To reach Peschiera for the Lake Garda route (see page 113), follow the S249 north from Valeggio sul Mincio. For Verona, travel north via the S62 from Mantua (Mantova).

Route: Leave **BRESCIA ❶** heading southeast on the S236, following signs to **Castiglione delle Stiviere**, but continuing past it about 9km to the left turning where signposted **SOLFERINO ❷**. Leave Solferino on the unnumbered road signposted **VALEGGIO SUL MINCIO ❸**. On arriving in Valeggio sul Mincio, turn right, but before following the road across Ponte Visconteo, divert to the left, alongside the river, to visit Borghetto. Returning to cross Ponte Visconteo, Castello Scaligeri will be straight ahead. To reach it, turn left at the end, then go right, following signs to the castle. From Valeggio sul Mincio, head south on the S249, through **Roverbella** until its intersection with the S62, where you turn right, following signs to **MANTUA** (Mantova) ❹ (28km). Leave Mantua travelling west on the S10 to **CREMONA ❺**. Return to Brescia on the S45B, or the faster A21 (113km).

Detour: History enthusiasts can leave Valeggio sul Mincio on the unnumbered road east, signposted **Villafranca**. The town centre is dominated by a large castle, scene of the 1859 conference where Habsburg Austria lost its Italian provinces. Follow the S62 south to Mantua (Mantova) (25km).

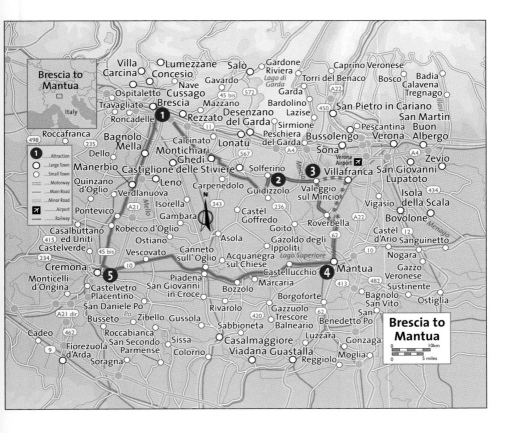

Also worth exploring

ⓘ **Turismo Comune
di Sabbioneta** *Pza
Ducale 2; tel: 0375 223 011;
fax: 0375 220 000; www.
comune.sabbioneta.mn.it.
Guided tours €€.*

The failed 16th-century Utopia of **Sabbioneta** still stands, although its monumental buildings seem as oddly out of place in the agricultural Po plain as they did when built. You must take a tour, organised by the AAST, which includes two palaces, a church with a surprising *trompe l'œil* ceiling, and a copy of Vicenza's *Teatro Olimpico*. To reach Sabbioneta, travel southwest from Mantua on the S420.

Lake Garda

Ratings

Scenery	●●●●●
Boat trips	●●●●○
Castles	●●●●○
Children	●●●●○
Mountains	●●●●○
Outdoor activities	●●●●○
Markets	●●●○○
Beaches	●●○○○

The largest lake in Italy, Garda covers more than 350sq km, its water in places as deep as 346m. It is 84km long, narrow at its northern end, widening out at the south. Palms, agaves and olive trees adorn the slopes that cradle it, growing north of their usual range because of the mild year-round climate. Mountains rise steeply from its northern portion, making stunning scenery from nearly any vantage. La Gardesana, the 50km road that hugs the lake's western shore from Riva del Garda to Salò, is wilder than the more developed eastern shore route. The road pops in and out of tunnels, and tiny towns cling to the steep hillside above or below it. Nearly every town on the shore can be easily reached by boats that circle the lake and shuttle from point to point throughout the day.

BARDOLINO

ℹ️ **APT** *Pzle Aldo Moro; tel: 045 721 0078; www.lagodigarda.it*

➡️ A cycling and walking path follows the lake shore from Bardolino to Torre del Benaco.

🅿️ Parking € just north of town, signposted from the S249.

🏛️ **Museo dell'Olio d'Oliva** *V. Peschiera 54, S249, Cisano di Bardolino; tel: 045 622 9047; www.lakegarda.com. Open Mon–Fri 0900–1230, 1430–1900, Sun & hols 0900–1230. Free.*

Bardolino's shaded benches invite visitors to enjoy the view of the tidy little marina and lake front. Olive trees grow on the shores of the lake, some distance north of their usual range. Locally pressed olive oil is highly prized and at the **Museo dell'Olio d'Oliva (Olive Oil Museum)** visitors can compare the flavours of various oils and purchase them in the shop. Two churches are of special interest: the 9th-century Carolingian **San Zeno** and the 11th-century Romanesque **San Severo**, with a frescoed interior. South of Bardolino, the beautiful little enclosed harbour of **Lazise** is bordered by ochre buildings and a venerable stone church. A Scaligeri castle guards the southern edge, its 11th-century walls wrapping around the core of the old town.

Accommodation and food in Bardolino

Restaurants and tavernas line the waterfront.

Pizzeria La Strambata €–€€ *V. Fosse 24; tel: 045 721 0110.* More than

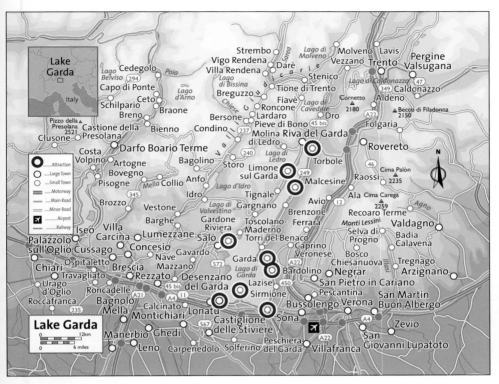

pizzas, this friendly place is where locals go for a full meal or for a glass of wine and a snack. There's plenty of outdoor seating in the summer.

Hotel Capri €€ *V. Mirabello 21; tel: 045 721 0106; fax: 045 621 2088; email: info@hotel-capri.com; www.hotel-capri.com. Open Apr–Oct.* Contemporary rooms with balconies, safes, satellite TV, access for guests with disabilities. Dining room **€€**.

DESENZANO DEL GARDA

While it is not as 'cute' as some of Garda's other lakeside towns, Desenzano is hard to beat as a base for exploring the lake. Hotels are plentiful and well located, and it has both bus and boat connections to every town on the lake and is the only one with train access. Abundant restaurants, cafés and shops, as well as a pretty marina and stunning views of the lake and mountains, add to its attraction. A small Roman villa with some excellent mosaics, **Villa Romana**, has

Parking € in a secured garage is on Via Scavi Romani, off Via Antonio Gramsci, the main route from the A4, signposted.

Villa Romana €
V. Crocefisso 22; tel: 030 914 3547. Open Mar–mid-Oct Tue–Sun 0830–1900; mid-Oct–Feb Tue–Sun 0830–1630.

been excavated and nicely interpreted. The **Museo Archeologico Rambotti (Archaeological Museum)** has finds from Roman and earlier eras, and the parish church has a painting by Tiepolo.

Accommodation and food in Desenzano del Garda

Hotel Piroscafo € *V. Porto Vecchio 11; tel: 0309 141 128; fax: 030 991 2586; www.hotelpiroscafo.it.* On the small harbour, this family-run hotel has bright rooms, some with balconies. The restaurant **€€** offers indoor or arcade dining. Parking available.

Bagatta alla Lepre Ristorante/Wine Bar €–€€ *V. Bagatta 33; tel: 030 914 2313; www.lalepre.com. Open Wed–Mon.* Mediterranean cuisine with emphasis on fish, mushrooms and truffles. The wine bar is a less expensive option, serving risotto inside a *grana* cheese and fresh pasta.

Museo Archeologico Rambotti € *Vle T da Molin; tel: 030 914 4520; www.museiarcheologici.net; Open Tue–Fri 1500–1900, Sat–Sun 1430–1900.*

Market day: Tue.

Left
Hotel Vittorio, Desenzano

Ristorante la Villetta €–€€ *V. del Colli Storici 8–10; tel: 030 911 0618. Open Tue–Sun.* The speciality is porcini mushrooms, which are featured in several dishes.

Trattoria La Biocca €–€€ *Vicolo Molino 6; tel: 030 914 3658. Open Fri–Wed.* Our favourite place in Desenzano, serving local specialities with flair. Reservations suggested during high season. Try the pumpkin ravioli or carpaccio.

Hotel Vittorio €€ *V. Porto Vecchio 4; tel: 030 991 2245; fax: 030 991 2270; www.hotelvittorio.it.* Almost every room of this Art Deco hotel has views of the lake or small marina, while most have balconies. Room 410 has the best view. Friendly and helpful staff, breakfast included in the room price, garage parking 200m.

Palazzo Arzaga €€€ *Carzago; tel: 030 680 600; fax: 030 680 6270; www.palazzoarzaga.it.* A 15th-century monastery turned luxury hotel with a Saturnia spa, Jack Nicklaus- and Gary Player-designed golf courses and fine dining. Guest rooms and public areas are furnished with 18th-century Venetian antiques.

GARDA

APT *Lungolago Regina Adelaide 3; tel: 045 627 0384; www.aptgardaveneto.com. Open daily.*

Parking € *in a large car park at the east side of the S249, limited 1-hr spaces* € *at the lake in front of Casa de Comune.*

San Vigilio *S249, 2km west of Garda, parking in summer along the S249, rest of year at point.*

Museo del Castello Scaligero € *Tel: 045 657 0333. Open Apr–May & Oct daily 0930–1230, 1430–1800; Jun–Sept daily 0930–1300, 1630–1930.*

It's hard to find a more pleasant lakeside town to laze about in than Garda, which makes no pretence of being anything else. Benches face the lake from a fringe of shade trees, a walking and cycling path borders the shore, while behind sprawls an assortment of cafés where no one minds if you sit for hours over one espresso. There's no must-see sight except the lake, open 24/7. Evening brings music, alfresco dinners and the general air of people relaxing and enjoying life. Those who feel guilty about not visiting a museums can take comfort in the **Museo Civico** (*Pza C Battisti 3; tel: 0464 573 869. Open daily 1030–1830. Free*), featuring prehistoric inscriptions, at **San Vigilio**, a scenic point of land overlooking the lake. Although its pebble beach is very crowded in the summer, the point is particularly beautiful, with its 16th-century palace framed by tall cypresses. Just north is **Torri del Benaco**, with its 14th-century castle, built by the ubiquitous Scaligeri of Verona. The **Museo del Castello Scaligero** overlooks a little marina of fishing and pleasure boats. A ferry carries cars across the midpoint of the lake, to Gardone Riviera.

Accommodation and food in Garda

Caffè Bar Taverna € *Pza Catullo.* An old favourite updated, and an enjoyable place to spend an evening sampling local wines.

Hotel Roma €–€€ *Lungolago Regina Adelaide 8; tel: 045 725 5025; fax: 045 627 0266; www.hotelromagarda.it. Open Mar–Oct.* You couldn't

⊖ Look for brightly
painted local
tableware and decorative
ceramics along Via Spagna
and other streets leading
from the lake promenade.
Market day: Fri.

have a more central location, right on the lake, next to a loggia and with cafés at its feet. Parking is available.

Taverna Fregoso €–€€ *Corso Vittorio Emanuele 39; tel: 045 725 6622. Open Thur–Tue.* A cosy restaurant/taverna/pizzeria where you can sit outdoors and watch the world go by. Live music summer, nightly 2100–0200.

Hotel-Ristorante Gardesana €€ *Pza Calderini 20, Torre del Benaco; tel: 045 722 5411; fax: 045 722 5771; www.gardesana.eu.* Beautiful view over the marina, and a restaurant that is part of the Buon Ricordo group: chefs committed to offering traditional regional dishes. Here the specialities include the delicate, white, lake fish *lavarello.*

Locanda San Vigilio €€€ *Punta San Vigilio; tel: 045 725 6688; fax: 045 725 6551; email: sanvigilio@gardalake.it; www.gardalake.it/sanvigilio. Open Apr–mid-Oct.* The peninsula and villa are equally lovely and the hotel has an excellent restaurant **€€€.** Sporting activities are available.

GARDONE RIVIERA

❶ **ARPT** *Corso Repubblica 8, Gardone; tel: 0365 20 347; www.lagodigarda.it. Open daily.* **ARPT** *Pza San Antonio, Salò; tel: 0365 21 423; www.lagodigarda.it. Open summer daily.*

🏛 **Hruska Botanical Gardens €** *V. Roma. Open Mar–Oct daily.*

Il Vittoriale degli Italiani €€ *V. Vittoriale; tel: 0365 296 511; www.vittoriale.it. Open Apr–Sept daily 0800–2000; Oct–Mar daily 0900–1700; House (Priora) open Tue–Sun, War Museum open Thur–Tue.*

Gardone is elegantly turned out around public gardens, which cascade in terraces of stately trees. Plants from all around the Mediterranean and from as far away as Africa grow in the **Hruska Botanical Gardens.** The mild lake climate favours plants that would ordinarily not survive this latitude, and made Gardone a popular site for villas. Lake Garda's most famous villa – **Il Vittoriale degli Italiani** – overlooks the lake, built for the eccentric poet Gabriele d'Annunzio. It eschews the usual villa architecture for Art Deco, and is filled with proof of the poet's unusual tastes: a coffin-shaped bed, black-covered windows and a ship embedded in the extensive gardens. Although neighbouring **Salò** is best known for Mussolini's puppet Salò Republic, in the final years of World War II, the town has much more to be remembered for. Its pastel buildings form a decorative frame for the lake, and its duomo has a fine wooden altarpiece and Renaissance portal. Salò also has a small archaeological museum.

Accommodation and food in Gardone Riviera

Hotel Monte Baldo, Villa Acquarone € *V. Zanardelli 110; tel: 0365 20 951; fax: 0365 20 952; email: info@hotelmontebaldo.com; www.hotelmontebaldo.it. Open Apr–late-Oct.* An attractive hotel facing on to the lake, with a restaurant serving local specialities.

Locanda Agli Angeli € *Via Dosso 7; tel: 0365 20 991; fax: 0365 20 746; www.agliangeli.com. Open year-round.* Attractive guest rooms in an older, well-kept, building, with parking. It has its own restaurant **€.**

Opposite
Lake front, Garda

Market day: Wed.

Agli Angeli €–€€ *V. Dosso 7; tel: 0365 20 991; www.agliangeli.com. Open mid-Mar–mid-Apr Tue–Sun; mid-Apr–mid-Oct daily; mid-Oct–mid-Mar Tue & Thur–Sun.* Call to book a table at weekends, since this outstanding informal restaurant is no secret.

Grand Hotel Gardone €€€ *V. Zanardelli 84; tel: 0365 20 261; fax: 0365 22 695; email: ghg@grangardone.it; www.grangardone.it.* Its elegant façade adorns a long stretch of the shore, and its balconies offer sweeping views of the lake. Dance there in the evening or dine in the excellent restaurant. Private beach and lots of extras for guests.

Ristorante Laurin €€€ *Vle Landi 9, Salò; tel: 0365 22 022.* A stylish citified menu that does not overlook its local roots, featuring traditional trout dishes rarely found elsewhere.

La Veranda della Spiaggia d'Oro €€€ *V. Spiaggia d'Oro 15; tel: 0365 290 034; www.hotelspiaggiadoro.com.* The menu offers the usual Italian and continental selections, but the chef's insistence on fresh local ingredients sets them apart.

Villa Del Sogno €€€ *V. Zanardelli 107; tel: 0365 290 181; fax: 0365 290 230; www.villadelsogno.it.* The gracious – and spacious – villa overlooks the lake; the restaurant is outstanding, with creative preparations of local ingredients, and an excellent wine list.

LIMONE SUL GARDA

ARPT *5545 (main road); tel: 0365 918 987; www.lagodigarda.it*

Market days: 1st & 3rd Tue of each month.

St Peter's Day 29 Jun, brings a fair and fireworks.

The climate on the steep, east-facing slopes is even milder than on the opposite shore, making Limone an ideal place for the groves of lemon trees that give it its name. Terraces were cut into the hillside for the trees, some of which still thrive above the picturesque old town that clusters around the port. Despite the onion-shaped domes of the churches, Limone is a classic little Italian town, a patchwork of pastel stucco buildings ascending the mountainside. While it has no 'sights' in particular, it is a relaxed and pleasant town for browsing in shops and lazing in cafés.

Accommodation and food in Limone sul Garda

Villa la Gardenia € *V. IV Novembre 47; tel: 0365 954 178; fax: 0365 954 214; www.hotellagardenia.com.* The hotel sits in a wooded garden setting on the west side of the autostrada above the town and lake. It has a well-respected restaurant with vegetarian offerings.

MALCESINE

ARPT *V. Gardesana 238; tel: 045 740 0044, fax: 045 740 1633; www.lagodigarda.it. Open daily.*

Parking € *is in the tiered garage on the hillside above the S249.*

Museo de Castello Scaligero € *Tel: 045 657 0333. Open daily 0930–1800.*

Funivia €€ *Tel: 045 740 0206; www.funiviedelbaldo. com. Open Apr–mid-Sept daily 0800–1900; mid-Sept–Oct daily 0800–1800; Oct–Nov daily 0800–1700 (last descent 15 mins before closing).*

Artists' studios and boutiques line several of the narrow streets leading to the castle.

It's hard to be this handsome and unaware of it, so if Malcesine is a bit too tarted up and tidied, it can – like Sirmione – be forgiven. Its narrow streets wind upward; from the boat-landing to the castle, passing under arches and past artists' studios, restaurants and boutiques. The German poet Goethe had much to say of Malcesine, where he was arrested as a spy for drawing a picture of **Castello Scaligero**, on one of the finest settings in all Italy. Lake views are splendid from the terrace just below the entrance, which overlooks a tiny beach (reached by stairs from Via Posterna). On a clear day, the 10-minute ride by the ultra-modern revolving *funivia* (cable car) to an elevation of more than 1,700m on **Monte Baldo** rewards with views to distant Dolomite peaks and access to scenic walking trails.

Accommodation and food in Malcesine

Osteria alla Rosa €–€€ *Piazzetta Boccara 5; tel: 045 657 0783; www.osteriaallarosa.it.* Polenta dishes with salami, sausage or fish from the lake.

Ristorante Taverna Agli Scaligeri €–€€ *V. Caselunghe 12; tel: 045 657 0166 or 347 257 4739; www.agliscaligeri.com.* Specialising in Lombard and Trentino dishes, including *risotto giallo con ossobuco, cassoela, cotoletta alla Milanese* and *tonco del Pontesél*.

Hotel Alpi €€ *Campogra. nge; tel: 045 740 0717; fax: 045 740 0529; www.alpihotel.info.* A modern hotel, on the main road and an easy walk to the centre of town. Restaurant **€€**.

Below
Castello Scaligero, Malcesine

Market day: Sat.

Hotel Garni Diana €€ *V. Scoisse 8; tel: 045 740 0192; fax: 045 740 0415; www.dianamalcesine.com.* On the hill overlooking the medieval town, a 5-minute walk below; modern and bright with a pool and restaurant €€.

PESCHIERA DEL GARDA

APT *Pzle Betteloni 15; tel: 045 755 1673. Open daily.*

Parking € is along the lake front at the port, opposite the TIC.

La Rocca € *Complesso Monumentale. Open Apr–Sept daily 0900–1900; Oct–Mar daily 0830–1630.*

Market day: Mon.

Anniversario della Liberazione *25 Apr,* the town celebrates the anniversary of its liberation in 1945.

Where the River Mincio flows from the southern end of Lake Garda, the Austrians fortified the fine **Port of Peschiera** to defend the position during Italy's war for independence in the mid-19th century. Italy won, and kept the fort, now more scenic than defensive, a fine backdrop for the colourful little boat basin. The romantically crumbling old palazzo was a German command headquarters during World War II, which explains the town's enthusiastic celebration of Liberation Day. You can tour the whole fort complex, **La Rocca**, whose grass-topped walls form a bridge over the end of Peschiera's river-mouth harbour. Peschiera is in two parts, and it is the western, fortified section you should head to. Coming from the A4, bear left and pass through the impressive main gate, **Porta Verona**.

Accommodation and food in Peschiera del Garda

Camping Cappuccini € *V. Arrigo Boito 2, Località Cappuccini; tel/fax: 045 755 1592; email: info@camp-cappuccini.com; www.camp-cappuccini. com. Open Mar–Sept.* Showers, caravan and tent pitches, shelters, beaches, swimming and other sports. No campfires.

Hotel Bell'Arrivo €–€€ *Piazzetta Benacense 2; tel: 045 640 1322; fax: 045 640 1311; www.hotelbellarrivo.it.* This small hotel has been completely refurbished and is right on the marina, at the Port of Peschiera, which its café overlooks.

Vecchio Viola €€ *V. Milano 7; tel: 045 755 1666. Open Wed–Mon.* Local dishes are a speciality, with lake fish and traditional filled ravioli. Guest rooms are also available.

La Vela Blu €€ *V. Benaco 8; tel: 045 640 1485; www.albergolavelablu.it.* Specialising in seafood and fresh fish from the lake itself.

Ristorante al Fiore €€–€€€ *Lungolago Garibaldi 9; tel: 045 755 0113.* A reliable standard menu, well prepared.

Left
Via Posterna, Malcesine

RIVA DEL GARDA AND TORBOLE

ⓘ ARPT *Largo Medaglie d'Oro al Valor Militare 5; tel: 0464 554 444; www. gardatrentino.it. Open daily.*

ⓟ Parking € is at the eastern entrance to Riva, connected to the lake front by a walking path. Limited parking € is also at Piazza Cesare Battista.

ⓗ Museo Civico, Rocca di Riva € *Pza Cesare Battista; tel: 0464 573 869. Open Mar–Jun & Oct–Nov Tue–Sun 1000–1230, 1330–1800; Jul–Sept daily 1000–1230, 1330–1800.* The castle museum is accessible to people with disabilities.

Cascata de Varone € *Tel: 0464 521 421; www.cascata-varone.com. Open Jan–Feb & Nov–Dec Sun & hols 1000–1700; Mar & Oct daily 0900– 1700; Apr & Sept daily 0900–1800; May–Aug daily 0900–1900.*

Arboreto di Arco *V. Lomego. Open Apr–Sept daily 0800–1900; Oct–Mar daily 0900–1600. Free.*

Castel Drena € *Drena S45B; tel: 0464 541 220. Open Feb–Jun & Sept daily 1000–1800; Jul–Aug daily 1000–1900; Oct daily 1000–1700; Nov–Dec Sat–Sun 1000–1700.*

Museo delle Palafitte € *Molina de Ledro; tel: 0464 508 182. Open Mar–Jun & Sept–Nov Tue–Sun 0900– 1700; Jul–Aug Tue–Sun 1000–1800.*

ⓜ Market days: 2nd & 3rd Wed in summer.

Riva's palm-lined hotel grounds spread eastward around the head of the lake, extending right to **Torbole**, because they have very little room to grow to the west. The sheer face of Monte Brione rises above the town on that side, overlooking the attractive old town centre. The **Museo Civico, Rocca di Riva** sits behind its moat, a solid castle built by the Scaligeri, now housing a very good museum. Featured are finds and interpretative displays on the prehistoric settlement here, and armour. Follow brown signs from Riva to find **Cascata de Varone**, one of Europe's most dramatic waterfalls, plunging out of a lake suspended almost directly overhead. The falls have carved a swirling corkscrew tunnel through the mountain and created an ecosystem all their own, so cool and wet that you will need a waterproof jacket. Excellent signage in English. The area is a centre for watersports, especially in Torbole, a favourite of the younger set where windsurfing is king. Hire equipment is plentiful in both towns, and sailing-boat hire establishments line the S249 to the south.

North of Riva in Arco, **Arboreto di Arco** contains mature trees from all over the world, which flourish in the microclimate of a large park created by a Habsburg duke in the 1800s. Walk from the attractive little village up to **Castello di Arco**, high on a rock cliff, with good views all along the way. Perched over the Salagoni Gorge in nearby Drena, the tall single tower and curtain walls of **Castel Drena** date at least to the 1100s and its museum includes Bronze Age archaeological finds and later historical artefacts. In Molina di Ledro, the **Museo delle Palafitte** houses a remarkable collection from the archaeological excavations of Bronze Age lake dwellings from the second millennium BC. One of these dwellings has been reconstructed nearby to complete the picture.

Accommodation and food in Riva del Garda and Torbole

Cafés and pastry shops line the lake front, many of them serving sandwiches.

Albergo Ancora € *V. Dante 47, Riva del Garda; tel: 0464 567 099; fax: 0464 560 288; www.rivadelgarda.com/ancora.* A small, cosy hotel with a nice restaurant and roof terrace, in the centre of town.

Hotel Europa €€ *Pza Catena 13, Riva del Garda; tel: 0464 555 433; fax: 0464 521 777; www.hoteleuropariva.it.* Perfectly located on the quay in the old town centre, where the boats arrive. It has been completely renovated.

Ristorante Picolo Mondo €€–€€€ *V. Matteotti 7, Torbole; tel: 0464 505 271.* Along with its innovative dishes, the restaurant is known for its rendition of a traditional local meat and bean salad.

SIRMIONE

ⓘ ARPT *Vle Marconi;
tel: 030 916 114;
www.sirmione.it.
Open summer daily;
Nov–Mar Mon–Sat morning.*

ⓟ Parking € is on the
mainland side of the
moat; only foot traffic is
allowed inside the gates.

**ⓗ Rocca Scaligera
and Museo dei
Castello** € *Tel: 030 916
468. Open Mar–mid-Oct
Tue–Sun 0830–1900; mid-
Oct–Feb Tue–Sun
0830–1700.*

Grotte di Catullo € *Tel:
030 916 157. Open
Apr–Sept Tue–Sun
0900–1800; Oct–Mar
Tue–Sun 0900–1600.*

ⓜ Market day: Fri.

To many travellers, Sirmione is the highlight of the lake, as it certainly
was to the Romans. To others, it is a Hollywood set overflowing with
boutiques and tourists. However you see it, you will not deny that it
has a perfect setting, at the end of a long narrow point of land, water
whichever way you look. **Rocca Scaligera**, a 13th-century moated
castle, fairly begs for at least one photograph. You can cross its
drawbridge for a tour, as well. Its harbour inside the castle's defensive
walls provided safe refuge for fishing boats and the Scaligeri ships. At
the end of the scenic point, reached via a lakeside promenade, is
Grotte di Catullo, a retreat built by Roman poet Catullus in the 1st
century BC. More than a villa, it was a full-scale resort, with the Roman
equivalents of apartments, a spa and shopping mall. Artefacts
discovered here are in the small **Antiquarium**. **San Pietro** is built on a
rise, and preserves 12th-century frescoes.

Accommodation and food in Sirmione

Amid Sirmione's swish boutiques and cafés, don't expect to find
budget dining.

Hotel Marconi €–€€ *V. Giuseppe Vittorio Emanuele II 51; tel: 030 916
007; fax: 030 916 587; www.hotelmarconi.net. Open May–Sept.* A good
location right on the lake in the town centre, with parking.

Osteria al Pescatore €–€€ *V. Piana 18; tel: 030 916 216;
www.ristorantealpescatore.com.* Reasonably priced seafood.

Hotel Broglia €€ *V. Giuseppe Piana 34–36; tel: 030 916 172; fax: 030
916 586; www.hotelbroglia.it. Open late Mar–late Oct.* A full-service,
upmarket hotel with a restaurant €€, bar, parking and gardens.

Suggested tour

Total distance: 161km, with detours 288km.

Time: 6 hours' driving. Allow 2 days for the main route, 3 days with
detours. Those with limited time should tour the lake on a day trip by
boat, stopping at Sirmione and Malcesine.

Links: To reach Lake Garda from Brescia (*see page 94*), take the A4,
which also leads on to Verona (*see page 116*). To connect to the Alto
Adige route (*see page 142*), follow the S45B north from Riva to Trento,
or the S240 east from Torbole to Rovereto.

Route: Leave **DESENZANO DEL GARDA ❶** heading east on the S11
to **Colombare**, turning left to visit **SIRMIONE ❷**, return to
Colombare and continue on the S11 to **PESCHIERA ❸**. Continue to

follow the lake shore along the S249, north to **Lazise, BARDOLINO** and **GARDA** ❹. (*See Detour 1 below.*) From Garda, the road swings west to round the beautiful point of **San Vigilio**, turning north again to **Torri del Benaco** (54km). The various little settlements that make up **Brenzone** and its northern neighbours all blend together as they line the shore. The prettiest of these is easy to spot from the S249 by the little river that cascades through it. Parking is scarce, but worth finding to follow this stream on foot to the beautiful little port at its mouth. A charming ensemble of brightly painted houses, an arched bridge and a round stone tower surround the basin. There are few prettier vignettes on the lake. The road continues to border the lake closely with a succession of glorious views of the western shore and its steep mountain slopes. At **MALCESINE** ❺, these views are framed by a medieval castle on a wooded point. The S249 continues north, hugging the lake shore and through a series of tunnels, before emerging at **TORBOLE** and **RIVA DEL GARDA** ❻ (39km). (*See Detour 2 below.*) Go south from Riva on the S45B again closely following the shore through a series of tunnels to **LIMONE SUL GARDA** ❼. Several small towns cling to the shore north of **GARDONE RIVIERA** ❽ and **Salò** (47km). South of Salò the S572 continues south travelling inland but with fine views all the way to your starting point at Desenzano del Garda (21km).

Detour 1: From Garda, follow the signposted road east to **Caprino Veronese**, then north to **Spiazzi**. Here the sanctuary of **Madonna della Corona** overlooks the Adige Valley. Continue to **Ferrara di Monte Baldo** to visit the **Orto Botanica del Monte Baldo**. The gardens display the plants indigenous (and many endemic) to this pre-Alpine mountain range, including edelweiss, Alpine lilies and wild roses. Backtrack through this high valley to Garda (45km).

Detour 2: From Riva del Garda, the S45B heads north past the castellated towns of **Arco** and **Drena**, both worth visiting. North of Drena the road becomes increasingly scenic as views of the surrounding Dolomites open out in all directions and continues to be scenic all the way to **Trento** (*see page 138*). For a different series of views of the same area, backtrack to Riva (82km).

Getting out of the car

Boat options range from slow and scenic 'steamers' to fast hydrofoils and catamarans. The problem, of course, with touring by boat is that the time in each town is limited (or extended) according to the departure of the next boat. In general, towns on the southern end of the lake are more easily explored by boat, since there are many options without having to wait for the next round-the-lake steamer.

Ⓘ Orto Botanico di Novazzina (Orto Botanico d'Europa).
V. General Graziani 10, Novezzina, Ferrara di Monte Baldo; tel: 045 624 7288; www. ortobotanicomontebaldo.org

---

Ⓝ Navigazione Lago di Garda €–€€
Tel: 030 914 9511; www.navigazionelaghi.it. Operates Jun–mid-Sept. Schedules and connections for boat travel on Lake Garda.

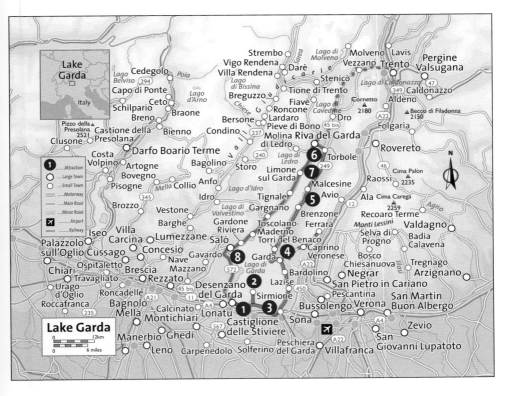

Also worth exploring

Ristorante Miralago
€€ *Pza A Cozzaglio 2, Tremosine; tel: 0365 953 001; www.miralago.it.* Those with acrophobia might not appreciate the setting, suspended above 300m of thin air, but the lake views are unmatched. A hotel adjoins, with an equally good prospect.

From Limone, a narrow, but very scenic, mountain road climbs to the village of **Vessio** and winds along a high terrace to **Tignale** before rejoining the S45B north of **Gargnano**. This road gives a different set of views down over the lake, and passes the sanctuary of **Monte Castello**, just beyond **Gardola**.

Right
Limone sul Garda

Verona

Ratings

Architecture	●●●●○
Art	●●●●○
Food and drink	●●●●○
Historical sights	●●●●○
Museums	●●●○○
Walking	●●●○○
Castles	●●○○○
Children	●○○○○

'There is no world without Verona walls' lamented Romeo in Shakespeare's *Romeo and Juliet*. While that's not quite true today, the traveller will find many of the city's attractions in the historic centre the walls enclose. Others – a Roman theatre and the church of San Zeno – lie within a pleasant walk along the Adige's banks. Although Shakespeare never set foot in Verona, he set two plays there, and gave Verona's tourism officials an icon that they have not failed to exploit. You will hear of the mythical Juliet everywhere, and be shown her tomb and her balcony in a courtyard now trashed by graffiti. Latter-day legends surround both. Far more interesting are Verona's Roman, medieval and Renaissance relics, which include the best-preserved Roman arena in Italy, still in use for everything from grand opera to rock concerts.

Getting around

ⓘ **APT** V. *Alpini 9 (off Pza Brà); tel: 045 806 8680; fax: 045 800 3638 Mon–Fri. Good for lodging recommendations, but not much else.*

The old city, which is also today's busy centre, lies between the huge Piazza Brà, where the Arena is, and the river, which describes a large, graceful curve through Verona. Via Mazzini, the main shopping street, leads from the arena to Piazza Erbe, the former Roman forum, now a lively morning vegetable market. Most streets between the two are closed to traffic, unless you are staying at one of the hotels, in which case you can unload baggage and park, if the hotel has permits. North from Piazza Brà, historic Castelvecchio stretches along the river, which is spanned by a graceful medieval castellated bridge. Verona's historic centre is small enough to explore on foot.

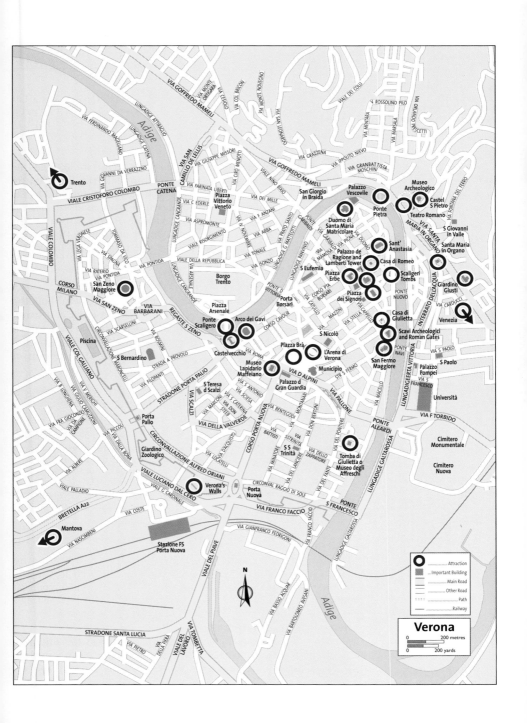

Sights

Turismo *Ponte Aleardi at V. Pallone and V. Macello. Open Mon–Fri 0900–1800, Sat–Sun 0900–1230, 1400–1730. More useful than the APT.*

L'Arena di Verona *€ Pza Brà. Open daily 0900–1800, opera days 1000–1500.*

Casa di Giulietta, house *€, courtyard free. Tel: 045 803 4303. Open Tue–Sun 0800–1900.*

Castelvecchio *€ Corso Castelvecchio 2 (end of Corso Cavour). Open Tue–Sun 0900–1900 (last entry 1800). Get the room-by-room guide.*

Arco dei Gavi
Close to Castelvecchio, between the river and Corso Cavour, sits a 1st-century AD arched gateway from a Roman road. It was moved in 1933, complete with the stone road bearing chariot tracks.

L'Arena di Verona
The Arena has been part of Verona life since about AD 30, when its 22,000-plus seating capacity could accommodate the city's entire population. It was used for combat between gladiators and wild beasts and for grand expositions; St Fermo may have been martyred here. A place of refuge during barbarian invasion, it was also used for executions. It is the third-largest Roman arena and the best preserved. Since 1913, each August it has been home to a world-class opera festival.

Casa di Giulietta (Juliet's House)
The setting was once sweetly romantic, a restored medieval building with stone balcony (added in the 1930s) facing a quiet courtyard. Today it's a mob scene crammed with young tourists who have turned the walls into a polychromed madness of graffiti. The delicate bronze statue of the heroine is disfigured by the rubbing of thousands of hands.

The Juliet connection

The story of the young lovers Romeo and Juliet comes to us from Vicenza, where Italian writer Luigi da Porto chose names from two local families for his characters. English poet Arthur Brooke took up the tale in 1562, drawing the attention of William Shakespeare, whose play is considered the best version. Although entirely fictional, the story draws tourists, and the city has obliged by creating homes for the pair and a tomb for the heroine.

Casa di Romeo (Romeo's House)
Not well marked (*V. Arche Scaligere 4*), not open and bearing no apparent relationship to the young hero who has been lost in the Juliet hubris, this house is nevertheless an interesting walled medieval building.

Castelvecchio and Ponte Scaligero
The castle was built by Cangrande II (1355–75), as was the adjoining Ponte Scaligero, a castellated bridge. The castle has been converted into one of Italy's finest museum spaces, housing a remarkable art

Duomo € *Pza Duomo. Open Mar–Oct Mon–Sat 1000–1730, Sun 1330–1730; Nov–Feb Tue–Sat 1000–1300, 1330–1600, Sun 1300–1700.*

Giardino Giusti €
V. Giardini Giusti 2; tel: 045 803 4029. Open daily daylight hours.

collection, the majority of which are from city palaces, churches and monasteries. Most are from the 13th–19th centuries and include works by Bellini, Pisano, Francheschi, Rubens, Falconetti, Montagna, Tintoretto, Tiepolo and Guardi.

Duomo di Santa Maria Matricolare

The cathedral, on the site of a 5th-century church built over a Roman temple, was begun in 1139, combining Gothic, Romanesque and Renaissance styles. The two-storey Romanesque portal shows the knights Roland and Oliver surrounded by stern-faced saints, created by medieval sculptor Nicolo. In the first chapel (left) is Titian's *Assumption*.

Giardino Giusti (Gusto Gardens)

An easy walk from the Roman Theatre, Giusti Gardens are among the finest Renaissance gardens in Italy, designed in the 15th and 16th centuries. On the lower level are formal parterres of clipped hedges, walkways, cypress trees and grottoes. The steep hillside above is a more natural setting. It's a cool, shaded place to wander or picnic under the eyes of Renaissance statues.

Museo Lapidario Maffeiano € *Pza Brà 28; tel: 045 590 087. Open Mon 1330–1930 Tue–Sun 0830–1930. Buy tickets at Castelvecchio.*

Lamberti Tower € *Pza dei Signori. Open Sun–Sat 0900–1800, first Sun of each month free.*

Throughout Verona you will see a shield with a ladder on the escutcheon. This is the symbol of the della Scala family (*scala* means 'ladder'), rulers of the city and immediate area during medieval times (1263–1390). Collectively they, and their works, are referred to as Scaligeri and their style dominates the city. It is recognised particularly by the fish-tail crenellations along the tops of castle walls.

San Fermo Maggiore € *Stradone San Fermo (near Ponte Navi). Open Mon–Sat 1000–1800, Sun 1300–1800.*

Museo Lapidario Maffeiano

The stones here are from Roman Verona, a reliquary of architectural fragments that show the city of 2,000 years ago.

Palazzo de Ragione and Lamberti Tower

Rising above Piazza Erbe, the 83.82m Lamberti Tower marks the location of the medieval palace used as law courts. The palace and the lower courses of the tower are of striped layers of pink brick and white tufa. Look into the courtyard for the fine Renaissance staircase to the courtrooms. Climb the tower or use the lift for views of the Dolomites.

Piazza Brà

At the centre of old Verona lies this large open square, which has the huge Roman arena as a focal point. On the east is the large neoclassical municipal building, while opposite is a row of colourful 19th-century buildings housing cafés, from whose tables the Veronese enjoy the wide promenade. The 14th-century Palazzo delle Gran Guardia and the arched gateway, **Portone della Brà**, complete the southern side. Look for Shakespeare's quote inscribed on the Portone.

Piazza dei Signori

Palaces of the medieval della Scala family surround this elegant square. At its centre stands an 1865 statue of Dante (always with a pigeon on his head), who stayed here during his exile from Florence. Behind Dante the **Loggia del Consiglia** has frescoes on the upper façade and statues of Veronese notables. On the wall of the Palazzo de Ragione is a denunciation box, a good way to get even with enemies.

Piazza Erbe

For more than 2,000 years a market has filled this spot, which once adjoined the Roman forum. It is still a vibrant marketplace with cafés spreading into it in the evening. In the centre is the **Madonna of Verona**, actually a Roman statue given a new persona in 1368. At the end is a column surmounted by the Lion of St Mark, erected in 1528 when *La Serenissima* ruled. Behind the lion rises **Palazzo Maffei**, 17th-century palace of the Maffei family, its façade topped by a balustrade of Roman gods. Now a hotel and restaurant, it occupies the site of the Roman Temple to Jupiter, excavated beneath.

San Fermo Maggiore

Erected in the 8th century to honour Sts Fermo and Rustico (alleged to have been martyred in the Arena), the church was covered in the 11th century by a new one of pink brick and white tufa. The original church remains as the crypt. Originally Romanesque, San Fermo has 14th-century Gothic elements superimposed. Above the Brenzoni mausoleum are Pisanello frescoes and the ornate pulpit is also

Right
Piazza Erbe

surrounded by frescoes. Statues of saints sit in niches. Alessandro Turchi's *Adoration of the Shepherds* is in the St Joseph chapel.

San Zeno Maggiore *Pza San Zeno (west of the centre, near Porta San Zeno). Open Mar–Oct Mon–Sat 0830–1800, Sun 1300–1800; winter shorter hours. Free.*

San Zeno Maggiore

San Zeno, 1123–35, is one of the finest examples of Italian Romanesque churches to be found, built of alternate layers of pink brick and white tufa. You see San Zeno's first artistic masterpiece as you enter: 48 bronze door panels, some dating from an earlier 1039 church, depicting biblical scenes and the life of San Zeno, first bishop of Verona. The portico roof is supported by columns resting on lions, below a 12th-century Wheel of Fortune rose window. The outstanding wooden, arched, polychromed ceiling of the nave dates from 1386. On the main altar is a fine triptych: *Virgin and Child with Saints* by Andrea Mantegna. A crypt contains the tomb of San Zeno, and the cloister has Romanesque and Gothic columns.

🔊 Sant'Anastasia €
Pza Sant'Anastasia.
Open Mar–Oct Mon–Sat
0900–1800, Sun
1300–1800; Nov–Feb
Tue–Sat 1000–1300,
1330–1600, Sun
1300–1700.

Santa Maria in Organo
Pza Isolo Sorge, V. San
Chiara (south of the Roman
Theatre).

Santa Maria Antica € V.
Arche Scaligeri (behind Pza
dei Signori). Open daily
0730–1230, 1500–1900.
The tombs are outdoors
and always visible.

Teatro Romano €
Regaste Redentore 2; tel:
045 806 6485. Open
Mon–Sat 1030–1300,
1600–1900. Museum open
Tue–Sun 0900–1900.

Tomba di Giulietta €
V. Shakespeare (off
V. del Pontiere). Open
Mon 1330–1930, Tue–Sun
0830–1900.

Sant'Anastasia

The late 13th-century Gothic church has a portal carved with scenes from the life of St Peter, surmounted by 15th-century frescoes. Just inside, a pair of marble hunchbacks support holy water fonts; the one on the left (1495) is by Gabriele Caliari, father of painter Paolo Veronese. A highlight is the Pisanello fresco *St George and the Princess*.

Santa Maria in Organo

The highlight of the 15th-century church is the 1477–1501 wood marquetry by Fra Giovanni da Verona. The inlay in the choir stalls, lectern and sacristy is outstanding for its precision and realistic perspective. Some panels appear to be shelves of books or display cupboards; others show lifelike chickens and rabbits.

Scaligeri Tombs

The ornate pinnacled tombs of Verona's leading military family are just behind Piazza dei Signori, outside tiny **Santa Maria Antica**. The church, consecrated in 1185, became the family church of the della Scala princes. Their tombs are topped by fully armoured effigies.

Scavi Archeologici and Roman Gates

Verona has recently uncovered more of its Roman past, and integrated them skilfully into its busy shopping district. In Via Cappello, off Piazza Erbe, are parts of a Roman city gate, **Porta Leoni**. On the opposite end of Piazza Erbe, Via Corso Porta Borsari leads west to the other remaining Roman gate, **Porta Borsari**.

Teatro Romano, Ponte Pietra and Museo Archeologico

Dating from the 1st century BC, the stage is gone but the semicircular seating area overlooking the Adige River is substantially intact. Shakespeare plays are performed here as well as other plays, ballet and jazz concerts. Above, in a converted monastery, is the **Archaeological Museum**, showing Roman statuary, mosaics, architectural fragments, pottery and glassware. Nearby, the five-arch span of **Ponte Pietra** was painstakingly restored after destruction in 1945.

Tomba di Giulietta e Museo degli Affreschi

Juliet's 'tomb' is in a crypt of San Francesco al Corso, its stone sarcophagus empty but in atmospheric surroundings. The museum exhibits frescoes, which, for those not questing after the mythical heroine, may be more interesting. Some of the rooms are beautifully decorated.

Verona's Walls

Verona has always been in the path of invaders, so its rulers reinforced the natural protection of the river with substantial walls. Unusually

The main shopping street is Via Mazzini, a double row of smart shops filled with the latest fashions. Around the corner, at the foot of Piazza Erbe, another pedestrianised street has more practical shops, including a department store. Look especially for gloves and fine leather goods. Each morning the vegetable market fills Piazza Erbe.

The Arena is the scene of one of Italy's major opera festivals each summer, as well as other festivals and special events. Teatro Romano is a smaller venue, perfect for Shakespeare and more intimate concerts and ballet. For Arena schedules and tickets, contact *Fondazione Arena di Verona, Pza Brà 28; tel: 045 805 1811; tickets: V. Dietro Anfiteatro 61B; tel: 045 800 5151; fax: 045 801 3287.* The TIC has schedules for other venues.

Below
Veronese courtyard

complete, these date from the 12th and 13th centuries. Five 16th-century gates provide monumental entrances. These are **Porta Nuova** in white marble, **Porta Pailo** in brown tufa and **Porta San Zeno** in white tufa and brick, all three designed by Michele Sanmicheli. Across the river are **Porta San Giorgio** (also called Porta Trento), of tufa faced in white stone, and **Porta Vescovo**, enlarged in 1860, site of the liberation of Verona from Austria in 1866.

Accommodation and food

Catullo € *V. Valerio Catullo 1; tel: 045 800 2786.* A good, basic 3rd-floor walk-up, in the centre of the old town, with nearby parking. Private and shared bathrooms.

Ristorante Greppia €–€€ *Vicolo Samaritana 3 (off V. Mazzini); tel: 045 800 4577; www.ristorantegreppia.it. Open Tue–Sun.* This family-owned restaurant overflows into the adjacent *piazzetta*, serving pasta stuffed with pumpkin, almonds and nutmeg in a light cheese sauce or tender *tortellini mascarpone* with thinly sliced radicchio.

Trattoria alla Pigna €–€€ *V. Pigna 4; tel: 045 800 4080; www. osteriapigna.com.* A secret the Veronese rarely share, La Pigna serves creative dishes such as steelhead trout sauced in brandied courgette flowers, or creamy white *panacotta* with a purée of woodland berries. The atmosphere is elegant, the service personal, the menu translated.

Hotel Aurora €€ *Pza Erbe; tel: 045 594 717 or 597 834; fax: 045 801 0860; www.hotelaurora.biz.* A comfortable, family-run hotel with a terrace bar overlooking the market. All rooms have en-suite baths, satellite TV and air conditioning. Parking nearby.

Hotel San Luca €€ *Vicolo Volto San Luca 8; tel: 045 591 333; www. hotelsanluca.it.* Just off Piazza Brà, this hotel has inviting public spaces and well-decorated rooms. The friendly staff, high-speed Internet access and enclosed parking make this a top choice.

Dodici Apostoli €€–€€€ *Corticella S. Marco 3; tel: 045 596 999; www. 12apostoli.com. Closed Sun evening & Mon.* Verona's best-known restaurant, holding its pre-eminent position for decades with a generous list of local dishes and fine classic Italian cuisine. The wine cellars are exceptional.

Due Torri Hotel Baglioni €€€ *Pza Sant'Anastasia 4; tel: 045 595 0444; http://duetorrihotel.hotelsinverona.com.* The city's finest, this former palace is furnished with period antiques, each room unique. Service is impeccable, as is the restaurant.

Ristorante Maffei €€€ *Pza Erbe 38; tel: 045 801 0015; www.ristorantemaffei.it. Open Tue–Sun.* In the beautiful Palazzo Maffei, serving traditional dishes with flair, in an elegant setting.

Walking tour

P Metered parking is along the river on Lungadige Capuleti, beyond the Ponte Aleardi bridge. A 24-hr car park is at Piazza Cittadella, just south of Piazza Brà. Some hotels in the historic centre have parking permits, but you should ask when reserving a room.

Time: 1½ hours, 3 hours with detours.

Route: Begin at **PIAZZA BRÀ ①** and the **ARENA ②**, following Via D'Alpini, on the south side of the piazza, and walk east. Turn left on to Via Maffei, which becomes Stradone San Fermo. Near the river, the church of **SAN FERMO MAJOR ③** is on the right. Continue towards Ponte Navi turning left on Via Leoni, which becomes Via Cappello, looking into the courtyard of **CASA DI GIULIETTA ④** before reaching **PIAZZA ERBE ⑤**, with the **Madonna de Verona** in the centre and **Palazzo Maffei** at the opposite end. There are good **frescoes** on the buildings along the side. Follow the passageway under the **LAMBERTI TOWER** into **PIAZZA DEI SIGNORI ⑥**. Opposite Dante is the entrance to the **PALAZZO DE RAGIONE** and the tower. Return to Piazza dei Signori, turning right and through the arch to the **SCALIGERI TOMBS** and **Santa Maria Antica**. Past the tombs turn left to Corso Sant'Anastasia, then turning right on to the Corso to the church of **SANT'ANASTASIA ⑦**, opposite the **Hotel Due Torri**. (*See Detour 1 below.*) Follow Corso Sant'Anastasia back to Piazza Erbe, past Palazzo Maffei, where the street becomes Corso Porta Borsari. This was the main street of Roman Verona, and you will pass through Roman **Porta Borsari ⑧**. Here the name changes to Corso Cavour, which you follow past **ARCO DEI GAVI ⑨** to **CASTELVECCHIO ⑩** and **PONTE SCALIGERO**. (*See Detour 2 below.*) Opposite the castle gate, Via Roma will return you to Piazza Brà ①, where you can visit the **MUSEO LAPIDARIO MAFFEIANO ⑪**.

Detour 1: To see the **DUOMO ⑫**, take Via Duomo from the small piazza in front of Sant'Anastasia, walking north three blocks. Follow the street behind the duomo, crossing **PONTE PIETRA ⑬** to the **TEATRO ROMANO** and **MUSEO ARCHEOLOGICO ⑭**. Backtrack to Sant'Anastasia ⑦.

Detour 2: From the gate of Castelvecchio, turn right and follow the building around to the right, on to Regaste San Zeno, following it along the river. Follow Via Barbarani when it angles off to the left. This long but pleasant walk takes you to **SAN ZENO MAJOR ⑮**. Follow Via San Zeno a short way to see **Porta San Zeno**. Backtrack to Castelvecchio.

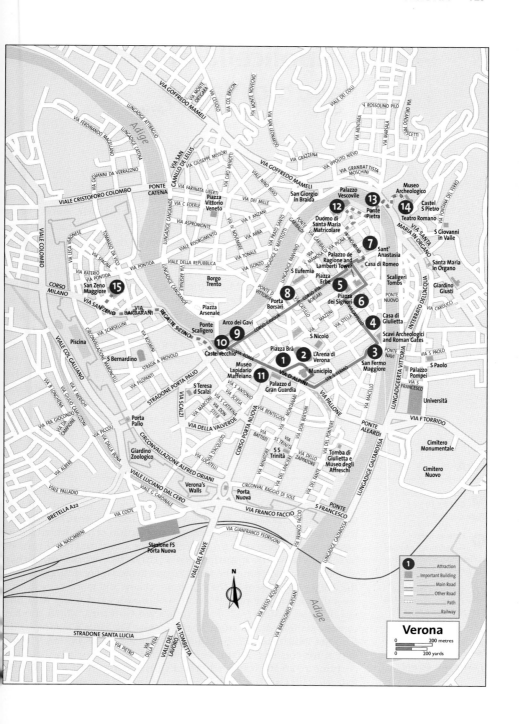

Valpolicella and Pasubio Valley

Ratings

Castles	●●●●●
Scenery	●●●●●
Vineyards	●●●●●
Geology	●●●●○
History	●●●●○
Mountains	●●●●○
Nature	●●●●○
Architecture	●●●○○

The region along the great sweeping curve of the River Adige has been inhabited since prehistoric times, with Neolithic settlements followed by those of the Etruscans and later Romans. The Ostrogoths and Lombards also left their mark, as did the Scaligeri of Verona, the Venetians and even, briefly, Napoleon. The Valpolicella region, formed by the valleys of the Fumane, Negrar and Marano rivers as they flow south from the Lessini mountains, is home to some of the most popular Italian red wines. Along with its vineyards are natural attractions and some surprisingly rugged terrain. Few more dramatic roads challenge the driver than those through the Pasubio Valley, to the north. The Adige Valley opens the main route from the Mediterranean through the Dolomites to Bavaria, via the Brenner Pass; its rich history is evidenced in the towns of Avio and Ala.

ALA

ⓘ Informazione *Tel: 0464 430 363. Open seasonally.*

Ⓟ Park in Largo Giuseppi Vicentina, as the road enters the old town.

Ⓗ Cantina Sociale *V. Bolzano; tel: 0464 671 168. Open Mon–Fri. € for group visits.*

Ⓐ Unusual painted ceramics are sold at **Il Coccio** *V. Carerra 11.*

The Romans saw immediately that Ala's location controlled the narrow valley, the only passage north through the Dolomites. It was the Venetians, however, who launched the industry that brought Ala its fortune and its fame. This was the production of silk, which led in turn to high-quality velvet, a necessity to the courts and nobility of all Europe. Eight silk-spinning mills, three dye works and other manufactories lay along the short Roggia River, where it dropped into the Adige. The palaces of the velvet merchants still grace Ala's streets, several with good stonework, some with frescoes and many with fine wooden doors. More frescoes are inside **San Giovanni**, which also has ceramic stations of the cross. At the foot of Via Santa Catarina is the Baroque **Palazzo de Pizzini**, housing a piano museum, rarely open except for concerts. In the summer, actors and musicians in period costume re-create scenes from Ala's history and lead tours of the palaces. The **Cantina Sociale** winery is open for tastings. North of

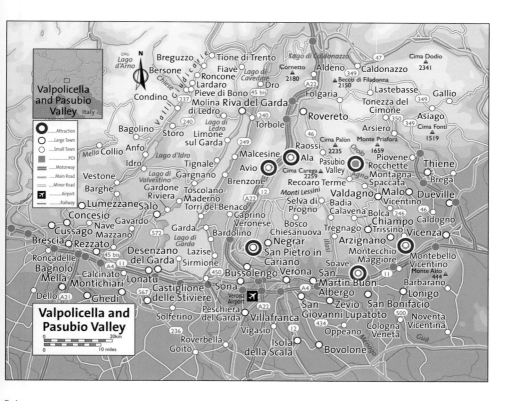

Valpolicella and Pasubio Valley Italy

Below
Balcony and doorway, Ala

town, along the old Roman road, stands a shrine to **St Anthony**, an onion-domed Baroque church.

Accommodation and food in Ala

Trattoria La Luna Piena € *V. Carrera 7; tel: 0464 673 030. Closed Mon, Tue lunch & Sun evening.* The wide variety on the menu may include hearty country fare, such as sausage and beans or more sophisticated dishes like scaloppine in balsamic vinegar.

Viennese € *S12 near Ala turn-off; tel: 0464 672 530; fax: 0464 672 312; www.hotelviennese.com.* A plain, but pleasant hotel with access for guests with disabilities, and parking.

Bar Di's Club €–€€ *Piazzetta Erbe 2; tel: 0464 674 106. Open Tue–Sun 0700–0100.* The best lunches in town, with delectable bruschetta and focaccia sandwiches; full dinner menu, as well.

AVIO

Castello di Avio €
Tel: 0464 684 453.
Open Mar–Sept Wed–Sun
1000–1800; Oct–Nov
Wed–Sun 1000–1700.

Cantina Sociale
V. Dante 14; tel: 0464 684
008; www.cantinaavio.it.
Open Mon–Fri 0800–1200,
1400–1800.

Guerrieri Gonzaga
San Leonardo Borghetto;
tel: 0464 689 004. Open
Mon–Fri 0800–1200,
1400–1700.

**Buy local cheeses at
the cooperative,**
V. Al Parco 10, Sabbionara
d'Avio; tel: 0464 684 641.

Castello di Avio (Avio Castle) guards the town and valley from a majestic mountainside perch, posing for photos with its tall tower and vineyards enclosed by a ring of well-preserved walls. It makes the transition from a medieval fortress to the more liveable palace-castles of the early Renaissance. Frescoes are in the main tower and guardroom, the latter cycle a rare view of 13th-century men-at-arms. A short, steep path back to the car park leads past a small cascade. The local **Cantina Sociale** is open for wine tastings, as is **Guerrieri Gonzaga**, in nearby Borghetto. The latter winery has an interesting museum of old farm equipment.

Food in Avio

Dai Menegheti € V. Morielle 37, Sabbionara d'Avio; tel: 0464 684 646. Open Wed–Sun. Antonelli Gianni presents the freshest and best of local produce.

Trattoria Castelbarco € V. Castelbarco, Sabbionara d'Avio; tel: 0464 684 134; www.castelbarco.it. Traditional local dishes, in an informal setting.

Ristorante Castellum Ava €–€€ Castello di Avio; tel: 0464 684 299. No views from inside the castle walls, but a pleasant arbour-covered terrace and good veal and lamb choices.

MONTECCHIO MAGGIORE

Informazione V.
Leonardo da Vinci;
tel: 0444 696 546.

**Restaurant
d'Amore €€€**
Castello di Bella Guardia; tel:
0444 496 6172. Open
Thur–Tue lunch & dinner.
Booking essential.

**Villa Cordellina-
Lombardi €** V.
Lovara 36; tel: 0444 696
075. Open mid-Apr–mid-Oct
Tue–Fri 0900–1300,
Sat–Sun 0900–1200,
1500–1800.

Travellers following the trail of Juliet should stop at the two castles that local lore hold to be the homes of the supposed rival families. These Scaligeri castles are thought to have inspired Luigi da Porto, whose villa was within sight of both castles, to write the original story. Castello della Villa (tel: 0444 492 259) is used for performances and Castello di Bella Guardia contains Restaurant d'Amore. Follow signs upward from the centre of town to the two castles – and to fine views. Just east in a garden park is the Palladian-style **Villa Cordellina-Lombardi**, built in the early 1700s, with large Tiepolo frescoes in the central reception hall. A 6km trip northward leads to **Arzignano** and an interesting black stone castle.

Accommodation and food in Montecchio Maggiore

Castelli €€–€€€ Vle Trieste 89; tel: 0444 697 366; fax: 0444 490 489; www.hotelcastelli.it. A full range of services and amenities, as well as a restaurant (€€–€€€ Open evenings).

Opposite
Avio Castle

PASUBIO VALLEY

ⓘ Informazione *V. Roma 25, Recoaro Terme; tel: 0445 75 070; http://turismo.provincia. vicenza.it*

Monte Pasubio was one of the hardest-fought battle lines of World War I, and the traces of war are still found along its heights. Defensive positions carved out by the Italian and Austrian armies still pockmark the mountainsides. The route through the Pasubio Valley is misleading on a map. Although it follows the river, don't picture a serene valley road; instead, the narrow (but well-surfaced) road is carved out of the steep bank, hundreds of metres above the river. The trip is much less hair-raising if travelled from southeast to northwest, on the inside of the S46. The scenery (which the driver must use a lay-by to enjoy) is splendid throughout. Above the top of **Passo Pian di Fugazze** (1,159m) is a war memorial, the **Ossuary Pasubio**. The remains of gun emplacements and fortifications are also visible, and a ruined fort is above **Sant'Antonio**. **Recoaro Terme** is an old spa town laid out in well-kept parks and gardens. It is also an active winter-sports centre, with a tramway, ski lifts and cross-country trails centred at **Recoaro Mille**.

Accommodation and food in the Pasubio Valley

Carla €€ *V. Cavour 55, Recoaro Terme; tel: 0445 780 700; fax: 0445 780 777; www.hotelcarla.it.* A modest hotel with good local dishes in its restaurant (*€€ Closed Sun evening & Mon*).

SOAVE

ⓘ IAT *Foro Boario 1; tel: 045 619 0773; www.comunesoave.it. Open summer only.*

ⓟ Parking € *outside the town gates, in the large piazza; also at the castle.*

ⓗ La Rocca € *V. Castello Scaligero; tel: 045 786 0036. Open Tue–Sun 0900–1200, 1400–1600.*

One of the finest of the several castles that dot the countryside around Verona, Soave's **La Rocca** commands and encircles the town. Crenellations march in neat rows down the hillside and around the cluster of stone buildings. The castle, sometimes inaccurately called 'Rocca Scaligeri', actually predates that Verona family, who enlarged it in the 1200s. Inside, the rooms are furnished to the early Renaissance. Soave, first settled by the Romans, but built by the Lombards, has several distinguished buildings within the walled town. On the way into town, you cannot miss the huge plant whence Bolla's popular white wine makes its way around the world.

Accommodation and food in Soave

Al Gambero € *Corso Vittorio Emanuele; tel: 045 768 0010; www.ristorantealgambero.it. Closed Tue evening, Wed & late Aug.* A pleasant restaurant serving local dishes, with 12 comfortable guest rooms **€**.

VALPOLICELLA WINE TOWNS

ℹ️ APT *Pza Brà at V.*
degli Alpini 9, Verona;
tel: 045 806 8680;
fax: 045 800 3638;
www.tourism.verona.it

🏛 Villa Mosconi-
Bertani *Novare*
(Negrar); tel: 045 601 1211.
Open Mon–Fri 0900–1200,
1400–1800, Sat
0900–1300.

Casa Vinicola Sartori *V.*
Casette 2, Negrar; tel: 045
602 8001;
www.sartorinet.com

Museo Botanico della
Lessinia *€ Parco delle*
Cascate; tel: 045 772 0185;
www.cascatemolina.it

Tommasi Viticoltori
V. Ronchetto 2, Pedemonte;
tel: 045 770 1266;
www.tommasiwine.it. Call
for tours of the winery.

Vivere Molino *V. Bacilieri*
1; tel: 045 770 2185;
www.cascatemolina.it

🔵 Palio del Recioto
festival, mid-Apr,
Negrar; tel: 045 600 0330;
www.paliodelrecioto.org

Those who enjoy wines will find many vineyards in the Valpolicella region, where they can sample the product; others will enjoy the scenery, villas, churches and natural attractions. The primary town is **San Pietro in Cariano**, and the whole area is scattered with distinguished villas. **Villa Mosconi-Bertani**, in Novare, was built by a follower of Palladio; Bertani wines, sold at the villa, are among Valpolicella's finest and you can schedule a tasting €€€, with accompanying food. You can dine and spend the night at the Renaissance **Villa del Quar**, in Pedemonte, listed as an Italian National Monument (*see Accommodation below*). The 18th-century **Villa Rizzardi**, in Negrar, has particularly fine Italianate and English gardens. Nearby, at **Casa Vinicola Sartori**, you can visit the gardens and taste the wines. Quarries at **Sant'Ambrogio di Valpolicella** are the source of the most prized building stone used in Verona's churches and even the arena. **San Giorgio**, just to the north, is known for the Lombard Romanesque **Pieve San Giorgio**, with a fine cloister and a museum showing Roman and earlier finds, along with fossils. Inside the church is the rare 8th-century Lombard **ciborio**. **Molina Falls Park**, in the Fumane Valley, includes several waterfalls, with nature trails along a wooded brook. The **Museo Botanico della Lessinia** identifies the many indigenous plants. The most remarkable natural site is the huge **Ponte di Veja**, a natural bridge that formed the entry to a cave where prehistoric artefacts were found. The entire area is filled with fossils, and the **Museo dei Fossili** in Sant'Anna has a 7m shark, 70 million years old.

Accommodation and food in the Valpolicella wine towns

Ai Parcheggi € *Parco della Cascate; tel: 045 772 0078*. Right at the entrance to the park, this bar-restaurant is a good refreshment stop after walking the trails to waterfalls.

Trattoria da Nicola € *V. Valle 41, Monte, Sant'Ambrogio di Valpolicella; tel: 045 776 0180*. Try the local *sopressa* salami as a starter.

Trattoria dalla Rosa Alda € *Strada Garibaldi 4, San Giorgio di Valpolicella; tel: 045 770 1018*. Friendly trattoria with local dishes, such as wild rabbit or pheasant with polenta.

Villa del Quar €€€ *V. Quar 12, Pedemonte (Verona); tel: 045 680 0681; fax: 045 680 0604; www.hotelvilladelquar.it*. Well-appointed guest rooms in a beautifully maintained Renaissance villa. The Michelin-starred Arquade €€€ restaurant is among the finest in northern Italy.

Suggested tour

Informazione
Vle Trento, Valdagno;
tel: 0445 401 190.

A road tunnel connects Valdagno with Schio and the S46, a faster but less scenic route to the Pasubio Valley.

Villa Trissino Marzotto €€
Trissino; tel: 0445 962 029;
www.villatrissinomarzotto.it.
Open Mon–Fri by appointment.

Total distance: 202km, with detours 342km.

Time: 5 hours' driving. Allow 3 days for the main route, 4 days with detours. Those with limited time should concentrate on Valpolicella.

Links: The Lake Garda route (*see page 113*) begins a few kilometres west of Verona, via the A4. The Alto Adige route (*see page 142*) begins on the S12 in Rovigo. Vicenza (*see page 213*) is close to Montecchio Maggiore via the S11 or A4.

Route: Leave Verona ❶ (*see page 116*), heading east and following signs to Venice (Venezia), on the A4 autostrada (thus avoiding frequent traffic tie-ups on the S11), exiting at **SOAVE ❷**. (*See Detours 1 and 2 below and on page 133.*) Head south to rejoin the A4. Continue northeast on the A4 until the exit for Montecchio. Turn off and travel north on the S246, following signs to **MONTECCHIO MAGGIORE ❸** (44km). Continue north on the S246, signposted **Valdagno**. Although visits require advance booking, **Villa Trissino Marzotto** is worth the effort of a 2km sidetrack, left, signposted to **Trissino**. Two villas, one an atmospheric ruin, are set in a splendid Italianate garden park. Continue north on the S246 to Valdagno (20km). Just northwest, follow signs to **Montagna Spaccata**, with a 100m-deep gorge and waterfall. From Valdagno, follow the scenic valley north to **Recoaro Terme**, where you turn right to climb the 671m **Passo Xon**, following signs to **Valli del Pasubio** (23km). Here you enter the historic **PASUBIO VALLEY ❹** and, after turning west (left), begin climbing immediately up the **Passo Pian delle Fugazze**. As the road levels out on the western side, the river valley lies hundreds of metres directly below. This scenery continues all the way to the outskirts of **Rovereto** (*see page 137*), where you reach the old Brenner Pass road, the S12 (39km). Head south (left) on the S12, to **ALA ❺**, whose historic centre lies just east of the main road. From Ala, continue south on the S12 to **AVIO ❻**, following brown signs up winding narrow streets to the castle. Returning to the S12, continue south through the Adige Valley to **Domegliara**, turning east (left) to **Sant'Ambrogio di Valpolicella**, and the vineyards of the **VALPOLICELLA WINE TOWNS** (49km). Continue on the unnumbered road east to **San Pietro in Cariano**, past **Pedemonte** and back to the S12 just outside Verona, your starting point (25km).

Detour 1: To explore the **Monti Lessini plateau**, follow the unnumbered road west from the north side of Soave, beyond the castle, or take the S11 west, in either case following signs to **Colognola ai Colli**. Turn north (right) following signs to **Tregnago** and **Giazza**, in a beautiful setting along a valley. It is one of several in the Monti Lessini plateau that were settled by Bavarian farmers in the 13th century. The local **Museo Etnografico** (€ *V. dei Boschi 62. Open summer daily; winter Sat–Sun*) tells their story. Backtrack south to the S11 and Soave (80km).

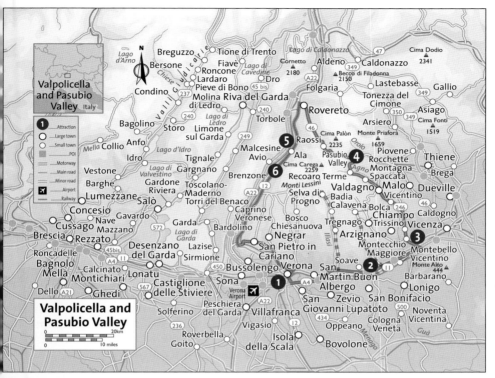

Valpolicella and Pasubio Valley Italy

- ❶ ....Attraction
- ○ ....Large town
- ○ ....Small town
- ....POI
- ....Motorway
- ....Main road
- ....Minor road
- ✈ ....Airport
- ....Railway

Valpolicella and Pasubio Valley

0 _____ 20km
0 _____ 10 miles

🏛 **Museo dei Fossili €**
V. San Giovanni Battista.
Open Tue–Sun.

🍴 **La Terrazza €€€**
V. Cesare I, Montecchia di Crosara;
tel: 045 745 0940. The panoramic view vies on even terms with the food – look for the speciality: scallops with black truffles in port.

ℹ **IAT** *Pza della Chiesa 34, Bosco Chiesanuova;* tel: 045 705 0088. Open year-round.

Detour 2: To explore another of the long valleys that drop from the Monti Lessini plateau, follow the S11 east from Soave to a turning north (left) signposted **Monteforte d'Alpone**. Head north along the river through **Montecchia di Crosara** to **Bolca**, on the plateau. This entire area is a fossil centre (many are in Verona's Museo Civico) and the **Museo dei Fossili** has a large collection of reptiles, fish and plants. Ask at the museum for directions for the 3km loop to quarries where fossils were found. Return by the same road to the S11 (60km).

Also worth exploring

Any one of the valleys that stretch between the Lessini plateau and the S12 between Verona and Vicenza bear investigation. In **Grezzana** is the 13th-century **Santa Maria** church with Romanesque font and campanili of multicoloured limestone. At **Cuzzano**, nearby, is Baroque **Villa Allegri-Arvedi**, built in the 1600s (*tel: 045 907 045. Open Tue morning*). South, **Santa Maria in Stelle** is a Roman nymphaeum, beside a church. **Bosco Chiesanuova** is a popular ski resort with downhill lifts and cross-country trails. East of Bosco, near **Camposilvano**, is **Valle delle Sfingi**, filled with large rock formations.

The Alto Adige

Ratings

Castles	●●●●●
Geology	●●●●●
Scenery	●●●●●
Vineyards	●●●●●
History	●●●●○
Mountains	●●●●○
Architecture	●●●○○
Villages	●●●○○

The Adige's valley was for centuries the main route from northern Europe to the Mediterranean. Its strategic and commercial importance was tremendous, and its history is filled with the movements of traders, travellers and armies. The legacy of that history is the astonishing string of castles that seem to crown every crag. Although today's traveller sees many of these – the great white walls of Beseno and elegant towers of Avio are hard to miss – dozens more hide in side valleys, or simply blend into the rocky landscape. Mountains rise on every side, and on their lower slopes and protected valleys grow vineyards that produce outstanding wines: red and white, dry and sweet, still and *frissante*. Even without the dinosaur footprints, the medieval frescoes, the hiking trails and the magnificent views, the traveller could spend a very pleasant holiday here just seeking its wines and castles.

BOLZANO

ⓘ APT *Pza Walther 8; tel: 0471 307 000; www.bolzano-bozen.it. Open posted hours Mon–Fri 0900–1830, in reality closed 1230–1400, Sat 0900–1230.*

Club Alpino Italiano *Pza delle Erbe 46.* Has information on hiking and climbing.

Ⓟ Parking € is plentiful in underground car parks at Piazza Walther and the bus terminal nearby.

Ringed by mountains, Bolzano looks more Austrian than Italian – not surprising, since the city spent its formative centuries under Austrian and Bavarian rulers. The eye-catching patterned roof and carved spire of the **duomo** overlook spacious **Piazza Walther**, Bolzano's lively centre of everyday life. Inside, the duomo is soaring Gothic, with fine polychrome and gilt carving in the ambulatory chapel. At nearby **Chiesa dei Domenicani**, the Dominican cloister is decorated in 15th-century frescoes; those in Capella di San Giovanni are from the Giotto school. Follow Via Goethe from the Dominican church, through **Piazza delle Erbe**, bounded by an assortment of architectural styles and enlivened by a morning market. Directly beyond, Via dei Francescani leads to **Chiesa dei Francescani**, a 14th-century church with a fine Gothic wooden altarpiece and frescoed cloisters.

Across the river in **Vecchia Chiesa Parrocchiale di Gries** is an exceptional polychrome carved altarpiece from the 15th century,

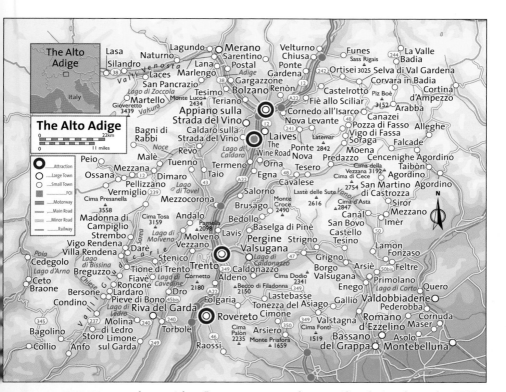

Duomo Tel: 0471
978 676. Open
Mon–Fri 1000–1200,
1400–1700, Sat
1000–1200. Treasury open
Tue–Sat 1000–1200. Free.

Chiesa dei Domenicani
Open Mon–Sat 0930–1700,
Sun 1200–1700. Free.

Chiesa dei Francescani
Tel: 0471 289 089. Open
daily 0815–1200,
1430–1900. Free.

**Vecchia Chiesa
Parrocchiale di Gries**
V. M Knoller; tel: 0471 283
089. Open Apr–Oct Mon–Fri
1030–1200, 1430–1600.

along with a Romanesque wooden crucifix, dating from the 1200s. The museum exhibit few visitors can resist seeing is 'Frozen Fritz', the 5,300-year-old man found on a nearby glacier. The Ice Man and his equipment are displayed, along with other pre-medieval finds, at the **Museo Archeologico**. Opposite, at the **Museo Civico**, you can learn about local life through arts, costumes and furnishings. **Castel Roncolo** presents a rare picture of 13th-century life, with the largest collection of medieval secular frescoes in existence. For many, the greatest pleasure of Bolzano is simply wandering the streets and squares of its old town, with their ornate buildings, cafés and shops. **Via dei Bottai**, **Piazza del Municipio** and **Via dei Portici** all have frescoed façades, balconies and plasterwork.

Accommodation and food in Bolzano

Vogele € V. Goethe 3; tel: 0471 973 938. Small restaurant popular with the locals, serving home-style regional specialities.

Albergo Figl €–€€ Pza del Grano 9; tel: 0471 978 412; fax: 0471 978 413; www.figl.net. Starkly modern, the hotel is centrally located in a

🏛 **Museo Archeologico** € *V. Museo; tel: 0471 320 100; www.iceman.it. Open Jan–Jun & Sept–Nov Tue–Sun 1000–1800; Jul–Aug & Dec daily 1000–1800.*

Museo Civico € *V. Cassa di Risparmio. Tel: 0471 997 960; www.bolzano.net/ museocivico.htm. Open Tue–Sun 1000–1700.*

Castel Roncolo €€ *V. Santo Antonio 14; tel: 0471 329 808. Open mid-Apr–Oct Tue–Sun 1000–1800. Free shuttle from Hotel Greif, on Piazza Walther.*

⛪ **Christmas Market** *1–23 Dec*, brings rows of colourful street stalls.

Flower Market *30 Apr– 1 May*, fills Piazza Walther with bloom.

Market day: Sat, in Piazza della Vittoria, just over the Talvera Bridge; food *Pza delle Erbe; Mon–Sat 0800–1900.*

pedestrian area, parking € at nearby Garage Walther 3. Café with outdoor seating.

Ristorante Argentieri €€–€€€ *V. Argentieri 14; tel: 0471 981 718. Open Mon–Sat.* Smart restaurant with pavement tables and an upmarket menu.

Hotel Greif €€€ *Pza Walther; tel: 0471 318 000; fax: 0471 318 148; email: info@greif.it; www.greif.it.* The stylishly designed rooms may be traditional or modern in décor, all have computer workstations, some have whirlpools. Excellent restaurant €€€ serves both Italian and German dishes, including smoked venison.

Right
Piazza delle Erbe, Bolzano

ROVERETO

APT *V. Corso Rosmini
6A; tel: 0464 430 363;
www.aptrovereto.it.
Open daily.*

**Parking is at Largo
Posta**, and at the foot
of Viale de Colli at the
base of the old town;
limited parking behind
the castle.

**Museo Storico,
Castello de
Rovereto** € *V. Castelbarco
7; tel: 0464 438 100;
www.museodellaguerra.it.
Open Jan–Jun & Oct–Dec
Tue–Sun 1000–1800;
Jul–Sept Tue–Fri
1000–1800, Sat–Sun
0930–1830.*

Museo Civico € *Borgo
S Caterina 41; tel: 0464
452 800; www.
museocivico.rovereto.tn.it.
Open mid-Jun–mid-Oct
Tue–Thur & Sat
0900–1200, 1500–1800,
Fri & Sun 0900–1200,
1500–2200; mid-Oct–
mid-Jun Tue–Sun
0900–1200, 1500–1800.*

Santa Maria Assunta
*Villa Lagarina. Open
Mon–Sat 0900–1300,
1500–1900, Sun for
worship.*

Vini Vallagarina
*V. Brancolino 4, Nogaredo;
tel: 0464 412 073. Open
Mon–Fri 0800–1200,
1400–1800; guided tours.*

Castel Beseno €
*Besenello; tel: 0464 834
600. Open Mar–May & Nov
daily 0930–1700; Jun–Oct
daily 1000–1800; Dec–Feb
Sat–Sun 0930–1700.*

St Mark's Lion on the old city gate reminds travellers that they are back in the lands of *La Serenissima* – the Venetian Empire. Crowning a hill, 13th-century **Castello de Rovereto** gives views over the red-roofed town to mountains that rise steeply from the Adige Valley. Inside is an extraordinary history of the impact of World War I on the whole of northern Italy. Artefacts, photographs and posters are so graphic and well arranged that you don't need to read Italian. Look especially at the racks of photographs showing the liberation of towns you might visit – Trento, Gorizia, Riva and Udine. **Strada degli Artiglieri** is named after the World War I artillery that Italian forces dragged and pushed up this steep route, literally digging their defensive positions into the mountainside. Memorials to the men lost here, among them a count of Savoy, line the road. Following signs to the dinosaur tracks (*see below*), almost under the power line, a short trail leads to one of the defensive caves. Each evening Rovereto remembers the thousands of lives lost, with the ringing of the **Maria Dolens**, a huge bell cast from cannons contributed by both sides.

Greek and Roman archaeology, local dinosaur finds and silk manufacture are themes of the **Museo Civico**, much of it donated by archaeologist Paolo Orsi. To see the **dinosaur tracks** on a mountainside south of town, follow signs for the **Ossario di Castel Dante** (war memorial), then follow Strada degli Artiglieri to the car park, clearly marked. The first footprint is about a 15-minute walk from the road. Along with distinct imprints of single tracks are entire paths of footprints – about 350 – dating back 200 million years. Although it may seem presumptuous for tiny Villa Lagarina, across the Adige, to bill itself as 'Little Salzburg', its church of **Santa Maria Assunta** was designed by the same artists who created Salzburg Cathedral. The fine Baroque interior has elaborate stuccowork and a high altar of coloured marble. To its south are several wineries, including **Vini Vallagarina**, where you can taste and purchase all the local varieties. A short distance north of Rovereto, **Castel Beseno** covers an entire hilltop, a magnificent sight from the valley below. One of the largest castles south of the Alps, it was owned by the Trapp family until 1973. Fortifications enclose three medieval compounds, 'modernised' to reflect Renaissance refinements. After seeing Palazzo dei Mesi's 15th-century frescoes and the inner courtyards, you can walk the defensive walls surrounding a large tournament field.

Accommodation and food in Rovereto

Hotel Rovereto €–€€ *Corso Rosmini 82D; tel: 0464 435 222; fax: 0464 439 644; www.hotelrovereto.it.* Traditional hotel, well located between the motorway and the town centre, with indoor car park.

Above
Old town, Rovereto

Vecchia Trattoria Scala della Torre 7
€–€€ *Scala della Torre 5 (off Pza della Erbe);*
tel: 0464 437 100. Open daily 1200–1430,
1930–2100. Veal *tonato*, wild boar with
polenta, and a nod to its northern
clientele with goulash.

Leon d'Oro €€ *V. Tacchi 2; tel: 0464 437*
333; www.hotelleondoro.it. Located in the
centre of town, all rooms are comfortable,
well furnished and have a private bath.
Parking available.

Novecento €€–€€€ *Corso Rosmini 82; tel:*
0464 435 222. Open Mon–Sat. The *canederle*
(gnocchi) with three cheeses is excellent,
as are the tortellini and freshwater fish.

Al Borgo €€€ *V. Garibaldi 13; tel: 0464 436*
300. Closed Sun evening & Mon. Pricey, but
known as one of the region's best, serving
dishes such as quail roasted in acacia
honey and balsamic vinegar.

TRENTO

ⓘ APT *V. Manci 2;*
tel: 0461 216 000;
www.apt.trento.it.
Open Mon–Sat 0900–1800,
Sun 0900–1300.

ⓒ Trento Card
Available in 24 hr
(€10) or 48 hr (€15)
denominations and includes
major attractions in Trento
and Rovereto, public
transport, wine tastings
and discounts on bicycle
rental, taxis, dining and
more. Buy at the TIC, or at
major sites.

ⓗ Castello
Buonconsiglio € *V.*
B Clesio 5; tel: 0461 233
770; fax: 0461 239 497;
www.buonconsiglio.it. Open
Tue–Sun 1000–1800.

Castello Buonconsiglio houses several museums in a walled complex
that includes the 13th-century **Castelvecchio**, 16th-century **Palazzo
Magno**, the **Torre Grande** and the **Torre dell'Aquila**. Once the
residence of the prince-bishops, the buildings not only contain their
considerable art collections, but are themselves works of art, especially
the richly frescoed Castelvecchio. Frescoes also adorn the rooms
throughout the Palazzo Magno, but the most remarkable are in Torre
dell'Aquila, a beautiful fresco cycle dating from 1400–1539, known as
the *Ciclo dei Mesi*, or Cycle of Months, hard to find without asking. Also
at the castle is the **Museo Storico**, covering local history from
Napoleon to World War II, when Trento was a centre for the resistance.

Trento is best known for the Council of Trent, which took place in
the castle and **duomo** 1545–63, and began the Counter-Reformation.
Its decrees were announced in front of the large wooden crucifix in
the side chapel. Unusual are the colonnaded stairs in this Lombard
Romanesque church. In the 13th century, it replaced the earlier
Basilica di San Vigilio, still beneath the present duomo. Enter from
the north transept to see fragments of mosaics and the tombs,
including that of San Vigilio. Adjoining the duomo is the **Palazzo
Pretorio**, a 13th-century episcopal palace housing the **Museo**

Museo Storico €
*V. Torre d'Augusto
35–41; tel: 0461 230 482;
www.museostorico.tn.it.
Open Mon–Thur 0900–
1700, Fri 0900–1300.*

Basilica di San Vigilio €
*Pza Duomo; tel: 0461 980
132. Open daily
0630–1200, 1400–2000.*

Museo Diocesano €
*Pza Duomo; tel: 0461 234
419; fax: 0461 260 133;
www.
museodiocesanotridentino.it.
Open Jun–Sept daily
0930–1230, 1430–1800;
Oct–May daily 0930–1230,
1430–1730.*

**Museo Tridentino di
Scienze Naturali €**
*V. Calepina 14; tel: 0461
270 311; www.mtsn.tn.it.
Open Tue–Wed & Fri–Sun
1000–1800, Thur
1000–2200.*

**Museo dell'Aeronautica
Gianni Caproni €**
*V. Lidorno 3, Mattarrello at
the airport; tel: 0461 944
888; www.museocaproni.it.
Open Tue–Sun 0900–1300,
1400–1800. Accessible for
people with disabilities.*

**Giardino Botanico
Alpino €** *Rifugio Viote,
Monte Bondone; tel: 0461
948 050. Open Jun–Sept
daily 0900–1200,
1430–1700.*

**Museo degli Usi e
Costumi della Gente
Trentina €** *V. Edmondo
Mach 1; tel: 0461 650 314;
www.museosanmichele.it.
Open Tue–Sun 0900–1230,
1430–1800.*

Diocesano. The diocesan treasury includes 15th–19th-century goldwork and outstanding 16th-century Flemish tapestries, hung in the cathedral during the council meetings. In the centre of Piazza Duomo is the Baroque **Neptune Fountain**, and facing the square are façades with 16th-century frescoes. Frescoes are also along Via Manci and Via Belenzani. On nearby Via Cavour, another Council of Trent venue, **Santa Maria Maggiore**, has good frescoes in the ceiling and over-altar dome.

Museo Tridentino di Scienze Naturali (Natural Science Museum) contains minerals, fossils, dinosaur footprints, local reptiles, birds, mammals and botanical displays, mostly relating to the Dolomite region. Look for the 16th-century frescoed ceilings in rooms flanking the entrance hall. The **Museo dell'Aeronautica Gianni Caproni** contains a remarkable collection of 20 planes built between 1910 and 1980, nine of which are the only surviving examples in the world – the personal collection of pioneering aircraft designer Gianni Caproni. Multi media exhibits show the history of flight using early flight films with English captions.

On Monte Bondone, high above the Adige west of Trento, is **Giardino Botanico Alpino**, near Rifugio Viote. The garden displays over 2,000 species of Alpine flora, with ecosystem signage in English. In San Michele all'Adige, north of Trento, **Museo degli Usi e Costumi della Gente Trentina** is housed in a 12th-century Augustinian monastery that was once a hospice for Rome-bound pilgrims. One of the most important ethnographic museums in all of Europe, it contains displays and artefacts that show the farming, wine-making, metal-working, weaving, woodcarving, pottery, costumes and many other facets of local culture over several centuries, with English signage.

Accommodation and food in Trento

Antica Trattoria due Mori € *V. San Marco 11; tel: 0461 984 251; www.ristoranteduemori.com. Open Tue–Sun.* Appealing dishes, such as risotto with rocket and gnocchi with pumpkin blossoms. Near the castle.

Rifugio Viote € *Viote, Monte Bondone; tel: 0461 948 162.* A pleasant bar and restaurant at an altitude of over 1,500m.

Ristorante la Cantinota € *V. San Marco 22–24; tel: 0461 238 527; www.cantinota.editarea.com. Open Fri–Wed.* Venison marinated with lavender and served with polenta, courgette blossoms filled with herbed ricotta – not your ordinary chef.

Hotel America €€ *V. Torre Verde 50; tel: 0461 983 010; fax: 0461 230 603; www.hotelamerica.it.* Close to the cathedral and to the castle, rooms are pleasant and the staff welcoming. The hotel has a good restaurant €–€€ with local specialities. Parking available.

Ristorante Le Tire-Bouchon €€ *V. Milano 148; tel: 0461 261 456. Open Mon–Fri lunch, 1830–0100, Sat 1830–0100.* You might find goat's cheese gnocchi with a salad of fresh herbs and an entrée of loin of rabbit with *pignoli* and thyme.

Hotel Buonconsiglio €€–€€€ *V. Romagnosi 14–16; tel: 0461 272 888; fax: 0461 272 889; www.hotelbuonconsiglio.it.* A fine and genial hotel, well situated, with many services and enclosed parking.

THE WINE ROAD

ⓘ APT *Pza Principale 8, Caldaro sulla Strada del Vino (Kaltern); tel: 0471 963 169; www.kaltern.com.* Open Mon–Sat 0930–1200, 1430–1700

Ⓗ Gewürztraminer tasting May, Termeno. A chance to compare this wine from around the world, in the town of its origin.

The road west of the Adige below Bolzano is designated 'Strada del Vino' ('Wine Road'), for good reason. Vineyards cover entire landscapes, broken only by picturesque towns clustered around onion-domed churches. The attractions are the scenery, the castles and the wineries, where you can taste and often dine, under leafy arbours. About midway is **Lago di Caldaro (Lake Caldaro)**, the warmest lake for swimming in all the Alps, and well equipped with lake-front amusements and walking trails. A **wine museum**, at **Caldaro**, traces the history of wine growing here from Roman times. At nearby **Castelvecchio (Altenburg)** are the ruins of the 4th-century church of **St Peter**, and a view of the lake and the Sud Tyrol peaks.

Castles overlook every valley: in **Appiano** there are 12 and in **Missiano** you can stand on the terrace of **Castel Corba (Schloss Korb)** and see two others along the same slope. A trail connects the three. From Castel Corba's terrace is one of the region's loveliest panoramas, dropping away to vineyards that stretch across the broad valley to the tree-clad foothills. Beyond, as though standing on tiptoes to see, are the snow-covered Dolomites; and in the middle, where the mountains break for the Adige, lies Bolzano, compressed into a tidy red and white mosaic. **San Paolo** is a typical village, its rural Renaissance buildings surrounding a parish church with a melodious peal of bells. The cloister churchyard seems more like a garden, with fresh flowers decorating graceful iron crosses.

Accommodation and food on the Wine Road

Hotel Schloss Korb €€€ *Missiano, Appiano; tel: 0471 636 000; fax: 0471 636 033; www.schloss-hotel-korb.com.* Surrounded by vineyards, with views over Bolzano and the Dolomites, the setting doesn't get better. The charm of a medieval castle, with all mod cons and an outstanding restaurant **€€€**.

Suggested tour

Total distance: 96km, with detours 154km.

Opposite
Piazza Duomo, Trento

Time: 2½ hours' driving. Allow 3 days for the main route, 4 days with detours. If time is limited, concentrate on Bolzano and Trento.

A mountain lift climbs from **Caldaro** to the summit of **Passo di Mendola** for a 360-degree panoramic view, saving a tortuous climb via the S42.

Links: From Verona (*see page 116*), follow the Valpolicella and Pasubio Valley route (*see page 132*) to Rovereto. To Cortina d'Ampezzo, follow the Dolomite Road route (*see page 150*) from Bolzano.

Route: Follow the S12 north from **ROVERETO ❶**, continuing to **TRENTO ❷**, along the historic Adige Valley. Mountains rise dramatically on either side, more scenic than the valley floor's industry (21km). (*See Detour 1 below.*) North of **San Michele all'Adige**, at Salorno, follow brown signs for **THE WINE ROAD ❸** (Strada del Vino) left over the river, turning right to **Termeno** and **Lago di Caldaro**. Continue north to the town of **Caldaro**. Head north again to **Appiano** and follow the small road left, signposted **San Paolo**. At the church, bear right to Missiano. Backtrack to the S42, which leads left into **BOLZANO ❹** (75km). (*See Detour 2 below.*)

Detour 1: For a more challenging and scenic drive, circle the slopes of **Monte Paradiso**, between Rovereto and Trento. On a map the road looks like a plate of spaghetti as it twists through the mountains. At **Besenello**, turn east (right) on to the S350, which winds to **Folgarìa** and over the **Passo di Sommo**. Turn north (left) on the S349 through **Centa San Nicolo** to **Trento** (48km).

Detour 2: Before entering **Bolzano**, turn left on to the S38, signposted **Merano**. The road follows the Adige to the spa town favoured by Austrian Empress Elisabeth. The town is a centre for winter sports and

Below
Vineyards and church, San Paolo

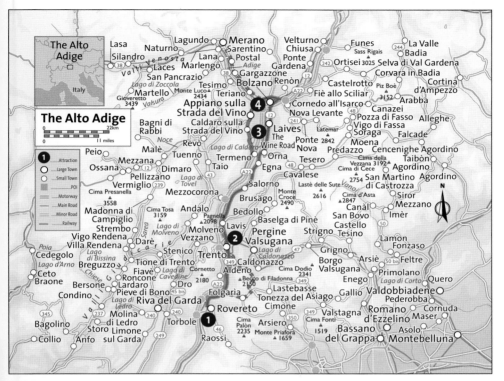

The Alto Adige

Italy

The Alto Adige

- **1** Attraction
- ○ Large Town
- ○ Small Town
- ■ POI
- Motorway
- Main Road
- Minor Road
- Railway

Alpine walking, and for garden lovers, who can stroll the flower-bordered promenades and visit the new botanic gardens at **Castel Trauttmansdorff**. Backtrack on the S38 or follow the unnumbered local road on the Adige's west bank back to Bolzano (52km).

Also worth exploring

East of Trento is a beautiful area of mountains and lakes reached via the S47 or the smaller S349. The S47 leads to the **Val Sugana** and eventually to **Bassano del Grappa** (*see page 201*). In Lavarone on the S349, is a rare remaining highland Austrian fort, **Forte Belvedere**, a three-storey pillbox from World War I. Its interior is largely intact, as are the deep tunnels which were dug into the bedrock.

Castel Trauttmansdorff
€€ *V. San Valentino 51; 0473 235 730; www.trauttmansdorff.it. Open mid-Mar–mid-Nov daily 0900–2100.*

Forte Belvedere € *Oseli Lavarone; tel: 0464 780 005; www.fortebelvedere.org. Open Apr–Jun & Sept–Oct Tue–Sun 1000–1200, 1430–1800; Jul–Aug daily 1000–1800.*

Villa Madruzzo
€€–€€€ *V. Ponte Alto 26, Cognola; tel: 0461 986 220; www.villamadruzzo.it. Open Tue–Sun. On the S47, not far out of Trento, this stylish restaurant is set in a 19th-century villa; specialities include venison with bilberries.*

The Dolomite Road

Ratings

Geology	●●●●●
Mountains	●●●●●
Nature	●●●●●
Outdoor activities	●●●●●
Scenery	●●●●●
Walking	●●●●●
Villages	●●●●○
Architecture	●●○○○

Although this route from Bolzano to Cortina is designated 'Strada delle Dolomiti', its views are typical of those seen from nearly any road in this remarkable mountain massif. It begins with a bang, leaving Bolzano along the Ega River through a dramatically carved gorge, whose convoluted rock walls rise on both sides. The whole of the Val d'Ega is scenic, and mountain views begin almost immediately. The route crosses three passes, first the Passo di Costalunga, then the higher Passo Pordoi, under the magnificent Gruppo di Sella, one of several such clusters of peaks to come. The third is Passo di Falzarego, near Cortina. All along the way, side roads beckon with tempting signs pointing to other passes. Adventurous travellers, who are not afraid of narrow and winding mountain roads, could spend weeks exploring these.

ARABBA AND THE CORDEVOLE VALLEY

ⓘ **APT Arabba** V. Mesdì 38, Livinallongo; tel: 0436 79 130; www.apt-dolomiti-cortina.it. A hotel connection board in the centre of Arabba assists with accommodation.

By contrast with the passes on either side, the road along the Cordevole Valley between mountain villages seems almost straight. **Arabba**, an attractive resort town, stretches along the S48 with views from every window. A funicular climbs **Col Burz**, the 1,943m mountain north of town, for even more panoramic views. Towns dot the valley below, its bright green slopes looking like well-kept – but quite vertical – lawns, its houses and churches like toys. **Pieve di Livinallongo** is a typical Dolomite town filled with Tyrolean-style buildings, but it is larger than most, with restaurants and cafés. Tiny **Andraz**, with its onion-domed church, has fewer services for travellers, but takes the prize for its ruined **Castello di Andraz**, built in the 14th century. From its picturesque perch on a rocky crag, it controlled access to the pass ahead, and helped protect it from bandits. **Falzarego Pass** was the scene of bitter fighting as Italy struggled against Austria in World War I. Several sites are marked by memorials.

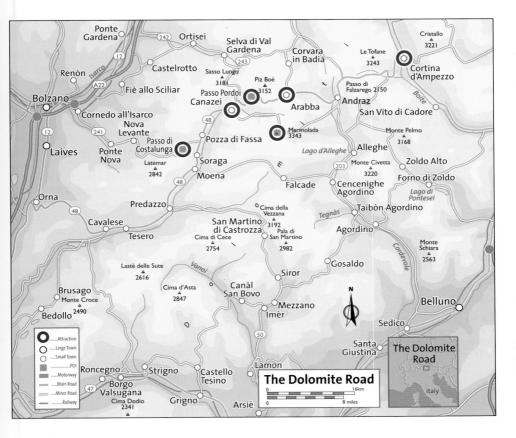

The Dolomite Road

Accommodation and food in Arabba and the Cordevole Valley

Note that hotel rates are higher during winter than in summer.

Cesa Padon €–€€ *Loc. Pieve 62, Livinallongo; tel: 0436 7109; fax: 0436 7460; www.cesa-padon.it. Open Dec–mid-Oct.* Local specialities include sausage and Tyrolean ham.

Hotel Evaldo €–€€ *V. Mesdi 3, Arabba; tel: 0436 79 109; fax: 0436 79 358; www.hotelevaldo.it.* Chalet near the slopes, with wooden balconies and après-ski luxuries, including whirlpool baths. Restaurant serves local and continental dishes.

Hotel-Ristorante Al Forte €€ *V. Pezzei 66, Pieve di Livinallongo; tel: 0436 79 329; fax: 0436 79 440; www.alforte.com.* Contemporary Alpine-style hotel near ski slopes, with whirlpool baths and playground. Accessible for guests with disabilities.

CANAZEI AND PASSO PORDOI

APT *Pza Risorgimento 2, Alba; tel: 0173 35 833; fax: 0173 363 878; www.langheroero.it.* Open Apr–mid-Sept Mon–Fri 0900–1300, 1430–1830, Sat–Sun & hols 0930–1330, 1430–1830; mid-Sept–mid-Nov Mon–Fri 0900–1300, 1430–1830, Sat, Sun & hols 0900–2000; mid-Nov–Mar Mon–Fri 0900–1800, Sat–Sun & hols 1000–1800.

Col Rodella (and other cable cars) € Open 20 Jun–20 Sept daily.

Museo degli Sci Col Rodella cable-car departure station; tel: 0462 609 620. Open Dec–Apr daily 0800–1830.

La Sia (sawmill) *Penia di Canazei.* Open mid-Jun–mid-Sept Mon–Sat 1000–1200, 1500–1900.

Canazei is an attractive ski and mountain-climbing resort, whose profile – unlike neighbouring Cortina's – has remained low enough that mountains can be seen even from the village centre. A waterfall drops almost directly into the town, and many houses are painted with lively Tyrolean frescoes. For those who prefer a slightly less jet-set atmosphere, Canazei is an excellent alternative to Cortina as a centre for exploring the Dolomites. In neighbouring Campitello di Fassa is the family-owned **Museo degli Sci**, which shows ski and winter-sports equipment spanning the entire 20th century, plus even older wooden skates. A 16th-century Venetian sawmill, **La Sia**, which provided lumber for building the Venetian navy, is the last of its type existing in this region. The restored mill is not just a museum, but is used by local residents. North of Canazei, **Passo de Sella** leads north to the Val Gardena and the town of **Ortisei**, heart of the Ladino country, where remnants of the Roman legions settled. The road must climb to an elevation of 2,239m to scale **Passo Pordoi**, the lowest point between the Gruppo di Sella (3,152m) to the north, and the Gran Vernal (3,210m) to the south. Views stretch in every direction at the top, although the foreground is less photogenic than the backdrop: walls of jagged rock rising vertically like teeth on every side. La Funivia, a cable car, carries skiers and hikers from here to **Sass Pordoi**, where **Refugio Maria** perches on a terrace at 2,950m.

Accommodation and food in Canazei and Passo Pordoi

From Easter–mid-June to mid-September–November, many hotels and restaurants close for maintenance.

La Bolp € *V. Costa 62, Alba; tel: 0462 602 313. Open daily for lunch & dinner.* One of the few restaurants open off season, serving a fixed menu. In season, La Bolp serves dishes such as Tyrolean ham, polenta with venison and the local sausage, *luganegahe.*

Enoteca Valentini € *V. Antermont 2, Canazei; tel: 0462 601 134; www.enotecavalentini.com. Open summer and winter daily, 1530–1930.* A cosy wine bar for après-ski.

Hotel Miramonti € *Strèda de Costa 199, Alba; tel: 0462 601 325; fax: 0462 601 066; www.hotelmiramonti.it.* A small hotel with good views and a dining room €–€€ serving hearty mountain dishes.

La Stua dei Ladins € *V. Pareda 35, Canazei; tel: 0462 600 052.* Near the lifts, serving simple, good food; noted for their bruschetta.

Stella Alpina €–€€ *V. Antermont 4, Canzaei; tel: 0462 601 127; fax: 0462 602 172; www.stella-alpina.net.* This beautifully restored Alpine home offers a rare chance to see a traditionally decorated interior, with hand-painted furniture, antiques and fine woodcarving in the breakfast room. Corner room 204 has good mountain views.

Above
Alpine decoration in Canazei

Lupo Bianco Hotel €€ *Strada del Pordoi 9, Canazei; tel: 0462 601 330; fax: 0462 602 755; www.hotellupobianco.it.* In a little glen on the road to Ortesei, the hotel has a dining room and lounge.

La Stalla Ristorante €€ *V. Col da Ronch 43, Canazei; tel: 0462 600 173.* In the centre of town; the choice for fine dining.

CORTINA D'AMPEZZO

ℹ **APT** *Piazzetta San Francisco 8; tel: 0436 3231; www.apt-dolomiti-cortina.it. Open daily.*

The 1956 Winter Olympics put Cortina on the jet-set map and turned a secret hideout of serious skiers into an international resort to rival the Swiss Alps. The only unfortunate result of all this attention is that Cortina is now crowded, both with visitors and with buildings that sometimes obscure the stunning scenery. But a few steps from nearly any place in town will bring an opening to the Cinque Torri, the five peaks that tower above. The scenery from the ski slopes is so

P Parking is plentiful at the Apollonio Stadium below the Tondi di Faloria lift, and in several places in the town centre.

◑ Shop for smart ski-wear and local woodcarving.

Market days: Tue & Fri.

Below
Cortina d'Ampezzo

breathtaking that it's difficult to concentrate on skiing. Along with the downhill thrills are many kilometres of cross-country trails through equally spectacular snowscapes. Bobsleighing (the run ends at Via Ronco) joins sports such as skating in the Olympic rink, **Stadio del Ghiaccio**. Lifts lead from the town to mountains in all directions, used in summer by walkers to access high mountain trails, and by those who just wish to admire the **views**.

Accommodation and food in Cortina d'Ampezzo

Ra Stua € *V. Grohmann 2; tel: 0436 868 341.* A good place for hearty simple food, well prepared.

Leone e Anna €–€€ *V. Alverá 112; tel: 0436 2768. Open Dec–Apr & Jul–Oct & Dec–Apr Wed–Mon.* A comfortable little restaurant that serves mountain food with a Sardinian twist.

Da Beppe Sello €€–€€€ *V. Ronco 68; tel: 0436 3236; www.beppesello.it. Open Wed–Mon.* Across the river from the centre, the speciality of its talented chef is a well-seasoned loin of venison.

Hotel Natale €€–€€€ *Corso Italia 229; tel: 0436 861 210; fax: 0436 867 730; www.hotelnatale.it.* A small hotel with fine views over the town and mountains from its carved wooden balconies.

Hotel Parc Victoria €€–€€€ *Corso Italia 1; tel: 0436 3246; fax: 0436 4734; www.hotelvictoriacortina.com.* Five-storey chalet-style hotel, most rooms with balconies overlooking town. Fine dining in their restaurant.

Miramonti Majestic Grand Hotel €€€ *V. Pezie 103 (above the S48); tel: 0436 4201; fax: 0436 867 019; www. miramontimajestic.it.* It really is grand, on a hillside with a golf course, stunning views and a good dining room. Minimum stay of three days.

Savoia Grand Hotel €€€ *V. Roma 62; tel: 0436 3201; fax: 0436 869 186; www.grandhotelsavoiacortina.it.* A four-star hotel in the heart of the town, it has friendly, English-speaking staff and fine dining.

MARMOLADA

ⓘ APT *V. Marmolada 11, Rocca Pietore; tel: 0437 722 277; www.marmolada.com*

ⓜ Museo della Guerra *€ Refuge Passo Fedaia, V. Malga Ciapela 58, Rocca Pietore; www.museodellaguerra-marmolada.com. Open Jun–Sept & Dec–Easter daily 1000–1230, 1400–1830.*

While snow on the surrounding ski trails lasts only November–May, the high slopes of Marmolada, the Dolomites' highest at 3,343m, offer year-round skiing. Access is easy via several tramways, which leave from the S641. At the **Fedaia Pass** is the **Museo della Guerra (War Museum)**, a small private collection including a field kitchen, for those with a particular interest in World War I. On the other side of Marmolada, at the terminal of the **Malga Ciapela** cable car, is a monument zone with machine-gun postings, trenches, artillery posts and huts intact. The caves and passages of the Punta Serauta are open to view (*Jun–Sept*).

Accommodation and food in Marmolada

Hotel Garni Roberta € *Malga Ciapela 68, Malga Ciapela; tel: 0437 522 980; fax: 0437 522 980; www.garniroberta.com.* Small hotel close to the ski lifts.

Rosalpina €–€€ *V. Bosco Verde, Rocca Pietore; tel: 0437 722 004; fax: 0437 722 049; www.rosalpinahotel.com. Open Jun–Sept & Dec–Apr.* A cosy inn with mountain views and a restaurant €–€€ serving hearty Tyrolean food.

PASSO DI COSTALUNGA AND VAL DI FASSA

ⓘ APT *V. Carezza 21, Nova Levante; tel: 0471 613 126; www.welschnofen.com. Open daily.* Good information on hiking and skiing.

ⓜ Museo Ladino di Fassa € *San Giovanni Vigo di Fassa; tel: 0462 760 182; www.istladin.net. Open Jan–May daily 1500–1900; mid-Jun–mid-Sept & Dec daily 1000–1230, 1500–1900. Closed Nov.*

Molin de Pezol (watermill) *V. Jumela 6, Pera di Fassa. Open mid-Jun–mid-Sept Mon–Sat 1000–1200, 1500–1900; shorter hours off season. Free.*

The summit of **Passo di Costalunga** is one of the loveliest on the route, wooded rather than open, with two attractive stone hotels clad in wooden Alpine balconies. Tall pine trees frame views of surrounding peaks. To the west of the pass, nestled in a wooded vale, is the bright blue **Lake Carezza**, at the village of Carezza al Lago. Nearby is **Nova Levante** with a tiny historic **onion-domed church** below the road level. A number of walking trails lead into the surrounding hills, past green meadows filled with wild flowers. A few tiny villages perch high above, overlooking the river and valley. **Chiesa Santa Elena**, in Nova Ponente, has extensive 14th-century frescoes. The **Val di Fassa**, east of the pass, is a centre for the Ladino culture, and the **Museo Ladino di Fassa**, in Vigo di Fassa, looks at the traditions of this unique ethnic group. Restored rooms show how people lived and worked, as well as their religion, music and festivals. A watermill, **Molin de Pezol**, in Pera di Fassa has millstones for grinding cereals, powered by three large paddle wheels.

Accommodation and food in Passo di Costalunga and Val di Fassa

Hotel Pension Diana € *V. Carezza 94, Nova Levante; tel: 0471 613 160; fax: 0471 614 403; www.diana-hotel.it.* Modern Alpine hotel known for its wine cellar and its restaurant.

Hotel Savoy €–€€ *S48, Passo di Costalunga 5; tel: 0471 612 124; fax: 0471 612 132; www.hotelsavoycarezza.it.* Wooded mountain setting and panoramic views. Restaurant €€ with a cosy atmosphere.

Tscheinerhutte €–€€ *Nigerstrasse, Nova Levante; tel: 0471 612 612.* Serves home-style Tyrolean specialities, including dumplings.

Hotel Monti Pallidi €€ *Strada de Sen Pelegrin, Moena; tel: 0462 573 221; fax: 0462 573 578; www.montipallidi.com.* Traditional hotel with comfortable rooms, a sauna and hydromassage, restaurant and parking. Special packages include dining and skiing.

Suggested tour

Total distance: 100km, with detours 130km.

Time: 3 hours' driving. Allow 2 days for the main route, 3 days with detours. Those with limited time should concentrate on the scenery instead of the towns.

Links: From Lake Garda (*see page 102*), the Alto Adige route (*see page 142*) leads to Bolzano. Continue to Udine to reach the Borderlands route (*see page 168*) via the Dolomite Road route from Cortina d'Ampezzo.

Route: Leave **BOLZANO ❶** on the S241, along the Ega River through a deep, narrow gorge that the river has carved through the rock, forming undulating curves, caves and walls on both sides. A waterfall pours unexpectedly from a cave into the river. Be sure to pull into the small lay-by to look back – and almost straight up – at **Castel Cornedo**, perched on solid rock. The road climbs to **Nova Levante** and continues climbing past the beautiful **Lake Carezza**. The lake is surrounded by majestic evergreens, which continue to line the road as it climbs **PASSO DI COSTALUNGA ❷**, which, unlike the other passes on this route, has summit views framed by trees. From the pass, the road plunges sharply into the **VAL DI FASSA**, meeting the S48 in Pozza di Fassa, where you turn left, following signs to **CANAZEI ❸**. (*See **Detour** opposite.*) Look for waterfalls dropping through the lower forested slopes and from rock ledges high above (47km). Continue east from Canazei on the S48, climbing the 2,239m **PASSO PORDOI ❹**. From **ARABBA ❺**, the road drops suddenly to the valley floor, bordering the river before rising to **Pieve di Livinallongo**. At **Andraz**, the narrow road (poorly signposted) to **Castello di Andraz**, which you can see on the left at the head of the valley, offers the only views of the castle from a safe stopping place. It leaves the S48 to the left at a dangerous curve, so you might wish to continue to a safe turning point and approach it from the other direction. The S48 ascends to yet another panoramic viewpoint at **Pocol** before arriving at **CORTINA D'AMPEZZO ❻** (53km).

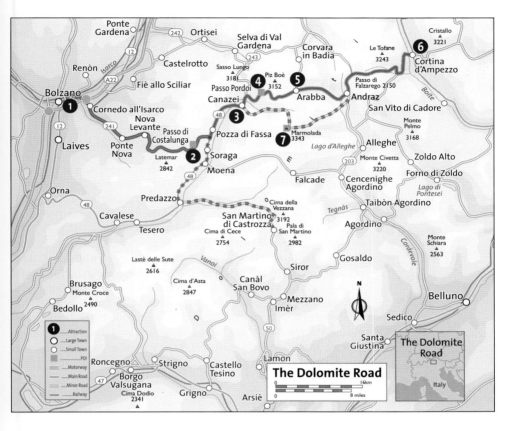

The Dolomite Road

Detour: For wild, open scenery along the shoulder of **MARMOLADA** ❼, leave Canazei on the S641, through the settlement of Alba, climbing the 2,057m **Passo Fedaia**. Continue through Sottoguda and Rocca Pietore; bear right at Salesei on to the S48. Follow signposts for Andraz to your right.

Also worth exploring

The area south of Vigo di Fassa along the Aviso River is reached by turning south (right) on the S48 towards **Moena**, instead of left to Canazei. This craggy mountain area has a very interesting geology and is rich in minerals. The **Museo Civico** in **Predazzo** displays some of the more famous minerals and thousands of fossils, some as old as 270 million years. It offers a number of walking itineraries, interesting even to those without a background in geology. A chairlift from Predazzo climbs the 2,264m **Doss Capel**. To the south is the particularly scenic **Paneveggio-Pale Nature Park** in **San Martino**.

Eastern Dolomites

Ratings

Mountains	●●●●●
Outdoor activities	●●●●●
Scenery	●●●●●
Walking	●●●●○
Nature	●●●●○
Villages	●●●●○
Architecture	●●●○○
Historical sights	●○○○○

Scenery is what this region is all about, and it doesn't get any better. Traditional tourist sights are rare, but the Dolomites more than compensate with stunning panoramas, walking paths, cable-car rides and ski trails. In the spring, Alpine meadows are dotted with bright wild flowers. Driving the winding, steep and often narrow roads is a full-time job, as they weave through tiny villages and zigzag over high mountain passes. The roads are often abuzz with motorcycles (often in the wrong lane), which seem to operate on a blend of petrol and testosterone. Although tourism is newer to the ski resorts on this eastern side of the Dolomites, many of the hotels and mountain tramways are aimed at skiers and summer climbers, closing in spring and autumn. Many of the mountain passes are closed in winter, when snowfall becomes too great for maintenance.

THE CADORE VALLEY

APT *Pza Venezia 22, Pieve di Cadore;* tel: 0437 940 084; *www.infodolomiti.it.* *Open summer daily.*

Tourist Service *V. Nazionale S52, San Vito di Cadore; tel: 0436 9119; www.infodolomiti.it.* *Open Wed–Sun 0930–1230, 1600–1900.* Accommodation information and assistance.

A long string of towns with 'Cadore' ending their names, are all located on or above the River Piave and its tributary, the Boite. Each stands at between 800 and 1,100m elevation, and all around them soar peaks topping 3,000m. Each has its charms, with Alpine architecture and a different set of stunning mountain views. **Pieve di Cadore** has the greatest claim to fame, as the birthplace of the artist Titian, whose house, **Casa di Tiziano**, and the **Museo Archeologico** make interesting stops. The parish church has a Titian painting of the Madonna. Between Pieve di Cadore and **Vigo di Cadore**, the Piave's course is through a steep, narrow ravine. From **Venas di Cadore** to Cortina d'Ampezzo (*see page 147*), the road lies along the north slope of a deep valley, with **views** to Monte Pelma and others. **San Vito di Cadore** is a ski resort, less crowded than nearby Cortina.

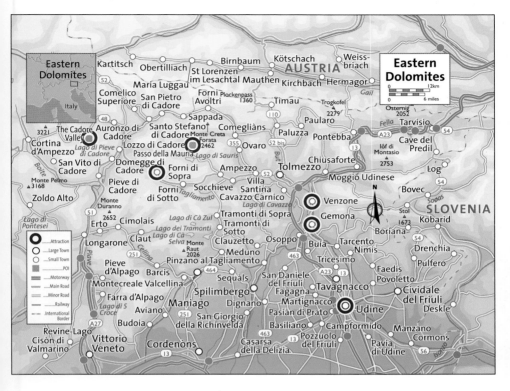

Accommodation and food in the Cadore Valley

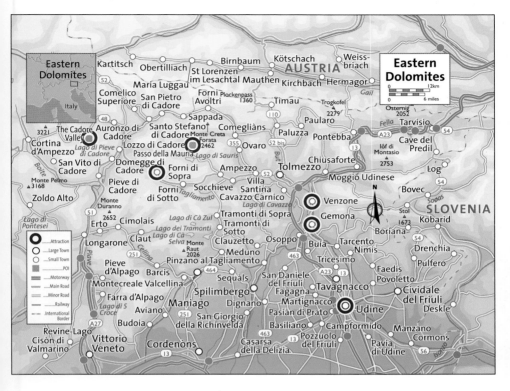
Casa di Tiziano €
V. Arsenale 4. Open Jun–Aug Tue–Sun 0930–1230, 1600–1900.

Museo Archeologico €
Pza Tiziano. Open Jun–Aug Tue–Sun 0930–1230, 1600–1900.

Market day: Mon in Pieve di Cadore.

Italia € *V. IV Novembre 39, Vigo di Cadore; tel: 043 577 643; fax: 0435 77 764.* A well-kept chalet-style hotel with balconies and a restaurant.

Hotel Cima Belpra €–€€ *V. Calvi 1, San Vito di Cadore; tel: 0436 890 444; fax: 0436 898 315; www.hotelcimabelpra.com.* Easy to find, this modern hotel has balconies on some rooms, good views from all.

La Scaletta €–€€ *V. Calvi, San Vito di Cadore; tel: 0436 890 469.* Local dishes with a Germanic accent.

GEMONA AND VENZONE

On 6 May 1976, an earthquake registering 6.4 struck the upper Tagliamento Valley. When the dust had settled, the 14th-century **duomo** in the historic centre of **Gemona** lay in ruins. Only one wall of its bell tower remained, the entire west side of the church was

Informazioni
*V. Caneva 15, Gemona;
tel/fax: 0432 981 441.
Open weekdays.*

Parking is available
at the duomo in
Gemona, and outside
the walls of Venzone.

**Agosto medievale
a Gemona**, *Aug first
weekend*. Gemona's
citizens re-enact life in the
14th century.

collapsed and open, and the apse wall was gone. Around the church, the medieval centre lay in rubble, with 400 lives lost. A quarter of a century later, the duomo stands again, the gigantic **St Christopher statue** – one of the few things left undamaged – dwarfing its portal, both original to the 1300s. To the same period belong the large central **rose window** and the two smaller ones at each side. Inside, original features include sections of the gilded, carved 14th-century **altarpiece**, to the right of the main door. The rest of the town centre has been as carefully restored, and the streets are well worth exploring to see the fine arcaded buildings, especially **Palazzo Boton**, at the far end of Via G Bini. A short distance north of Gemona is **Venzone**, a rare 13th-century fortified town. The walls are intact, as are several of the gates. The small church of **Santa Caterina** stands atop a crag, the road to which offers good views of the wall-enclosed town.

Accommodation and food in Gemona

Da Si-Si € *V. Piovega 15, Gemona; tel: 0432 981 158.* Serves local dishes and Friulian wines.

Hotel Pittini € *Pzle della Stazione, Gemona; tel: 0432 971 195; fax: 0432 971 380; www.hotelpittini.com.* Convenient for the historic centre and easy to find from the S13.

PASSO DELLA MAURIA AND TAGLIAMENTO VALLEY

APT *V. Cadore 1,
Forni di Sopra;
tel: 0438 86 767.*

Villa Santina is a
centre for mushroom
growing, and you can buy
bags of these dried *funghi*
in most shops (*closed Sat
afternoon*).

Before dropping into the **Tagliamento Valley**, the S52 climbs out of the Cadore region, over the 1,300m **Passo della Mauria** and through the **Friuli Dolomites National Park**. The road falls steeply from the pass, then levels out somewhat before winding its scenic way down through a land of Alpine meadows and spruce forests. The backdrop of limestone crags retain their white colour even when not covered in winter snow. The wide, pale-blue Tagliamento River loops back and forth under the road through its valley, east of the Passo della Mauria. In **Enemonzo**, not far from the town of **Ampezzo**, the 13th-century church of **Santilario e Taziano** was reconstructed after an earthquake in 1700, and has a Domenico Fabris fresco of the Ascension of Christ. A brook runs below its stone bell tower and a chestnut tree shades a nice picnic spot.

Accommodation and food in Passo della Mauria and Tagliamento Valley

Albergo al Pura € *V. Nazionale 12, Ampezzo; tel: 0433 811 168; fax: 0433 819 914; www.albergoalpura.it.* Fine views of Ampezzo, below, from this Alpine hotel and restaurant.

Left
The Cadore Valley

Cridola € *V. Nazionale 6, Forni di Sopra; tel/fax: 0433 88 015.* Inexpensive rooms, with a million-euro view.

Edelweiss € *V. Nazionale 19, Forni di Sopra; tel: 0433 88 016; fax: 0433 88 017; http://edelweiss-forni.it.* On the western edge of town, with a good restaurant **€**.

UDINE

🛈 *Pza 1 Maggio, northeast of the castle; tel: 0432 295 972; www.turismofvg.it. Open Mon–Sat 0900–1300, 1500–1700, Sun 0900–1300.*

🅿 Parking **€** is available in Piazza 1 Maggio, Piazza Duomo and several other places close to the historic centre.

🏛 **Galleria d'Arte Antica €** *Castello; tel: 0432 288 588. Open Tue–Sat 0930–1230, 1500–1800, Sun 0930–1230.*

Museo Archeologico € *Castello; tel: 0432 271 591. Open Tue–Sat 0930–1230, 1500–1800, Sun 0930–1230.*

Palazzo Arcivescovile € *Pza Patriarcato. Open Wed–Sun 1000–1200, 1530–1830.*

🛍 The main shopping street is Via Mercatovecchio, near Piazza Matteotti, where a morning market brings vendors of cheese and local sausages.

Reminders that this was once part of the Venetian Empire fill **Piazza della Libertà** – in the three bibliophilic lions, in the Moors that strike the bells on the **clock tower**, and in the beautiful pink-and-white-stone façade of the 15th-century **Loggia del Lionello**. The oldest part of town – where most of the attractions are – lies below the **castle**, whose walls surround a broad park. Inside the castle is the **Galleria d'Arte Antica** and the **Museo Archeologico**. The former has works by several of the great Venetian painters, including Carpaccio, Caravaggio and Tiepolo. The climb to the castle from **Piazza della Libertà**, through a gate designed by Palladio and along an ascending stone arcade, passes the lovely **Santa Maria del Castello**. Built in the 13th century, it is decorated with frescoes of the period. Behind the loggia, narrow streets lead to **Piazza Matteotti**, the busy market square. Surrounding it are tall, arcaded buildings in fascinating architectural variety. South (downhill) from the Piazza della Libertà is the **duomo**, looking a bit crowded in its small piazza. Its portals are especially fine, and inside are frescoes by Tiepolo. The most unusual is in the chapel on the right, nearest the altar. Over the tabernacle is a painting of the Resurrection, also by Tiepolo, who lived for many years in Udine. Nearby is the **Palazzo Arcivescovile**, with Tiepolo frescoes of scenes from the Old Testament.

Accommodation and food in Udine

Osteria Al Cappello € *V. Sarpi at the Fish Market; tel: 0432 299 327; www.osteriaalcappello.it.* A popular and noisy wine bar that spills out on to the street.

Villa Coren € *V. Cividale 1, Siacco di Povoletto; tel/fax: 0432 679 078; www.villacoren.com.* No credit cards. An old winery which has been converted into guest rooms and two apartments, with kitchens. Ask for a vineyard tour.

Trattoria Le Maddalene Sporcje €–€€ *V. Pellicerie 4 (off Pza Matteotti); tel: 0432 500 544. Closed Sun evening & Mon.* Dine street-side or upstairs in this smart wine bar, whose inspired daily menu may include ravioli with asparagus and walnuts, toothsome tagliatelle with pesto, and fish cooked to the moment of perfection.

Hotel Cristallo €€ *Pzle d'Annunzio; tel: 0432 501 919; fax: 0432 501 673; www.cristallohotel.com*

Right
Market,
Piazza Matteotti, Udine

How the Dolomites were formed

In the Triassic Period – 250 million years ago, give or take a few – a seabed of coral, shellfish, seaweed and fish was slowly thrust upward by the collision of the African and European tectonic plates. The land cracked, folded and was further disrupted by volcanic eruptions as it rose. In the millennia since, water, weather and glaciers – once more than 1,500m thick here – wore and eroded the soft limestone, which was compacted into layers alternating with calcium carbonates. These layers eroded at different rates, accounting for the rough, jagged and uneven textures of the rock, and the mountains they form.

Hotel Principe €€ *Vle Europa Unita 51; tel: 0432 506 000; fax: 0432 502 221; www.principe-hotel.it.* Well-appointed rooms and off-street parking, a 5-minute walk from the historic area, but right on the circumferential street for easy access.

Vitello d'Oro €€–€€€ *V. Valvason 4; tel: 0432 508 982; www.vitellodoro.com. Closed Tue evening, Wed & Jul.* Seafood and lamb are specialities, or opt for the full-course regional menu, with local wines. A vine-draped terrace overlooks the street.

Suggested tour

International Access:
In **Tolmezzo**, the S52 intersects with the S52B, which heads north over the **Passo di Monte Croce Carnico** (Plockenpass) into Austria, and on to **Lienz**. Just to the east, near **Amaro**, the A23 autostrada heads east to the border town of **Tarvisio**, and on to **Villach**, also in Austria. To reach the Slovenian resort of **Bled**, leave the A23 at **Tarvisio** and follow the signs to the frontier and **Jesinice**.

Shortly before reaching **Forni di Sopra**, a cable car climbs the southern slope of the 2,865m Monte Tudaio di Razzo.

Al Plan Paluz
€–€€ V. Malignani, Tarcento; tel: 0432 784 120. Open Tue–Sun. This agriturismo restaurant, on a farm about 3km from the S13 via the S356, serves local specialities, such as gnocchi with ragù, at lunch and dinner.

Total distance: 159km, with detours 187km.

Time: 5 hours' driving. Allow 2 days for the main route, 2–3 days with detours. Those with limited time should concentrate on Udine and the route over the mountains to Cortina.

Links: The Dolomite Road route (*see page 150*) ends in Cortina. Cividale and Gorizia (*see pages 161–3*) are a few kilometres east of Udine via the S54.

Route: Leave Cortina ❶ on the S51, following signs to **San Vito di Cadore**. As you descend from Cortina, you'll see ahead the pyramidal Antelao, 3,263m high ahead, forming a backdrop for San Vito. To the south along this entire route through THE CADORE VALLEY, mountains tower above the Valle d'Ampezzo, and towns string out along the hillside road to **Tai di Cadore** (30km). (*See Detour 1 below.*) At Tai di Cadore, head north (left) on the S51B to **Pieve di Cadore** ❷. Leave Pieve di Cadore travelling north on the S51B to **Lozzo di Cadore** (12km). Just past Lozzo, turn east (right) on to the S52, signposted **PASSO DELLA MAURIA** and Ampezzo. Follow this scenic road through a series of panoramic views, over the 1,298m pass and down the other side to **Forni di Sopra**. Continue through the mountain scenery, through **Forni di Sotto** dropping suddenly into Ampezzo ❸ (47km). (*See Detour 2 below.*) Leave Ampezzo, on the S52, following signs to **Tolmezzo** (17km). Make your way through the confusing roundabout, following signs to **Tarvisio**, but at **Carnia**, turn south (right) on to the S13, signposted **Udine**. Follow the S13 south, stopping in **VENZONE**, to **Ospedaleto**, there turning left on a road signposted **GEMONA** ❹ (26km). Leave **Gemona** via the southern approach, returning to the S13 and on south to **UDINE** ❺ (27km). Alternatively, enter the A23 autostrada here for a quicker trip through this flat countryside.

Detour 1: Shortly past **San Vito di Cadore**, turn south (right) on the S347, signposted **Passo Cibiana**. After a steep, winding climb, stop in **Cibiana di Cadore** to admire the unique paintings on the walls of traditional local stone and wood *tabia*. All created since 1980, several of the paintings are works of internationally known artists. Return to the S51 by the same road (10km).

Detour 2: If you are up for more mountain driving, on even narrower and steeper roads, make the scenic loop from just west of **Ampezzo**, turning north (left) on an unnumbered road signposted Passo del Pura. After topping the 1,425m pass, descend to the crystal waters of **Lago di Sauris**. Continue to the right, looping back south into Ampezzo (18km).

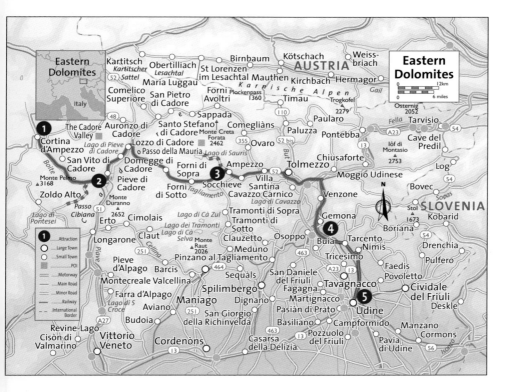

Also worth exploring

ℹ **ATP** *V. Misurina;*
tel: 0436 39 016.
Open summer daily.

🍴 **Malga Misurina**
€–€€ Cella de Dan
Innocente; tel: 0435 9247.
Local meats and cheeses
are featured in dishes such
as *gnocchi ricotta* or polenta
with cheese.

The waters of **Lake Misurina**, north of Cortina, reflect the peaks of the Tre Cime di Lavaredo and Cristallo, a photographer's dream. High above the town, reached by a steep mountain road past **Lake Antorno**, at the **Refugio Auronzo** is a simply splendid panorama of jagged peaks. Travellers come here for the views and to walk along the high trails. The trip to Misurina from Cortina is short, about 14km over the **Tre Croce Pass**, a particularly scenic route. From Misurina, continue north on the S48B, turning south (left) on to the S51 to return to **Cortina**. On the S51, about 6km north of Cortina, a small car park sits at the head of the walking trail to **Fanes Waterfall**, where a long stream of frothy water pours off a ragged rock wall. The walk is about 30 minutes, and a perfect venue for a picnic.

The Borderlands

Ratings

Historical sights	●●●● ○
Architecture	●●● ○○
Beaches	●●● ○○
Food and drink	●●● ○○
Museums	●●● ○○
Nature	●●● ○○
Scenery	●●● ○○
Geology	●● ○○○

The part of the Veneto known as Friuli-Venezia Giulia is seldom visited by foreign travellers, except those bound for its fine-sanded Adriatic beaches. But this land had its fill of other invasions since the Romans first built their towns here, long before the Venetian lagoon was settled. Travellers with a nose for history can almost see the successive eastern hordes that swept through during the early Middle Ages, and get a rare glimpse of their civilisation. Just as visible is the process of their Christianisation, as they built their basilicas, interpreting Christian/Roman forms through their own Eastern eyes. The architecture of the Austro-Hungarian Empire overlays the Roman, but has an almost Slavic touch. Museums give vivid accounts of World War I, hard fought among the limestone hills.

AQUILEIA

ℹ Proloco Aquileia
Pza Capitolo 1;
tel: 0431 91 067;
www.prolocoaquileia.it.
Open daily.

P Parking is free at the basilica.

🍷 A winery, Vini Catullio, and the Botega della Grappa distillery welcome visitors with samples.

St Mark is believed to have spread Christianity to the Roman town of Aquileia, and although greatly altered over the years, the 9th-century **basilica** is impressive. This church replaced the one that Attila the Hun burnt in AD 425. **Mosaic floors**, discovered in 1909, are from the 4th century, the largest palaeo-Christian mosaic floor known in Western Europe. Below the sanctuary is a 9th-century **crypt**, whose walls and ceiling are covered in Byzantine-style frescoes from the 12th century. To the left of the entry is another remarkable series of **mosaic floors**, their bird and animal designs intricate (even to facial expressions on animals) and condition near perfect. After admiring the **baptistery** and **campanile**, walk round the back to see the **World War I cemetery**, with rows of iron crosses and gripping memorial statuary. Follow the path behind the walls to the ruins of the city's former port, once washed by the Natisone. Later constructions overlay it somewhat, built of bits and pieces of Roman stonework. Remains of

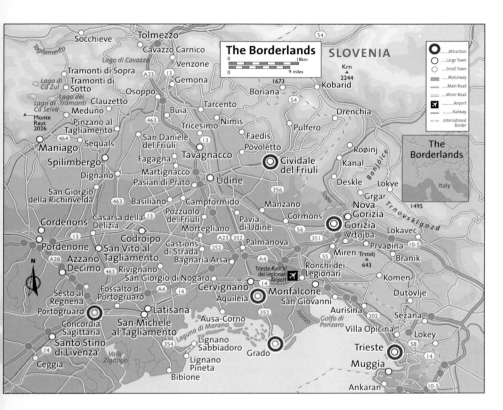

The Borderlands

SLOVENIA

Italy

The Borderlands

a **forum** stand along the S352, as does the **Museo Archeologico**, with excellent sculptures, mosaics, glass and other Roman artefacts.

Accommodation and food in Aquileia

Trattoria Al Morar €–€€ *V. Beligna 66; tel: 0431 919 340.* Friendly little place with good fresh seafood.

Ai Patriarchi €€ *V. Giulia Augusta 12; tel: 0431 919 595; fax: 0431 919 596.* In the town centre, close to the basilica, this hotel has a restaurant serving fresh seafood and grilled meats €–€€.

Basilica di Aquileia
€ *Open Mon–Fri 0900–1300, 1400–1700, Sat–Sun 0900–1700. Closed for Mass Sun 1015–1130.* An excellent brochure is available in English.

Museo Archeologico €
V. Roma 1; tel: 0431 91 016. Open Mon 0830– 1400, Tue–Sun 0830–1930.

Several *agriturismo* farms along the S352 have restaurants.

CIVIDALE DEL FRIULI

Cividale hangs on the edge of a ravine carved by the final efforts of the Natisone to burst out of its rocky confines into freedom on the

ℹ **ARPT** *V. Iulia; tel/fax: 0432 815 111; www.turismofvg.it*

℗ Limited free parking near the Tempietto Longobardo, and by timed ticket (ticket machines are well hidden) around the market square.

🏛 **Tempietto Longobardo** € *Off Pza San Biagio; tel: 0432 701 211. Open Apr–Sept Mon–Sat 0930–1230, 1500–1830, Sun & hols 0930–1300, 1500–1930; Oct–Mar daily 0930–1230, 1430–1830. Actual hours may vary.*

Museo Archeologico € *Pza del Duomo; tel: 0432 700 700. Open Mon–Fri 0900–1330, Sat–Sun 0630–1930.*

Museo Cristiano *Pza del Duomo. Open Mon–Sat 0930–1200, 1500–1700, Sun 1000–1300, 1500–1900. Free.*

Ipogeo Celtico *V. Monastero Maggiore. Free. Ask for the key at Bar al Ipogeo, around the corner near the bridge.*

Friulian Plain. The city was founded by Julius Caesar in 50 BC and was a Lombard capital 500 years later, reaching its apex in the 8th and 9th centuries as the seat of the bishop of Aquileia. **Ponte del Diavolo (Devil's Bridge)** spans the chasm, with views of houses crowning the convoluted limestone cliffs. Cividale's streets climb and twist among buildings straight from the Middle Ages – and before. The **Tempietto Longobardo**, a gem of 8th-century construction, was rebuilt after a 13th-century earthquake. Look especially for the saints' statues and the stucco arch – rare surviving examples of Lombard art. To appreciate even further the degree of civilisation these conquering tribes had achieved, see the 5th- and 6th-century jewellery and weaponry at the **Museo Archeologico**. In the **duomo**, along with a masterful silver altarpiece and an octagonal baptistery, is the small **Museo Cristiano**, with the 8th-century Altar of Ratchis and newly discovered fresco panels. Perhaps the most unusual attraction in town is its least known, hidden behind an unremarkable door, just around the corner from the Ponte del Diavolo. The 4th- or 3rd-century BC **Ipogeo Celtico** is a Celtic burial chamber, with graves set into the walls of a series of caves in the cliff above the river. Access to this spooky crypt is down several flights of narrow stairs.

Accommodation and food in Cividale del Friuli

Roma € *Pza Picco; tel: 0432 731 871; fax: 0432 701 033; www.hotelroma-cividale.it.* On a quiet square in the centre of Cividale, the Roma is handy for sights and dining.

Osteria Alla Terrazza €–€€ *Streta C Gallo 3; tel: 0432 700 288; www.laterrazza.it.* Excellent sandwiches and full meals featuring local products. Opening on to the street opposite, a wine bar gives samples of local cheeses, smoked meats and pastries.

Frasca di Gianni €€ *V. Valli del Matisone 38; tel: 0432 732 319. Open Fri–Wed.* Serves lunch and dinner of locally cured meats, a Friulian speciality, and other local farm produce.

Locanda al Castello €€ *V. del Castello 20; tel: 0432 733 242; fax: 0432 700 901; www.alcastello.net.* About 2km from the centre, this former monastery stands on a hillside with fine views. A terrace restaurant serves local specialities and continental dishes.

Opposite
River view, Cividale

GORIZIA

ℹ **ARPT** *Corso Italia 9; tel: 0481 535 764; fax: 0481 539 294; www.turismofvg.it*

Looking more like part of Austria, which it was until World War I, Gorizia sits on the Slovenian border. The former Yugoslavia built Nova Gorizia on its side of the line after World War II. You can visit the Slovenian town, although there's not much to see there. Gorizia's main sight is the medieval **Castello**, on a hill with good views. Around

Castello € *Borgo Castello; tel: 0481 535 146. Open Apr–Sept Tue–Sun 0930–1330, 1500–1930; Oct–Mar Tue–Sun 0930–1800.*

Museo de Storia e Arte *€ Borgo Castello; tel: 0481 533 926. Open Tue–Sun 1000–1300, 1400–1900.*

Sant'Ignazio *Pza della Vittoria. Open daily 0900–1230, 1530–1800.*

Shopping is geared mostly to the Slovenians who throng across the border for Western goods.

the castle, which was fortified during a short Venetian rule, is **Borgo Castello**, a quarter also built by the Venetians. Here you will find **Chiesa di Santo Spirito**, a small 14th-century church, and the **Museo de Storia e Arte**, with local crafts, a costume collection and good World War I exhibits. The best of the churches, however, is **Sant'Ignazio**, replete with onion domes and clearly a product of the Austrian years. Over in Nova Gorizia, Francophiles will want to visit the **Castagnavizza**, called Kostanjevica in Slovenian, the crypt of the last of the French Bourbons. The family spent its final years here in exile.

Accommodation and food in Gorizia

Gorizia Palace Hotel €–€€ *Corso Italia 63; tel: 0481 82 166; fax: 0481 31 658; www.goriziapalace.com.* Centrally located, this large hotel has parking and bicycles.

Osteria Korsic €–€€ *S Floriano del Collio; tel: 0481 884 248.* Almost on the Slovenian border, this *osteria* serves excellent grilled lamb; sample three local pastas in *tre pasti*.

Ristorante Alla Transalpina €€ *V. Caprin 30; tel: 0481 530 291.* Specialises in local dishes and wines; they have rooms € as well.

Golf Hotel Castello Formentini €€€ *V. Oslavia 2, San Floriano del Collio (6km from Gorizia's centre); tel: 0481 884 051; fax: 0481 884 052; www.golfhotelformentini.com.* Contessa Isabella Fiorentini makes guests feel at home in her castle with a complimentary 24-hour buffet of local food and drink specialities. The view from the hilltop golf course makes it hard to concentrate on the game.

GRADO

APT *Vle Dante 72; tel: 0431 877 111. Open Mar–Nov daily 0800–1900; winter Mon–Fri.*

P Parking € is available around the fishing port.

Duomo and baptistery *Open daily 0830–1815.*

Motonave Christina €€€ *Riva San Vito; tel/fax: 0431 81 412. Open Mon–Sat 1030–1230 lagoon tour, 1530–1830 islands.*

Perdon *Jul 1st Sun.* A colourful votive procession of boats.

Above
Doorway, Grado

When the barbarian hordes made life too dangerous for the Romans in Aquileia, they decamped hastily to the more easily defended tip of the peninsula. Grado, the town they built there, is still a pleasant one, for all the holiday crowds that flock to its beaches. In the centre of its old quarter, several blocks of narrow lanes, is the 6th-century Romanesque **duomo**, with outstanding columns topped by Byzantine capitals. Its mosaic floor, although not as impressive as the one in Aquileia, is well worth seeing, and you can look through a hole in the floor to see more from the 4th century. The Venetian silver **altarpiece** is also interesting. More capitals, plus a collection of ancient **stone carving** (many of the intertwined designs have a distinctly Celtic look), are displayed in a stone courtyard, with good identifying signs. Next to the duomo is a 6th-century **baptistery**, also with mosaics, and facing the same square is **Santa Maria delle Grazie**, a basilica from the period. Close by is the very picturesque **fishing port**, where Motonave *Christina* leaves for excursions around the lagoon, with refreshments available on board.

Accommodation and food in Grado

Lodging is scarce in summer, and booked well in advance. Most hotels insist on full board; many close November–March.

Serena € *Riva Sant'Andrea, Fraz. Isola della Schuisa; tel: 0431 80 697; fax: 0431 85 199; www.gradohotelserena.it.* Quieter than the busy centre, located on a nearby island in the lagoon. The hotel has a restaurant.

Ambriabella €€ *Riva Slataper 2; tel: 0431 81 479; fax: 0431 82 257.* In the centre, and open all year, this small hotel has a garden and pleasant restaurant serving local dishes.

Trattoria al Marinaio €€ *Campo Porta Nova; tel: 0431 85 882.* Has a covered patio and serves a mixed grill of fish, grilled shrimp and calamari.

Trattoria Santa Lucia €€ *Campo Porta Nova; tel: 0431 85 639. Open Wed–Mon.* Dine outdoors or inside, from a full menu of fresh fish.

PORTOGRUARO AND CONCORDIA SAGITTARIA

APT *V. Martiri della Libertà 19, Portogruaro; tel: 0421 73 558; www.turismovenezia.it/ bibionecaorle. Open daily.*

Palaeo-Christian excavations *Pza Duomo, Concordia Sagittaria; tel: 0421 275 677. Open daily 0900–2000. Free.*

Museo Nazionale Concordiese € *V. Seminario 22, Portogruaro; tel: 0421 72 674. Open daily 0900–2000.*

Market day: Thur.

Festival della Città *Tel: 0421 71 352. Mid-Aug–Sept.* Brings together music groups of local and international repute.

One of the several 'little Venices' that grace the region, Portogruaro sits along a river that is often visible only through the gateways of the 15th-century **palazzi** that line its main street. These reflect the graceful lines of the Venetian palaces in their arched windows and Gothic doorways. Many of them are arcaded, one supported by columns with carved capitals. When a view of the river does open out, it's worth waiting for. Behind the **duomo**, whose tall, leaning bell tower follows the design of St Mark's campanile, is as pretty an ensemble of architecture and water as you will find in the Veneto. The **fish market** is under a loggia, and a medieval building overlooking the river has a tiny votive chapel tucked into its lower floor. A pair of old **mills with large waterwheels** are connected by a footbridge to the other bank, and the whole is framed in weeping willows. The best views are from the path through a tiny linear garden that borders the river's opposite bank.

Before Portogruaro was founded in medieval times, Concordia Sagittaria, just south of the S14, was a thriving Roman city. Beside and under its **duomo** (with an 11th-century **baptistery**) is the excavation of **Roman and palaeo-Christian buildings**, including a porticoed burial chamber and mosaic floors. Descriptive signage is in English. Ask there for a brochure showing other Roman sites, such as a **stone oven** and **Roman bridge**. The many finds from the various Roman sites in Concordia are in

Festa della Madonna della Pescheria *Tel: 0421 71 399. Mid-Aug.* A colourful event along the river.

the **Museo Nazionale Concordiese**, in Portogruaro. This impressive collection includes statuary, capitals, mosaics and bronzes.

Accommodation and food in Portogruaro and Concordia Sagittaria

Antico Spessotto € *V. Roma 2, Portogruaro; tel: 0421 71 040; fax: 0421 71 053; www.hotelspessotto.it.* In the town centre, 120 well-furnished rooms, and a friendly staff.

Right
Fish market and campanile, Portogruaro

Antica Locanda Campanile €–€€ *V. Roma 13, Portogruaro; tel: 0421 74 997; www.alcampanile.it. Open Tue–Sun.* Right under the leaning campanile, with a full menu of stylish and casual dishes, including sandwiches.

TRIESTE

APT *Stazione Centrale, Pza della Libertà, at the northern approach to the city and V. San Nicolo 20; tel: 0432 734 100; www. triestetourism.it. Pza dell'Unita; tel: 0463 478 312.*

Parking € is at Piazza dell'Unità d'Italia and on either side of it along the port. There is also parking at the castle.

Bus No 24 goes to the castle.

Castello and Museo Civico € *Castello Open winter daily 0900–1800, later in summer.* **Museum** *Open daily 0900–1300.*

Museo di Storia e d'Arte € *V. Cattedrale 1; tel: 040 310 500. Open Tue & Thur–Sun 0900–1300, Wed 0900–1900.*

The daily market is in Piazza Ponterosso, beside the Canal Grande.

Teatro Verdi *Pza Verde 1; tel: 040 672 2111.* The opera house.

Even more telling for Trieste than its location at the far edge of Italy, it is also at the point where Slavic East meets Latin West. The city has been fought over since the Illyrians and Celts tussled for it, and as late as 1954 it was not a part of Italy. The city has a distinct Eastern feel to it, quite different from its Italian neighbours. While the Romans left their mark, it's the imprint of Empress Maria Theresa and the Austro-Hungarian Empire that you see today, in its Baroque and neoclassical buildings, and in the **Piazza dell'Unità d'Italia**. This square, bounded by three elegant buildings and the sea, is a natural focal point, as is the elevation which rises inland. This **Capitoline Hill** was the heart of Roman Trieste, and continued to be so through medieval times. Beside the remains of the **forum** stands the 11th-century **Basilica di San Giusto**, featuring mosaics and early medieval frescoes, set in a melange of architectural styles and periods. Also crowning the hill is the **Castello**, built when the Venetians were in residence, in the 15th century. Walk its high walls for fine views. The **Museo di Storia e d'Arte** has old stonework displayed in its garden. Two other churches are of particular note: **Chiesa di Santa Maria Maggiore**, a Baroque gem about halfway between the castle and Piazza dell'Unita; and **Chiesa di Santo Spiridone**, near the end of Canal Grande. Below, a Roman amphitheatre is set into the steep hillside.

Accommodation and food in Trieste

Try to avoid Trieste at weekends, when cars from Belgrade flood the city to shop.

Caffè San Marco € *V. Cesare Battisti 18.* A traditional Austrian-style café with generations of Trieste tradition.

Antica Trattoria Suban €€€ *V. Emilio Comici 2; tel: 040 543 68.* Possibly the city's oldest restaurant, it's been a favourite since 1865.

Continentale €€€ *V. San Nicolò 25; tel: 040 631 717; fax: 040 368 816; www.continentalehotel.com.* Overlooking the Canal Grande, close to restaurants and sights.

Grand Hotel Duchi d'Aosta €€€ *Pza dell'Unità d'Italia; tel: 040 760 0011; fax: 040 366 092; www.grandhotelduchidaosta.com.* Stay in a style that Empress Maria Theresa would have enjoyed, with all the extras from whirlpool tubs to a parking garage, all in a prime location.

Suggested tour

Castello Duino €€
*Open Mar–Sept
Tue–Sun 0930–1730; Oct
Tue–Sun 0930–1700; Nov
Sat–Sun & hols 0930–1600.*

Castello Miramare €€
*Tel: 040 224 143;
www.castello-miramare.it.
Open summer daily
0900–1900; winter daily
0900–1600.*

Villa Manin € *V. Dei Dogi
1; tel: 0432 821 211;
www.villamanincontemporan
ea.it. Open Tue–Fri
0930–1230, 1430–1800,
Sat–Sun 1000–1830. Hours
vary; best to call in advance.*

Borgo Grotta Gigante
*€€ Tel: 0432 7312;
www.grottagigante.it. Open
summer daily 0900–1200,
1400–1900; winter shorter
hours.*

**Dal Diaul €€–
€€€** *V. Garibaldi 20,
Rovignano; tel: 0432 776
674; www.daldiaul.com.
Open Thur–Fri dinner,
Sat–Wed lunch and dinner.
6km north of Latisana, this
rustic restaurant has a
garden terrace for alfresco
summer dining on dishes
such as risotto with
truffled pigeon.*

**Al Mulino del
Conte €** *V.
Tagliamento 268, Cisterna di
Coseano; tel: 0432 86 22
40; www.mulinodelconte.it.
North of Codroipo, with
modern rooms and an
outstanding restaurant,
both at unbelievably low
prices.*

Total distance: 251km, using detours 248km.

Time: 5 hours' driving. Allow 2–3 days with or without detours. Those with limited time should concentrate on Aquileia and Cividale.

Links: Udine (*see page 156*) is connected to Cortina via the Eastern Dolomites route. Venice (Venezia) (*see page 170*) is only a few kilometres west of Portogruaro, via the S14 or A4.

Route: Leave Udine ❶ on the S54, following signs to **CIVIDALE DEL FRIULI** ❷ (17km). Head south from Cividale on the S356, turning east (left) upon reaching the S56 in **Cormons** and continuing on to **GORIZIA** ❸ (30km). From Gorizia, head south on the scenic S55 until it intersects with the S14 at **San Giovanni**, on the Adriatic coast. Head south (left), stopping at the beautifully located **Castello Duino** and at **Castello Miramare**, a white confection of a Habsburg palace set in gardens overlooking the sea. Continue south into **TRIESTE** ❹ (41km). (*See **Detour 1** below.*) Leave Trieste by retracing your route north on the S14 to **Monfalcone** (17km). (*See **Detour 2** below.*) From Monfalcone, follow the S14 west to **Cervignano del Friuli** (18km). Turn south (left) on the S352 to **AQUILEIA** and **GRADO** ❺ (19km). Leave Grado travelling north on the S352. On returning to Cervignano, turn west (left) on the S14, through **Latisana** and on to **PORTOGRUARO** ❻ and **CONCORDIA SAGITTARIA** (52km). Take the S463 north from Portogruaro to **Casarsa della Delizia**, turning east (right) on the S13 to **Codroipo**: worth a stop to see the gigantic **Villa Manin**, built for the last doge of Venice, and continuing on the S13 back to Udine (57km).

Detour 1: At 4.5km north of **Trieste**, turn left on to the S58, signposted to **Villa Opicina**, where there are views, then bear left again following signs to **Borgo Grotta Gigante**, billed as the world's largest accessible cave (13km). Return to the coastal S14, following signs to **Prosecco** and head north to **Monfalcone**.

Detour 2: For a shorter, slower, and more interesting drive, from **Monfalcone** follow the unnumbered road south, signposted to **Grado** (24km). Birdwatching is especially good in the delta marshlands and lagoon.

Getting out of the car

An excellent brochure, *In Bici 165km de Percorsi Ciclabili*, is available from local TICs. It maps 165km of cycling routes between Grado and Palmanova, with good details on sights en route.

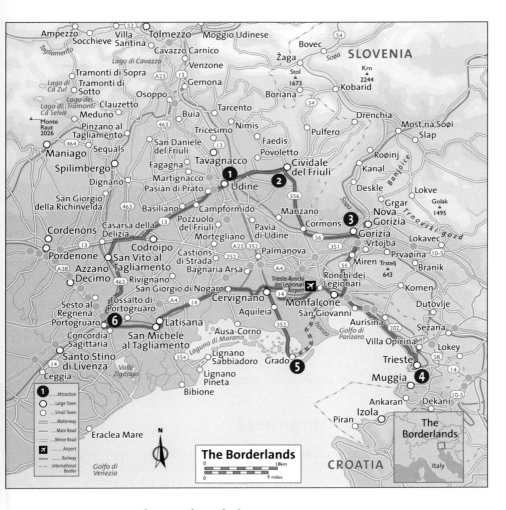

The Borderlands

0 _____ 18km
0 _____ 9 miles

Also worth exploring

APT V. Maia 37, Bibione; tel: 0431 411 111; www.bibioneturismo.it

From Jesolo's 15km-long beach to Bibione's 6km of wide beach backed by pine forest, nearly any road you follow southward will lead to a beach. Forming the barrier for the Venetian lagoon is the Litorale del Cavallino; Punta Sabbione at its end has regular boat access to Venice and its islands. The fine-sand beaches slope gently, with no sudden drop-offs, and birdlife is abundant in the reedy marshlands bordering the lagoons.

Venice

Ratings

Architecture	●●●●●
Boat trips	●●●●●
Museums	●●●●●
Art and craft	●●●●○
Scenery	●●●●○
Children	●●●○○
Historical sights	●●●○○
Walking	●●●○○

Venice is unique. In the span of 1,100 years this tiny city-state at the edge of the Adriatic Sea rose to become the Serene Republic, *La Serenissima*, conqueror of Constantinople. Long a magnet to European royalty, it also drew artists, poets and writers. The centre, heart and soul of the empire was Piazza San Marco. Here were Palazzo Ducale, home of the ruling doges, and the basilica of San Marco, the spiritual centre of the city. Even today, a café on Piazza San Marco is the place to be. The Accademia, museums and churches of the city are the repository of the best of 12th–19th-century art. Works by Tintoretto and other Venetian masters are almost commonplace and even the smallest church has its masterpiece. But it is the city itself that charms, for its canals, bridges, passageways and campos have no match.

Getting there

ⓘ **APT** *Pza San Marco; tel: 041 529 8711.* Crowded but not especially useful. Ask for *Un Ospite di Venezia* for current events, opening times and gondola rates. The TIC at the train station is more helpful with lodging.

Transport information: *www.hellovenizia.it* includes transport and hours of museums and attractions. *www.actv.it* has vaporetto lines, and *direzione@actv.it* will give specific directions.

International flights arrive at Marco Polo airport, small and easy to navigate. Boats to the city are pricey, but a bus to Porta Roma vaporetto stop is cheap. Buy a ticket at the newsstand near the door. Those arriving by car can park at Porta Roma (expensive) or at one of the car parks near Marco Polo airport (free shuttle to the airport bus stop). In any case, leave nothing in your car.

Getting around

Venice spreads across several islands, and the only ways to get from one place to another are by boat or on foot. Count on getting lost. That's part of the fun, and locals will point you on your way cheerfully. Vaporetto boats ply the Grand Canal and around the edges of the islands, encircling the entire city on route No 52. Maps,

W A very useful website, packed with information and links, all frequently updated, is www.veniceforvisitors.com

available at the TIC, are easy to follow. Be sure the boat is going in the right direction or you'll have to circle the whole route. If you plan to use the vaporetto more than twice within 24 hours, an all-day pass saves money. It includes all the islands and Porta Roma car park. Venice also has picturesque gondola ferries crossing the Grand Canal. Traghetto rides are so cheap you will want to cross just for fun. Romantic rides in your own gondola are pricey, but rates are regulated and published.

Sights

Finding an address

Venice is divided into six *sestieri* or neighbourhoods, so it is important to know which *sestiere* an address is in. From there, if you cannot locate an address on the map, ask someone. Directions and addresses often include the nearest church as a landmark. The sights below are divided alphabetically into the six *sestieri*, which can be reached on foot from one another. The gazetteer concludes with a selection of the best of the outlying islands, which can only be reached by boat. Streets have many designations, including *fondamenta* and *riva* (paved waterside paths) and *sottopassagio* (a tunnel passageway). These wander into campi (singular campo), often little more than courtyards, but sometimes large squares. Venice has only one piazza – San Marco.

CANNAREGIO

Beyond the usual tourist path, Cannaregio forms an arch across the north side of the Grand Canal. It is one of the quieter quarters, with a more measured pace. On the east and south it abuts Castello.

Museo Ebraico €
Campo del Ghetto Nuovo; tel: 041 715 359. Open Jun–Sept Sun–Fri 1000–1900; Oct–May; Sun–Fri 1000–1730; guided tours hourly.

Ghetto and Museo Ebraico

The Venetians called the foundry here *geto* and in 1516 it was decreed that all Jews in the city would live on this islet, the original use of the word. While their numbers have dwindled, the area still bears the tone of their culture with Jewish libraries, food stores and synagogues. The museum has artefacts of 17th–19th-century Jewish life and schedules tours of three synagogues.

Santa Maria dei Miracoli € *Campo dei Miracoli. Open Mon–Sat 1000–1700, Sun 1300–1700.*

Santa Maria dei Miracoli

This Early Renaissance jewel box has a three-part façade faced in pink, green and white marble. The lower has Corinthian columns with panels of coloured marble between, the second level Ionic columns with arched windows and the third a marble lunette with rose windows. Interior walls are geometric patterns of coloured marble.

CASTELLO

Immediately east of San Marco, bordered also by Cannaregio and Canale di San Marco on the south and Canale delle Fondamente Nuove on the north.

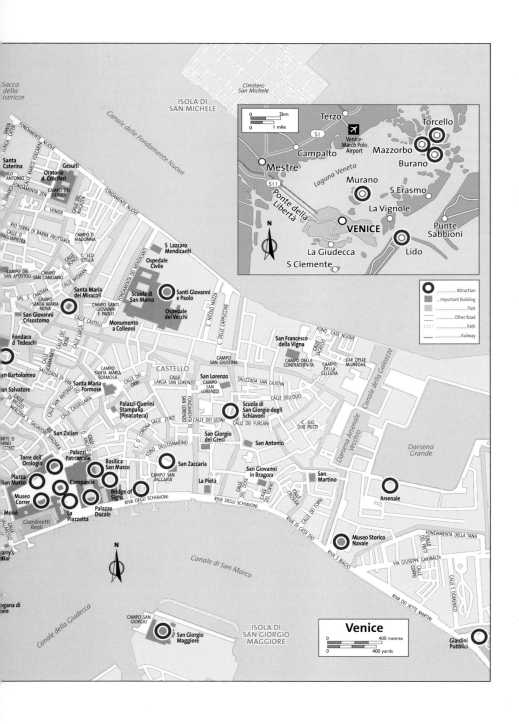

Sacca della isericor

ISOLA DI SAN MICHELE

Cimitero San Michele

Canale delle Fondamente Nuove

Santa Caterina
ELO ANTONIO
Gesuiti
Oratorio d'Crociferi
CAMPO DEI GESUITI

Inset map:

Terzo
Torcello
S1
Venice-Marco Polo Airport
Campalto
Mazzorbo
Mestre
Burano
S11
Murano
S Erasmo
Ponte della Libertà
La Vignole
N
VENICE
Punte Sabbioni
La Giudecca
Lido
S Clemente

Laguna Veneta

S Lazzaro Mendicanti
Ospedale Civile

Santa Maria dei Miracoli
Scuola di San Marco
Santi Giovanni e Paolo
Ospedale dei Vecchi

San Giovanni Crisostomo
Monumento a Colleoni

Fondaco d'Tedeschi

San Francesco della Vigna

CAMPO DELLA CONFRATERNITA
CAR DELLE MUNEGHE

an Bartolomeo
CASTELLO
CAMPO SANTA MARIA FORMOSA
San Lorenzo
CAMPO SAN LORENZO

an Salvatore
Santa Maria Formosa
Scuola di San Giorgio degli Schiavoni

San Zulian
Palazzi Querini Stampalia (Pinacoteca)
San Giorgio dei Greci
San Antonio

Torre dell'Orologio
Palazzo Patriarcale
Basilica San Marco
San Zaccaria
San Giovanni in Bragora
San Martino

Piazza San Marco
Campanile
CAMPO SAN ZACCARIA
La Pietà
Arsenale

Museo Correr
Bridge of Sighs
RIVA DEGLI SCHIAVONI

Moisè
La Piazzetta
Palazzo Ducale
RIVA DEGLI SCHIAVONI

Giardinetti Reali

arry's Bar

Museo Storico Navale
RIVA S BIAGIO
FONDAMENTA DELLA TANA

N

Canale di San Marco

gana di are

Canale della Giudecca

CAMPO SAN GIORGIO
San Giorgio Maggiore
ISOLA DI SAN GIORGIO MAGGIORE

Darsena Grande

VIA GIUSEPPE GARIBALDI

Giardini Pubblici

Legend:

Attraction
Important Building
Park
Other Road
Path
Railway

Scale:

Venice
0 — 400 metres
0 — 400 yards

🛈 **Museo Storico Navale** € *Campo San Biagio at Fondamenta dell'Arsenale; tel: 041 520 0276. Open Mon–Fri 0845–1330, 0845–1300 Sat.*

San Zaccaria € and **chapels** *Campo San Zacccaria. Open Mon–Sat 1000–1200, 1600–1800, Sun 1100–1200, 1600–1800. San Zaccaria vaporetto: through the Sottopassagio San Zaccaria on the Riva degli Schiavoni.*

Santi Giovanni e Paolo *Campo Santi Giovanni e Paolo, Vaporetto Fondamente Nuove; tel: 041 5223 7510. Open Mon–Sat 0830–1230, 1530–1900.*

Scuola di San Giorgio degli Schiavoni € *Ponte dei Greci at Rio de San Lorenzo. Open Apr–Oct Tue–Sat 0930–1230, 1530–1830, Sun 0930–1230; Nov–Mar Tue–Sat 1000–1230, 1500–1800, Sun 1000–1230.*

Arsenale

The great navy of the Venetian Republic was born here, using one of the first production-line techniques in history. Unfortunately it is not open, but you can see much of it from the high bridge over the Riva dell'Arsenale. Ships were moved from station to station (the recesses along the canal) during construction. The arched gate dates from 1460, and in front are a pair of lions snatched from Piraeus and a strange-looking lion, thought to be Scandinavian in origin, from a 1040 war with Byzantium.

Giardini Pubblici

The tree-shaded gardens are a cool getaway from sun-warmed buildings and pavements. Summers of odd-numbered years fill the pavilions with an international art show, the Bienniale.

Museo Storico Navale

Bringing together artefacts of Venice's glory days of naval power, the fascinating collection is user-friendly, with good English signage. It includes original ship models created and used in the Arsenale (*see above*), a model of the doge's ceremonial barge *Bucintoro*, as well as equipment and uniforms of the Italian navy into modern times.

Riva degli Schiavoni

The Riva is the high street and front window of Venice, a long quay extending from Piazzetta San Marco to the Riva di Ca'di Dio. The Schiavoni always seems packed with people, walking and talking. The colourful buzz is most intense near Piazza San Marco, where people go to promenade. Artists sell their paintings (some quite good), others hawk souvenir trinkets. The waterfront is a constant hubbub of gondolas, vaporetti and *motoscafi*.

San Zaccaria

Begun as a Gothic building, by the time San Zaccaria was completed in 1515 it included classical elements of the Renaissance, a mix that continues inside. The second altar to the left has a fine *Madonna and Saints* by Giovanni Bellini and opposite is an early Tintoretto, *The Birth of Saint John the Baptist*. Eight doges are entombed, two of whom died here. More treasure fills the adjacent chapels.

Santi Giovanni e Paolo (San Zanipolo)

From the mid-13th to the late 18th century, 25 doges were buried here. The cross-vaulted interior, more than 91m long, is supported by ten stone columns. Tombs flanking the entrance are by the three Lombardos. On the right side in the chapel closest to the front is a unique ceiling, *The Glory of Saint Dominic*, by Giovanni Piazzetta, who influenced the young Tiepolo.

Scuola di San Giorgio degli Schiavoni

Venice colonised the Dalmatian coast and many Slavs (*schiavoni*) became Venetians. In the 15th century, they were numerous and

Right
The gondoliers

🅘 **Ca'Rezzonico €**
Fondamenta Rezzonico;
tel: 041 241 0100. Open
Apr–Oct Wed–Mon
1000–1800; Nov–Mar
Wed–Mon 1000–1700 (last
admission 1 hr before
closing).

wealthy enough to build this meeting house, commissioning Vittore Carpaccio to paint the life cycles of the Slav saints George, Tryphone and Jerome. Of his three Venetian cyclic paintings, this is considered the finest.

DORSODURO

West of the San Marco district, Dorsoduro is bounded by the Canale della Giudecca on the south, the Grand Canal on the east, Santa Croce/San Polo on the north and the cruise port district on the west.

Campo San Barnaba

This charming square faces Rio San Barnaba, close to the Grand Canal, but worlds away. Moored alongside Fondamenta Gherardini is usually a barge loaded with fruit and vegetables. On the bridge look for footprints in the white stone, memorialising furious fist fights here in the 1600s. On a more civilised note, look for **Pasticceria Colussi**, locally popular for its sweets.

Ca'Rezzonico

This is a rare opportunity to see the interior of one of the major Venetian residential palaces. Begun in 1667 and finished at staggering

ⓘ Gallerie dell'Accademia €€
Grand Canal at Accademia Bridge; 041 522 2247; www.gallerieaccademia.org. Open Mon 0815–1400, Tue–Sun 0815–1915.

Peggy Guggenheim Collection €€
Fondamenta Venier dei Leoni; tel: 041 240 5411; www.guggenheim-venice.it. Open Wed–Mon 1000–1800.

Most museums do not accept credit cards; keep a supply of paper notes. Admission prices are low, usually under €4, and several have combined admission schemes.

Basilica San Marco
(€ Treasury, € Pala d'Oro) Pza San Marco. Open Mon–Sat 0945–1700, Sun & hols 1400–1600. Treasury and Pala d'Oro may close a bit earlier. To avoid long queues in summer and holidays, arrive well before opening time or late in the afternoon. Private worship through the Piazzetta dei Leoncini portal before 0945.

Opposite
The Grand Canal

expense in 1758, it is now the museum of 18th-century Venice. Poet Robert Browning lived here. It is filled with frescoes, paintings by Guardi, Tiepolo, Canaletto and Longhi, and period furnishings. The ballroom ceiling is in *trompe l'oeil*, other rooms are by Tiepolo.

Gallerie dell'Accademia
The Accademia's 24 galleries house the largest collection of Venetian art in the world. Spanning the 14th–18th centuries, much of it was brought from monasteries and churches suppressed during the Napoleonic period. Artists include Longhi, Carpaccio, Giorgione, Tintoretto, Veronese, Veneziano, and Jacopo, Giovanni and Gentile Bellini, and scores of others.

Peggy Guggenheim Collection
This museum is an exciting counterpoint to the Renaissance art elsewhere. Collector Peggy Guggenheim lived here from the late 1940s until 1979, gathering works of modern artists such as Pollock, Picasso, Ernst, Miró, Kandinsky and Mondrian. Sculpture is displayed throughout the house and gardens.

Squero di San Trovaso
One of very few gondola construction and repair shops remaining, this *squero* behind the Accademia always seems busy. While you can't go on tour, you can see the gondolas in progress and watch the work across the narrow canal from the Fondamenta Maravegie. The workers who built the shop were from the Dolomites, hence the Alpine-style buildings.

SAN MARCO
In the centre of Venice, its borders are the Grand Canal and the waterfront, except on the east, where Rio di Palazzo, San Zulian and della Fava border it.

Basilica San Marco
Even those who 'don't do churches' marvel at this one. Whether reflecting the midday sun or floodlit at night, the sight is magical, especially when high tides flood the piazza to reflect the lighted façade. Built 1063–94, San Marco is Romanesque with a strong Byzantine accent. Five lower arches support a portico for replicas of the famed **bronze horses** from Constantinople (the originals are inside). The whole is topped off with five domes, each with its own parachute-like mini-dome.

To the left, in **Piazzetta dei Leoncini**, are two porphyry lions, more spoils of war, worn smooth by children posing for photographs. Inside, the basilica overwhelms with gold; glittering mosaics dating from the 12th century cover domes, columns and walls. Behind the alabaster high altar is the **Pala d'Oro**, a 250-panel altarpiece created by 10th-century goldsmiths, set with precious stones. The **Treasury** is filled with more silver and gold objects, many collected in conquest.

Bridge of Sighs

This sad landmark derives its name from the prisoners passing from the Palazzo Ducale to the dank cells of the adjacent prison. The best view of it is from Ponte d'Paglia along the Riva degli Schiavoni, in morning light.

🅷 **Campanile** € *Pza San Marco.* Open Jul–Sept 0900–2100; Oct 0900–1900; Nov–Easter 0930–1545; Easter–Jun 0900–1900. Note that there are usually queues for the ascent.

Campanile

Rebuilt following its dramatic collapse in 1902, the campanile offers views over the entire archipelago, and to the Dolomites on clear days. Originally erected as a lighthouse in 1153, it was also used to suspend prisoners in cages. Contemplate this during a ride to the top in the 14-passenger lift.

During the heyday of the Republic, the Piazzetta was called the *broglio*. In the morning it was limited to the use of scheming nobles, hence *imbroglio*.

Museo Correr

Designed by Napoleon as a grand ballroom, the building now houses Venice's civic museum with bits and pieces of its long history. The story of the Republic is on the first floor. You can watch Venetian art blossom on the second, in a fine collection of works by Paolo Veneziano, Cosmè Tura, Antonello da Messina, Gentile Bellini and Vittorio Carpaccio.

Museo Correr €€€ *Pza San Marco.* Open Apr–Oct daily 1000–1900; Nov–Mar daily 1000–1700 (last admission 1 hr before closing).

Palazzo Ducale €€€ (combined ticket) *Piazzetta San Marco; tel: 041 271 5911.* Open Apr–Oct daily 0900–1900; Nov–Mar daily 0900–1800 (last admission 2 hrs before closing).

Tickets for the Palazzo Ducale include admission to the Museo Correr.

➋ To reach Piazza San Marco, take vaporetto 1, 52 or 82 to San Marco or San Zaccaria.

Palazzo Ducale

The candy-coloured marble confection, built throughout the 1400s, was the home of Venice's elected noble rulers. Its Byzantine-influenced Gothic epitomises the Venetian style, which influenced architecture throughout the Veneto. Above the street-level arcade is an arched loggia, surmounted by a solid wall of pink and white marble in geometric shapes, with fine carvings on the capitals and corners. Enter through the 1442 **Porta della Carta** into a Renaissance courtyard. The first level above the courtyard was the **Doge's apartments**, with paintings by Bellini, Bosch and Tiepolo. Above were the official government chambers, with Veronese's masterpiece, *The Rape of Europa*, a ceiling also by Veronese and several works by Tintoretto. The **Grand Council Chamber** is spectacular for both its size – 52m long – and its rich decoration. Over the throne is Tintoretto's immense *Paradise* and on the ceiling *The Apotheosis of Venice*, by Veronese. Cross over the Bridge of Sighs to see the prison.

Piazza San Marco

Once the seat of power, today San Marco is the cultural and social centre of Venetian life. The basilica of San Marco commands the east end of the square, while the other three sides are formed by three exquisite colonnaded Renaissance buildings, built at different times. On the north is the **Procuratie Vecchie**, anchored at the east end by the Torre dell'Orologio (clock tower). The south wall is the colonnaded **Procuratei Nuove**, home to **Caffé Florian**, favoured by Byron, Dickens, Proust and countless others. **Ala Napoleonica**, built in the same style during the Napoleonic occupation, forms the end wall. The campanile punctuates the square.

Above
Basilica of San Marco and
Piazza San Marco

**San Giorgio
Maggiore**
*Open Apr–Sept Mon–Sat
0900–1230, 1430–1830,
Sun 0930–1030,
1430–1630; Oct–Mar
Mon–Sat 1000–1230,
1430–1700, Sun
0930–1030, 1430–1630.*
Campanile € *same
hours.*

La Piazzetta

Joining Piazza San Marco at the campanile, this was the great formal
entrance from the sea, at the beginning of the Grand Canal. It is
marked by two columns, San Marco and San Teodoro. The focal point
is the quintessentially Venetian façade of Palazzo Ducale, the Doges'
Palace, beside the basilica of San Marco.

San Giorgio Maggiore

A masterpiece of Andrea Palladio, San Giorgio sits across the lagoon
from the Piazzetta, pure Renaissance with a façade of superimposed
classical temples. Inside, Corinthian columns support arches, which in
turn support the gallery. Two of Tintoretto's late paintings, *The Last
Supper* and *The Gathering of Manna*, are on the chancel side walls. His
last, *The Deposition*, is in the Chapel of the Dead. He and his son,
Domenico, painted the *Martyrdom of Saint Stephen* in the left transept.

Torre dell'Orologio

Calle Mercerei leaves Piazza San Marco, passing under this 15th-
century clock tower. The gilt-and-blue clock face shows phases of the
moon and the zodiac, surmounted by a statue of the Madonna.
Ascension Week brings figures of the magi from side doors to pay
homage. Atop the tower, a pair of Moors, *Due Mori*, strike the large bell
each hour.

Ca'Pesaro €
*Canal Grande, Santa
Croce. Open Apr–Oct
Tue–Sun 1000–1800;
Nov–Mar Tue–Sun
0900–1700. San Stae
vaporetto stop.*

**Santa Maria Gloriosa dei
Frari €** *Campo dei Frari.
Open Mon–Sat 0900–1800,
Sun 1300–1800. Vaporetto to
San Tomà.*

**Scuola Grande di San
Rocco €€** *Campo San
Rocco; tel: 041 523 4864;
www.scuolagrandesanrocco.it.
Open daily 0930–1730
(except during special
exhibitions) (last entrance
30 mins before closing).*

SAN POLO AND SANTA CROCE

Located on the west side of the Grand Canal, which forms their boundary, except in the south where the boundaries are the Rio Nuovo and the Rio di Ca'Foscari.

Ca'Pesaro, Galleria d'Arte Moderna

The Pesaro family were prominent Venetians, and their 1710 palazzo was given to the community to exhibit works by unknown artists. It now displays works by Klimt, Klee, Bonnard, Matisse and Miró, along with works of lesser-known Italian painters of the last two centuries.

Ponte Rialto and Rialto markets

Since 1591 this graceful bridge has been one of only two ways of crossing the Grand Canal on foot. The single arch span has balustraded staircases of 42 steps rising along each side. In the centre are two rows of shops, now largely selling souvenirs. It's a fascinating place for watching water traffic on the canal as gondolas, *motoscafi*, rowing boats, vaporetti and work-a-day barges and delivery boats perform a water ballet vying for space. Watch housewives and chefs in the **Rialto markets** choose from the myriad fish and fresh produce from lagoon farms to learn what the evening's menu specials will be. Barges loaded with radicchio, artichokes, sole, squid and sardines begin to arrive at dawn. The colourful spectacle is all over and closed up by noon. Cross the Rialto Bridge from San Marco and take the first right along the Grand Canal.

Santa Maria Gloriosa dei Frari

When the Franciscans built this brown brick Gothic church in the mid-15th century, they made it big. The 97m nave was big enough to accommodate some of the finest art in the city. At the centre of the high altar is a magnificent *Assumption of the Virgin*, by Titian; his *Madonna di Ca'Pesaro* hangs by the side entrance. Pietro Lombardo's exquisitely carved **rood screen** hides an unusual set of relief-carved **choir stalls** of Venetian scenes and saints. Flanking the main altar are the tombs of two doges and in the first chapel to the right of the altar is a fine carved wooden St John the Baptist by Donatello. Tombs and monuments commemorate Titian, Canova, Monteverde and other greats. The former monastery has two cloisters, one by Sansovino, the other by Palladio.

Scuola Grande di San Rocco

The 16th-century *scuola* in tribute to San Rocco was a hedge against the return of the plague. Tintoretto was commissioned to decorate, and reached new heights in the treatment of light, colour and perspective. Ceilings and walls in three large chambers are covered with his work. In Venice, a *scuola* was a building housing charitable organisations for the city's poor or a meeting place for a minority population. Their ornate décor shows the attention that was lavished on them.

Right
Gondolas at San
Zaccaria, Riva degli
Schiavoni

THE ISLANDS

While most of the lagoons have been filled, leaving only canals to separate them, a few islands still exist and they make a delightful day excursion. Boats leave from San Zaccaria, but before setting out, verify the return schedule so you will not be stranded.

Museo del Merletti
€ *Pza Galuppi. Open Apr–Oct Wed–Mon 1000–1700; Nov–Mar Wed–Mon 1000–1400.*

Trattoria da Gatto Nero €–€€
Da Ruggero. Sits along the canal with views of bright coloured houses and the tilting Campanile di San Martin.

Burano and Mazzorbo

Smaller than Murano island, but far more colourful and interesting, Burano is famed for its lace. **Museo del Merletti**, in the former lacemaking school, has demonstrations and historic examples of the art and a school where lacemaking is taught. The small houses that line Burano's canals are painted in brilliant colours, as are its fishing boats. Somewhat startling is the dramatic tilt of the **Campanile di San Martin**, which seems ready to topple into the lagoon. Cross to the island of **Mazzorbo**, for a nice walk through a garden and along a *fondamenta*, where you can catch the ferry.

Lido

Lido was the favoured beach of the crowned heads of Europe; everyone who was anyone came to try the new sport of sea bathing on its 11km of beach. Although past its social prime, Lido still draws crowds to its casino, film festival and hotels. To explore its quiet roads and canal, hire a bicycle opposite the vaporetto quay.

Museo Vetrario €
Fondamenta Giustinian.
Open winter Thur–Tue
1000–1700.

Santa Maria Assunta €
Open same hours as museum.

Museo dell'Estuario €
Pza di Torcello; tel: 041 730 761. Open Apr–Sept Tue–Sun 1030–1230, 1400–1730; Oct–Mar Tue–Sun 1030–1230, 1400–1600.

Murano

Famed for glass-blowing, Murano is thronged by tourists. Beware of people touting free tours: they will lead you to places of inferior quality. Leave the main *fondamenta* to see the real Murano, and visit **Museo Vetrario (Glass Museum)** to see the glass-blowers' art in a 17th-century palazzo. When the shops close, the island shuts down.

Torcello

When the Veneti escaped into the lagoon in the 5th century they first set up shop at Torcello, but soon outgrew it. The highlight of the marshy island is their basilica, **Santa Maria Assunta**, parts of which date from 638. Its tall campanile stands out above the lagoon. The church has an exquisite 9th- to 12th-century floor and wall mosaics, including a Madonna on a gold ground and a frightening rendition of the Last Judgement. The small church nearby is **Santa Fosca** (11th-century). In the piazza is the **Museo dell'Estuario**, with an excellent collection of ancient artefacts from around the lagoon and, in a second building, mosaics and Byzantine and medieval art.

Accommodation and food

Nearly every campo of any size has at least one restaurant, and they cluster in droves along the Grand Canal near the Rialto and in the streets close to San Marco. But those in heavy tourist areas are not necessarily the best. Better to browse in the narrow streets away from the Grand Canal.

Above
Italian festive cakes and sweets

Trattoria alla Madonna €–€€ *Calle della Madonna 594; tel: 041 522 3824. Open Thur–Tue.* The big, unpretentious dining room is known for the high quality of its seafood; try risotto, fried baby whitefish or *anguilla frita* (eel).

Hotel Alex €€ *Friari, S Polo 2606; tel/fax: 041 523 1341; www.hotelalexinvenice.com.* A short walk from the S Toma vaporetto stop, this new hotel has attractive rooms at budget prices for Venice.

Hotel Caneva €€ *Castello 5515; tel: 041 522 8118; fax: 041 520 8676; www.hotelcaneva.com.* Hospitable, clean and inexpensive hotel perfectly located on the shortest route between the Rialto and San Marco.

Hotel Gallini €€ *Calle della Verona 3673, San Marco; tel: 041 520 4515; fax: 041 520 9103; www.hotelgallini.it.* Near La Fenice theatre, with a friendly staff.

Trattoria Casa Mia
€–€€ Calle de L'Oca. Open Wed–Mon. An inviting dining room with wainscot and stucco walls; Venetian specialities are marked on the menu and include *sarde in saor* (marinated sardines).

Osteria alla Botte €€ *Calle de la Bissa, (off Campo San Bartolomeo); tel: 041 520 0623. Open Thur–Tue.* Small and cosy, with dark panelling and friendly service. Good *cicchetti* (traditional snacks) include creamed salt cod with grilled white-corn polenta.

Bar alla Toletta € *Calle Toletta; tel: 041 520 0196.* Delicious panini near San Trovaso and the Accademia. Very popular with locals.

Osteria Alberto € *Calle Giacinto Gallina (near Santa Maria dei Miracoli); tel: 041 523 8153.* Menu includes aubergine *parmegian*, gnocchi with four cheeses and *fegato Venetiana* (veal liver). It's popular, so expect a wait.

Signor Blum *Campo San Barnaba, Dorsoduro; tel: 041 522 6367; www.signorblum.com.* Captivating, intricate wooden puzzles in natural finishes and bright colours.

Tragicomica *Calle dei Nomboli 2800, San Polo; tel: 041 721 102; www.tragicomica.it.* Maker of outstanding masks and costumes.

Osteria Vivaldi €€ *Calle de la Madoneta, S Polo; tel: 041 523 8185.* The menu changes daily and always includes local seafood dishes. Cash only.

Fiaschetteria Toscana €€–€€€ *Salizzada San Giovanni Crisostomo 5719; tel: 041 528 5281.* Near the Marco Polo house, this restaurant serves regional specialities. Look for scallops with almonds or more traditional *frito misto*.

Pensione Accademia-Villa Maravege €€–€€€ *Fondamenta Bollani 1058, Dorsoduro; tel: 041 521 0188; fax: 041 523 9152; www. pensioneaccademia.it.* San Trovaso and the Accademia are just a few steps away from this fine small hotel facing the Grand Canal over gardens.

Hotel Ca'Maria Adele €€€ *Dorsoduro 111; tel: 041 520 3078; www.camariaadele.it.* A charming palazzo beautifully adapted to an inn, with free Internet in the lobby, lavish breakfasts and a convenient location in a quiet neighbourhood, a few steps from the Vaporetto No 1 landing at Salute.

Shopping

Among the warren of streets are excellent shops and craftsmen's studios. Streets called *Ruga* are good places to look, since the word indicates that the street is lined with shops.

La Bottega dei Mascareri *San Polo 80 (near the Ponte Rialto); tel: 041 522 3857, and Calle Saoneri; tel: 041 524 2887.* A fine mask shop with two locations.

Franco Furlanetto *Calle dei Nomboli (corner of Rio Terra Nomboli); tel: 041 520 9544; email: ffranco01@libero.it.* Woodcarver makes *forcola*, the oar supports for gondolas, and gondola details. A fascinating place to visit.

Karisima *Rio Terra de Nomboli 2752 (corner of Calle dei Saoneri).* Speciality papers including botanicals, blank books and leather-bound books, at excellent prices.

Il Pavone *Campiello dei Meoni, Calle de Mezzo 1478 (between the Rialto and Campo San Polo); tel: 041 522 4296.* Some of the finest paper goods in the city.

Punto Arte *Calle dei Saonere 2721, S Polo; tel: 041 522 7979; www.etchingvenice.com.* Hand-printed etchings in the traditional technique capture Venice's unique light refractions with aquatint.

Walking tour – San Marco and Castello

Time: About 3 hours.

Route: Start at **PIAZZA SAN MARCO** ❶ in front of **PALAZZO DUCALE** ❷ and head towards the water, turning left on to **RIVA DEGLI SCHIAVONI** ❸, created 600 years ago. Cross a bridge over the Rio del Palazzo, looking left to see the **BRIDGE OF SIGHS** ❹. Just before the next bridge is the former **Palazzo Dandolo, now Hotel Danieli**. Cross the bridge and directly ahead is the monumental statue of **Vittorio Emanuele II**, the first king of a united Italy. On the left, opposite the San Zaccaria vaporetto stop, a *sottopassagio* through a building leads to the campo and church of **SAN ZACCARIA** ❺.

Leave the **Campo San Zaccaria** at the top left corner, passing through the **Campo San Provolo** and along the **Fondamenta dell'Osmarino**, look for the pink **Palazzo Pruili** on the opposite side. Turn left, crossing **Rio San Provolo** at **Rio dei Greci**. While crossing it, look to the right, at the precariously leaning campanile of **San Giorgio dei Greci**. Follow **Fondamenta di San Lorenzo** along the canal to **Calle dei Leoni**, going right across the canal and continuing across **Rio della Pietà** to the **SCUOLA DI SAN GIORGIO DEGLI SCHIAVONI** ❻. Backtrack across Rio dei Greci on Calle dei Leoni and turn right on to **Fondamenta di San Lorenzo** along the canal to the second left, **Calle Larga San Lorenzo**. Follow it, turning right at the **Palazzo Cavagnis** and following **Calle Ospedale** as it twists to the left and right crossing three canals on the way. At the **Salizzada SS Giovanni e Paolo**, go left and the extraordinary mounted statue of **Colleoni** is ahead when you reach **Campo Santi Giovanni e Paolo**. In this square you will find the **Scuola di San Marco** ❼ and **SANTI GIOVANNI E PAOLO** ❽.

Leave by the northwest corner of the campo and cross **Rio dei Mendicanti** on **Calle Larga G Gallina**, which leads into the beautiful **Campo Santa Maria Nova**, a good place for a café break. Across the bridge and **Rio dei Miracoli** is **SANTA MARIA DEI MIRACOLI** ❾. From its front door, take **Calle dei Miracoli** across **Rio dei Miracoli** to **Salizzada San Canzian**, turning left and following it to **Campo di San Giovanni Crisostomo**. Here follow **Salizzada San Giovanni Crisostomo** to the left to **Campo San Bartolomeo**, an active place at any hour. Follow **Salizzada Pio X** right to **PONTE RIALTO** ❿ for a good vantage point over the busy **Grand Canal**. At the foot of the bridge, follow the shore a few metres right on **Riva di Ferro** to **Via Mazzini**, following it to **Merceria San Salvatore**, **Merceria San Zulian** and **Merceria di Orologio**, shopping streets, all signposted, back to Piazza San Marco.

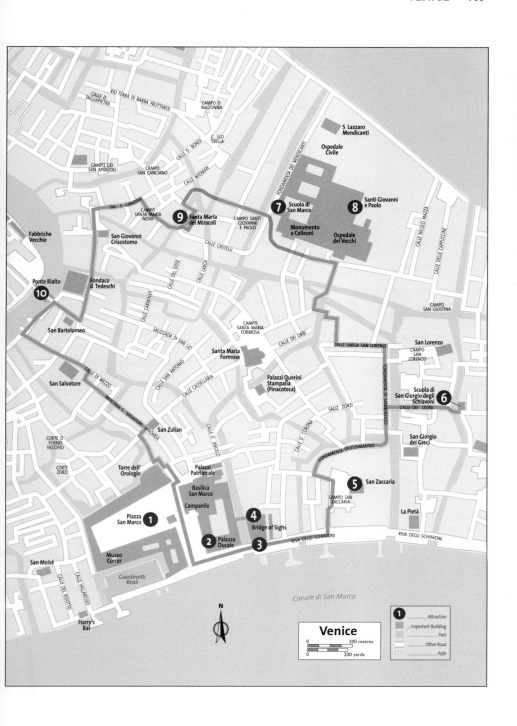

Venice

●	Attraction
	Important Building
	Park
	Other Road
	Path

0 — 200 metres
0 — 200 yards

N

Canale di San Marco

Eastern Alpine foothills

Ratings

Architecture	●●●●○
Food and drink	●●●●○
Mountains	●●●●○
Scenery	●●●●○
Vineyards	●●●●○
Art	●●●○○
Markets	●●○○○
Villages	●○○○○

At the height of the Venetian Republic, *La Serenissima*, as it was called, spread its influence over most of northeastern Italy. St Mark's Lion gazed benevolently over places far from the Adriatic lagoons, bringing art, culture and – for its time – an enlightened civil government. That influence is still so evident that many of the cities are known as 'little Venices' and today's visitor will recognise them first by their architecture. Graceful curved windows and balconies, often traced in delicate stonework, recall the palazzi that overlook the Grand Canal. Along with the physical signs, these small cities bear a cultured grace that makes them exceedingly pleasant places to be. They are rarely crowded, except by a festival celebrating a local harvest or the day of a patron saint. The rich farmlands of the Treviso province assure a varied seasonal cuisine.

BELLUNO

APT *Pza dei Martiri 8; tel: 0437 940 083; www.dolomiti.it/apt. Open Mon–Sat 1000–1230, 1430–1730.*

P Arriving from the south, cross the river and enter a tunnel under the city, which you can see directly above. Immediately out of the tunnel is the entrance to a car park, **Parcheggio Lambioi €**, and to the steep stairlift that takes you to the old town. Take a token from the machine

Belluno's setting, high above the confluence of the Piave and the Ardo, surrounded by mountains, is reason enough for a visit. The steep stairlift from the car park deposits you in front of Belluno's most elegant building, the Venetian **Palazzo Rettori**. Now governmental offices, this palazzo was built between 1491 and 1536, with a nine-arch colonnade and clock tower. Next to it is the 12th-century **Torre Civica**, the battlemented remnant of a medieval castle. Opposite is the **duomo**, designed by Lombardo, with a tall campanile, which you can ascend for splendid mountain views. Construction began on the cathedral in 1517 in a combination of both the Renaissance and Baroque styles. The unfinished bronze doors honour Bellunese Albino Luciani, who became Pope John Paul I.

Facing the duomo is the **baptistery**, with a magnificent carved font cover. Also facing the duomo is the **Museo Civico**, which has archaeological artefacts and paintings by the master Montagna. Just

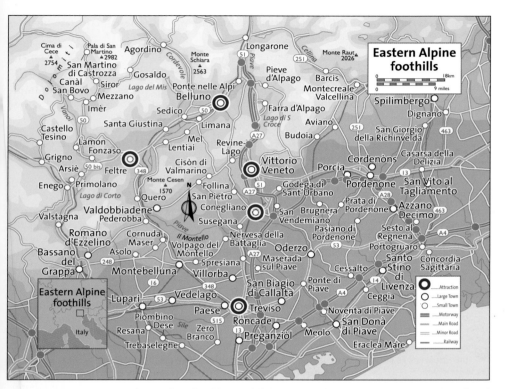

Eastern Alpine foothills

on entering the car park and take it with you to the lift. As you leave the lift on your way back, put the token into the machine at the door and it literally tells you what to pay (in English). If you drive into the upper town, parking is on Piazza di Martiri.

Duomo *Pza del Duomo. Open daily 0700–1230, 1500–1900.* **Baptistery** *open daily 0800–1230, 1500–1900. Free.*

Museo Civico € *Pza del Duomo; tel: 0437 944 836. Open May–Sept Tue–Sun 1000–1300, 1600–1900; Oct–Apr Mon–Sat 0900–1300, Thur–Sun 1500–1800.*

beyond is the **Piazza del Mercato** (also called the Piazza Erbe), faced by the **Loggia dei Ghibellini**, dating from the 15th and 16th centuries. A barely discernible Lion of St Mark is on the wall, put there when the Venetians were in control and defaced in 1797. In the centre is an early 15th-century fountain. Along Via Rialto is **Porta Dojona**, a gate whose southern side was built in 1289 and north side in 1533. Attractive **Piazza dei Martiri** with its cafés and public gardens is north of the duomo. The streets in old Belluno are well worth wandering as they wind between and under Renaissance buildings. The church of **San Pietro** has altars carved by Brustolon, who did the font cover in the baptistery, and a side chapel with a fresco cycle by Ricci. The church of **Santo Stefano** also has some of Brustolon's carving, and sits in a pleasant shaded garden not far from Piazza dei Martiri.

Accommodation and food in Belluno

Enoteca Mazzini € *Off Pza Mazzini; tel: 0437 948 313.* A good place to sample local wines in a very traditional atmosphere.

Hotel Alle Dolomiti € *V. Carrera 46; tel: 0437 941 660; fax: 0437 941 436.* Well located between the Piazza dei Martiri and San Stefano.

San Pietro *Pza San Pietro (east of V. Mezzaterra); tel: 0437 941 853. Open for festivities and weddings only. Call for visits. Free.*

Santo Stefano *V. Roma at Pza San Stefano. Open Mon–Sat 0900–1230, 1600–1900. Free.*

Market day: *Sat.*

Comfortable, attractive and bright, with a restaurant; rate includes breakfast.

Ristorante Taverna € *V. Cipro 7; tel: 0437 25 192.* A good menu and pleasant patio for alfresco dining, plus bar.

Trattoria Moretto € *V. P Valeriano 8; tel: 0437 943 476.* Simple surroundings and simply delicious food. Pasta with smoked cheese filling may be on the menu, which changes daily.

Hotel Astor €–€€ *Pza dei Martiri 26E; tel: 0437 942 094; fax: 0437 942 493; www.astorhotelbelluno.com.* Nicely located in a modern building on the historic piazza.

CONEGLIANO

APCT *V. XX Settembre 61; tel: 0438 21 230; fax: 0438 428 777; www.conegliano2000.it. Open Mon & Wed 0900–1230, Tue & Thur–Fri 0900–1230, 1500–1800, Sat–Sun 0930–1230, 1500–1800.*

Parking *is plentiful at the castle, less so in the lower town.*

Museo Castelvecchio € *Pzle Castelvecchio; tel: 0438 22 871. Open May–Jun & Sept daily 1000–1230, 1530–1900; Jul–Aug Wed–Sat 2130–2300; Oct–Apr Wed–Sat 1000–1230, 1500–1830.*

Scuola di Santa Maria dei Battuti € *V. XX Settembre. Open Sun & hols 1500–1830, or enquire at the duomo.*

Galleria Civica dell'Arte *€ V. XX Settembre; tel: 0438 413 312. Open Mon 1330–1530, Thur 1430–1800, Fri 0800–1100.*

Conegliano rolls down a hillside in three terraces, crowned at the summit by **Castelvecchio**, a walled enclosure with a square tower, shown in some of the paintings of Cima da Conegliano. Inside the tower, **Museo Castelvecchio** contains frescoes and 16th-century paintings, among other works of art. This castle's walls are a good place to get an up-close look at the unique 'fishtail' crenellations that are the hallmark of castles built by the Scaligeri family of Verona. Here they frame views of the town and the beautiful rolling countryside of vineyards, where Prosecco, one of Italy's finest sparkling white wines, is produced. Views from the castle's terrace extend over a vineyard-filled valley to the Dolomites, best savoured from a table at **Bar Ristorante Al Castello**, designated as the first stop on the 'Strada del Vino Bianco', the 'White Wine Road' (maps at tourist offices en route).

The castle is connected to the town below via a cobbled walkway, Calle Madonna della Neve, bordered by the arcaded wall of the former San Francesco monastery. It passes the appealing little **Oratorio Madonna della Neve**. Conegliano's middle terrace is its heart, the curving and arcaded Via XX Settembre. Here are the best of the town's palazzi, many from the 15th century. Some are decorated in frescoes, some have distinctive windows in the Venetian style. Opening on to this street under a deep loggia is the **duomo**, which is highlighted by the only major work to remain in the city by its most noted artist, Cima da Conegliano. This **altarpiece**, of the Virgin and Child, was created by commission of the brotherhood of flagellants, the *Battuti*, whose headquarters is next door. Reached from a passageway beside the cathedral, the **Scuola di Santa Maria dei Battuti** is at the top of a flight of stone stairs. It is lined with a most unusual cycle of 15th- and 16th-century frescoes, in which the Dolomites are recognisable. Listen for the *duomo* bell, which clearly rings out 'Figaro, Figaro, Figaro'.

On the opposite side of Via XX Settembre is the **Galleria Civica dell'Arte**, where you should at least step into the courtyard to see the unusual wooden statue of the Madonna, with a door enclosing the

Casa di Cima €
*V. Cima; tel: 0438 21
660 or 0438 413 254.
Open Sat–Sun 1500–1900.*

Market day: Fri.

infant Christ. Although it has no originals, Cima's birthplace, **Casa di Cima**, has reproductions of many of his works, in which it's easy to recognise the landscapes of his hometown region. At its centre, Via XX Settembre opens out into a terraced plaza, in front of the **Accademia**, a neoclassical theatre guarded by two buxom and oft-photographed sphinxes. Below is a wide passageway leading down to the town's business area, much of which lies along Corso G Mazzini, bordered by a swathe of greenery with cafés overlooking it.

Right
Accademia, Conegliano

Accommodation and food in Conegliano

Caffè Centrale € *Piazzetta XVIII Luglio 8; tel: 0438 22 488.* Good for sandwiches, light meals and people-watching from a terrace above Corso G Mazzini.

Cristallo € *Corso G Mazzini 45; tel: 0438 35 445; fax: 0438 24 434; www.hotelcristallo.tv.it.* A full-service hotel with restaurant and bar, and with parking for guests.

Canon d'Oro €–€€ *V. XX Settembre 129; tel: 0438 34 246; fax: 0438 34 249; email: canondoro@sevenonline.it; www.hotelcanondoro.it.* The rooms in this historic frescoed building are very nicely furnished. Enclosed parking and a secluded garden terrace.

Osteria/Trattoria Città di Venezia €–€€ *V. XX Settembre 77/79; tel: 0438 23 186. Closed Sun night, Mon & late Aug.* Although the speciality is seafood, they usually have four options, including pasta and meat dishes, all well prepared.

Restaurante Canon d'Oro €–€€ *V. XX Settembre 129; tel: 0438 415 166. Open Jun–Aug Mon–Sat; Sept–May Sat–Thur.* By the hotel, separately owned, is excellent, serving starters such as risotto with shellfish and mixed grilled fish *en brochette*, along with several good veal dishes.

Trattoria Stella €–€€ *V. Accademia 3; tel: 0438 22 178. Closed Wed lunch & Sun.* No menu, but genial host will describe the day's specials, which might be veal, or crêpes with asparagus.

Tre Panoce €€ *V. Vecchia Trevigiana 50; tel: 0438 60 071; www. trepanocekiri.com. Closed Sun evening & Mon.* Wooden ceiling beams and warm lighting create an inviting atmosphere. A speciality is duck with Prosecco.

FELTRE

ⓘ ARPT *Pza Trento e Trieste 9; tel: 0439 2540. Open summer daily 0900–1230, 1530–1830; winter daily 0900–1230 only.*

🏛 Museo Civico € *V. Lorezzo Luzzo; tel: 0439 885 241. Open Tue–Fri 1030–1230, 1600–1900, Sat–Sun 0930–1230, 1600–1900.*

Galleria Rizzarda € *V. del Paradiso 8; tel: 0439 885 242. Open Tue–Sun 1030–1230, 1500–1800.*

⬤ Market days: Tue, Fri morning.

The steeply roofed 16th-century houses that line the streets of Feltre reflect the shapes of the mountains that rise behind it. The homogeneous architecture results from Feltre's rebuilding by Venice after it was sacked by enemies of the empire. This, of course, accounts for the Lion of St Mark, prominent on a column in the central square. Only a part of the medieval castle is left of the earlier city, also found on **Piazza Maggiore**, along with a Lombardo **fountain**. A row of Renaissance palazzi lines one side of the square. The **Museo Civico** tells the town's tumultuous history since the Romans and Etruscans, in addition to paintings by arch-rivals Bellini and Cima da Conegliano and local artist Lorenzo Luzzo. More palaces lie along the main street, **Via Mezzaterra**, many with frescoed walls by Luzzo. In the lower part of the town, reached by arcaded steps, is the **duomo**, which has an outstanding **Byzantine cross** carved in the 6th century, showing 52 New Testament scenes. **Galleria Rizzarda** exhibits modern art and wrought-ironwork by the local master Carlo Rizzarda.

Accommodation and food in Feltre

Hotel Nuovo de Cesaro € *V. Fornere Pazze 5; tel: 0439 81 345; fax: 0439 89 241; www.hotelnuovo.it.* Located near the historic centre, this full-service hotel is comfortable and has a bar; parking is available for guests.

Osteria Novecento € *V. Mezzaterra 24; tel: 0439 83 043. Open Tue–Sun.* Sample local wines with well-prepared seafood.

TREVISO

ⓘ APT *Palazzo Scotti, V. San Andrea 3; tel: 0422 547 632; fax: 0422 656 236; www. provincia.treviso.it. Open Tue–Thur 0930–1230, Fri–Sat 0930–1230, 1500–1800.*

Below
Houses along one of Treviso's canals

Descriptions of Treviso that bill it as a mini-Venice don't do it justice. While it does have a river and two canals running through its centre, it looks and feels very little like Venice. It is quite pretty in its own right, with flower-draped balconies and graceful willows overhanging the water and wide, tree-lined streets. In addition to the trees, it differs from Venice in that it is a completely walled town, entered over a moat and through monumental gates. It's clear who built the protective walls, however: lions look down from the gates. Small enough to explore easily on foot, Treviso is level, compact and a pleasure to walk in.

The Lion of St Mark

Wherever you go in the Veneto, you are likely to find the symbol of *La Serenissima*, Venice's name for its republic. The lion, often standing atop a column, but also found in bas-relief on a prominent wall overlooking a square, holds a book in one paw. If the book is open, Venice is at peace. When the book is closed, Venice is at war. Many of these lions are gone, victims of war, neglect or development, but a careful search will turn them up, even in such unexpected places as carved on a pulpit.

🅿 Parking is in Piazza Duomo €, Piazza Matteotti €, just inside the north town wall € and along most of the broad streets with entrance gates.

🅗 **Duomo** *Pza del Duomo. Open daily 0900–1200, 1500–1800. Free.*

San Nicolò *V. San Nicolò. Open daily 0900–1200, 1500–1800. Free.*

⬤ A Sunday antiques market is set up along Via Liberale.

Market days: Tue, Sat morning.

The **duomo** has been rebuilt several times since its beginnings in the 1100s. In the chapel to the right of the high altar is a Titian painting, and the church also has an excellent Pordenone fresco and a Lombardo tomb. At the church of **San Nicolò** and chapter house of the adjacent Dominican monastery, are paintings by Thomas of Modena as well as a number of frescoes, decorated columns and monumental tombs. The chapter-house wall friezes and frescoes are particularly notable, as is the Byzantine crucifix. Modena frescoes decorate several other Treviso churches.

Treviso is the home of an Italian family business success story: **Benetton.** To see what's new in the Kingdom of United Colours, visit their store, prominently located next to the fine old **Palazzo dei Trecento,** built in the 13th century. It was severely damaged in World War II bombings, and you can see the line of rebuilding. Behind the palazzo is the colourful arcaded **Pescheria,** a daily food market on an island in the canal. Behind that is the rebuilt 13th-century church of **San Francesco,** with more Modena frescoes in a chapel adjacent to the chancel.

Accommodation and food in Treviso

Albergo Il Focolare € *Pza G Ancilotto 8; tel: 0422 56 601; fax: 0422 540 871; www.albergoilfocolare.net.* A good, comfortable hotel in the town centre, behind the Palazzo dei Trecento, but without guest parking.

Il Cascinale € *Strada Torre d'Orlando 6B, Sant'Angelo; tel/fax: 0422 402 203; www.agriturismoilcascinale.it. Restaurant open Fri–Sun and by advance booking.* A bright new *agriturismo* lodging and restaurant, 3km south from the centre of Treviso. The gnocchi with local red endive, fresh asparagus or other seasonal vegetable is delectable.

Hotel Al Giardino € *Strada di Sant Antonino 300A, 31100; tel: 0422 406 406; fax: 0422 406 406; www.hotelgiardino.it.* Out of town a bit, but

Above
Clock tower with Lion of St Mark, Treviso

with easy access and plentiful parking. Inexpensive comfortable rooms, a restaurant and bar.

Antica Osteria al Cavallino €–€€ *Borgo Cavour 52 at town gate, Porta Quaranta; tel: 0422 412 801. Open Wed–Mon.* The fish is delectable, the owners good-natured and the atmosphere cosy. Sunday afternoon favourite of local families, who fill the vine-draped terrace with laughter.

Al Fogher €€ *Vle della Repubblica 10; tel: 0422 432 950; fax: 0422 430 391; www.hotelalfogher.it.* A full-service hotel with restaurant, serving local specialities. Parking available for guests, and accessible for guests with disabilities. Outside the town walls to the west.

Osteria alla Pasina €€ *V. Marie 3; tel: 0422 382 112; www.pasina.it. Closed Sun evening & Mon.* In season, try the courgette blossoms filled with fresh fish.

VITTORIO VENETO

ℹ ARPT *V. della Vittoria 110; tel: 0438 57 243; www.comune.vittorio-veneto.tv.it. Open Tue–Thur 0930–1230, Fri–Sat 0930–1230, 1500–1800.*

Ⓟ Parking is difficult in old Serravalle, and nearly impossible on Mon; park well south of town and walk to the old centre.

Ⓜ Market day: Mon.

Museo della Battaglia € *Pza Giovanni Paolo I, Ceneda; tel: 0438 57 695. Open May–Sept Tue–Sun 0930–1230, 1600–1900; Oct–Apr 0930–1230, 1400–1700.*

Museo del Cenedese € *Pza Marcantonio Flaminio I; tel: 0438 57 103; www.museocenedese.it. Open May–Sept Tue–Sun 0930–1230, 1600–1900; Oct–Apr 0930–1230, 1400–1700.*

Ⓓ Duomo *Off Pza Marcantonio Flaminio. Open Mon–Sat 0900–1300, 1500–1900. Free.*

Really two towns, **Serravalle** and **Ceneda** could not be more different, despite their close proximity. Apart from the **Museo della Battaglia**, of particular interest to those questing World War I history, there is little in the southern Ceneda worth stopping for. Serravalle, however, is a delight to explore, with slightly lopsided stone buildings, venerable wooden doors beneath low arched arcades, and frescoes decorating its walls. At the northern end, just before the town ends abruptly at a sheer rock face, is one of the Veneto's loveliest squares, **Piazza Marcantonio Flaminio**. At one end is the **Museo del Cenedese**, worth a visit, but more notable for its elaborately decorated exterior than for the mixture of archaeology, sculpture and frescoes inside. Other buildings around the square are adorned with frescoes and balconies and a Lion of St Mark surveys it all from his customary pillar. Occasional market stalls sell local sausages and cheeses from nearby farms. Just across the bridge from the piazza, the **duomo** has a Madonna by Titian. The **Oratorio di San Lorenzo dei Battuti** is decorated by a remarkably well-preserved cycle of mid-15th-century frescoes.

Accommodation and food in Vittorio Veneto

Hotel Flora € *V. Trento e Trieste; tel: 0438 53 625; fax: 0438 941 440; www.albergoristoranteflora.it.* Close to the railway station and in the centre of town, this is a comfortable and convenient venue from which to explore. Breakfast is included in the rate and the hotel has a restaurant, bar and garage.

Trattoria alla Cerva € *Pza Marcantonio Flaminio; tel: 0438 57 353. Open Tue–Sun.* In the centre of town on a square that looks like a stage set. Serves well-prepared local specialities.

 **Oratorio di San Lorenzo dei Battuti** *Open Tue–Sun 1400–1500. Tour begins at Museo del Cenedese.*

 **Casa Caldart €€** *V. Erizzo 165, Valdobbiadene; tel: 0423 980 333; www. ristorantecasacaldart.it.* Dine indoors or out on their terrace. Well-prepared local dishes.

 **Hotel Diana €–€€** *V. Roma 49, Valdobbiadene; tel: 0423 976 222; fax: 0423 972 237; www. hoteldiana.org.* Comfortable accommodation in town with a restaurant and bar, garage parking. Accessible for guests with disabilities. Breakfast *€.*

Al Ben Star €–€€ *V. Piandera, Nogarola, village just west of Vittorio Veneto; tel: 0438 583 659.* Two guest rooms on a lovely farm just west of town, with a restaurant open at weekends or with advance notice. Specialities are farm-fresh vegetables and grilled meats. Children are welcomed with a full playground.

Suggested tour

Total distance: 140km, with detours 179km.

Time: 3¹/₂ hours' driving. Allow 3 days for the main route, 3 days with detours. Those with limited time should concentrate on Treviso.

Links: From Venice (Venezia) (*see page 170*), the S13 leads north to Treviso. Connect to the Western Alpine foothills route (*see page 206*) through Asolo via the S248 from Montebelluna.

Route: Leave **TREVISO ❶** heading north on the S13, crossing the wide River Piave before arriving at **CONEGLIANO ❷**. Return to the S13 and continue north a short distance, turning north (left) on to the S51. Follow it to **VITTORIO VENETO ❸**. Note that the autostrada A27 bypasses the town of Vittorio Veneto (41km). Continue north

Left
Piazza Marcantonio Flaminio,
Vittorio Veneto

Right
Museo del Cenedese,
Vittorio Veneto

from Vittorio Veneto on the S51 through a scenic valley past the lake of Santa Croce to **Ponte nelle Alpi**, where you again cross the Piave, and immediately turn left on the S50 signposted for **BELLUNO** ❹ (39km). Leave Belluno heading west on the S50 to **FELTRE** ❺ (31km).

Da Nani *V. Maseral Fabri 14, Solighetto di Pieve di Soligo; tel: 0438 842 078. Open Mar–Dec Fri–Sun. A pleasant, rustic restaurant, where you can sample Prosecco with your sausage or grilled chicken.*

Backtrack from Feltre as far as **Busche**, turning south (right) on the S348, which parallels the Piave River. At **Fener** turn left to cross the Piave, following signs to San Vito and **Valdobbiadene**. (*See Detour below.*) From Valdobbiadene, backtrack through San Vito and across the Piave to the S348, turning south (left). Follow the S348 past **Montebelluna** and back to Treviso ❶ (60km).

Detour: From Valdobbiadene, the Strada del Vino Bianco, the White Wine Road, should be easy to follow, but is not. Signs lead in all directions, much to the traveller's confusion; but the detour is enjoyable, and if you get lost, simply follow signs or ask directions to

This region is the centre for *Cartizze*, a DOC (*denominazione di origine controllata*) of Prosecco, a sparkling white wine, which you can taste and buy at vineyards along the way from Valdobbiadene to Conegliano. The area has a number of *agriturismo* farm restaurants, open only at weekends, most of which specialise in grilled meats, sausages, and fresh vegetables and fruit from their farms – and, of course, the local white wines.

Right
Belluno

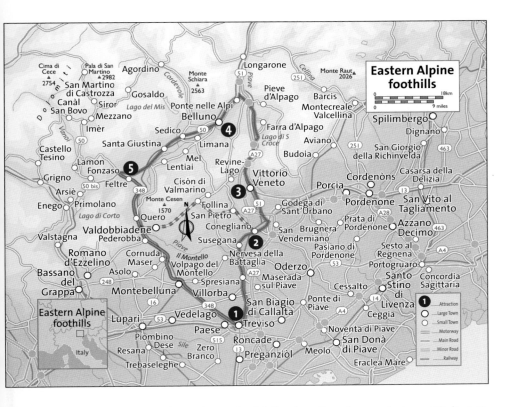

Conegliano. Instead of following the wine road signs, it's best to follow town signs east from Valdobbiadene to Miane and **Follina**. In Follina turn south (right) to Solighetto, then left to see the Romanesque frescoes in the parish church at **San Pietro di Foletto**. From San Pietro, follow signs south to Conegliano. You can return to Treviso by heading south on the S13 (39km).

Also worth exploring

The **Valzoldana** is the valley north of Belluno, formed by the Zolda River as it flows from the Dolomites into the valley of the Piave. Its principal resort centre is **Forno di Zoldo**. Villages are distinctly Tyrolean in appearance, with balconied chalets in wood and stone, roadside shrines and woodcarving shops. A benign foreground of green meadows dotted with wild flowers is set against a background of rock cliffs and jagged peaks.

Western Alpine foothills

Ratings

Architecture	●●●●●
Castles	●●●●○
Art and craft	●●●○○
Children	●●●○○
Historical sights	●●●○○
Scenery	●●●○○
Villages	●●●○○
Mountains	●●○○○

This short route packs some very interesting towns into a tight circle. The landscapes through the two walled southern towns – Castelfranco and Cittadella – are flat, while the northern loop is along the foothills of the Dolomites, which rise quite suddenly from the plain. Steep streets of Asolo and Marostica lead to castles, from which are splendid views over the towns and across the hilly landscapes. Behind lie the mountain towns, and nearly any road headed north will climb immediately into a jagged terrain of steep slopes dotted with secluded valleys. This route combines some of the most interesting and visual elements of northern Italy: castles, walled towns, Palladian villas and medieval pageantry. Signs of Venice's empire, which once spread its influence here, are legion: a Venetian balcony, a wall of the characteristic windows, or St Mark's Lion looking down from a pillar or façade.

ASOLO

ⓘ **APT** *Municipio, Pza Gabriele d'Annunzio 2; tel: 0423 55 045; www.asolo.it. Open Mon–Sat 0900–1230, 1500–1800.* A rare TIC where they let visitors browse racks of information rather than having to beg for each scrap.

The climb from the lower car park is a steep one, and seems steeper on a hot afternoon, but that doesn't discourage throngs of locals, for whom it is a favourite Sunday outing. One suspects that it was a bit less crowded and precious when Robert Browning fell in love with it. The main activity is strolling along the arcaded streets and admiring the frescoed walls and views of surrounding hillsides. That and stopping at the many *osterie* to sample Prosecco.

Two women feature prominently in Asolo's story, one a queen of Cyprus and the other a queen of the stage. Queen Caterina, a Venetian married to the king of Cyprus, was given Asolo in exchange for Venetian control of the island, and lived here until the Austrians claimed Asolo. Elenora Duse, an early 20th-century stage actress, sought quiet here between tours. A **Museo Civico**, in the elegant 15th-century **Loggia della Ragione**, has personal mementos of the actress,

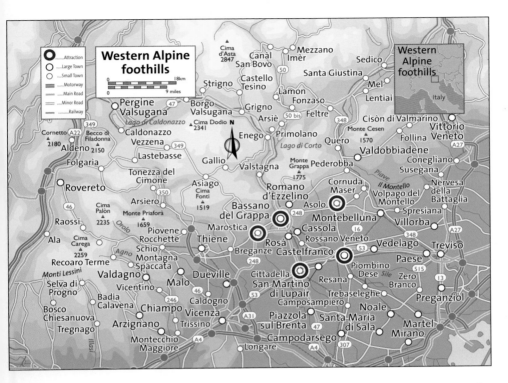

P Parking € is in two large car parks, well signposted as you enter town. Only those with overnight lodging may drive further.

Museo Civico € V. Regina Cornaro 74; tel: 0423 952 313. Open Sat–Sun 1000–1230, 1500–1900.

Villa Barbaro €€ V. Cornuda 7, Maser; tel: 0423 923 004; www.villadimaser.it. Open Mar & Jul–Aug Tue, Thur & Sat 1030–1800; Apr–Jun & Sept Tue–Sat 1000–1800; Dec–Feb Sat–Sun 1100–1700.

Museo Canova € Possagno; tel: 0423 544 323; www.museocanova.it. Open Tue–Sun 0930–1800.

the queen, and the poets and artists who made their homes here, plus paintings and sculpture. Follow signs to Bar Castello, to reach Queen Caterina's **Castello della Regina**, from whose walls are good views over the town, at their best bathed in afternoon light. At the top of the hill opposite is **Rocca di Asolo**, a solid fortress shaped like a ship. Stairways lead to its ramparts, for another set of views over the town (**€** Sat–Sun).

In nearby **Maser**, clearly signposted, is **Villa Barbaro**, perhaps the most perfect marriage of painting and architecture of any villa. Palladio worked with Veronese, and the result highlights the genius of each. The interior's 'architectural' details are actually *trompe l'œil* frescoes, adding a playful touch to the sense of light and air and spaciousness. To many, this is the pinnacle of perfection in the Veneto's villas. On the grounds are the **Tempietto**, Palladio's only church outside of Rome, and a carriage museum. An equal distance north of Asolo, in Passagno, is the birthplace of the neoclassical sculptor Canova, whose plaster casts, terracotta models, drawings and paintings are in the **Museo Canova** and whose remains rest in an outsized mausoleum.

Accommodation and food in Asolo

Pricey boutiques, antique shops and studios line the streets. In summer, buy fresh sweet cherries from the *agriturismo* farm below the gate.

Market day: Sat. On the second weekend of Sept–Jun the main square is filled with an antiques market (pricey).

Bar al Castello €–€€ *Castello della Regina. Open Tue–Sun 1000–0200.* A pleasant café inside the castle walls.

Melo in Fiore €–€€ *V. Caldretta 41, Maser (1km from Villa Barbaro); tel: 0423 565 205; www.meloinfiore.it. Guest rooms open all year, restaurant Fri–Sun or by advance booking.* A wine estate with comfortable rooms and a restaurant serving grilled meats, seasonal vegetables and fruit from the farm.

Due Mori €€ *Pza Gabriele d'Annunzio (next to the TIC); tel: 0423 952 256; www.ristoranteduemori.it. Open Thur–Tue 1800.* Begin with pasta and porcini before moving on to game birds with polenta. Tables on the terrace have nice views.

Albergo Al Sole €€–€€€ *V. Collegio 33; tel: 0423 951 332; fax: 0423 951 007; www.albergoalsole.com.* A Venetian red building set just above the main *piazza*, with fine castle views from its spreading porch.

Right
Antique shop, Asolo

The villas of the Veneto

In the 16th century, it was fashionable to quit the city of Venice in the summer and retire to a cooler country estate on the mainland. To house them there, wealthy Venetians built villas, sprawling palaces far larger than the cramped confines of Venice allowed. The favoured architect for these was, of course, Palladio, and of all those he conceived, no two are alike. His creativity seemed boundless, but always within the classical and Roman villa traditions. The architect often worked with one of the master painters of the day – Veronese, Tiepolo, Zelotti – who created frescoes to adorn the interiors.

BASSANO DEL GRAPPA

ⓘ APT *Largo Corona d'Italia 35; tel: 0424 524 351. Open daily 0900–1300, 1400–1800.* One of the most accommodating and helpful in all Italy.

ⓟ Parking € is just east of the old city, off Viale delle Parolini.

ⓜ Museo della Grappa
V. Gamba 6; tel: 0424 524 426. Open daily 0900–1930. Free.

Museo degli Alpini
Ponte degli Alpini; tel: 0424 503 662. Open Tue–Sun 0800–2000. Free.

Museo Civico €
Pza Garibaldi; tel: 0424 522 235. Open Tue–Sat 0900–1230, 1530–1830, Sun 1530–1830.

Museo della Ceramica, Palazzo Sturm €
V. Schiavonetti; tel: 0424 524 933; www. museobassano.it. Open Apr–Oct Tue–Sat 0900–1200, 1530–1830, Sun 1530–1830.

ⓐ Asparagus Festival *Late Apr, early May.*

Bassano del Grappa was not named after the drink, nor vice versa, although you can learn about its making at the Poli distillery in the **Museo della Grappa**. Steps away is Bassano's best-loved landmark, the covered bridge, **Ponte degli Alpini**, designed by Palladio. Destroyed in the World War II by Italian partisans (two of whom were executed by the Germans for doing so), it was faithfully reproduced by Alpini soldiers. The **Museo degli Alpini**, downstairs from the cheerful Taverna Al Ponte, at the bridge, has weapons, uniforms and photographs from both World Wars and material relating to the reconstruction of the bridge. The bridge is Bassano's favoured place for the evening passeggiata, especially in summer, when it catches the slightest breeze. The 13th-century **Torre Civica** overlooks Piazza Garibaldi, opposite the church of **San Francesco** (*Open daily 0800–1200, 1500–1900*), built in the 1200s and with a fine portico and 15th-century frescoes. On its exterior wall is a town map showing where bombs fell, a poignant memorial. The **Museo Civico**, set in the cloister and convent of a 14th-century Franciscan church, shows works by artist Jacobo Bassano and sculptor Canova, archaeology of Bassano's Roman era, and the evolution of the local ceramics. At **Palazzo Sturm** are more local decorated ceramics, housed in a rococo setting of frescoes and stucco work.

Accommodation and food in Bassano del Grappa

Hotel al Castello € *Pza Terraglio 19; tel/fax: 0424 228 665; www.hotelalcastello.it.* A bowl of glistening fresh fruit is offered at breakfast (included), a thoughtful touch at this friendly and well-located hotel.

Hotel Positano € *Vle Asiago 196; tel: 0424 502 060; fax: 0424 502 615; www.hotelpositanobassano.it.* Minutes from central Bassano, the Positano has spacious rooms, a restaurant with a terrace and is good value for money.

🍄 Look for dried porcini and other mushrooms, honey and jars of delicious condiments in **El Melario** at the foot of Ponte degli Alpini. Grappa (brandy) and pottery are found in several shops at the upper end of the bridge. Buy elegant picnic items, salads, pâtés and pastries at **Lino Santi** *V. Da Ponte 14.*

Market days: Thur, Sat.

Taverna Al Alpini € *Ponte degli Alpini.* The best view in town, from tables on its tiny balcony over the river.

Trattoria Alla Veneziana € *V. Menarola 22; tel: 0424 522 525. Closed Mon eve & Tue.* This is food you hope to find and seldom do: vegetables and fish grilled to perfection, gnocchi with courgettes and shrimps, tender pasta with salmon.

Trattoria El Piron €€ *V. Z Bricito 12; tel: 0424 525 306. Open Fri–Wed. Bigoli* (a locally popular fat spaghetti) is served with duck; tender gnocchi is prepared with porcini mushrooms.

CASTELFRANCO

ⓘ **ARPT** *V. Francesco M Preti 39; tel: 0423 491 416; www. comunecastelfranco.it. Open year-round Tue–Sat 0930–1230; also Feb–Mar, Aug & Nov–Dec Fri–Sat 1500–1800; Apr–Jul & Sept–Oct Fri–Sun 1500–1800.*

ⓟ Parking is between the wall and moat near the west gate, often on the east side as well.

🅗 **Casa di Giorgione €** *Pza Duomo; tel: 0423 725 022; fax: 0423 735 689; www. museogiorgione.it. Open Tue–Sun 0900–1200, 1500–1800.*

Duomo *Pza Duomo. Open daily 0900–1200, 1500–1800. Free.*

Villa Emo €€ *Fanzolo di Vedelago; tel: 0423 476 334; fax: 0423 487 043. Open Apr–Oct Mon–Fri 1500–1830, Sat–Sun & hols 1000–1230, 1500–1830; Nov–Mar Mon–Wed 1400–1600, Sat–Sun & hols 1400–1730.*

🍄 **Market days:** Thur, Fri morning.

Opposite
The duomo of Cittadella

Defensive walls rising intact above portions of a moat are Castelfranco's hallmark and most interesting feature, built in 1199 to defend against Paduans. **Casa di Giorgione** was the home of Titian's teacher, whose masterpiece *Madonna and Child* hangs in the **duomo**, opposite. Coins in the adjacent box will illuminate the painting. At **Villa Emo** in nearby **Fanzolo**, Palladio created a spacious, spreading design that perfectly incorporates the farm and residence. Mid-1500s-interior frescoes by Zelotti show scenes from mythology. A farm museum of implements and local crafts is on the grounds.

Accommodation and food in Castelfranco

Alla Torre € *Piazzetta Trento e Trieste 7; tel: 0423 498 707; fax: 0423 498 737; www.hotelallatorre.it.* At the eastern tower of the city's impressive walls, this is the most centrally located hotel.

Al Pozzo €–€€ *V. Cal di Monte 7, San Floriano di Castelfranco; tel: 0423 487 251. Open Fri & Sat evenings, Sun & hols.* A farm restaurant, 4km from Castelfranco centre. Dine on risotto with quail, mixed grill and other local specialities.

Ferraro €–€€ *V. Larghe 4, San Floriano di Castelfranco; tel: 0423 476 492. Open Fri & Sat evenings, Sun & hols, other days by advance booking.* A rural restaurant serving spit-roasted meats and seasonal dishes.

Ristorante Alle Mura €€–€€€ *V. F M Preti 69; tel: 0423 498 098; www.ristoranteallemura.com. Open Fri–Wed.* In the shadow of the walls at the west gate, this classy restaurant specialises in pricey fish, although you can order other dishes – from a menu in English.

CITTADELLA

ℹ Tourist Board Pro Cittadella Porte
Bassanesi 2;
tel: 049 940 4485;
www.comune.cittadella.pd.it.
Open Apr–Oct Mon &
Wed–Fri 0900–1300,
1400–1800, Sat–Sun
0900–1230, 1430–1900;
Nov–Mar Mon & Wed–Fri
0900–1300, 1400–1600,
Sat–Sun 0900–1230,
1430–1700.

⬤ Market day: Mon
morning.

Opposite
Castello Inferiore, Marostica

The 13th-century **walls** and **moat** at Cittadella were the Paduans' response to the similar fortifications built by Trevisans at Castelfranco. Its four gates and thirty-two towers provided a good view of approaching danger. Today they and the parapets provide lots of leg exercise, and good aerial views. Viewers will notice that the gates don't match the walls. In the 1800s, demolition of the walls was begun. Fortunately, preservationists won the day, and the gates were rebuilt, but in the Romantic style of the time. The tower of the **Padua Gate** has the bicycle-like symbol of the Carraresi family on it. The **duomo**, which faces a large piazza near the centre of the enclosed town, has several paintings by 19th-century Veneto artists.

Accommodation and food in Cittadella

Due Mori € Borgo Bassano 141; tel: 049 940 1422; www.hotelduemori.it. Restaurant closed Sun evening & Mon. Two dozen guest rooms and a good restaurant serving traditional local dishes.

Hotel Filanda €€ V. Palladio 34; tel: 049 940 0000; fax: 049 940 2111; www.hotelfilanda.it. Restaurant closed Sun evening & Mon. Reliable hotel, but best known for its excellent restaurant, **Alle Antiche Mura**, whose chef is an active promoter of the use of fresh, locally grown products. Look for white asparagus April–May, woodland mushrooms in autumn.

MAROSTICA

ℹ ARPT 94 Pza
Castello; tel: 0424 72
127; fax: 0424 72 800.
Open daily 1000–1200,
1500–1800. Helpful staff
and plentiful information.

Ⓟ Parking is usually
available around the
square at the Lower
Castle.

🏛 Castello Inferiore
€ Pza Castello; tel:
0424 472 127. Open daily
0930–1200, 1430–1800.

Museo della Ceramica
€ Nove; tel: 0424 829 807;
www.ceramics.it/museo.nove.
Open Tue–Sat 0900–1300,
Sun 1500–1900.

One of the finest remaining castellated towns, Marostica's **Castello Superiore** crowns a hilltop, with **Castello Inferiore** directly below it on the town's famous chessboard square. For fine views, walk the medieval walls connecting the two. Finding the road to drive up to Castello Superiore is trickier. Follow Via Mazzini to the left (as you face the Upper Castle), exiting through Porta Breganze. Turn right, ascending Via Can Grande della Scala and keeping to the right until you reach the gate in the castle walls. Inside the Lower Castle are the costumes worn by the 'chessmen' and other participants in the biennial re-enactment of a 1454 chess game. Surrounding the chessboard pavement is a fine ensemble of buildings: the castle, faced by its former armoury, now a covered market, and along one side a row of arcaded buildings. Near the eastern gate, along Via Mazzini, is a row of medieval arcade buildings with decorative brickwork. Nearby **Nove** is a ceramics centre, an industry and craft made possible by mills built in the 1700s on the Brenta River, which crushed rock quarried nearby into the fine powder needed for pottery. Today Nove is a major source of the colourful ceramic table and decorative ware found in

Nearby **Nove** is a ceramics centre, with workshops. Many do not have signs advertising their work. An employee will show you in.

Maer *V. Padre Roberto 26; tel: 0424 828 064.* Has especially good prices.

Market day: Tue.

Partita a Scacchi The famous human chess game is played on the town square; *tel: 0424 72 127; fax: 0424 72 800; www.marosticascacchi.it.* Sept 2nd weekend, even-numbered years.

shops all over northern Italy. You can tour the workshops to buy blems (factory seconds) and surplus stock. **Museo della Ceramica** shows examples of the art and craft over its three-century history.

Accommodation and food in Marostica

Trattoria Alla Fortuna € *V. Capitelli 28; tel: 0424 77 220. Open Tue–Sun.*

Hotel Europa €–€€ *V. Pizzamano 19; tel: 0424 77 842; fax: 0424 72 480; www.hoteleuropa.biz.* A full-service hotel with secure parking, a restaurant and convenient location just outside the walls, near the lower castle.

Ristorante Due Mori €–€€ *V. Mazzini 73; tel: 0424 471 777; www.duemori.it*

La Rosina €–€€ *V. Maretti, Valle San Floriano; tel: 0424 470 360; fax: 0424 470 290; www.larosina.it.* Twelve rooms and a fine restaurant, featuring fresh local ingredients and views of the hills between Marostica and Bassano.

Suggested tour

Sample the local sweet, *treccia d'oro*, at **Signorini**, a café near Castello Porto-Colleoni, Thiene.

Thiene market day: Mon morning.

Total distance: 116km, with detours 253km.

Time: 4 hours' driving. Allow 3 days for the main route, 5 days with detours. Those with limited time should concentrate on Bassano del Grappa and Asolo (with Villa Barbaro), and a quick stop in Marostica.

Links: From the Valpolicella and Pasubio Valley route (*see page 132*), connect via Schio to Thiene. Treviso, the starting point for the Eastern Alpine foothills route (*see page 194*), is almost directly west of Castelfranco via the S53.

Route: Leave Vicenza ❶ (*see page 213*), heading northeast on the S53 and following signs to **CITTADELLA** ❷. Several access roads lead from the S53 into Cittadella as it skirts the town. Continue on the S53, following signs to **CASTELFRANCO** ❸, which is just south of the S53 on the S667. Backtrack to the S53, crossing it and continuing to Valla (40km). (*See Detour 1 below.*) In Valla turn left following signs to Asolo and **Riese Pio X**, named after native son Giuseppe Sarto, elected Pope Pius X in 1903 and canonised in 1954. **Museo San Pio X** memorialises his birthplace (*open summer daily 0800–1200, 1500–1900; shorter winter hours. Free*). Continue through San Vito, turning right on the S248 and immediately left, signposted **ASOLO** ❹. Leaving Asolo, return towards the S248, turning left just short of its intersection and following signs to **Maser** and **Villa Barbaro**.

Malga Cason Vecio €–€€ V. Cenghia, Bassano del Grappa; tel: 0423 542 051. Open May & Oct Sun; Jun–Sept daily. The speciality of this mountain restaurant (apart from the panoramic view) is polenta served with the local hard sausage, *sopressa*, but the onion soup and apple tart are equally good.

Travel south from Maser, signposted Montebelluna, only until you reach the S248, turning west (right) and following signs into **BASSANO DEL GRAPPA** ❺ (42km). (*See Detour 2 below.*) Leave Bassano heading south on the S47, turning right on to the S248. Shortly after crossing the Brenta River follow signs left into **Nove**, the region's ceramic centre (some signs read 'Nove de Bassano'). Leave Nove heading west from its centre, following signs to **MAROSTICA** ❻ (you will cross the S248). Leave Marostica heading west on the unnumbered route signposted Mason Vicentino, continuing on through **Breganze** to **Thiene** ❼. (*See Detour 3 opposite.*) In the historic centre of Thiene is the 15th-century battlemented **Castello Porto Colleoni**, in the Venetian Gothic style, with good frescoes in the great hall and excellent 18th-century stables by Muttoni (€€ *Corso Garibaldi 21, guided tours Sun*). Return to Vicenza following the S349 south from Thiene to Motta, where you meet the S46 into the city (34km).

Detour 1: In Valla turn right, following signs to **Fanzolo**, to visit Villa Emo. Backtrack to Valla (8km).

Detour 2: Leave Bassano heading north on the S47, turning right on the outskirts of town and following signs for **Monte Grappa** via the S141. This winding and often steep mountain road ascends the

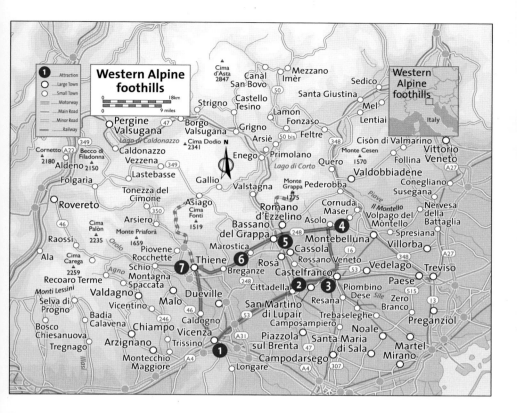

1,775m Monte Grappa, from which are panoramic views. Built in 1935, the huge circular memorial commemorates the 12,000 soldiers who died in battle here during World War I, both Italians and members of the Austro-Hungarian army. Via Eroica leads to a war museum. Return to Bassano via the S141 (62km).

Detour 3: From Thiene, travel north on the S349 signposted to **Asiago**. This hilly mountain road leads to the **Altopiano di Asiago**, a region at the centre of a World War I engagement, and the site of five British cemeteries. The hill towns are rich in local culture, with a full calendar of festivals. Many good walking trails through the Dolomite foothills begin here, as do cross-country and Alpine ski trails and lifts. Backtrack to Thiene (67km).

Also worth exploring

Northwest of Asiago, bordering the **Val Sugana**, the S349 winds scenically (and often precipitously) through the foothills and over Passo di Vezzena.

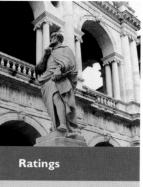

Vicenza and the Euganean Hills

Ratings

Architecture	●●●●●
Villas	●●●●●
Art	●●●●○
Gardens	●●●●○
Historical sights	●●●○○
Scenery	●●●○○
Villages	●●●○○
Vineyards	●●●○○

The gracious, lively and architecturally superb city of Vicenza is, unaccountably, not on most travellers' 'must-see' list of Italy. That's a shame, because the city and the hillsides above it have so much to offer. Much of its appeal derives from the work of native son Andrea Palladio, who gave his name to the style of architecture that has inspired buildings all over the world. Southeast of the city lie the Euganean Hills, a scenic cluster of near-perfect cones formed by long-extinct volcanoes. Remains of this thermal activity make this one of the largest hydro-geological basins in Italy. Thermal springs here have been used for bathing and therapy since the Romans languished in the warmth of their waters. Vineyards and farms are also common along the surprisingly steep roads that meander through these hills.

ABANO TERME AND MONTEGROTTO TERME

ⓘ IAT V. P d'Abano 18, Abano Terme; tel: 049 866 9055. Open Mon–Sat 0830–1300, Sun 0900–1200, 1500–1800. Brochures are mostly in French and German.

ⓘ Scavi Romani V. Scavi; tel: 049 979 3700. Tours at 0900, 1000, 1100 & occasionally Sat afternoon.

The name of **Abano** – the largest and best-known spa centre – is thought to derive from the Greek, meaning 'Removal of Pain'. Mineral-laden, 87°C waters are slightly radioactive and muds from the thermal lakes have been used for a wide variety of complaints. For those not booked into a treatment programme, a glance at the pricey spa hotels is the only reason to stop. In **Montegrotto Terme** are **Scavi Romani**, extensive ruins of Roman baths and theatre. A live butterfly collection is shown at **Casa delle Farfalle**. Just west of Abano is the 15th-century Benedictine monastery **Abbazia di Praglia**, whose brothers offer tours of the Renaissance church and its cloisters. The monastery grows herbs for market and is a botanic garden. East, in Due Carrare, **Castello di San Pelagio** is a surprising venue for a museum of air and space. The connection between this villa and flight is not so tenuous as one might imagine – it was from here that the

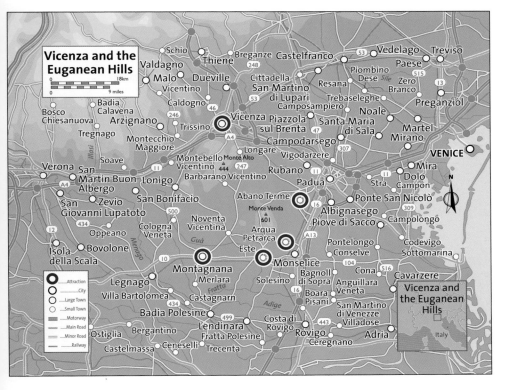

Vicenza and the Euganean Hills

Casa delle Farfalle

€€ *V. delle Scavi 21, Montegrotto; tel: 049 891 0189. Open Mar & Sept daily 0900–1230, 1430–1630; Apr–Aug daily 0900–1230, 1430–1730.*

Abbazia di Praglia

Bresseo de Teolo *6km west of Abano; tel: 049 999 9300. Open Apr–Sept Tue–Sun 1530–1730; Nov–Mar daily 1430–1630; tours every 30 mins. Free.*

Castello di San Pelagio

€€ *Due Carrare; tel: 049 912 5008; www. museodellaria.it. Open summer Tue–Sun 0900–1230, 1430–1900; winter Tue–Sun 0900–1230, 1400–1800.*

poet Gabriele d'Annunzio and his World War I squadron began their 1918 flight over Vienna.

Accommodation and food in Abano Terme and Montegrotto Terme

Throughout the hills are *agriturismo* restaurants, some open weekends only. Nearly every village has its trattoria serving local wine.

Terme Mamma Margherita € *V. Monteortone 63 (Teolo village of Monteortone); tel: 049 866 9350; fax: 049 667 286; www.termesalesiani.it.* With its own thermal baths, this amiable hotel and restaurant is a pleasant distance from Abano.

Caffè Bar Lucia € *V. Stazione 97, Montegrotto; tel: 0380 351 8060.* Good sandwiches and a wide street-side terrace.

Above
Chessboard, Abano Terme

ARQUA PETRARCA AND EUGANEAN HILLS

P Parking in Arqua
Petrarca is uphill
from the main square.

Casa di Petrarca €
V. Valleselle 4; tel: 0429
718 294. Open Mar–Oct
Tue–Sun 0900–1230,
1500–1900; Nov–Feb
0900–1230, 1430–1730.

**Villa Barbarigo
Valsanzibio €** Valsanzibio;
tel: 049 805 9224. Open
Mar–Nov daily 0900–1200,
1330–sunset.

**Museo Naturalistico di
Villa Beatrice €**
V. Monte Gemola, Baone;
tel: 0429 647 157;

The centre of this hill town looks much as it did in the Middle Ages, when the poet Petrarch spent his last years at **Casa di Petrarca**, amid the landscapes he had described in his poetry. The frescoed, bucolic scenes from his works date from the 1500s. Note especially the fine painted and panelled ceilings. From the balcony you can look down at the well-kept gardens. The church of the **Assumption** has frescoes from as early as the 11th century. Wealthy Paduans and Venetians chose these hills for their summer villas, one of which, **Villa Barbarigo**, is surrounded by some of the finest Baroque gardens in Italy. The 17th-century **Valsanzibio**, as the beautifully kept gardens are now called, are filled with statuary, trick fountains, a labyrinth and a monumental Baroque gate, the Arch of Diana. At the crest of Monte Gemola, west of Arqua, is the **old convent** of Beatrice d'Este, in a lovely setting with views of surrounding **Euganean Hills**. **Villa Beatrice** contains a natural history museum showing the botany and zoology of this microclimate ecosystem. The adjacent nature reserve protects a population of rare hedgehogs. In Cinto Euganeo, the old

mob: 348 874 6424.
Open Mon–Fri 0900–1300.

**Museo Geo-
Paleontologico Cava
Bomba €** *V. Bomba, Cinto
Euganeo; tel: 0429 647 166.
Open Apr–Oct Sat
1500–1900, Sun
1000–1300, 1400–1900;
Nov–Mar Sat 1400–1800,
Sun 0900–1300,
1400–1900. Group bookings
Tue–Fri 0900–1300,
1400–1900.*

🏺 Jujubes preserved in
local liqueurs, other
fruit preserves and wines
are at **Enoteca Da Loris**
*V. Valleselle. Open daily
0930–1200, 1430–1930.*

🏺 **Jujube Festival** *First
two Suns in Oct.*
Celebrates local fruit, wine
and chestnuts, with food
vendors and floral
decoration.

furnace of **Cava Bomba** works as a museum of fossils dating to the
Cretaceous period, and reveals the unique geology of the hills.

Accommodation and food in Arqua Petrarca and Euganean Hills

Alla Loggia € *Pza San Marco, Arqua Petrarca; tel: 0428 718 385. Open
Thur–Tue.* Sandwiches and gelati are served overlooking the quiet
square or on a flower-draped terrace.

Serena € *V. Bignano 90, Arqua Petrarca; tel: 0429 718 044; fax: 0429 718
045.* A small hotel with restaurant €, in a quiet setting.

Hotel Piccolo Marte €–€€ *V. Casteletto 51, Torreglia; tel: 049 521 1177;
www.piccolomarte.it. Restaurant open Thur–Tue.* In a beautiful green
setting, overlooking the hills and farms, the hotel is a good base for
exploring the area, with a restaurant **€–€€** specialising in veal
scaloppine and mixed grills.

Trattoria Alla Vigna €–€€ *V. Scagliara, Montegrotto (Turri); tel: 049 891
0782. Open Tue–Sun.* Order their speciality, *carne alla brace* (meats
roasted over a wood fire).

ESTE

ℹ️ **ARPT** *V. Negri 9; tel:
0429 600 462. Open in
theory Mon–Fri 0900–1230,
Sat 1000–1230.*

🏛️ **Museo Nazionale
Atestino €** *Castello
d'Este; tel: 0429 2085.
Open Tue–Sun 0900–2000.*
Children will like the
playground in the castle
grounds, reserved for the
under-12s.

Torre Civica € *Castello;
tel: 0429 931 5711. Guided
tours mid-May–Nov Sat
1600–1900, Sun
1000–1200, 1600–1900.
Gardens open Apr–Sept until
2300; Oct–Mar 0900–1800.*

🏺 **Market day:** Thur.

One of the two oldest settlements in the Veneto (Adria is the other), Este
was home to the Ateste people for five centuries, before the Romans
conquered them in the 4th century BC. Artefacts unearthed in Este –
bronze vessels, jewellery, tools, architectural details – are shown in the
Museo Nazionale Atestino, built into the walls of **Castello d'Este**. Also
in the museum are examples of arts from Roman to medieval times. The
castle overlooks Este's main square and inside its circling walls are
gardens that rise to the keep, the **Torre Civica**. The main interest in the
duomo is a Tiepolo altar painting of Saint Tecla. The campanile of the
11th-century church of **San Martino** lists disconcertingly.

Accommodation and food in Este

Albergo Centrale € *Pza Beata Beatrice 15; tel: 0429 3930; fax: 0429 603
209.* Facing the main square, this convenient hotel has a most
accommodating staff and parking close by.

Caffè Borsa € *Pza Maggiore 5; tel: 0429 603 529.* Smart, modern décor
and a spot overlooking the main square.

Below
Castle and gardens, Este

Sapio € *V. Madonnetta; tel: 0429 602 565. Open Tue–Sun.* The enclosed (and air-conditioned) terrace surrounds a giant tree. Expect to savour the likes of ravioli filled with pears and sauced in Gorgonzola. There's no written menu, but the genial staff will make sure you understand the evening's choices.

MONTAGNANA

ⓘ ARPT *Castel San Zeno; tel: 0429 81 320. Open Jul–Aug Tue 1600–1900, Wed–Sat 0930–1230, 1600–1900, Sun 1000–1300, 1600–1900; Sept–Jun Tue 1500–1800, Wed–Sat 0930–1230, 1500–1800, Sun 1000–1300, 1500–1800.*

ⓟ Parking is plentiful around the Piazza Duomo.

ⓓ Duomo *Pza Vittorio Emanuele II. Open daily 0800–1230, 1600–1730.*

Castel San Zeno, Mastio di Ezzelino € *Padua Gate; tel: 0429 81 320. Open Jun–Sept Tue 1500–1800, Wed, Thur & Sat 0930–1230, 1500–1800, Sun 1000–1300, 1500–1800; Oct–May Tue 1600–1900, Wed–Sat 0930–1230, 1600–1900, Sun 1000–1300, 1600–1900.*

Museo Civico € *Castel San Zeno; tel: 0429 804 128. Tours Jun–Sept Wed–Fri 1100–1200, Sat–Sun & hols 1000–1300, 1600–1900; Oct–May Wed–Fri 1100–1200, Sat–Sun & hols 1100–1200, 1600–1800.*

ⓐ Market day: Thur.

ⓐ Il Palio *First Sun Sept.* A horse race around the town walls, preceded by a week of medieval costumes and market.

The entire town is enclosed by a solid medieval brick wall with four gates and twenty-four towers, all still in good repair, making this one of the finest walled towns in northern Italy. The whole ensemble is surrounded by a grassy moat, begging photographs from every angle. The **duomo** is not only architecturally significant, but is almost an art museum as well. Its highly successful transition between Gothic and Renaissance shows some of the best of both. The art begins at the Sansovino portal and includes a Veronese altarpiece painting of the Transfiguration. Nearly every artist of note from the period has been credited with the panels that flank the entrance. Much of the vaulting is covered in early 16th-century frescoes. Choir stalls have delicately painted wood panels above them, and the main altar is flanked by a pair of fine semicircular transept chapels with good frescoes, lit by a coin box beside the right transept. The Rosary Chapel has unusual frescoes on an astrology theme. The arcaded **loggia** on the east side of **Piazza Vittorio Emanuele** has an excellent ceiling, with frescoes under the arches; and to remind you that this was once part of the Venetian empire, a lion of St Mark looks down from the wall above it. From the main square you can see the fine Gothic brick bell tower of **San Francesco Grande**. At the Padua Gate, inside **Castel San Zeno**, are museums with a variety of finds that include those from a Roman necropolis discovered in the 1980s. Clearly visible just outside the same gate is Palladio's **Villa Pisani**, which is not open to view.

Accommodation and food in Montagnana

Trattoria da Stona €–€€ *V. Carrarese 2; tel: 042 981 532. Open Tue–Sun.* Local favourites include peppered rabbit with polenta.

Hotel Aldo Moro €€ *V. Marconi (just off Pza Duomo); tel: 0429 81 351; fax: 0429 82 842; www.hotelaldomoro.com. Restaurant open Tue–Sun.* The only hotel inside the walled town also has a good restaurant.

VICENZA

ⓘ IAT *Pza Matteotti 12; tel: 0445 320 854. Open daily 0900–1300, 1400–1800.*

About halfway between Verona and Padua, Vicenza seems to suffer from 'middle-child syndrome' as tourists whizz past it on the autostrada. Without the mythical Juliet or the mystical St Anthony,

A Vicenza Card includes admission to most of the major sights, including Teatro Olimpico and the museums.

Palazzo della Ragione € (Basilica) *Pza dei Signori; tel: 049 820 5006. Open Feb–Oct Tue–Sun 0900–1900; Nov–Jan Tue–Sun 0900–1800.*

Santa Corona *Corso Palladio. Church open daily 0830–1200, 1430–1830. Museum open Jul–Aug Tue–Sat 1000–1900, Sun 0900–1200; Sept–Jun Tue–Sat 0930–1200, 1415–1700. Free.*

San Lorenzo *V. Montagna. Open Mon–Sat 1030–1200, 1530–1800, Sun 1530–1800. Free.*

Teatro Olimpico €€ *Pza Matteotti; tel: 0444 326 598; www.olimpico.vicenza.it. Open Tue–Sun 0900–1700. Ticket includes admission to museums and other attractions.*

Museo Civico €€ *Pza Matteotti; tel: 0444 321 348. Open Tue–Sun 0900–1700. Ticket includes admission to Teatro Olimpico and other attractions.*

Left
Teatro Olimpico, Vicenza

Vicenza must rely on its native son, Andrea Palladio. Not a weak reed on which to lean, Palladio's revolutionary approach to architecture transformed the way the world looked at buildings. Some of his most outstanding works are in his home town. The city's gracious historic centre spreads around the 15th-century **Palazzo della Ragione**, better known as the **basilica**, whose soaring loggia was built by Palladio in 1549, when he was assigned the job of supporting Vicenza's sinking town hall. His larger-than-life statue contemplates his accomplishment, often looking over market stalls that spill from adjacent **Piazza dell'Erbe**, a busy marketplace behind the basilica. In this piazza stands a crenellated medieval tower, **Torre del Tormento**, looking a bit uncomfortable among all the Palladiana.

On the opposite side of the basilica is **Piazza dei Signori**, one of the most architecturally pleasing squares in all Italy. Above rises the slender **Torre di Piazza**, whose height increased over the course of three centuries, to its present 82m. Opposite stands the **Loggia del Capitaniato**, an arcade designed by Palladio. Behind this, especially along Contra Porti, are elegant palazzi built by Vicenza's leading families, showing both the 14th-century Venetian style and a number of Palladio's designs. Between Piazza dell'Erbe and the River Retrone are more of these older Venetian-style palaces; more of Palladio's works are along Corso Palladio. Vicenza's **duomo** was largely reconstructed after severe damage in World War II. Also worth seeing is **Santa Corona**, a 13th-century Gothic church built as a home for a thorn from Christ's Crown of Thorns. It contains paintings by Bellini and Veronese; coin boxes adjacent to side altars illuminate these. Go behind the high altar to see the intricate marble work and the inlaid wood choir stalls. The former convent houses a museum of natural history and archaeology. **San Lorenzo** has some excellent tombs and an outstanding carved stone doorway. Its cloister is one of the loveliest in the city.

Facing Piazza Matteotti is the last of Palladio's works, unfinished at his death. **Teatro Olimpico** would be enough reason for visiting Vicenza, if Palladio had done nothing else there. Opened in 1589, it is the oldest indoor theatre surviving in Europe. The theatre is designed to feel like a Greek open-air amphitheatre, with the ceiling painted to look like sky and seats replicating the stone steps. The **stage**, designed by Palladio's student, Vincenzo Scamozzi, suggests the city of Thebes, its 'streets' so cleverly proportioned and raised that they appear to be many times longer than they are. Looking into the arches of the grand, statue-studded 'façade' is like looking down the streets of a town. The theatre is entered through the **Odeon**, a concert chamber richly decorated in frescoes. Opposite Teatro Olimpico is a grand Palladian palazzo, now home to the **Museo Civico**. At least step inside to see Carpione's magnificent frescoed entrance hall ceiling. The museum contains art from local churches and works by Montagna, Tiepolo, Veronese, Bellini and others.

Villa Valmarana
€€ V. dei Nani 8; tel:
0444 321 803. Open mid-Mar–early Nov Tue–Sun
1000–1200, 1500–1800;
mid-Nov–early Mar Sat–Sun
1000–1200, 1400–1630.

Villa Rotunda € V. della Rotunda (off the S247); tel:
0444 321 793. Grounds
open mid-Mar–mid-Oct daily
1000–1200, 1500–1800.
Interior open Wed
1000–1200, 1500–1800.

Market days in
Piazza dell'Erbe: Tue,
Thur.

The Feast of the Epiphany (6 Jan) is
celebrated in colourful
processions. The annual
Gold Fair, the first week in
Jun, is a good time to avoid
Vicenza, since the area is
filled to overflowing.

Three of Vicenza's sights are on **Monte Berico**, a hillside
overlooking the city, two of them connected by a pleasant stone path.
The whole ensemble can be reached on foot from central Vicenza, via
a shaded colonnade, punctuated by chapels. Follow Viale X Giugno
from Piazza X Giugno, south of the old city centre. The colonnade
leads to **Basilica di Monte Berico**, a pilgrimage church begun in the
15th century commemorating Vicenza's being spared from the plague.
The ornately embellished interior is illuminated by votive candles,
which hang around the high altar, giving it a distinctly Byzantine feel.
Montagna's fine *Pietà* fresco is to the right, beside a mosaic of framed
votives. In the refectory are Veronese's *The Supper of Gregory the Great*
and an incongruous – but fascinating – fossil collection. An anteroom
displays unusual needlework votives. Opposite the basilica is a park
with two notable monuments, one to the local Alpini battalion and
the other an appealing bronze statue of a woman playing with a child.

Villa Valmarana is surrounded by a wall guarded by stubby statues,
giving rise to the nickname 'Villa dei Nani', or 'Villa of the Dwarfs'.
Inside, each room is decorated with frescoes by Tiepolo, based on
mythology, including the *Iliad* and Virgil's *Aeneid*. Plentiful light from
large windows underscores Tiepolo's light and airy style, and the
frescoes and grisaille work are in fine condition. In the Forestierre, a
smaller building across the garden, are pastoral frescoes by the
younger Tiepolo in a very different, more representational style. A
short stone path leads from the front gate of Villa Valmarana down to
Villa Rotunda, perhaps Palladio's most famous single work. Its perfect
symmetry, clean lines and graceful proportions have inspired
buildings on nearly every continent. The two best views for
photographing the building are from the front approach, framed in
roses, or from the bosky corner to the left at the top of the walk, both
best in the afternoon. The interior is lavishly decorated.

Right
Villa Rotunda, Vicenza

Thomas Jefferson and La Rotunda

American travellers may wish to sit on the conveniently placed bench under the trees and contemplate why Jefferson was so impressed with Palladio's masterpiece that he adapted it for his own home, Monticello, in Virginia, and promoted the use of the style in America's new public buildings. Palladio's design was the very essence of Jefferson's philosophical vision for his new United States: dignity without pomp, everything in balanced proportion, and enough of the classical to satisfy the Federalist mind.

Accommodation and food in Vicenza

Pizzeria Vesuvio € *Corso Palladio 204; tel: 0444 324 546.* Close to Teatro Olimpico, with a lovely little courtyard, the restaurant is almost hidden down a small passageway. Pizza and many other options.

Antica Osteria al Bersagliere €–€€ *Corso Pescaria 11; tel: 0444 323 507. Open Mon–Sat.* Just below Piazza dell'Erbe, the *osteria* has only a few tables, usually filled with locals feasting on roasted kid or seabass baked in black olives.

Gran Caffè Garibaldi €–€€ *Pza dei Signori (next to Loggia del Capitaniato).* The most elegant and stylish place to watch Vicenza go by.

Giardini €€ *V. Giuriolo 10; tel/fax: 0444 326 458; www. hotelgiardini.com.* A small hotel with parking and a very convenient location near the Teatro Olimpico and TIC.

Villa Michelangelo €€–€€€ *V. Sacco 35, Arcugnano; tel: 0444 550 300; fax: 0444 550 490; www.villamichelangelo.it.* High in the Berici Hills south of the city, this stately villa has beautifully furnished rooms and an outstanding restaurant. The chef excels with seafood and paper-thin agnolotti, a delicately thin ravioli.

Suggested tour

Total distance: 162km, with detours 173km.

Time: 4 hours' driving. Allow 3 days for the main route, 3–4 days with detours. Those with limited time should concentrate on Vicenza.

Links: Vicenza is connected to Verona (*see page 116*) and Venice (Venezia) (*see page 170*) via the S11 or A4. The Euganean Hills are just south of Padua (Padova) (*see page 220*), reached via the S10.

Route: Leave Padua (Padova) ❶ via its inner ring road, following signs south to Rovigo and **ABANO TERME** ❷. Continue to **MONTEGROTTO TERME**. Leave on the unnumbered road signposted **Torreglia**, turning left at its centre, to **Galzignano Terme**. The gardens at **Valsanzibio** are

ARPT V. Roma 2,
Monselice; tel: 0447
5171. Open daily.

Ristorante Torre
€–€€ Pza Mazzini,
Monselice; tel: 0429 737
529. No surprises on the
menu, but a reliable stop.

**La Giostra della
Rocca** Monselice. First
three Suns in Sept brings
medieval merriment.

a short distance to the south (*see page 210*). Continue through
Galzignano, to **Faedo** and **Fontanafredda**, turning left, following signs
to **Cinto Euganeo**. In about 1km, turn left, following signs to **Villa
Beatrice** (49km). Return and continue south through Cinto Euganeo,
turning left and following signs to **ARQUA PETRARCA** ❸. Leave Arqua,
turning right at the T-junction and following signs to **ESTE** ❹. (*See
Detour 1 below.*) Leave Este, heading west on the S10 to
MONTAGNANA ❺. Leave Montagnana via the Padua (Padova) (east)
Gate, turning left immediately and heading north on the S19 to **Pojana
Maggiore**. On the southern end of the town, the road passes between
the 16th-century **Villa Pojana** (*open Tue–Sun, 1000–1800*) and the older,
castellated villa/farm opposite. Follow signs from Pojana to Noventa
Vicentina, turning north (left) on the S247, signposted **VICENZA** ❻.
(*See Detour 2 below.*) Follow the S247 into the city, passing the left turns
for Villa Rotunda and Villa Valmarana, both well signposted (84km).
From Villa Valmarana, follow Via Tiepolo to Borgo Berga, turn right and
follow signs right to **Villa Rotunda**. Return to Borgo Berga, turning left
and following it into Vicenza (26km). To return to Padua (Padova), use
the A4 to avoid the heavy traffic on the S11 (29km).

Detour 1: Instead of turning right to **Este**, turn left, signposted
Monselice. The town clusters around its 13th-century **duomo**, with a
fine, high altar painting depicting St Justine. Climb the **Via del
Santuario** to visit the **Santuario San Giorgio**, whose interior is
decorated in delicate designs of inlaid marble. The six chapels along the
way were also designed by Vincenzo Scamozzi, Palladio's student. Inside
the sanctuary church are tombs of early Christian martyrs. **Ca'Marcello**
(€€ *Hourly tours Tue–Sun morning & afternoon*), includes a castle, a chapel
and two palaces, with good frescoes, armour, tapestries and Renaissance
furnishings. Continue to Este on the S10 (17km).

Detour 2: North of **Noventa Vicentina**, in **Ponte di Barbarano**, turn
left on a road signposted **Barbarano Vicentino**. The road climbs from
the town into the Berici Hills, signposted for Vicenza. After passing
through **Perarolo** and **San Gottardo**, the road drops to **Monte Berico**
and its sanctuary, overlooking Vicenza. Follow Via d'Azeglio downhill,
turning right on to Via San Bastiano to its end at **Villa Valmarana**.

Also worth exploring

Ostello Amolara
€–€€ V. Capitello 11,
Adria; tel: 0426 943 035.
Simple food in an old mill
with a small museum.

Opposite
Bar, Arqua Petrarca

Southeast of the Euganean Hills lies the low, canal-webbed farmland
between the Po and Adige deltas, called the Polesine. **Rovigo** has the
fine octagonal **La Rotunda** church, with paintings and statues in
niches. **Adria**, 22km east, joins Este as the oldest settlements in the
Veneto. When the Po delta wandered at will over thousands of acres,
the town of Adria was a thriving port, but alluvial deposits have left it
more than 25km from the Adriatic Sea. Its **Museo Archeologico** (€ *V.
Badini 59; tel: 0425 21612. Open daily*) has a complete iron chariot
from the 4th century BC.

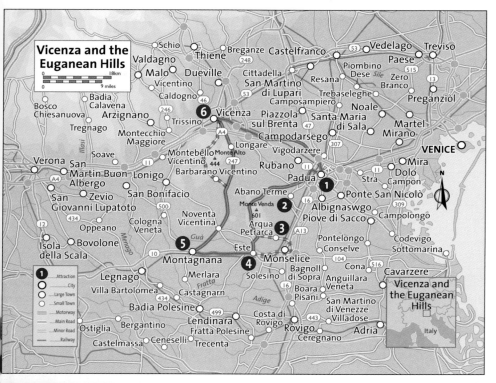

Vicenza and the Euganean Hills

Schio · Valdagno · Thiene · Breganze · Castelfranco · Vedelago · Treviso · Paese · Piombino Dese · Zero Branco · Preganziol · Malo · Dueville · Vicentino · Cittadella · San Martino di Lupari · Resana · Trebaseleghe · Noale · Martel Mirano · VENICE · Caldogno · Camposampiero · Santa Maria di Sala · Mira · Dolo · Campon · Stra · Ponte San Nicolò · Campolongo · Codevigo · Sottomarina · Cavarzere · Adria

Bosco Chiesanuova · Badia Calavena · Arzignano · Tregnago · Montecchio Maggiore · Trissino · Piazzola sul Brenta · Campodarsego · Longare · Vigodarzere · Padua · Albignaswgo · Piove di Sacco · Pontelongo · Conselve · Cona

Verona · San Martin Buon Albergo · Soave · Lonigo · Montebello Vicentino · Barbarano Vicentino · Monte Alto · Rubano · Abano Terme · Monte Venda · Arqua Petrarca · Este · Monselice · Bagnoll di Sopra · Anguillara Veneta · Villadose · Adria

San Giovanni Lupatoto · Zevio · San Bonifacio · Noventa Vicentina · Montagnana · Merlara · Solesino · Boara Pisani · San Martino di Venezze · Cerognano

Oppeano · Cologna Veneta · Bovolone · Isola della Scala · Legnago · Villa Bartolomea · Castagnarn · Badia Polesine · Lendinara · Fratta Polesine · Costa di Rovigo · Rovigo

Ostiglia · Bergantino · Castelmassa · Ceneselli · Trecenta

Map legend:
- Attraction
- City
- Large Town
- Small Town
- Motorway
- Main Road
- Minor Road
- Railway

Italy

Padua and the Brenta Canal

Ratings

Architecture	●●●●●
Art	●●●●○
Boat trips	●●●●○
Historical sights	●●●●○
History	●●●●○
Religious interest	●●●●○
Gardens	●●●○○
Food and drink	●●○○○

Saint Anthony was born in Lisbon, Portugal, but that has not stopped Padua from making him very much their own. The basilica built to honour his relics is one of Europe's major pilgrimage sites. Saint Anthony is not Padua's only claim to fame, however. Its university is among the oldest in the world, and their pioneering medical school created Europe's first botanic garden in 1545 to study medicinal plants. The university also conferred the world's first degree awarded to a woman. The Risorgimento that finally freed Italy from Austrian control was planned in the Caffè Pedrocchi, still thriving, still stylish and still a place for a lively exchange of ideas. It sits in the centre of Padua's old city, surrounded by distinguished palaces and public buildings. Above all, Padua is pleasant and hospitable, well accustomed to its role as host after greeting centuries of pilgrims.

ℹ APT *Stazione Ferrovie Stato; tel: 049 875 2077; fax: 049 8755 0008; www.turismopadova.it. Open summer Mon–Sat 0915–1900, Sun 0900–1200; winter Mon–Sat 0920–1745, Sun 0900–1200. Pza del Santo; tel: 0438 753 087. Open Mar–Oct Mon–Sat 0830–1330, 1500–1900.*

Informazione *Galleria Pedrocchi; tel: 049 876 7927; fax: 049 836 3316. Open Mon–Sat 0900–1330, 1500–1900.*

Getting there

Most motorists arrive in Padua via the A4, which connects it to Venice, Milan, Verona and Vicenza. Autostrade encircle the city, and avenues describe an inner ring around the city's remaining walls.

Getting around

From the basilica, public transport runs to the historic centre. Alternatively, walk up Via del Santo (which becomes Via Zabarella) to the Scrovegni Chapel and Chiesa degli Eremitani (Eremitani Church), just under 1km.

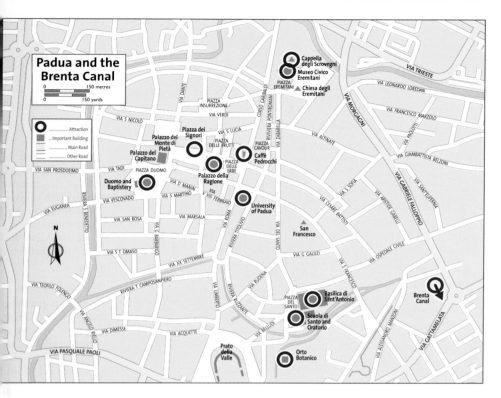

Sights

Basilica di Sant'Antonio

Construction began in 1232, only a year after St Anthony's death, and it immediately became a major pilgrimage site. The entombed relics in the Capella dell'Arca are the object of worshippers' devotion, set in a chapel of exquisite marble inlay and bas-relief by Sansovino, Tullio Lombardo and Giovanni Minello. Just beyond is the Cappella Beato Lucca Belludi, dedicated to the saint's companion, with frescoes by Giusto de'Menabuoi. In the ambulatory is a large Jesse Tree and several beautifully frescoed chapels. The Donatello bronze panels on the main altar are hard to see, but his stone bas-relief is visible. The Contarini and Bembo tombs, facing one another across the aisle, are by Sanmicheli. Cappella del Tesoro, in the apse, contains the saint's tunic and reliquaries, including his teeth and other remains. From the lovely cloister are fine views of the Pisan-style Romanesque church, which shows Gothic and heavy Byzantine influences. In the piazza, Donatello's *Gattamelata* was the first monumental equestrian statue since Roman times.

Caffè Pedrocchi €
V. VIII Febbraio 15; tel:
049 878 1231;
www.caffepedrocchi.it.
Museum open Tue–Sun
0930–1230, 1530–1800.

**Cappella degli
Scrovegni €€€**
Pza Eremitani 8; tel: 049
201 0020; www.
cappelladegliscrovegni.it.
Open daily 0900–1900.
Reservations must be made
48 hours in advance.

Duomo Pza Duomo;
tel: 049 662 814. Open
Mon–Sat 0730–1200,
1545–1930, Sun
0745–1300, 1545–2030.
Free. **Baptistery** Tel: 049
656 914. Open daily
0900–1800. Free.

**Museo Civico
Eremitani €€** Pza
Eremitani 8; tel: 049 820
4551. Open Tue–Sun
0900–1900.

Chiesa degli Eremitani
Pza Eremitani. Open
Mon–Sat 0815–1215,
1600–1800, Sun
0930–1215, 1600–1800.
Free.

Orto Botanico €
V. Orto Botanico 15 (near
the basilica). Open Apr–Oct
daily 0900–1300,
1500–1900; Nov–Mar daily
0900–1300.

Palazzo della Ragione
€€ Pza delle Erbe; tel: 049
820 5006. Open Feb–Oct
Tue–Sun 0900–1900;
Nov–Jan Tue–Sun
0900–1800.

Caffè Pedrocchi

The neoclassical building has housed this historic café since 1831. Manin and other Risorgimento leaders plotted the ousting of the Austrians, and students and intellectuals have gathered here ever since. Up a Greek stairway are theme-decorated rooms and a small **Risorgimento Museum**.

Cappella degli Scrovegni (Scrovegni Chapel)

When Dante consigned Reginaldo Scrovegni to hell in *L'Inferno* for usury, he may well have caused the building of this superb chapel. Finished in 1305 by the son to atone for his father's sins, the interior is covered with Giotto's most complete and outstanding fresco cycle. Beneath the luminescent blue ceiling, three rows of wall frescoes tell the story of Christ and of the Madonna with vivid Giotto colour on a cool blue background. Beneath, in monochrome, are the vices and virtues, while on the entry wall is the Last Judgement, a sobering reminder as worshippers left the chapel.

Duomo and Baptistery

The church itself is not the draw, although in the sacristy are paintings by Tiepolo, Bassano and others. The treasure is the **baptistery**, from an earlier 4th-century church, containing an astonishingly vivid cycle of frescoes by Menabuoi depicting the Creation, and Christ's miracles, Passion, Crucifixion and Resurrection. Facing Piazza Duomo is the splendid façade of the 16th-century **Palazzo del Monte di Pietà**.

Museo Civico Eremitani

Along with art and one of Italy's most outstanding archaeological collections, the complex includes the Eremitani Church and Scrovegni Chapel (*see above*). Archaeology covers Egyptian, Etruscan, Greek, Roman and later periods, including a 1st-century tomb of the Volumni family. Painting and sculpture is 13th to 17th century, with works by Giotto, Bellini, Veronese, Riccio and Jacopo Sansovino. The 13th-century Eremitani (Hermitage) Church was heavily damaged in 1944, destroying much of Mantegna's fresco work. Two outstanding panels and the altarpiece remain.

Orto Botanico (Botanic Garden)

Europe's oldest botanic garden dates from 1545, with trees from its first plantings. The garden is a pleasant place to stroll, fascinating for those interested in herbs and medicinal plants.

Palazzo della Ragione

Europe's largest medieval hall was created in 1218 as law courts. Reconstructed after a 1420 fire, the walls have frescoes by Nicola Miretto. Months of the year, mythology and the zodiac are depicted in 333 panels. Inside is a huge wooden horse made for a parade in 1466.

Above
Cloisters, Basilica of
St Anthony, Padua

The arcaded loggia, designed by Palladio in the 14th century, needs upkeep after use as a market.

Piazza dei Signori

Paduans savour city life in this gracious square surrounded by small shops, cafés and bars. At one end, **Palazzo del Capitano** has a clock tower (1599) and an astronomical clock (1344). Concerts are held in the adjacent 14th-century **Corte Capitano**, whose frescoes include a portrait of Petrarch.

Scuola di Santo
€ Pza del Santo 11.
Open daily 0900–1230,
1430–1700.

Scuola di Santo and Oratorio

Adjacent to the basilica, the Oratorio is a small chapel, its walls covered with elegant frescoes, two scenes of the life of St Anthony, by Titian (1511), and the lives of other saints and Christ, by Altichiero da Zevio and Jacopo Avenzo (1378–84).

University of Padua € V.
Marzolo 8. Guided tours
Mon, Wed & Fri hourly
1500–1700, Tue, Thur &
Sat hourly 0900–1100.

University of Padua

Italy's second-oldest university (1222), it was the first in the world to award a degree to a woman, Elena Piscopia, in 1678. Visit Palazzo del'Bo and the oval Anatomy Theatre built in 1594, the first in the world. The **Auola Magna (Great Hall)** is a Baroque room with walls completely covered in crests. Galileo worked here for 18 years, developing his law of accelerated motion and designing the first astronomical telescope lens.

Antiques Market
Prato della Valle, 3rd
Sun of each month.

Above
The Brenta Canal

Accommodation and food in Padua and the Brenta Canal

Hotel Maritan €–€€ *V. Gattamelata 34; tel: 049 850 177; fax: 049 850 506; www.hotelmaritan.it.* In the centre of town, it is near the station and public transport, with parking available.

Trattoria al Pero €–€€ *V. Santa Lucia 72; tel: 049 875 8794; www. trattoriaalperopadova.com.* Well-prepared local cuisine in a friendly atmosphere.

La Vecchia Enoteca €–€€ *V. San Martino e Solferino 32; tel: 049 875 2856.* A block south of the Piazza delle Erbe, popular so reservations are advised.

Hotel Donatello €€ *V. del Santo 102–104; tel: 049 875 0634; fax: 049 875 0829; www.hoteldonatello.net.* A full-service hotel opposite Basilica di Sant'Antonio. The restaurant serves local specialities, parking available and public transport nearby.

Relais Alcova del Doge €€ *V. Nazionale 39–40, Mira; tel: 041 424 816; fax: 041 560 9373; www.alcovadeldoge.it.* Attractive hotel overlooking the Brenta Canal, near the bus line to Venice.

Trattoria Porto Menai dall'Antonia €€ *V. Argine Destro, Gambarare di Mira; tel: 041 567 5618.* Very popular with locals for the extraordinary seafood; genial owners will bring you small samples of local specialities to try.

The Brenta Canal

Villa Pisani (Villa Nazionale) **€€** *V. Roma 19, Vescovana; tel: 0425 920 016; www.villapisani.com.* Open daily 0900–1800. Labyrinth open Apr–Oct.

Villa Foscari (La Malcontenta) **€€** *V. dei Turisti, Gambarare di Mira; tel: 041 5263 9666.* Open Apr–Oct Tue & Sat 0900–1200.

Battelli del Brenta **€€** *V. Porciglia 34, Padova; tel: 049 876 0233; fax: 049 876 3410; www.battellidelbrenta.it.* Guided cruises.

From Stra, just east of Padua, the Brenta Canal shortened the route to Venice and the Adriatic. Wealthy Venetians used it as their summer escape, creating the Brenta Riviera. Their sumptuous villas still line the canal, which is paralleled by the S11. Cruises on *burchielli*, named after the boats that once carried noble Venetians to their summer homes on the canal, depart from Venice and Padua on alternate days, stopping at two or all three of the villas open to the public. Return is by public transport. Motorists can visit the villas at more leisure, stopping at canal-side cafés. **Villa Pisani** (Villa Nazionale) is not by Palladio, which is remarkable for a major villa in this area. Built more than a century after Palladio's death, Pisani was designed by Girolamo Frigimelica, a 114-room mansion to rival any in the Veneto in size and splendour. Tiepolo (with his assistants) decorated the interior. Its garden contains one of the world's most difficult hedge mazes – so difficult that some visitors don't have time to see the other two villas. **Villa Foscari** (La Malcontenta) is one of Palladio's best-known, most admired and most copied villas, for its perfect proportions, temple portico and elegant double staircase. Elaborate Zelotti frescoes decorate the interior, only a small part of which is shown. The large salon that forms the core of the building is cross shaped, with light entering from all four of the building's sides. Its setting is splendid, with its best side looking on to the Brenta Canal, framed in willows. Beside the villa are parterre gardens.

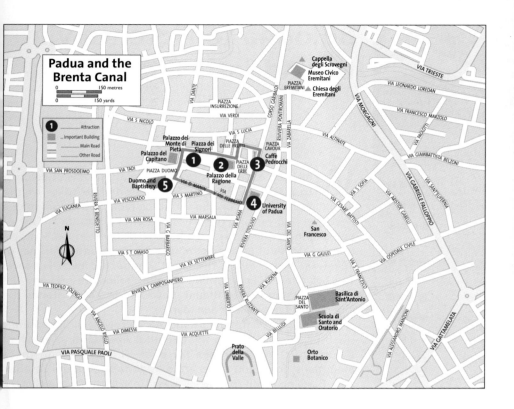

Padua and the Brenta Canal

0 _____ 150 metres
0 _____ 150 yards

① .... Attraction
◼ ....Important Building
.... Main Road
.... Other Road

Below
Basilica of St Anthony, Padua

Walking tour – Padua (Padova)

Time: 45 minutes.

Route: Start at the **Palazzo del Capitano** on the **PIAZZA DEI SIGNORI** ❶, crossing the street and travelling along the left side of the square on **Via San Clemente** into **Piazza delle Frutti** (the old fruit market). Diagonally across the square is the **Palazzo Communali** with its 13th-century tower, and directly across the square is the back of the **PALAZZO DELLA RAGIONE** ❷. Continue ahead, bearing left on to **Via Gorizia**. At the end of the street, on the right, is **CAFFÈ PEDROCCHI** ❸. Turn right on to **Via VIII Febbraio**, following it to the **UNIVERSITY OF PADUA** ❹ on the left. On your right you will pass **Piazza delle Erbe**; the front of Palazzo della Ragione encloses the piazza on the right. Turn right on to **Via Manin**, past arcaded shopfronts to **Via Monte di Pietà**, then turn left into **Piazza Duomo**. The **DUOMO** and **BAPTISTERY** ❺ are ahead on the right. Recross the piazza past the front of **Palazzo del Monte di Pietà** and turn left on to Via Monte di Pietà, which leads back into Piazza dei Signori.

Bologna to Florence via the Adriatic Coast

Ratings

Art	●●●●●
Beaches	●●●●○
Castles	●●●●○
Food and drink	●●●●○
Historical sights	●●●●○
Scenery	●●●●○
Children	●●●○○
Mountains	●●●○○

While you can rush from the many attractions of Bologna to Florence in a few hours along the spine of the Apennine mountains on the A1 autostrada, you would miss a beautiful and historic region of the Emilia-Romagna. East of Bologna, near the Adriatic Coast, one of Christendom's richest treasure troves of Byzantine mosaics illuminates the churches of Ravenna. South along the coast, connected by silver-sand beaches, are colourful fishing villages, holiday resorts and the ancient Roman city of Rimini. Beyond and above stands the independent Republic of San Marino.

Within sight of the deep blue Adriatic waters, increasingly steep hills rise quickly to the beautiful Apennines, over which this route climbs to reach Florence. Hidden among these mountains' folds and crags are hillside farms, nature reserves and charming castle-topped villages rarely visited by travellers.

BOLOGNA

ⓘ **CST** *Pza Maggiore; tel: 051 239 660; www.bolognaturismo.info. Open daily 0900–1900.* **Airport G Marconi** *Open daily 0900–1900.*

Ⓟ **Parking €** Cars are allowed in the city centre only with central-lodging reservations.

Ⓦ **Internet:** The Sala Borsa, opposite the Neptune Fountain, has free access for visitors.

Few cities offer such a concentration of art, history, gastronomy and culture, and yet remain so little visited by tourists as Bologna. Reminders of its rich history are everywhere. Begin at the **Basilica San Petronio**, designed to be larger than St Peter's in Rome and never finished, but still impressive. Each of its side chapels is like a small church. Ask in the small **museum** to see the drawings for completing the half-finished façade – especially numbers 10, 11 and 12 by Andrea Palladio. Along the floor of the nave is a meridian line.

Saint Dominic died in Bologna, in the convent of the order he founded, and his tomb is among the city's most important treasures, carved in marble by a remarkable ensemble that includes Pisano and Michelangelo. Also in **Basilica San Dominico**, the choir is highlighted by outstanding wood inlay. **San Stefano** contains five Romanesque churches in all, dating from the 11th to 13th centuries.

The tiny 1604 **Oratorio Santa Maria della Vita**, almost hidden upstairs off Via Clavature, has a fresco ceiling so incredible that two

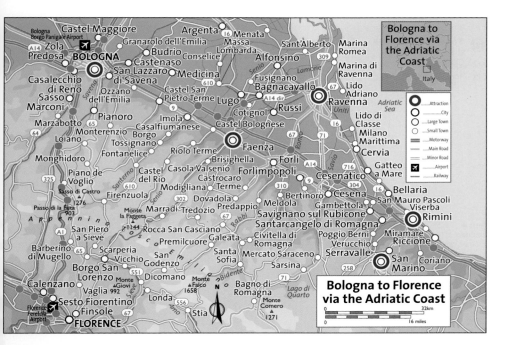

Bologna to Florence via the Adriatic Coast

Museo de Basilica
*Tel: 051 225 442.
Open Mon–Fri 0930–1230,
1530–1830, Sat
0930–1230, 1530–1730,
Sun 1530–1730.*

**Museo Civico
Archeologico € V.**
*dell'Archiginnasio 2; tel: 051
275 7211. Open Tue–Fri
0900–1500, Sat–Sun & hols
1000–1830.*

**Museo Civico
Medioevale € V.** *Manzoni
4; tel: 051 203 930. Open
Tue–Fri 0900–1500,
Sat–Sun & hols 1000–1830.*

Pinoteca Nazionale €
*V. Belle Arte 56; tel: 051
420 9411. Open Tue–Sun
0900–1900.*

**Palazzo
dell'Archiginnasio** *Pza
Galvani; tel: 051 276 811.
Open Mon–Fri 0900–1845,
Sat 0900–1345.*

benches are provided so you can admire it from flat on your back. At
one end is a gold altar, on the other terracotta relief. Another 'lost'
treasure situated on Via Zamboni, is the **Oratorio Santa Cecelia**, its
interior covered in a medieval fresco cycle.

Bologna's museum list is endless, boosted by the various university
collections. Primary among them are the **Archaeology and Medieval
museums** and the **Pinoteca Nazionale**, an outstanding art gallery. In
the **Palazzo dell'Archiginnasio**, the **Teatro Anatomico**, where
medical students once learned anatomy, is panelled in cedar wood.

Among the beauties of Bologna are its ornamented buildings and
colonnaded streets, which can be enjoyed during after-hours strolls.
Few remain of the many towers that once crowned the palaces, but
two stand side by side at alarming angles. The energetic can ascend
the taller, **Torre degli Asinelli**.

Accommodation and food in Bologna

Le Navate Cafe €€ *V. Val d'Aposa 7; tel: 051 262 793.* Cosy restaurant
with a piano bar.

Trattoria Leonida €€ *Vicolo Alemagna 2; tel: 051 239 742;
www.trattorialeonida.com. Open Mon–Sat.* Upholding the city's
gastronomic reputation with dishes such as veal scallops with
artichokes and pancetta in a delicate white wine sauce. Wines from
under €10.

Torre degli Asinelli
€ *Pza di Porta. Open Apr–Sept daily 0900–1800; Oct–Mar daily 0900–1700.*

Trattoria Romagnola €€ *V. Rialto 13; tel: 051 263 699. Open Mon–Sat.* Some distance past San Stefano, but worth it for creative seasonal dishes.

Trattoria Gianni €€–€€€ *V. Clavature 18; tel: 051 229 434. Closed Sun evening & Mon.* Tortelloni with marrow flowers and the definitive veal Bolognese.

Al Cappello Rosso €€€ *V. de'Fusari; tel: 051 261 891; fax: 051 227 179; www.alcappellorosso.it.* A few steps from Piazza Maggiore, this posh, modern hotel is among the few central hotels that offers parking.

City Hotel €€€ *V. Magenta 10; tel: 051 372 676; fax: 051 372 032; www.cityhotelbologna.it.* Comfortable rooms, a garden and free parking.

Below
Fountain of Neptune,
Piazza Maggiore, Bologna

Hotel Roma €€€ *V. d'Azeglio 9; tel: 051 226 322 or 800 219 868; fax: 051 239 909; www.hotelroma.biz.* One of the closest hotels to the sights, right in the historic centre.

FAENZA

TIC IAT *Pza del Popolo; tel/fax: 0546 25 231; www.terredifaenza.it*

Parking € *Pza San Francesco.*

Market days: Tue, Thur & Sat mornings.

Museo delle Ceramiche € *V. Baccarini 19; tel: 0546 697 311; www.micfaenza.org. Open Apr–Oct Tue–Sat 0900–1900; Nov–Mar Tue–Fri 0900–1330, Sat 0900–1330, 1500–1800.*

Shopping: Ceramics are the chief attraction; stop at **Antonio Liverani** *Corso Garibaldi 19; tel: 054 621 900.*

Known for the ceramics to which it gave its name, Faenza spreads gracefully around its long Piazza Repubblica, framed in arcaded buildings. The **duomo**, built 1474–1515, but with an unfinished façade, is filled with paintings and sculpture of the 15th to 19th centuries. **Museo delle Ceramiche** explores the history of ceramics, with worldwide as well as local examples and works by Matisse and Picasso.

Accommodation and food in Faenza

Osteria del Mercato €€ *Pza Martiri della Libertà 13; tel: 0546 680 797; www.osteriadelmercato.it.* Nice local restaurant specialising in grilled meats, churrasco, sausage and lamb spare ribs, but with many other choices.

Albergo Vittoria €€–€€€ *Corso Garibaldi; tel: 0546 21 508; fax: 0546 29 136.* The Liberty-style (Art Nouveau) interior has been restored; the dining room is a respected restaurant.

RAVENNA

TIC IAT *V. Salara 8; tel: 0544 35 404; www.turismo.ravenna.it. Open Mon–Sat 0830–1900, Sun & hols 1000–1600.*

Parking € is available at San Vitale and several other locations.

World Heritage mosaic sites €€ *Tel: 0544 541 688. Open daily 0900–1900.*

Museo Nazionale € *V. Fiandrini Benedetto; tel: 0544 543 711. Open Tue–Sun 0830–1930.*

Festivals: Jun–Jul, **Ravenna Festival** uses the churches and squares as venues for opera, symphony, dance and ethnic music.

The churches of Ravenna combine to form perhaps the world's richest collection of Byzantine mosaics, important enough to be named a World Heritage Site.

The interior of the 5th-century **Neonian Baptistery** is a riot of design, in tesserae so small that the pupils of the apostles' eyes are visible in the dome. Fine carved marble pieces, including a 6th-century pulpit, in the **cathedral** next door are easily overlooked among the city's mosaics.

Clustered at **San Vitale** are the mosaic-lined **basilica**, **Mausoleum Galla Placida** and **Museo Nazionale**. The basilica's large circular interior is covered in mosaics of astonishing finesse and brilliant colour. Equally vivid are the ceiling panels in the small mausoleum, illuminated in intricate designs of cobalt and gold.

For a break from Byzantine, stop at **Basilica di San Giovanni**, where the mosaics, many with animal themes, are older and more primitive. At **Sant'Apollinare**, the entire upper walls above the arches are devoted to larger-than-life images of saints and the nativity. In the cloister a fascinating display shows materials and techniques of mosaic art, including samples of 19 different shades of gold.

Dante's tomb is outside **Basilica di San Francesco**, where it's worthwhile to see the flooded 5th-century crypt, the stone-carved columns by Tullio Lombardo and *freschi* by Pietro da Rimini in the left aisle.

Accommodation and food in Ravenna

Cupido € *V. Cavour 43; tel: 0544 37 529*. Fast and inexpensive *piedini* (sandwiches), pizza and their own daily pastas (skip the gnocchi).

Ca de Ven €–€€ *V. Corrado Ricci 24; tel: 0544 30 163*. Traditional foods of the Romagna and a vegetable buffet are the specialities.

Albergo Cappello €€ *V. IV Novembre 41; tel: 0544 219 813; fax: 0544 219 814; www.albergocappello.it*. Well located opposite the market, the hotel has a restaurant **€–€€** serving grilled lamb chops, carpaccio and pasta dishes.

RIMINI

ⓘ IAT *FS Railway station, Pza Caesar Battisti 1; tel: 0541 51 331; www.riminiturismo.it. Open Mar–Oct Mon–Sat 0830–1900, Sun 0930–1230; Nov–Feb Mon–Sat 1000–1600.*

ⓟ Parking € *along city walls and outlying streets.*

ⓦ Internet *Email Beach Viale Vespucci 29C. Open Mon–Sat 1400–2000. Cyber Pub Viale Mantova 70. Open Mon–Sat 2000–2400.*

ⓣ Tempio Malatestiano (Duomo San Francesco) *V. IV Novembre; tel: 0541 51 130. Open Mon–Sat 0750–1230, 1530–1850, Sun & hols 0900–1300, 1530–1900. Free.*

An ancient Roman city, Rimini retains a surprising amount of its past, considering that its busy harbour was a major target for World War II bombs. The Roman Corso Augusto runs straight through its centre, from the striking **Porta Augusto** to the five-arched **Ponte Tiberini**, a Roman bridge. Halfway, it passes through the **Forum**, later the medieval marketplace and now Piazza Tre Martiri. Excavated segments of street, like other landmarks in the city, have historical signs in English.

Tempio Malatestiano, reconstructed by the Malatesta family in the 1400s, has carved marble works and a transept painting by Piero della Francesca. The elegant fountain in Piazza Cavour was admired by Leonardo da Vinci in 1502.

Stretching endlessly along the coast are fine beaches solidly lined with hotels, restaurants, cafés and shops.

Accommodation and food in Rimini

San Domingo € *Vle Dessié 7, Bellaria Igea Marina; tel: 0541 331 528; fax: 0541 332 124; www.hotelsandomingo.it*. Balconies overlook the Adriatic and the restaurant offers Romagnola specialities.

Café Teatro €–€€ *Pza Cavour; tel: 0541 781 528*. The place for a light meal, coffee or glass of wine and people-watching.

Hotel Rondinella €€ *V. Neri 3; tel/fax: 0541 380 567; fax: 0541 380 674; www.hotelrondinella.it*. At the beach, the hotel has a restaurant **€€** for its guests only.

Hotel de Londres €€€ *V. Vespucci 24; tel: 0541 50 114; fax: 0541 50 168; www.hoteldelondres.it*. A historic classic at the beach, completely refurbished to add all the mod cons.

SAN MARINO

ⓘ TIC Ufficio Turismo *Contrada Omagnano 20; tel: 0549 882 914; www.visitsanmarino.com. Open Mon–Fri 0830–1830, Sat–Sun 0900–1330, 1400–1830.*

ⓟ Parking Car parks € are located at various levels below the historic centre.

ⓙ Palazzo Pubblico and Museo Nazionale € *Tel: 0549 883 885. Open mid-Jun–Oct daily 0800–2000, shorter hours off-season.*

Rocca Malatestiana € *Verucchio. Open Apr–Sept daily 0800–2000; Oct–Mar daily 0900–1700.*

◖ Festivals Late Jul–early Aug, Medieval Days, filled with costumed pageantry.

Shopping Stamps and coins are popular with collectors.

◑ Market day: Thur morning.

◖ Relais Torre Pratesi *V. Cavina 11, Brisighella; tel: 335 694 2021 or 335 652 2841; fax: 0546 84 558; www.torrepratesi.it.* The medieval watchtower, converted to spacious lodgings, crowns a garden-painted hilltop with views to the sea. Multi-course dinners use only seasonal local ingredients, many grown in the chef's garden, accompanied by their own fine wines.

The views from this hilltop domain are splendid, especially from the castles that crown the long mountain top. The guard, in colourful uniforms, changes hourly at the half-hour in front of the **Palazzo Pubblico**, which can be toured on a combined ticket with the **Museo Nazionale**. Collections there include local Neolithic and later archaeological finds, paintings, sculpture, Egyptian antiquities and Byzantine icons. A paved walking route lined with eateries and kiosks connects the castles, beginning at the earliest, **Rocca Guaita** (1253). **Rocca Cesta**, at the highest point, contains an arms museum.

A short side trip to hilltop **Verucchio** is worthwhile, to see the 12th-century **Rocca Malatestiana**, with views of a string of other hilltop castles and the Adriatic.

Accommodation and food in San Marino

L'Angelo Divino € *Pza Malatesta 15, Verucchio; tel: 0541 679 407.* Very inexpensive sandwiches and wine.

Righi La Taverna €€ *Pza Libertà 10; tel: 0549 991 196; fax: 0549 990 597.* Café and meals at pavement tables or inside.

La Rocca €€ *V. Del Volta 10, Brisighela; tel: 0546 81 180; fax: 0546 80 289; www.albergo-larocca.com.* Attractive rooms with sweeping views and a restaurant serving local dishes.

Suggested tour

Total distance: 313km, with detours 458km.

Time: 12 hours' driving. Allow 4–5 days for the main route, 6 days with detours. Those with limited time should concentrate on Bologna and Ravenna.

Links: Florence (*see page 234*), the end point for this route, is the start of the Florence to Pisa route (*see page 252*).

Route: Leave **BOLOGNA ❶** on Via Massarenti to route S9, following signs to **FAENZA ❷** (50km). Leave Faenza by Via Garibaldi, following the S302 northeast to **RAVENNA ❸** (31km).

Leave Ravenna on the S16 heading south along the shore to **Cesenatico ❹**, whose charming old canal/fishing harbour is filled with a colourful collection of historic boats, described in English. Restaurants, shops and cafés line the banks and a tiny walk-on ferry crosses it. Continue south on the S16 to **RIMINI ❺**.

**🍴 Ca'de Be Museo
Enoteca €–€€**
*Belvedere, Bertinoro; tel:
0543 444 142. Shop open
daily 1030–1230, shop and
wine bar daily 1600–0030.
Serves local wine and light
snacks.*

Ristorante Magnolia
*€€ V. Trento 31,
Cesenatico; tel: 0547 81 598;
www.magnoliaristorante.it.
Just the right blend of
tradition and innovation in
the hands of an outstanding
chef; the signature roasted
rabbit balances a menu rich
in fresh seafood.*

Below
Faenza pottery

Leave Rimini on Via Flaminia, turning right to the S72, signposted to **SAN MARINO ❻** (24km). Follow signs ever upward to **Borgo Maggiore ❼**, then to **Centro Storico ❽**.

From San Marino, backtrack towards Rimini, exiting northwest on route S9 to **Cesena ❾** (30km).

After crossing the E45, follow signs south to the hilltop wine town of **Bertinoro ❿** for views from the belvedere and to see the curious hospitality pillar, where strangers once tied their horses. Descending, follow signs to Forlimpopoli to rejoin the S9.

Forlì is worth a stop to see the **Abazzia del Santa Maria**, facing its central piazza. The interior stone carving, in Istrian rock, resembles terracotta. The town is encircled by impressive bastioned walls.

Detour (52km): From Forlì, continue on the S9 to the Faenza access, but turn south on to the S302 to **Brisighella**. This hillside town is distinguished by a curious 14th-century covered gallery, **Via degli**

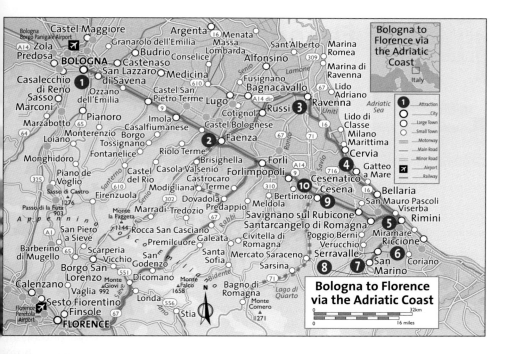

Bologna to Florence via the Adriatic Coast

TIC IAT *Pza Gabolo 5, Brisighella; tel/fax: 0546 81 166; www.comune.brisighella.ra.it. Open Apr–Oct Mon–Sat 0930–1230, 1600–1800; Nov–Mar Wed–Sat 1030–1230, Sun 1500–1700.*

Locanda Giovanna *€–€€ V. D Manin 35, Bagno di Romagna; tel: 0543 911 057.* The mixed grill and house-made pastas are excellent. Simple rooms include meals.

Hotel Tosco Romagnolo *€€–€€€ Pza Dante 2, Bagno di Romagna; tel: 0543 911 260; fax: 0543 911 014; www.paoloteverini.it.* Hospitable family-owned spa resort. Its restaurant, one of the region's finest, highlights local truffles, wild game, woodland berries and fresh seafood.

Asini, that overlooks Piazza Marconi. An even more compelling reason to visit this region is to stay and dine in the mountain-top eyrie of **Relais Torre Pratesi**, a perfect mid-trip respite.

To rejoin the main route, follow the vineyard-lined unnumbered road from Brisighella, following signs to Modigliana and Dovadola to the S67, just south of Dovadola. Turn right (southwest) on to the S67.

To continue on the main route, leave **Forlì** travelling southwest on the S67, signposted to Firenze (Florence) (105km). This route traversing the Apennines is relatively easy, passing the mountain resorts of **Rocca San Casciano** and **Benedetto in Alpi** before entering Florence along the River Arno.

Also worth exploring

Shortly past Cesena, the E45, signposted 'Roma', almost immediately enters the scenic and rugged Apennine foothills. The roadway remains relatively level via tunnels and bridges to **Bagno di Romagna** (51km). This appealing old spa town with Roman origins hides in a deep, shady valley, and lacks the pretensions of the better-known watering holes. Children love the free **Gnome Trail** in the wooded **Parco dell'Armina** across the river.

Florence

Ratings

Architecture	●●●●●
Art	●●●●●
Museums	●●●●●
Shopping	●●●●●
Food and drink	●●●○○
History	●●●○○
Children	●●○○○
Gardens	●●○○○

The showplace of the Italian Renaissance, Florence finds itself in a difficult position today. The largesse of important buildings and art makes it a magnet for tourists – many travellers place it ahead of Rome on their 'must-see' list. They come in hordes, so many that they often literally fill the streets in a solid mass. And Florence is caught between welcoming these cultural pilgrims and trying to maintain the treasures and their environment.

The traveller must overlook these obstacles and appreciate those masterpieces they came to see – the simply stunning Duomo-Battistero complex, the art-filled churches and galleries and icons such as Ponte Vecchio and the Boboli Gardens. There is so much to see in Florence that one trip cannot possibly do more than skim the surface, so don't try to do everything. Concentrate on absorbing a few sights – and come back often.

Getting there

ℹ **APT Firenze**
V. A Manzoni 16;
tel: 055 276 0852;
fax: 055 234 6286;
www.firenzeturismo.it

Comune de Firenze
Pza Stazione 4 (opposite the railway station); tel: 055 212 245. Open Mon–Sat 0830–1900, Sun & hols 0830–1400.

Borgo Santa Croce *29;*
tel: 0442 340 444. Open Mon–Sat 0900–1700, Sun & hols 0900–1400.

Arriving in Florence by plane is surprisingly difficult, as the city lacks a major airport. Its small airport, if used, connects to the centre via a regular bus. The nearest large airport with flights from abroad is in Pisa, from where one can ride directly to Florence on local trains – the travel time is approximately 1 hour. Longer-distance travellers may need to fly into Milan, then catch a train for Florence. Rail passengers arrive at Florence's handy railway station (also known as FMN), just a 800m walk from the duomo, the Arno and most of the major sites. There's luggage storage in the station, though fees are per piece and quickly add up.

Getting around

Florence is a very compact place, yet there's tremendous congestion for such a small city centre; driving is not advised, and there is no

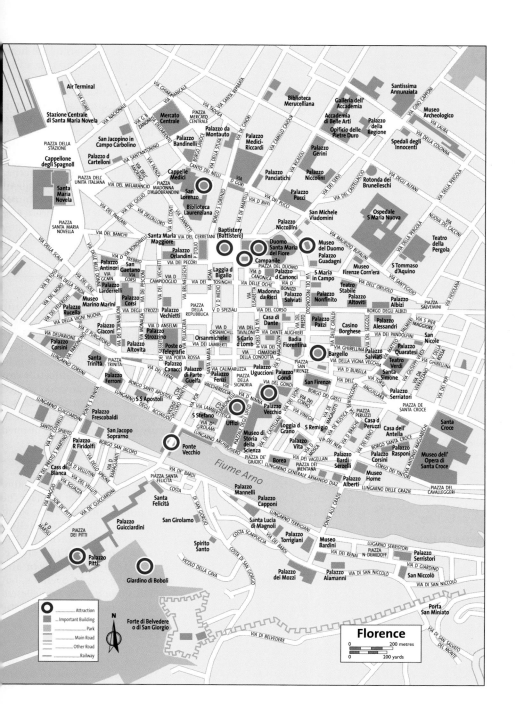

Florence

P Large car parks are near the main railway station (Fortezza da Basso) and the cheaper Piazza della Libertà (Parterre). Most of the city centre is *Zona Blu* (blue zone), meaning only residents are allowed to park on the streets; cars parked illegally in this zone are towed away and held for ransom at *V. dell'Arcovata 6; tel: 055 355 231*. Make sure signs don't say *ecetto residenti autorizatti* (no parking except for residents). Don't park in or near the notorious (for break-ins) Piazzale Michelangelo.

☺ Florence profits from its past but remains a working city engaged in an astonishing range of crafts and trades, particularly shoes, leather, handbags, textiles, nightgowns, bookbinding and art restoration. Most of the work is done in the Oltrarno (the left bank of the Arno) in small shops, some of them the size of a cupboard.

ⓘ Battistero € *Pza del Duomo/San Giovanni; www.operaduomo.firenze.it. Open Mon–Sat 1200–1900, Sun 0830–1400.*

Museo Nazionale del Bargello €€
V. del Proconsolo 4; tel: 055 238 8606; www.firenzemusei.it. Open daily 0815–1400.

Campanile €€ *Open daily 0830–1930 (last admission 40 mins before closing).*

Opposite
Piazza del Duomo

underground. That makes walking by far the best option in the heart of the city. Bridges cross the Arno at convenient points, making a visit to Oltrarno easy. The local buses are cheap; taxis are hard to find or call and cost more than they're worth in such a walkable place.

Driving: If Dante were alive today, he would surely add driving in Florence to the punishments of hell – a maelstrom of Vespa scooters, taxis, pedestrians and overly aggressive Italian drivers awaits. Avoid it at all costs, as you won't need a car anyway to see any of the important sights.

Buses: Florence's city buses can take you to the suburbs rather cheaply, though drivers drive like hellions and then make frequent stops. Among the options are single-ride tickets valid for 70 minutes (€1–€2), 24-hr tickets (about €5) and 48-hr tickets (about €9). *www.ataf.net*

Sights

Baptistery
The origins of the Baptistery (Battistero) are mysterious, but the foundations are probably from the 4th–8th centuries, while the current building dates from 1059–1128. Medieval Florentines, including Dante (baptised here in 1265), thought it was built by the Romans and it does, in fact, stand at the former intersection of the town's two main Roman roads. See all three sets of its bronze doors, especially Ghiberti's east door. His crowning achievement, it is one of the finest artworks created during the Renaissance (the original ten gilded panels are in the Museo del Duomo); even Michelangelo, normally a merciless critic, called them the 'Doors of Paradise'. Inside, 13th-century mosaics in the apse inspired Dante while writing *L'Inferno*.

Bargello
The Bargello is strangely neglected, though its collection of sculpture rivals that of any museum in the world. The ground floor displays the only bust Michelangelo ever carved, of *Brutus*, and the same room contains his *Tondo Pitti* and *David-Apollo*. Upstairs is Donatello's homoerotic, under-age *David* – the first nude statue of the Renaissance, and one of the most remarkable works of art in Florence. Other high points include Ammanati's *Leda and the Swan* and Ghiberti's powerful *The Sacrifice of Isaac*. They're easy to overlook, but on the wall of the first floor are two panels submitted by Brunelleschi and Ghiberti in fierce competition for the commission to do the baptistery doors.

Campanile
Giotto was appointed architect of Florence's cathedral in 1334, but never got beyond building this tower. He decorated it with octagonal

ⓘ Duomo *Pza del Duomo; www. operaduomo.firenze.it. Open May & Oct Mon–Wed & Fri 1000–1700, Thur 1000–1530; Jun–Sept Mon–Fri 1000–1700, Sat 1000–1645. Free.*

Dome €€ *Open Mon–Fri 0830–1900, Sat 0830–1740 (closes 1600 first Sat each month).*

Giardino di Boboli € *Palazzo Pitti; tel: 055 238 8786. Open Mar daily 0815–1730; Apr–May & Sep–Oct daily 0815–1830; Jun–Aug daily 0815–1930; Nov–Feb daily 0815–1630 (last admission 1 hr before closing).*

Museo del Duomo €€ *Open Apr–Oct Mon–Sat 0900–1930; in summer also Sun 0900–1340; Nov–Mar Mon–Sat 0900–1730. If you want to see the workshop that is now used to repair the duomo, walk around the corner to V. dello Studio 23r.*

Galleria Palatina €€ *Tel: 055 294 883; www.firenzemusei.it. Open Tue–Sun 0815–1850. Other museums in the Palazzo Pitti open Tue–Sat 0900–1400, Sun 0900–1300. (Hours may change often.)*

pilasters and a colour scheme that would later be applied to the cathedral – white marble (quarried in Carrara), green marble (from Prato) and red marble (from Maremma). The reliefs were added over the next century by Andrea Pisano, Luca della Robbia and Donatello, and portray the history of humanity.

Duomo Santa Maria del Fiore

When it was built, Florence's magnificently patterned duomo was the largest church in the world: 53m long and 38m wide. Today it is still the fourth-largest cathedral in Europe and tremendously impressive. Arnolfo di Cambio began the duomo in 1296, but it was Brunelleschi who put his stamp on it, winning a heated competition to design the ingenious double-shelled **dome** (1420–34). Climbing to the top of it is one of the most unforgettable experiences of a trip to Florence, for its simultaneous views of the city's red-tiled rooftops and a plunging look into the marble canyon of the church's interior.

Giardino di Boboli

The 16th-century Medici rulers used this vast fantasy-filled garden overlooking the city as a retreat; the public didn't get its first peek until 200 years later, and has been ambling happily through it ever since. Avenues lined with cypresses intersect ensembles of Roman and Renaissance statues, and stately cedars of Lebanon shade strange grottoes. Fountains are ubiquitous, and deeper inside beneath stalactites is Giambologna's well-endowed *Venus*. The steep climb to the top of the gardens is rewarded with a cinematic view of Florence and the surrounding Tuscan countryside.

Museo del Duomo

Many of the most impressive pieces of the baptistery, duomo and campanile are kept here to preserve them from pollution and vandalism. Sculptures from the unfinished cathedral façade torn down in 1587 line the walls of the ground floor, as do the original panels of Ghiberti's 'Doors of Paradise'.

The 80-year-old Michelangelo sculpted the moving *Pietà* (1548–55) for his own tomb in Rome, portraying himself in the figure of St Nicodemus. Donatello is represented by the early, powerful sculptures of prophets Jeremiah and Habakkuk (1420) and a late Mary Magdalene in wood (1455). It's interesting to note that the 13th-century building behind the duomo served as its workshop for centuries. Michelangelo sculpted *David* there in 1501–4.

Palazzo Pitti

The vast Pitti Palace was built at the edge of Florence by Luca Pitti and greatly expanded by Medici tyrant Cosimo. Today the palace contains no fewer than eight museums devoted to fashion, silver, coaches and other items. The **Galleria Palatina** is one of Europe's great art

Above
View of the duomo

🅸 **Palazzo Vecchio**
€€ *Pza della Signoria;*
tel: *055 276 8325;*
www.firenzemusei.it. Open
Mon–Wed & Fri–Sun
0900–1900, Thur
0900–1400. **Museo dei**
Ragazzi *(in Palazzo*
Vecchio) Tel: 055 276 8224.
Open daily 0930–1700.

museums, containing a brace of Caravaggios, more than a few
paintings by Raphael (such as *Portrait of a Lady*) and Titian, and other
works by Rubens (including *The Consequences of War*), Tintoretto and
Giorgione.

Palazzo Vecchio
The palace is still the City Hall of Florence. It was the work of di
Cambio (1299–1314), although Michelozzo added the Early
Renaissance courtyard in 1453. Two centuries after its completion,
Vasari decorated the walls with frescoes, now badly faded, of Austrian
cities to celebrate a wedding between the house of Medici and an
Austrian princess. The clock, added in 1667, still ticks.

Ponte Vecchio
One of Europe's most photographed structures, the 'Old Bridge'
occupies a place used in Roman times as a crossing over the Arno for

Capelle Medici €€
*Basilica San Lorenzo,
Pza Madonna degli
Aldobrandini 6; tel: 055 294
883; www.firenzemusei.it.
Open daily 0815–1800.*

Uffizi €€ *Pzle degli Uffizi;
Tel: 055 294 883; fax: 055
264 406; www.
firenzemusei.it. Open
Tue–Sun 0815–1850;
reservations Mon–Fri
0830–1830.* Booking a
ticket means you don't
have to queue but it costs
a little more. Opening
hours are subject to
change.

the Via Cassia. Today's bridge was built in 1345. Originally, there were butcher shops and tanners lining it, but Ferdinand I replaced them with upmarket jewellers and goldsmiths.

San Lorenzo

As parish churches go, San Lorenzo goes a long way. It was, after all, the parish of the Medicis, who dropped generous amounts into the collection plate. In the church are bronze pulpits by Donatello, and the old sacristy is crowned by another of Brunelleschi's domes, painted by Donatello, who also made the bronze doors. Michelangelo designed the stairs to the Medici's library and sculpted the tombs in the **Capelle Medici**, entered at the side of the church, and richly inlaid in coloured stone.

Uffizi

Giorgio Vasari designed the Uffizi ('Offices') for Medici ruler Cosimo I in the 16th century. Today it is Italy's most popular museum (around 1.5 million visitors a year and growing), with 1,000 works of art from the 13th to the 17th century displayed in 45 rooms. Its most famous icon, Botticelli's *Birth of Venus*, challenges the *Mona Lisa* for the status of the world's most recognised painting. If your focus is the Renaissance, plan to spend the day in the first 15 rooms alone; save another day for the tremendous international collections, which hold major works by such European masters as Dürer, Cranach, Brueghel the Elder and Rembrandt.

Accommodation and food

Culture shock

Something strange
happened to French
novelist Stendhal one day
in 1817 during a visit to
the Uffizi. His heart raced
and he began to sweat
and tremble; shortly
afterwards, he broke
down in tears. Florentine
doctors and psychologists
still treat dozens of cases
of *sindrome di Stendhal*
each year, a recognised
medical condition that is
basically a kind of nervous
breakdown brought on by
an overdose of culture.

There is no off season in Florence, merely busy and busier seasons; Apr–Jun & Sept–Oct are worst of all. Some hotels do drop rates 25–50 per cent in winter. Make advance reservations or day trip into the city.

Hotel Crocini € *Corso Italia 28; tel: 055 212 905; fax: 055 210 171; www.hotelcrocini.com.* The long-established Crocini is one of Florence's last 'authentic', English-style *pensiones*. Located in a quiet residential area, its rooms are spacious for Florence, and there is a back garden and parking area. A 10-minute walk from the centre of town.

Osteria Pepo € *V. Rosina 4; tel: 055 283 259; www.pepo.it.* Although à la carte dishes are inexpensive, the fixed daily menu is a real bargain and includes wine. It's a good idea to reserve.

La Pentola dell'Oro € *V. di Mezzo 24r; tel: 055 241 808; www.lapentoladelloro.it.* Chef Giuseppe Alessi goes one better than traditional by serving Renaissance-style dishes – *piatti Rinascimentale* – and vegetarian meals.

La Spada € *V. della Spada 62; tel: 055 218 757; www.laspadaitalia.com.* Begin with the *tris* (trio) of pastas to get the chef's daily favourites and

order the excellent side dish of grilled vegetables – main courses are so inexpensive that you can splurge on extras here.

La Torricella € *V. Vecchia di Pozzolatico 25; tel: 055 232 1818; fax: 055 204 7402; www. farmholidaylatorricella.it.* Two-night minimum stay. A B&B in a villa on the outskirts of Florence, run by the attentive and friendly Giannozzi family. It is an easy drive from the Certosa exit of the A1 autostrada. There is public transport to the city centre.

Trattoria Antichi Cancelli € *V. Faenza 73; tel: 055 218 927.* Tourists rarely find this pleasant little place near the market, where generous portions are well prepared and cheap.

Trattoria Marione €–€€ *V. della Spada 27; tel: 055 214 756; www.marione.firenze.net.* The queue waiting for tables doesn't come for the surly service, but for the prodigious plates of homey Florentine food.

Caffè Bigallo €€ *V. del Proconsolo 73; tel: 055 291 403; www.caffebigallo.com.* Close to the duomo, this restaurant claims 'the world's best bar', but we go for the carpaccio, offered in six varieties.

Il Cibreo €€ *V. del Verrocchio 8; tel: 055 234 1100. Closed Sun–Mon, last week of Jul & Aug. No reservations.* Trattoria attached to a more expensive restaurant next door; the food is outstanding at modest prices, but it doesn't accept reservations and is always packed. Arrive early, before 8pm. *Anatra ripiena al forno* (stuffed roast duck) is a speciality; they don't do pasta.

Pitti Gola e Cantina €€ *Pza Pitti 16; tel: 055 212 704.* A little pricier than some wine bars, but you're paying for the view of the Pitti Palace and for the delicious snacks that accompany the wine.

Cucina alla Fiorentina

Florentine cuisine is simplicity itself. Crostini – toasted Tuscan bread – with chicken-liver pâté, tomatoes or mushrooms, or simply dipped in indescribably good olive oil. Soup often takes preference over pasta, *ribollita* in winter and *pappa di pomodori* in summer. Florentines also like to eat hare, wild boar and pheasant. The *bistecca alla fiorentina* is simply a steak – of local Tuscan beef, from the Valdichiana – marinated in herbs, garlic and the finest olive oil, and cooked to perfection over wood coals. *Tortino di carciofi*, an artichoke omelette, and *funghi alla griglia* (grilled mushrooms) are among the few offerings for vegetarians. Expensive restaurants sometimes have bargain lunch menus, and many eateries charge for *pane e coperto* (a cover charge for sometimes stale bread) and sometimes for *servizio* (10 per cent); check the menu.

Royal €€ *V. delle Ruote 52; tel: 055 483 287; fax: 055 490 976; www.hotelroyalfirenze.it.* One of the more accessible hotels by car, yet central. You can drive here directly from the peripheral road between Fortezza da Basso and Piazza della Libertà. Parking is in the courtyard.

Grand Hotel Minerva €€€ *Pza Santa Maria Novella 16; tel: 055 27 230; fax: 055 268 281; www.grandhotelminerva.com.* City-centre location makes this historic hotel a short walk to all the sights; close to several moderately priced restaurants. The hotel is in a limited traffic zone.

Helvetia & Bristol €€€ *V. dei Pescioni 2; tel: 055 26 651; fax: 055 288 353; www.hotelhelvetiabristolfirenze.it.* Just as welcoming today as it was to the leading intellectuals of a century ago, whose favourite hotel it was. The décor is positively sumptuous.

Hotel J and J €€€ *V. di Mezzo 20; tel: 055 2631; fax: 055 240 282; http://jandj.hotelinfirenze.com.* Few hotels in Florence have such a beautiful setting: 19 rooms are located off the courtyard of a 16th-century convent and decorated with frescoes, plush seating and fine hardwood furniture. The duomo is just 500m away. Parking at a nearby garage.

Hotel Villa La Vedetta €€€ *V. Michelangelo 78; tel: 055 681 631; fax: 055 658 2544; www.villalavedettahotel.com.* On a breezy hillside overlooking the city, this Liberty-style villa hotel has it all – free parking, free shuttle to the centre of town, beautifully decorated rooms, a terrace swimming pool, gardens, hospitable staff and an excellent restaurant €€€.

Relais Certosa Hotel €€€ *V. di Colle Ramole 2 (Certosa); tel: 064 814 798 (from Italy and the EU: 800 860 004); fax: 064 824 976; www.florencehotelcertosa.it.* Also just off the Certosa exit of the A1, this rambling villa has spacious, attractive suites, a good restaurant and courtesy bus to the city centre.

Shopping

Florence is not a bargain-hunter's dream. If money is no object, walk down Via Tornabuoni or Via della Vigna Nuova for high fashion, and price tags to match. Leather lovers shop in Florence for high-quality coats and shoes – you can find an open-air market atmosphere at **San Lorenzo Market**, and modest prices in the shops around Piazza Santa Croce. Ponte Vecchio is lined with some of Italy's top gold and silver jewellers.

Alice's Masks *V. Faenza 72; tel: 055 287 370; www.alicemasks.com. Open Mon–Sat 0900–1300, 1530–1930.* As much a museum as a shop, this studio also has workshops in papier mâché mask-making.

Coin *V. dei Calzaiuoli 56r; tel: 055 280 531.* Four-storey department store featuring affordable, made-in-Italy goods.

Officina Profumo Farmaceutica di Santa Maria Novella *V. della Scala 16; tel: 055 216 276; www.smnovella.com. Open Mon–Fri 0930–1930, Sun 1030–1830.* Dominican friars operate this charming apothecary, one of the world's oldest, full of fragrant balms, herbal creams and medicinals.

Scuola del Cuoio (Leather School) *V. San Giuseppe 5r; www. scuoladelcuoio.com.* Preserving handcraft traditions, with reasonably priced leather goods such as wallets and handbags.

Entertainment

There's surprisingly little nightlife in Florence, although the classical music scene is far more lively. Churches are often venues for chamber music, and the **Teatro Comunale** divides its year between opera, ballet and orchestral performances (*tel: 055 211 158; www.maggiofiorentino.com*). Florence has quite a few Irish pubs catering to an American, British and Aussie audience. Among the most popular are **Fiddler's Elbow** (*Pza Santa Maria Novella 7r; tel: 055 215 056*) and **The Lion's Fountain** (*Borgo Albizi 34r; tel: 055 234 4412*). For wine, try one of the city's *enoteche* (wine bars), which offer light meals and often have no seating.

Walking tour

Total distance: 2km.

Time: To see everything on this route would require at least 3 days. If you only have a day, visit the duomo sights, walk the route below and, along the way, choose between the Uffizi or Bargello.

Links: Florence falls at the end of the Bologna to Florence route across the Apennines (*see page 231*) and at the beginning of the Florence to Pisa route (*see page 252*).

Note that this tour skips the Accademia, which holds the famous *David* statue, but little else of interest; queues here are invariably very long, not worth experiencing for the time-short traveller.

Route 1: Piazza del Duomo is the ancient heart of Florence, where two Roman roads once met. Begin here with a look at the **BAPTISTERY ❶**, then visit the **DUOMO SANTA MARIA DEL FIORE ❷** – to appreciate it fully, climb the steps to the dome. A second, even more dizzying view is possible over the edge of the **CAMPANILE ❸**. (*See Detour on page 244.*)

On the north side of the duomo, take Via de Martelli. After one short block, have a look at the **Palazzo Medici-Riccardi ❹** and walk into its arcaded courtyard, one of the finest in Florence. This was the family home of the Medici until they moved to the Palazzo Vecchio in 1659.

SAN LORENZO ❺ is just a stone's throw away on Canto dei Nelli. The unfinished façade hides one of the most perfectly proportioned buildings of the Renaissance. The entrance to the **Cappelle Medici** ❻ is behind the church. Just a few paces further on is Florence's gastronomic paradise, the elegant 19th-century iron and glass **Mercato Centrale** ❼ (*V. dell'Ariento. Open Mon–Fri 0730–1300, Sat 0730–1300, 1600–2000*). This is the city's main market and one of the best places in Italy to buy food. Around it are market stalls selling foods, silk, leather, paper goods and everything else.

Detour: Walk around the cathedral past the fascinating **MUSEO DEL DUOMO** ❽, where you can see Ghiberti's original 'Doors of Paradise'. Now enter **Via del Proconsolo**, a pedestrian zone, though you will have to dodge taxis and mopeds. The **Palazzo Nonfinito** ❾ contains the **Museo Nazionale di Antropologia e Etnologia**, the first anthropological museum in Italy (founded in 1869, free). The Romanesque cloister of **Badia Fiorentina** ❿ is a small oasis of peace where Dante once wistfully spied on Beatrice at Mass; the lanes around it are known as the Dante Quarter. Opposite the Badia is the grim façade and tower of the **BARGELLO** ⓫.

Route 2: The narrow street of Borgo dei Greci leads into Piazza de Santa Croce, a neighbourhood where residents actually outnumber tourists. The largest Franciscan church in Italy, **Santa Croce** ⓬ was the work of Arnolfo di Cambio (but the façade is 19th century). It has been called the Westminster Abbey of Florence; inside are masterpieces by artists from Giotto to Donatello, and tomb-spotters will quickly find Michelangelo, Machiavelli, Galileo and Rossini. Few pay the price of admission to see the **Cappella dei Pazzi** (1430–46) next door, now part of a museum – the **Museo dell'Opera di Santa Croce**. Yet it is arguably the most perfect of all the designs created by Brunelleschi, built according to the golden mean.

Walk right into the imposing open piazza and along Borgo dei Greci to **PALAZZO VECCHIO** ⓭. This was the scene of the Bonfire of the Vanities, when Savonarola convinced Florentines to burn their carnival costumes and licentious paintings only a few short months before they subjected him to the same treatment. The huge square fronting it, **Piazza della Signoria** ⓮, is Florence's open-air drawing room – a gathering place for locals and tour groups alike. The U-shaped **UFFIZI** ⓯ gallery stands at the southerly end of the square; allow several hours at the very least to explore what may be Italy's finest museum, or, if you're pressed for time, follow its length (and the waiting line of tourists) to the river and the **PONTE VECCHIO** ⓰. This bridge is lined with goldsmiths and people taking pictures. Across the bridge, it is just one block further to the **PALAZZO PITTI** ⓱. The **GIARDINO DI BOBOLI** ⓲ is behind the palace. From here, buses return to the central railway station.

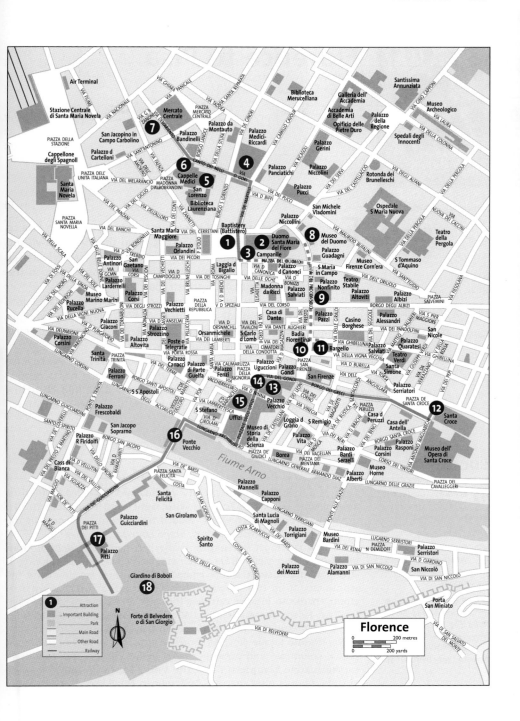

Florence

0 _____ 200 metres
0 _____ 200 yards

Florence to Pisa

Ratings

Architecture	●●●●●
Art	●●●●●
Gardens	●●●●○
Historical sights	●●●●○
Museums	●●●●○
Children	●●●○○
Crafts	●●●○○
Food and drink	●●●○○

From the almost too-well-known leaning campanile in Pisa to the secret treasures of lovely Lucca and the even less-visited towns of Prato and Pistoia, the short distance between Florence and the Mediterranean shore shouldn't be skipped past in the 2 hours it takes via the A11 autostrada.

While Pisa's closely grouped sights can be seen in a day, Lucca is a city to settle into for a few days. Follow the locals' example and hire a bike to explore it, or just wander to savour its architecture and friendly atmosphere.

Perhaps because they are so close to Florence, Prato and Pistoia go largely unnoticed by tourists. But each has a central core of attractions; Pistoia's collection of art-filled churches alone would have made it a tourist mecca in any other location.

LUCCA

ℹ APT *Pza Guidiccioni 2; tel: 0583 91 991; www.luccaturismo.it. Open daily.*

🅿 Parking is restricted within the city walls, but several car parks € lie just outside.

🏛 Palazzo Guinigi € *V. San Andrea 42; tel: 0583 316 846. Open May–Sept daily 0930–1930; Oct daily 0930–1730; Nov–Apr daily 0930–1630.*

Lucca is a thoroughly pleasant city, relaxed and not jaded by tourists. Manageable in size, it is filled with sights and enjoyable strolls, especially atop the **city walls**, shaded by large trees planted in the early 1800s by Napoleon's widow, Marie Louise.

Perhaps the most fascinating is the petrified shell of its **Roman amphitheatre**, visible inside as an oval piazza and outside as a ring of streets with odd stone arches embedded into their façades. View the whole city from tree-crowned **Torre Guinigi**, a surprisingly easy climb, thanks to historic cartoons that give an excuse to stop at each landing. In the separate Guinigi Villa is the **Museo Nazionale**, with Roman and Etruscan antiquities, medieval altarpieces and sculpture.

The **duomo** façade deserves more than passing notice for its arched porch, colonnade and ornately carved figures. Inside, the exquisitely carved marble **Tempieto** holds the **Volto Santo**, a simple wooden crucifix. Lucca's most precious holy relic, it is believed to be the only

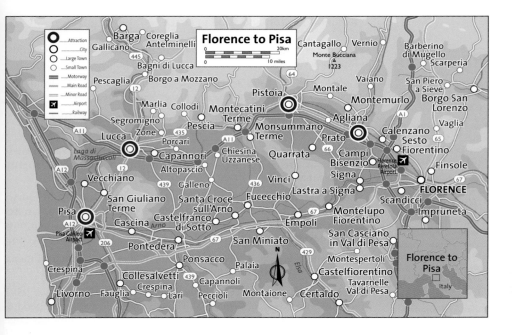

Florence to Pisa

Market: An antiques market fills several piazze the third weekend of each month.

Museo Nazionale di Villa Giuigi € *V. della Quarquonia; tel: 0583 496 033. Open Tue–Sat 0900–1900, Sun & hols 0900–1400.*

Duomo Sacristy € *Tel: 0583 957 068. Open Mon–Fri 0930–1745, Sat 0930–1845.*

Museo della Cattedrale € *V. Arcivescovado; tel: 0583 490 530. Open Apr–Oct Mon–Sat 1000–1800; Nov–Mar Mon–Fri 1000–1400, Sat–Sun 1000–1700.*

true portrait of Christ, sculpted by Nicodemus. In the Sacristy is the marble tomb of **Ilaria del Carretto** by Jacobo della Quercia. In a side chapel, Tintoretto's *Last Supper* takes an unusual perspective. The **Museo della Cattedrale** shows illuminated hymnals and intricate medieval goldwork, including a Pisani crucifix.

San Giovanni Reparata covers extensive excavations of a Roman bath, a first-century BC Roman home and stone sarcophagi. Enter through fragments of a baptistery floor (12th century) and palaeo-Christian mosaics – it is like descending through levels of time.

The **San Frediano** façade is crowned by a large mosaic, and inside is a baptismal font carved with fanciful creatures, a della Robbia panel and a chapel with incorrupt relics of St Zita. The carved and inlayed marble façade of **San Michele in Foro** seldom repeats a design on its pillars. Inside are works by della Robbia and Lippi; Puccini sang here as a choirboy. In Piazza Citadella, a statue of Puccini stands below **Casa Natale di Giacamo Puccini**, his birthplace and childhood home, with original music manuscripts and letters and the piano at which he composed *Turandot*.

Palazzo Pfanner combines ornately frescoed rooms with a beautiful garden that appears larger because of statue-lined walkways. At least look into it from the city wall.

Accommodation and food in Lucca

San Giovanni
Reparata € Open
Apr–Oct daily 1000–1800;
Nov–Mar Mon–Fri
1000–1400, Sat–Sun
1000–1700.

San Frediano Tel: 0583
493 627. Open Apr–Nov
Mon–Sat 0730–1200, 1500–
1700, Sun 1030–1700.

San Michele Tel: 0583 48
459. Open daily 0730–
1200, 1500–1800.

Casa Natale di
Giacamo Puccini €
Corte San Lorenzo; tel: 0583
584 028. Open Jun–Sept
daily 1000–1800 Nov–May
Tue–Sun 1000–1300,
1500–1800.

Palazzo Pfanner € V.
degli Asili 33. Open Apr–Nov
daily 1000–1800.

Opposite
Leaning Tower, Pisa

Lodging is scarce in Lucca, especially in the summer and at weekends. Reservations are a must.

Café l'Emiliana € *Pza dell'Anfiteatro 134; tel: 0583 496 767*. Inside the oval piazza, this is one of the few places serving breakfast.

La Luna €–€€ *Corte Compagni 12; tel: 0583 493 634; fax: 0583 490 021; www.hotellaluna.com*. Set inside the walls in two historic palazzi.

I Santi Vineria €–€€ *V. Anfiteatro 29A; tel: 0583 496 124*. Salad plates, vegetable terrine and lighter dishes are on the wine bar's highly creative menu.

Trattoria da Leo €–€€ *V. Tegrimi 1; tel: 0583 492 236; www. trattoriadaleo.it. Open daily 1200–1430, 1930–2230*. Friendly, family-run restaurant serving carpaccio with rocket or veal with *pignoli* nuts and red wine. No credit cards.

Canuleia €€ *V. Canuleia 14; tel: 0583 467 470*. A more upmarket menu than most of its neighbours, with a pleasant garden.

Grand Hotel Guinigi €€ *V. Romana 1247; tel: 0583 4991; fax: 0583 499 800; www.grandhotelguinigi.it*. Outside the walls, with free parking and easy to reach by car, the modern Art Deco-style hotel has large rooms and Internet access.

Locanda Buatino €€ *Borgo Giannotti 505; tel: 0583 343 207*. Outside the walls, this rustic restaurant offers rabbit cacciatore with olives, duck with mushrooms, risotto with trout. Modest rooms upstairs.

Locanda Prosciutto e Melone €€ *V. Anfiteatro 29; tel: 0583 48 805*. Huge cold plates, calzone, focaccie and pastas at pavement tables or the air-conditioned dining room.

Universo €€€ *Pza del Giglio 1; tel: 0583 493 678; fax: 0583 954 854; www.universolucca.com*. Near the duomo in the city centre, this venerable hotel has parking and a reliable restaurant.

PISA

APT Pza Vittorio
Emanuele II 16;
tel: 050 42 291;
www.pisaturismo.it. Open
Mon–Fri 0900–1900, Sat
0900–1600.

Parking near Campo
€, free Sundays.

The irony of the tilting campanile, **Torre Pendente**, is that even if it stood straight, its delicate arcaded form would make it one of Italy's most important monuments. But tilt it does, as it has from its construction. It is possible to climb the tower €€€, but expect a queue. Views from the top are fantastic.

The **duomo**, begun in the mid-11th century, is the definition of the Pisan-Romanesque architectural style that influenced churches throughout Tuscany. The mosaic in the apse is by Cimabue; Pisano created the pulpit.

🏛 **Combined tickets**
€–€€ are sold for monuments and museums, all of which charge for admission. It is best to verify times at *www.opapisa.it* close to the expected time of visit.
Ticket Office for Campo Miracoli monuments *tel: 050 560 547. Open Feb & Nov 0900–1700; Mar 0830–1730; Apr–Sept 0800–1930; Oct 0830–1900; Dec–Jan 0930–1630.*

Torre Pendente (Leaning Tower) €€€
Tel: 050 835 010; www.opapisa.it. Open for online reservations Mon–Fri 0800–1330. Tower hours for on-site tickets: Nov & Feb daily 0930–1730; Mar daily 0900–1730; Apr–Jun & Sept daily 0830–2000; Jul–Aug daily 0830–2300; Oct 0900–1900; Dec–Jan daily 1000–1630. Visits are limited to 30 minutes and must be booked in advance (best done online).

Duomo € *Tel: 050 560 547; www.opapisa.it. Open Mar daily 1000–1800; Apr–Sept daily 1000–2000; Oct daily 1000–1900; Nov–Feb daily 1000–1245, 1400–1700.*

Baptistery € *Tel: 050 560 547; www.opapisa.it. Open Feb & Nov daily 0900–1700; Mar daily 0830–1730; Apr–Sept daily 0800–1930; Oct daily 0830–1900; Dec–Jan daily 0930–1630.*

Camposanto € *Tel: 050 560 547; www.opapisa.it. Open Feb & Nov daily 0900–1700; Mar daily 0830–1730; Apr–Sept daily 0800–1930; Oct daily 0830–1900; Dec–Jan daily 0930–1630.*

The **Baptistery**, begun a century later, is largely the work of the Pisano family, with a magnificent pulpit by Nicolo Pisano. Shiploads of earth from the Holy Land were brought back by crusaders to fill the **Camposanto** so that influential Pisans could rest eternally in holy soil. Along with tombs and 2nd-century sarcophagi are ancient, restored frescoed walls. In adjoining chambers more *freschi* include vivid 14th-century depictions of the inferno.

The excellent **Museo dell'Opera del Duomo** displays an ivory Madonna by Giovanni Pisano, gold- and silver work and reliquaries, including a thorn from the *spina corona*. The view of the Leaning Tower from the courtyard balcony is among the best.

Not far from the Campo dei Miracoli, busy **Piazza dei Cavalieri** is surrounded by palaces.

Accommodation and food in Pisa

Many of Pisa's restaurants close for the month of August.

Trattoria La Mescita € *V. Cavalca 2 (Pza delle Vettovoglie); tel: 050 957 019; www.osterialamescitapisa.com. Open Tue–Sun.* Fresh vegetables rule at this crowded spot near the market, although fish and meats appear as well. Not your usual Tuscan menu.

Osteria dei Cavalieri €€ *V. San Frediano 16; tel: 050 580 858; www.osteriacavalieri.pisa.it. Closed Sat lunch, Sun & Aug.* Typical dishes, but with the chef's own creative flair. Excellent wine list, many by the glass.

Villa Kinzica €€ *Pza Arcivescovado; tel: 050 560 419; fax: 050 551 204; www.hotelvillakinzica.it.* Some rooms have views of the Leaning Tower and their **Restaurant Maiori €–€€** is better than expected in a busy tourist location.

Al Ristoro dei Vecchi Macelli €€€ *V. Volturno 49; tel: 050 204 24. Open Wed–Mon.* Fresh, local seafood and wild game are treated respectfully.

Museo dell'Opera del Duomo €

V. Arcivescovado; tel: 050 560 547; www.opapisa.it. Open Mar daily 0900–1800; Apr–Sept daily 0800–2000; Oct daily 0900–1900; Nov daily 1000–1700; Dec–Feb daily 1000–1700.

Royal Victoria Hotel €€€ *Lungarno Pacinotti 12; tel: 050 940 111; fax: 050 940 180; www.royalvictoria.it.* Beautifully maintained historic building (some parts are many centuries old) overlooking the Arno.

Villa di Corliano €€€ *S S Abetone 50; tel: 050 818 193; fax: 050 818 897; www.villacorliano.it.* Open Mar–Nov. The stately villa is set in gardens near the spa of San Giuliano, with a noted restaurant.

PISTOIA

AIT *Antico Palazzo dei Vescovi; Pza del Duomo; tel: 0573 21 622; www.turismo.pistoia.it*

Parking € is plentiful just outside the city walls, near the Fortezza di Santa Barbara.

Principal churches open 0830–1900. Baptistery closes 1200–1500.

Museo Civico € *Pza del Duomo; tel: 0573 371 296.* Open Tue & Thur 1500–1800, Wed & Fri 0900–1200, 1500–1800.

Giardio Zoologico € *V. di Pieve a Celle 160; tel: 0573 911 219; www.zoodipistoia.it.* Open Mon–Fri 0930–1800, Sat–Sun & hols 0900–1900.

The **duomo** is from the 11th century; apply at the Sacristy or look through the gate to see its masterpiece, the medieval silver altar with intricate depictions of saints. The **baptistery**, faced in carved and inlaid marble panels, has a coffered green and white marble interior with a 13th-century font. The **Museo Civico** is well worth the long climb to upper floors to see extraordinary medieval art.

Near Piazza del Duomo on Via Cavour, the church of **San Giovanni** has a pulpit supported on lion-held columns with intricate free-standing marble figures. A 5-minute walk in the opposite direction is the **Ospedale del Ceppo**, its façade surmounted by a wide ceramic frieze by della Robbia. The church of **Sant'Andrea** has a magnificent pulpit by Giovanni Pisano.

West of town is one of Italy's best zoos, **Giardio Zoologico di Pistoia**. In addition to jaguars (bred there), polar bears and elephants, a special section encourages children to approach animals safely and teaches about protecting rare domestic breeds.

Accommodation and food in Pistoia

La Torretta € *V. Provinciale Lucchese 488; tel: 0573 572 434.* West of town, in a 17th-century palazzo with a terrace. Serves updated Tuscan cuisine – old favourites with a flair.

Caffè San Giovanni €–€€ *V. Cavour 18; tel: 0573 21 623.* A relaxing stop for coffee and the local *cantuccini* (biscuits).

Hotel Firenze €–€€ *V. Curtatone e Montanara 42; tel/fax: 0573 23 141; www.hotel-firenze.it.* Close to the duomo, with parking and in-room Internet connections.

Liberty Cafe €–€€ *V. degli Orafi 54; tel: 0573 975 535.* In one of Tuscany's finest Art Nouveau buildings, serving light meals, cold dishes, waffles and pizza.

San Jacopo €–€€ *V. F Crispi 15; tel: 0573 27 786.* Homey local dishes, including Tuscan tripe.

Albergo Le Rose €€ *Vle Auda 87; tel: 0573 20 785; fax: 0573 976 161; www.lerose.it.* Just out of the town centre, with air conditioning and a good restaurant featuring local dishes.

Opposite
Duomo, Pistoia

Tenuta di Pieve a Celle €€ *V. Pieve a Celle 158; tel: 0573 913 087; fax: 0573 910 280; www.tenutadipieveacelle.it. Agriturismo* on a country estate with stylishly furnished rooms and swimming pool. Guests' meals by reservation.

PRATO

ℹ️ APT *Pza Duomo 8; tel/fax: 0574 24 112; www.prato.turismo. toscana.it. Open Apr–Sept Mon–Sat 0900–1330, 1430–1900, Sun & hols 1000–1300; Oct–Mar Mon–Fri 0900–1330, 1430–1830, Sat 0900–1330, 1430–1800, Sun & hols 1000–1300.*

Monday, when attractions are closed elsewhere, is a good day to visit Prato, which has Tuesday closings.

🅿 Parking € is in Piazza San Francesco and Piazza Mercanti.

🔔 Duomo *Tel: 0574 26 234. Open Mon–Sat 0700–1230, 1500–1830, Sun 0700–1230, 1500–1930.*

Museo dell'Opera del Duomo € *Tel: 0574 29 339. Open Mon & Wed–Sat 0930–1230, 1500–1800, Sun & hols 0930–1230.*

Castello Imperatore € *Pza Santa Maria delle Carceri. Open Apr–Sept daily 1000–1700; Oct–Mar daily 1000–1600.*

Museo del Tessuto (Textiles) € *V. Santa Chiara 24; tel: 0574 611 503; www. museodeltessuto.it. Open Mon & Wed–Fri 1000–1800, Sat 1000–1400, Sun 1600–1900.*

A centre for the woollen industry since the early Middle Ages, Prato grew rich and the results are seen in its churches and public buildings today. The green-and-white-striped **duomo** has an unusual broad pulpit on its façade, an exact replica of the original by Donatello (now in the **Museo dell'Opera del Duomo** in the adjoining Palazzo Vescovile). The church's sacred relic is a belt worn by the Virgin Mary, displayed in a chapel off the left nave, along with an outstanding marble and silver altar and a lovely Pisano Madonna. The high altar chapels are decorated by huge fresco cycles, including Filippo Lippi's *Banquet of Herod* with the dancing Salome.

The nearby **Piazza del Comune** is enclosed by the medieval **Palazzo Pretorio** and the **Palazzo del Comune**. The Gothic

🅘 **Luigi Pecci Centro**
€€ *V. della Repubblica 277; tel: 0574 5317; www.centropecci.it. Open Mon–Fri 1200–1900, Sat–Sun 1000–1900.*

Centro di Scienze Naturali € *Galceti (3km from Prato centre); tel: 0574 460 503; www.csn.prato.it. Open Jun–Oct Wed–Sat 0930–1230, 1500–1900, Sun 1500–1900; Nov–May Wed–Sat 0930–1230, 1500–1800, Sun 1500–1800. Park designated to rehabilitation of animals. Museum and Planetarium.*

🅧 **Ristorante Quaglino** €€–€€€
V. della Toretta, Montecatini Terme; tel: 0572 78 652. Grilled veal and frito misto del mare.

🅘 **Parco di Pinocchio**
€€ *V. San Gennaro 3, Collodi; tel: 0572 429 342; www.pinocchio.it. Open Mar–Oct daily 0830–sunset.*

🅢 **Shopping** Prato is the place to buy puppets, sold from shops and kiosks everywhere.

🅘 **Villa Torrigianni** €
V. del Gombreraio 3, Camigliano; tel: 0583 928 041. Open Mar–mid-Nov daily 1000–1300, 1500–1900, other days by appointment.

Villa Mansi € *V. delle Selvette 242, Capannori; tel: 0583 920 234. Open summer Tue–Sun 1000–1230, 1500–1900; winter Tue–Sun 1000–1230, 1500–1700.*

San Dominic houses a fresco museum off its cloister (€ *open Wed–Thur & Sun–Mon 0900–1300, Fri–Sat 0900–1300, 1500–1800*). The well-preserved 13th-century **Castello Imperatore** was built by Holy Roman Emperor Frederick II to impress his Italian subjects.

The new **Museo del Tessuto (Textile Museum)** shows more than 6,000 examples from all periods, and the **Luigi Pecci Contemporary Art Centre** proves Prato's continued dedication to art.

Accommodation and food in Prato

Caffè Buonamici € *V. Ricasoli 3; tel: 0574 30 170.* Generous sandwiches and a view of the duomo from pavement tables.

Giglio € *Pza San Marco 14; tel: 0574 37 049; fax: 0574 604 351; www.albergoilgiglio.it.* Close to the castle, modest but hospitable.

I'Rifrullo €–€€ *Pza Mercatale 18; tel: 0574 25 062. Open Tue–Sun.* Seafood and typical Tuscan dishes.

Hotel Flora €€–€€€ *V. Carioli 31; tel: 0574 33 521; fax: 0574 400 289; www.prathotels.it.* In the historic centre, with parking and all the mod cons.

Suggested tour

Total distance: 105km, with detours 124km.

Time: 4 hours' driving. Allow 3 days for the main route, 4 days with detours. Those with limited time should concentrate on Lucca and Pisa.

Links: Florence (*see page 234*), where this route begins, connects with the Bologna to Florence route (*see page 231*). Pisa, this route's end, is the starting point for the southern Riviera di Levante route (*see page 260*).

Route: Leave Florence ❶ on the A11 autostrada, exiting at **PRATO** ❷ (24km). Leave PRATO heading west on route S435 to **PISTOIA** ❸ (15km). Continue on route S435 to **Montecatini Terme** (15km).

Continue on route S435 through the plant and tree nurseries of **Pescia**, turning north on the unnumbered road signposted to **Collodi**, 'birthplace' of Pinocchio (14km).

Return to the S435, continuing west through **Zone** (*see Detour below*) and into **LUCCA** ❹. Leave **LUCCA** heading south on route S12 (beware of poor signage here), climbing the ridge of Monte Pisano and dropping into **San Giuliano Terme** before arriving in **PISA** ❺, where signs lead to **Campo dei Miracoli** (37km).

Detour: At **Zone**, turn north on the unnumbered road signposted **Segromigno**, following signs to **Villa Torrigianni** in **Camigliano**,

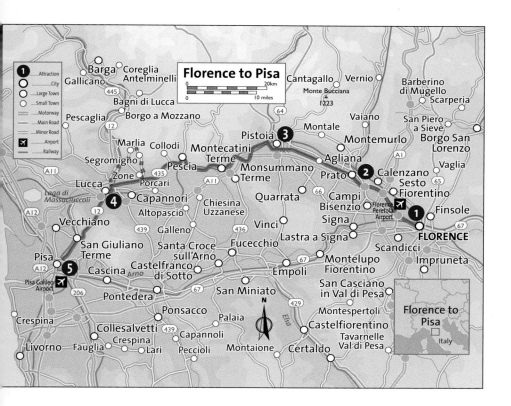

Villa Reale € *Località Villa Reale Marlia; tel: 0583 30 108; www.parcovillareale.it. Gardens open Mar–Nov 1000–1300, 1400–1800; guided tours Mar–Nov 1100, 1200, 1500, 1600, 1700 & 1800.*

Museo Archeologico € *Artimino; tel: 0558 718 124. Open Feb–Oct Mon–Tue & Thur–Sat 0930–1230, Sun 1000–1200; Nov–Jan Sun & ols 1000–1200, weekday mornings by appointment.*

Villa Mansi in **Segromigno** and **Villa Reale** in **Marlia**. Just past **Marlia**, turn south on route S12 into Lucca (19km).

Also worth exploring

Those with a passion for archaeology and early history will find the area south of Prato fascinating. A 7th-century BC Etruscan site has been excavated at Artimino, and artefacts from this and a number of necropoli and tumuli are shown in the **Museo Archeologico** at Artimino. You can visit the Etruscan **Montefortini Tumuli** (*tel: 0558 719 741. Open Mon–Sat 0900–1400*). From Prato, follow the SS325 and SS66 to Poggio a Caiano, then follow signs to Comeana and Artimino.

The southern Riviera di Levante

Ratings

Scenery	●●●●●
Villages	●●●●●
Walking	●●●●●
Children	●●●●○
Geology	●●●●○
Outdoor activities	●●●●○
Vineyards	●●●○○
Beaches	●●●○○

From the Art Nouveau pleasure palaces of the Ligurian beach towns to the rugged vertical cliffs of the Cinque Terre, this section of Mediterranean coast certainly doesn't lack variety. Nor does it lack history: Romans first coaxed marble out of the mountains of Carrara, from the same quarries that later supplied Michelangelo with his palette of stone.

Because of its golden beaches and scenery, and the attention that UNESCO recognition has brought the newly established Parco Nazionale delle Cinque Terre, the region can be very crowded in the summer. But the mild year-round climate makes the Ligurian Coast ideal for off-season travel, and the months of October, November, March and April bring good weather and uncrowded roads.

CARRARA

ℹ **TIC Marina de Carrara** V. A Vespucci 24 at Pza La Rotunda Paradiso; tel: 0585 240 063; www. aptmassacarrara.it

🏛 **Museo del Marmo** € Vle XX Sept; tel: 0585 845 746. Open May–Sept Mon–Sat 0930–1300, 1530–1800; Oct–Apr Mon–Sat 0900–1230, 1430–1700.

 **Market day:** Mon.

Its very name synonymous with marble – and not just any marble, but the world's finest – Carrara is also inextricably linked with the name of Michelangelo. The artist believed that the search for the right piece of stone was just as important as its sculpting, and he often explored the mountainsides above town. His efforts were rewarded, for his finest works are of the almost translucent Carrara marble. The **duomo** shows off the stone's architectural uses, with a delicate rose window whose tracery and frame seems like stone lace. At the **Museo del Marmo (Marble Museum)**, near the TIC between the town and the port, exhibits explore the quarries' history from Roman origins and show slabs of every imaginable variety of the stone. Above, the mountainsides look snow covered, so white are they with marble quarries. To visit these, ask at the TIC for a quarry map.

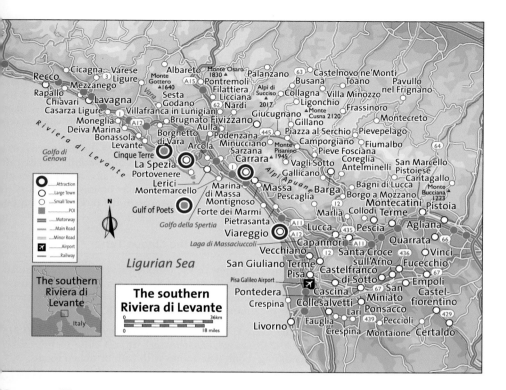

CINQUE TERRE

The region's only true TIC is at the railway station in Monterosso: V. Regina 38, Monterosso; tel: 0187 817 506; www.aptcinqueterre.sp.it or www.monterossonet.com. Open Easter–Oct.

Cinque Terre Card
€€–€€€
www.cinqueterre.com.
Allows free train and discounted boat travel, access to paths and use of shuttle buses in the park for 1, 3 or 7 days.

Cinque Terre National Park
: Telemaco Signorini 118, Riomaggiore; tel: 0187 76 031; www.parconazionale5terre.it

The Cinque Terre (Five Lands) includes five villages that cling to vertiginous slopes and cliffs that centuries of hard work have made arable and habitable. Many of the old vineyards are overgrown now, and the whole area is a national park and UNESCO World Heritage Site. Although the towns are packed with tourists and hikers, their charm endures, especially when you leave **Riomaggiore** and **Manarola**, the two connected by the shortest and easiest path, the **Via dell'Amore €**. This largely paved portion is relatively level and usually very crowded. The entire trail, the **Sentiero Azzurro €**, is more demanding – and interesting – but the views are stupendous from any part.

Most visit the towns by train, since the hair-raising road through the area runs along a corniche high above the towns, and it's a long, steep walk to the villages (and back up). Best to leave your car in La Spezia (*see page 258*) or Sestri Levante (*see page 267*) and ride the almost-hourly trains.

Riomaggiore is small – almost too small for the number of people that throng it. At the train station are murals by Silvio Benodetto,

P **Parking €** The only town you can reach by car is Corniglia, where a hefty fee €€€ discourages entering.

Hiking times:
Riomaggiore–Manarola
20 mins
Manarola–Corniglia
1 hr
Corniglia–Vernazza
1 hr 30 mins
Vernazza–Monterosso
2 hrs

depicting early life in the Cinque Terre. **Manarola** rises in steep terraces above a rocky pool where children swim. **Corniglia** sits high above the water, with few overlooks to admire the view. The climb from the train station below is scenic, but brutal; a bus is an alternative way to the top.

Beyond Corniglia the trail becomes its wildest, least crowded and loveliest. It is steep and very rough in places and several of the cornices are toe-curlingly narrow and without rails to separate hikers from the cliffs and ocean below. But it is bordered with wild flowers and passes through olive groves and vineyards.

Steep steps drop into **Vernazza**, the prettiest of the five towns, to a harbour lined with brightly painted boats and equally bright café umbrellas, under pink, yellow, red and ochre walls. Above is a castle tower, and a natural arch under the cliff has houses built across its top. The northernmost town, **Monterosso al Mare**, is the largest, flattest and least scenic.

Accommodation and food in the Cinque Terre

While formal hotels are few in the Cinque Terre, rooms are abundant in private homes and small informal B&Bs. They are not inexpensive, but staying in one brings you close to the life of the locals. Look for 'Affittacamere' or 'Zimmer' signs, or ask at the TIC for a list.

Hostel Cinque Terre € *V. B Riccobaldi 2, Manarola; tel: 0187 920 215; fax: 0187 920 218; www.hostel5terre.com.* Hostel close to the coastal path with a dining room; twin rooms with bath or shared rooms.

La Lanterna € *V. San Giacomo 46, Riomaggiore; tel: 0187 920 589; www.lalanterna.org. Open Dec–Oct daily to 2300.* Creative Ligurian dishes using local seafood.

Basso Stefania Apartments €–€€ *V. Fieschi 107, Corniglia; tel: 0187 812 364; fax: 0187 821 214.* Comfortable small apartments with kitchenettes.

B&B Da Baranin €–€€ *Manarola; online booking only: http://en.baranin.com.* Bright and contemporary B&B rooms and apartment accommodation.

Café Ananasso €–€€ *Pza Marconi 17, Vernazza.* A good stop for cool refreshment between hiking segments or for sandwiches; perfect for people-watching.

Locanda Cà dei Duxi €€ *V. Pecunia 19, Riomaggiore; tel: 0187 920 036; fax: 0187 920 036; www.duxi.it.* In the centre of the old town, the hotel dates from the 1600s and includes a restaurant €–€€.

Mike & Franca €€ *V. Carattino 16, Cinque Terre; tel: 0187 812 374; www.mike-franca.com.* Rooms with a garden terrace atop a cliff.

Villa l'Eremo sul Mare €€ *V. Gerai, Vernazza; tel: 339 268 5617; www.eremosulmare.com.* A bit of a hike uphill (about 0.5km), but right on the path, so you have a head start in the morning. The three guest rooms share facilities, but have kitchen privileges.

Above
Vernazza, Cinque Terre

Miky €€€ *V. Fegina 104, Monterosso al Mare; tel: 0187 817 608; www.ristorantemiky.it. Open summer daily for lunch & dinner; winter Wed–Mon for lunch & dinner.* Well-prepared seafood and pizza with sea views.

Porto Roca €€€ *V. Corone 1, Monterosso al Mare; tel: 0187 817 502; fax: 0187 817 692; www.portoroca.it.* Large villa furnished with antiques; 42 rooms and a suite, serenely with a restaurant.

GULF OF POETS

TIC Lerici, V. Biaggini 6 (on the seafront north of Pza Garibaldi); tel: 087 969 164; www.comune.lerici.sp.it. Open Mon–Sat 0900–1300, 1400–2000, Sun 1000–1300.

Portovenere Pza Bastreri 7; tel: 0187 790 691; fax: 0187 790 215; www.portovenere.it

The Gulf of Spezia earnt its more common name, the Gulf of Poets, nearly two centuries ago, when Shelley, Byron and their literary kin took villas here. La Spezia occupies the northern end of the bay and the attractive holiday towns of **Lerici** and **Portovenere** face each other across its entrance.

The buildings around Lerici's marina could fool you into thinking the architecture of their ornate façades was real. But it's all skilful *trompe l'œil* – the stonework quoins, window surrounds, corbels and cornices are all painted fakes. The 12th-century **castle** above is real, however, and contains a small museum of archaeology (Museo Geopaleontologico).

The road from La Spezia to Portovenere is so twisting and precipitous that most drivers prefer to arrive by boat, an easy trip from Lerici (**€€** *tel: 0187 967 676. Five return trips daily*). Portovenere clings to

ⓘ Museo Geopaleontologico
€ *Castello, Lerici; tel: 0187 967 346; www. museocastello.lerici.sp.it (Italian). Open mid-Mar–Jun & Sept–mid-Oct Tue–Sun & hols 1030–1300, 1430–1800; Jul–Aug Tue–Sun 1030–1230, 1830–2400; late Oct–mid-Mar Tue–Thur 1030–1230, Sat–Sun & hols 1030–1230, 1430–1730.*

ⓘ Corsorzio Marittimo Turistico *V. Don Minzoni 13, La Spezia; tel: 0187 732 987; fax: 0187 30 336; www. navigazionegolfodeipoeti.it. A consortium of 16 boat owners provide transport from La Spezia, Lerici and Portovenere to the towns of the Cinque Terre, Portofino and other destinations.*

a steep cliff, at the end of a peninsula, with islands set just off its shore. Tall, narrow houses in candy colours line the waterfront, and cafés sprawl along the quay below them. Two churches, **San Pietro**, with 4th-century origins, and **San Lorenzo** (*both open daily 0700–1800*) are worth visiting, as is the **castle**. The rocky point at the end of town is one of the best places in Italy to watch the sun set.

Boats from Portovenere connect to all the villages of the Cinque Terre, as well, a good alternative for visiting these and viewing them from the sea (€€ *tel: 0187 967 676. Six return trips daily*).

Accommodation and food in the Gulf of Poets

Punto Pizza € *Largo Marconi 6, Lerici; tel: 0187 967 269.* Good selection of bruschetta, seafood salads and wood-oven pizzas.

Staggering Pub € *Pza Caesar Battisti 14, Lerici; tel: 0187 967 539.* Serves good sandwiches.

Il Brigantino €€ *Pza Caesar Battisti 12, Lerici; tel/fax: 0187 969 012. Open Thur–Tue.* Good *frito misto del mare*.

Hotel Al Nido €€ *V. Fiascherino 75, Lerici; tel: 0187 969 263; fax: 0187 964 617; www.hotelnido.com.* The hotel has recently renovated rooms and a private beach.

Hotel Byron €€–€€€ *V. Biaggini 19, Lerici; tel: 0187 967 104; fax: 0187 967 409; www.byronhotel.com.* On the water, an easy walk to the marina and town centre.

LA SPEZIA

ⓘ *Vle Mazzini 45; tel: 0187 770 900; fax: 0187 770 908; www.aptcinqueterre.sp.it*

ⓘ Museo Tecnico Navale € *Tel: 0187 784 693; www. marina.difesa.it. Open Mon–Sat 0800–1845, Sun 0800–1300.*

Museo Amedeo Lia €€
V. Prione 234, tel: 0187 731 100; fax: 0187 731 408; www.castagna.it/mal. Open Tue–Sun 1000–1800.

When it seems as though everyone on the Ligurian Coast is either on holiday or catering to those that are, stop in work-a-day La Spezia for a reality check. It's also a good place to shop for practical items that beach-side boutiques don't have, or for provisions for a day's walking in the nearby Cinque Terre. The daily market is large and colourful, with cheeses, cured meats, breads and fruit for picnics. This is the jumping-off point for the Cinque Terre, with almost-hourly trains and lodgings when the five towns are overflowing in the summer.

La Spezia's importance and prosperity is based on the vast naval complex there, and maritime enthusiasts should visit the **Museo Tecnico Navale** to see ship models and exhibits on World War I.

Museo Amedeo Lia, in a converted convent, is a remarkable private collection recently donated to the city. Among its treasures are portraits by Titian and Bellini, bronzes by Giambologna and Ammannati and the star of the show, Benedetto da Maiano's 15th-century polychrome terracotta, *Addolorata*.

Accommodation and food in La Spezia

Firenze e Continentale €€ *V. Paleocapa 7; tel: 0187 713 210; fax: 0187 714 930; www.hotelfirenzecontinentale.it.* Spacious air-conditioned rooms with Carrara marble floors; parking available.

Paradiso €€ *V. Garibaldi, Portovenere 34–40 (about 13km south of La Spezia); tel: 0187 790 612; fax: 0187 792 582; www.hotelportovenere.it.* Family-owned *pensione* with restaurant €–€€.

Taverna del Corsaro €€–€€€ *Calata Doria 102, Portovenere (about 13km south of La Spezia); tel: 0187 790 622; fax: 0187 766 056. Open Feb–mid-Jun & early Aug–Oct Tue–Sun.* Housed in a converted 12th-century fort, the restaurant specialises in seafood.

Parodi €€€ *Vle Amendola 212; tel: 0187 715 777.* Booking is essential at this cutting-edge restaurant, where food is artfully presented. Look for star-shaped ravioli, for example.

VIAREGGIO AND THE BEACH TOWNS

Vle Carducci 10; tel: 0584 962 233.

TIC Forte dei Marmi *Tel: 0584 786 322. Open Mon–Sat 0900–1230.*

Warning: Red flags on the beach mean stay out of the water – even to wade – because of dangerous surf or undertow, which erodes sand from under your feet as you stand.

Lake tour boats € leave the landing in front of Villa Puccini in Torre de Lago; *tel: 0584 350 252.*

For admirers of Art Nouveau architecture and décor, **Viareggio** is a must-see. When fire destroyed the entire town in 1917, it was rebuilt in the latest mode, its buildings designed by none other than the father of Liberty style (as Italians call Art Nouveau), Galileo Chini, one of the founders of the style. Today these buildings still line the promenade: **Gran Caffè Margherita** and **Bagna Balina** are the icons, but in all 48 villas, hotels and public buildings are listed in that style, including the **Hotel Plaza e de Russie** (*see Accommodation*), the best in this part of Italy, but book early for a room.

As you continue north along the coast to **Forte dei Marmi**, through the string of beach towns, you will see other examples. Each of these towns has a somewhat different character, but each revolves around the wide golden beaches that stretch for many kilometres. Umbrellas and canopies are so thick on these that passers-by cannot see the sea. A spot of sand is expensive and the hotels have reserved the spots near the water for their guests. In July and August, it is difficult to get a space at all, and almost impossible to get one within sight of the sea. North of Forte dei Marmi, however, is one of the few good stretches of free beach. Forte dei Marmi is best known for shopping; designer shops and boutiques line the streets.

Villa Museo
Giacomo Puccini €
Tel: 0584 341 445;
www.giacomopuccini.it.
Open Apr–May Tue–Sun
1000–1230, 1500–1800;
Jun–Oct Tue–Sun
1000–1230, 1500–1830;
Dec–Mar Tue–Sun
1000–1230, 1430–1730.
The great composer
Puccini lived here.

Accommodation and food in Viareggio and the Beach Towns

In Forte dei Marmi, restaurant prices reflect the designer-shopping clientele. Few have posted menus, so ask to see one before taking a table. Check your bill carefully for 'mistakes'.

Ristorante Freddy €€ *Pza Garibaldi 2, Forte dei Marmi; tel: 0584 80 862.* One of the few restaurants in town that bothers with a menu; excellent seafood.

Hotel Il Negresco €€€ *Lungomare Italico 82, Forte dei Marmi; tel: 0584 78 820; fax: 0584 787 535; www.hotelilnegresco.com.* A beautifully maintained beachfront hotel with a garden-enclosed swimming pool and excellent restaurant. Well-appointed rooms have balconies overlooking the promenade and sea.

Plaza e de Russie €€€ *Pza d'Azeglio 1, Viareggio; tel: 0584 44 449; fax: 0584 44 031; www.plazaederussie.com.* Elegant and historic hotel on the promenade, with fine dining at its La Terrazza **€€€** restaurant.

Suggested tour

Below
Boat on a street at the
waterfront, Portovenere

Total distance: 90km with or without detours to La Spezia.

Time: 2 hours' driving. Allow 2 days in order to spend a day exploring the Cinque Terre. Those with limited time could use the A12 autostrada from Pisa to Carrara to save time.

Links: Pisa, the starting point for this route, is the western terminus of the Florence (Firenze) to Pisa route (*see page 252*). La Spezia, the end of this route and a convenient spot in which to drop your car, is the beginning of the northern Riviera di Levante route (*see page 268*).

Route: Leave Pisa ❶, heading north on the coastal S1 highway (also known as the Via Aurelia), perhaps stopping at **Torre del Lago Puccini** and then continuing north via **VIAREGGIO** ❷ to **Pietrasanta** (*see Detour 1 opposite*), **CARRARA** ❸, **Sarzana** and **LA SPEZIA** ❹ (*see Detour 2 opposite*). It's best to leave your car at La Spezia and catch a boat for the Gulf of Poets towns or a train for the five **CINQUE TERRE** towns ❺; once in **Portovenere**, you can also take a boat for any of the five towns. There's a winding road to Portovenere; and a worse one into Cinque Terre, rough, frequently closed and inconvenient to the towns below.

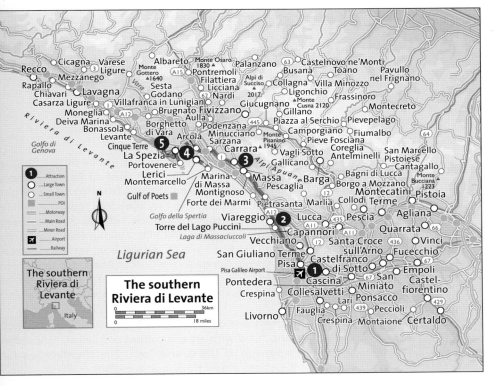

Detour 1: Instead of leaving **Viareggio** on the S1, follow the coastal promenade to see the elegant villas and hotels that line the beachfront as far as **Forte dei Marmi**, where a right turn signposted 'Serravezza' will take you back to the S1.

Detour 2: From Carrara, follow Viale XX Settembre to **Marina di Carrara**. Turn right at the junction, in front of the statue of a man carrying a slab of marble. Follow the coastal road to **Ameglia**, turning left at the signpost for **Montemarcello**. Follow the scenic wooded road through pretty Montemarcello and other cliff-top towns to **Lerici**, continuing on along the Gulf of Poets to La Spezia.

Also worth exploring

The mountains east of **Pietrasanta** and **Massa**, known as the **Alpi Apuane**, are part of a high natural region. A very scenic, although winding and often precipitous, route winds through these, heading west from the S1 at **Querceta**. The unnumbered road passes through **Seravezza**, to **Ami**, where it intersects with another unnumbered road heading west again into **Massa**. Here it rejoins the main route at the S1.

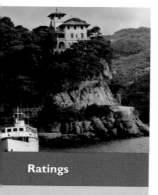

The northern Riviera di Levante

Ratings

Villages	●●●●●
Architecture	●●●● ○
Beaches	●●●● ○
Scenery	●●●● ○
Castles	●●● ○○
Geology	●●● ○○
Historical sights	●●● ○○
Walking	●●● ○○

After the rugged perpendicular landscapes of the Cinque Terre, the Gulf of Tigullio and Gulf of Paradise seem almost benign. Candy-coloured villages circle coves of bright blue water, small boats bob in tiny harbours, and the whole area has an air of prosperous seaside retreat. Behind these towns and villages rise green-clad hills, making them especially attractive viewed from the sea. A regular boat service connects the entire coast, from Genoa to the Gulf of Poets, but to explore the winding roads that connect them is part of the attraction, as are the views from the headlands that rise between and behind them.

At the northern end of the route is the sprawling port city of Genoa, historic, filled with art and culture and largely ignored in the modern version of the Grand Tour. The city deserves far more attention than it gets from most travellers.

CAMOGLI

ⓘ *V. XX Settembre 33; tel: 0185 771 066; fax: 0185 773 504; www.camogli.it (Italian). Open May–Sept Mon–Sat 0900–1230, 1530–1900, Sun & hols 0900–1230; Oct–Apr Sat–Sun 0900–1230, 1500–1830.*

🏛 **Museo Marinaro** *V. Gio Bono Ferrari 41; tel: 0185 771 570. Open Mon & Thur–Fri 0900–1200, Wed & Sat–Sun 0900–1200, 1500–1800. Free.*

Unlike some of its dandified neighbours, Camogli remains what it always was, a fishing town. Its beach and fishing port are backed with unusually tall buildings, all in a full palette of colours. An archway leads to the small working fishing port. Boats leave from here to tour San Fruttuoso. The town's fishing and marine heritage is explored in the good maritime museum, **Museo Marinaro**, that also has a reconstruction of an Iron Age settlement excavated nearby. Be sure to see the giant skillets used at the spring sardine festival, when huge pans of sardines are cooked and served free. The **basilica** is awash with gold inside, in votive offering from safely returned local seafarers.

Accommodation and food in Camogli

Bar Porticciolo € *V. al Porto 11; tel: 0185 771 629.* Under the arch, its terrace tables overlook the colourful little fishing harbour. Good sandwiches and seafood salads.

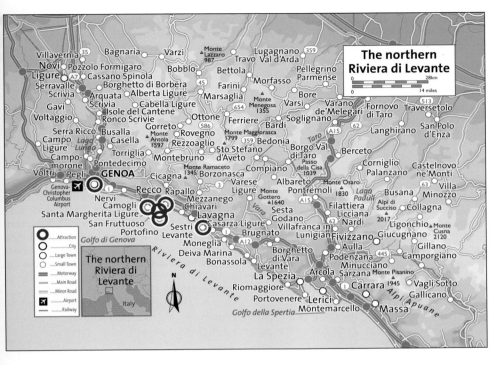

Albergo La Camogliese €€€ *V. Garibaldi 55; tel: 0185 771 402; fax: 0185 744 024; www.lacamogliese.it.* Attractive rooms overlook the beach in the town centre; seafood is happily paired with pasta in the restaurant.

Cenobio dei Dogi €€€ *V. Cuneo 34; tel: 0185 7241; fax: 0185 772 796; email: reception@cenobio.it; www.cenobio.it.* A palazzo originally built for Genoa's doges, this large hotel has rooms with balconies for outstanding water views.

GENOA

ⓘ APT *V. Garibaldi; tel: 010 557 2903 or 010 557 2751; www.genova-turismo.it. Open daily 0900–1300, 1430–1830.*

Also at Stazione Principe, the city's main railway station, west of the port area; *tel: 010 246 2633.*

Once a great naval power equal to Venice, Genoa remains a major port. And alongside a proud history that includes native son Christopher Columbus comes the somewhat unsavoury reputation of 'sailor towns'. Don't be put off by that; Genoa is a smart city of striking architecture and great culture. The **San Felice Opera House** is among Italy's finest, a new state-of-the art venue with flawless acoustics and approachable prices.

Stroll down Via XX Settembre and adjacent streets to see the outstanding Art Nouveau façades or along Via Balbi or Via Garibaldi to

P Parking is tight in this city of narrow lanes. Try Piazza Matteotti or Piazza Piccapietra (both just off the Piazza Ferrarri), or Via Turati just south of the Aquarium.

2 Frequent boat excursions, *tel: 010 2411*, leave from Genoa's docks to Portofino, Portovenere, the Cinque Terre and other towns described in this and the previous chapter. Especially in high tourist seasons, it's worth considering this form of transport over driving.

G **Galleria Nazionale di Palazzo Spinola**
€ *Pza Pellicceria 1; tel: 010 270 5300; www.palazzospinola.it. Open Tue–Sat 0830–1930, Sun 1330–1930.*

Museo di Palazzo Reale
€ *V. Balbi 10; tel: 010 271 0236; www.palazzorealegenova.it. Open Tue–Wed 0900–1330, Thur–Sun 0900–1900.*

Acquario €€€ *Ponte Spinola; tel: 010 234 5678; www.acquariodigenova.it. Open Mar–Jun & Sept–Oct Mon–Fri 0900–1930, Sat–Sun & hols 0845–2030; Jul–Aug daily 0830–2200; rest of year daily with varying hours.*

Cattedrale di San Lorenzo € *V. San Lorenzo; tel: 010 311 269. Open daily 0900–1200, 1500–1800.*

admire some of the palazzi of noble families. Two of these, **Galleria Nazionale di Palazzo Spinola** and **Palazzo Reale**, are open to tour the eye-boggling interiors of marble work, *trompe l'œil* decoration, crystal, mosaic floors and paintings. The Spinola Palace is in a maze of narrow streets known as the Sailors' Quarter, interesting to wander (but by daylight only, please – not all the city's reputation is unwarranted).

The top attraction in the port area must be the city's **Aquarium (Acquario)**, with widely admired collections of both native and unusual sea mammals and fish.

Of the city's many richly endowed churches, the most important is the **Cattedrale di San Lorenzo**, not far from the port. The striped marble of the arches in the nave reflect the striped façade; from the centre of the nave you can see the rose window and the excellent stone carvings over the largest of the side chapels. Dedicated to St John the Baptist, it was built to hold his remains, in the 13th-century carved ark at its centre. The saint's ashes, along with a bowl reputed to be the Holy Grail and the platter on which the saint's head was served up to Salome, are now in the **Museo del Tesoro della Cattedrale (€€** *Guided tours only, Mon–Sat 0900–1200, 1500–1800*), and more works of art from the church are in the **Museo Diocesano (€€** *Open Tue & Sat 1000–1300, 1500–1900, Wed–Fri & Sun 1500–1900*). Just up the hill, in the Jesuit church of **Sant'Ambrose**, is a theatrical painting by Rubens, just right for the exuberant High-Baroque interior of the church.

Accommodation and food in Genoa

For late night food, head for Piazza delle Erbe, near the duomo, where students gather at open-air bars and eateries until all hours.

Agnello d'Oro € *Vico delle Monchette 6; tel: 010 246 2084; fax: 010 246 2327; www.hotelagnellodoro.it.* Simple, friendly *pensione*, some rooms retaining touches of the building's 16th-century origins. Covered parking garage.

Da Genio € *Salita San Leonardo 61r (in the Carruggi area); tel: 010 588 463. Open Sept–Jul Mon–Sat.* Try *trenette al pesto* for a taste of the city's famous basil and pine nut sauce.

City Hotel €€€ *V. San Sebastiano 6; tel: 010 584 707; fax: 010 586 301; www.bwcityhotel-ge.it.* Perfectly located only a few steps from the duomo, opera house and shopping streets, but quiet and with parking.

PORTOFINO

V. Roma 35; tel: 0185 269 024; www. turismoinliguria.it. Open summer daily 1030–1330, 1430–1930; winter Tue–Sun 1030–1330, 1400–1630.

You can also use Santa Margherita's larger tourist office (*see page 266*) for Portofino when its own office is closed.

Castello di San Giorgio € *Tel: 0185 267 101. Open Apr–Sept Wed–Mon 1000–1800; Oct–Mar Wed–Mon 1000–1700.*

Entered via a highly scenic road from nearby Santa Margherita Ligure, Portofino lies below in such a studiedly perfect arrangement that it seems almost like a stage set. It fairly screams 'money' with its little round harbour full of classy pleasure yachts, pricey boutiques and well-tanned starlets. You'll have to park your four-wheeled yacht out of town (no room, and besides, it would spoil the view) and walk in. An alternative to this – and to the hourly parking fee – is to arrive by one of the boats that ply the area regularly.

While such a smashing setting doesn't really need attractions, Portofino provides them. First, head up to the patterned-stone terrace above for the best view of the harbour and surrounding painted houses – just like the postcards. Beyond the little church of San Giorgio is **Castello di San Giorgio**, originating from the 1500s. **Parco di Portofino** protects the wooded hillsides, the well-marked walking trails and the marine life of the peninsula. It's about a 2-hour walk through the park to **San Fruttuoso Abbey** (*see page 268*).

Accommodation and food in Portofino

There are far better places in the area to stay and to dine than crowded, pricey Portofino. But if you're hoping to spot a celeb or two when the sailing day is over, the cafés and restaurants here are the place.

Eden Hotel €€–€€€ *V. Vico Dritto 18; tel: 0185 269 091; fax: 0185 269 047; www. hoteledenportofino.com.* Bland, functional small hotel that's the least exorbitant option in town, and very close to the town's chic central square. There is a restaurant, too.

Ristorante Puny €€€ *Pza Martiri dell'Olivetta; tel: 0185 269 037. Open Wed–Fri.* Expect to wait a while for a table but to enjoy good pesto and seafood dishes.

Right
Villas near Portofino

Rapallo

ⓘ *Lungomare V. Veneto 7; tel: 0185 230 346; fax: 0185 63 051. Open Mon–Sat 0930–1230, 1500–1930, Sun & hols 0930–1230, 1630–1930.*

ⓜ **Museo Gaffoglio €** *Convento delle Clarisse, Pza Libia; tel: 0185 234 497. Open Tue–Wed & Fri–Sat 1500–1830, Thur 1000–1200.*

Museo del Merletto € *Villa Tigullio; tel: 0185 63 305. Open Oct–Aug Tue–Wed & Fri–Sat 1500–1800, Thur 1000–1130.*

Funivia € *Pza Solari; tel: 0185 52 341. Open daily 0900–1230, 1400–1800. Free parking.*

At first glance, you could mistake Rapallo's long, curving seafront **promenade**, backed by the gleaming white façades of balconied belle époque hotels, for one of its compatriots on the French Riviera. The little **castle** sitting on its rock, waves lapping at three sides, completes a very pretty picture, and there are plenty of terrace cafés near the castle from which to admire it.

The excellent **Museo Gaffoglio** exhibits a collection of rare jewellery, porcelain, enamels (including Fabergé eggs) and ivory carvings that range from a 15th-century Venetian box to sailors' scrimshaw. Rapallo was a major lacemaking town, and the **Museo del Merletto** shows more than 1,400 local and foreign examples of handmade lace dating back to the 1500s, along with lace patterns and drawings. Fine laces of silver and gold, christening dresses and a collection of high fashion clothing are displayed in the historic Villa Tigullio, set in **Parco Casale**, which is itself filled with rare plants and trees.

Views out over the Gulf of Paradise are the reward for a 7-minute ride on the **funivia**. At the top is the **Santuario Basilica di Montallegro**. From there, walkers have access to a good network of scenic trails, including one back down to the town centre.

Accommodation and food in Rapallo

Albergo Italia e Lido €€ *Lungomare Castello 1; tel: 0185 50 492; fax: 0185 504 494; www.italiaelido.com.* Unbeatable location facing the castle and the sea. Its restaurant **Grand Italia €** serves crispy *frito misto* and veal with asparagus.

Ristorante Monique €€ *Lungomare V. Veneto 5; tel: 0815 50 541; www.ristorantedamonique.com.* Offers a view of the castle and specialises in local seafood.

Riviera €€–€€€ *Pza IV Novembre 2; tel: 0185 50 248; fax: 0185 65 668; www.hotelrivierarapallo.com.* Many rooms have balconies, and there is parking and a restaurant.

Santa Margherita Ligure

ⓘ *V. XXV Apre 2B; tel: 0185 287 485; www.apttigullio.liguria.it. Open Mon–Sat 0900–1230, 1530–1830, Sun 0930–1230.*

Santa Margherita is an absolute gem of a town, more down-to-earth than chic next-door neighbour Portofino and yet possessing a rather beautiful beach and a rather genuine Italian character. This isn't the most historic village in Italy, but the beach is fine, a stroll uphill into the historic district is rewarding, and the village square is – as usual – the place for a coffee. **Parco di Villa Durazzo** (*open Apr–Sept daily 0900–1900; Oct–Mar daily 0900–1700*) is a typically fine Ligurian green space with English-style gardens and views of the sea; the villa (*open* *summer Tue–Sun 0900–1800; winter shorter hours*) is worth a look inside for its stucco work, Murano glass and tapestries.

Accommodation and food in Santa Margherita Ligure

Fasce €–€€ *V. Luigi Bozzo 3; tel: 0185 286 435; fax: 0185 283 580; www.hotelfasce.it.* Friendly, family-run hotel with lush courtyard. Spacious rooms, a car park and free bikes. Its restaurant € is good, too.

Il Faro €€ *V. Maragliano; tel: 0185 286 867. Open Wed–Mon.* Family-run restaurant with excellent seafood (try grilled fish with pesto).

SESTRI LEVANTE

Pza Sant'Antonio 10; tel: 0185 457 011; fax: 0185 459 575. Open Mon–Sat 0930–1230, 1500–1930, Sun 0930–1230, 1500–1630.

Galleria Rizzi € *V. Cappuccini 8; tel: 0185 41 300. Open Apr–Oct Sun 1000–1300; May–Aug Wed 1600–1900; late Jun–early Sept Fri–Sat 2130–2330; Nov–Mar by appointment.*

Coming from La Spezia, the S1 coastal highway plunges inland through rugged mountains bypassing the Cinque Terre, before rejoining the coast at Sestri Levante. Sestri is a decent-sized resort town, occupying a lovely position with a jutting point of land to one side and a long, sweeping bay to the other. Once upon a time it was, as so many other villages on this stretch of coast were, a strategic post. Later it became a fishing town.

Today it's a garden-filled resort town, but large enough to have a life of its own. It's a place to savour some of the finest hotels and restaurants on the entire coast, and an excellent option for lodging while visiting the Cinque Terre (*see page 255*). Access to the towns by train is as good as from La Spezia.

Sestri Levante's waterfront Piazza Matteotti and promenade are lined with colourful buildings whose elegant architectural detail is painted in *trompe l'œil*, and two of its outstanding buildings are the Suite Hotel Nettuno and Grand Hotel Villa Balbi, which face each other across Viale Rimembranza. At the piazza is the Baroque Santa Maria di Nazareth, whose primary treasure is a 12th-century crucifix. Those interested in art should visit the waterfront **Galleria Rizzi** containing works by Tiepolo, Rubens and Raphael.

The town ends in a steep, wooded, rock-bound promontory crowned by a castle-palazzo that is another hotel. Below is the little **Baiai del Silenzio** almost completely encircled by a free beach backed by pink and yellow houses, a former convent and church punctuating its point.

Right
The harbour, Portofino

Accommodation and food in Sestri Levante

Marina € *V. Fascie 100; tel/fax: 0185 487 332; email: marinahotel@ marinahotel.it. Open Mar–Dec.* Medium-sized *pensione* of 17 rooms; the least expensive choice in town.

Il Brigantino €–€€ *V. Rimembranza 38; tel: 0185 458 265. Open Tue–Sun.* Local fish *en brochette*, succulent grilled lamb steaks or creamy salmon with *trofie*, the local pasta speciality, are served by a particularly genial staff.

Vis à Vis €€€ *V. della Chiusa 28; tel: 0185 42 661; fax: 0185 480 853; www.hotelvisavis.com.* One of Italy's finest hotels, crowning the hilltop with views into the postcard-perfect Bay of Silence, the Vis à Vis descends in stunning layers from its swimming pool set in an olive grove, past terraced cafés to balconied guest rooms. Its **Restaurant Olympia** €€€ is superb, with service to match the creative menu. If you can afford only one magnificent meal on your trip, savour it here.

Suggested tour

Total distance: 125km.

Time: 2–3 hours' driving. Allow 1–2 days with or without detour. Those with limited time can save a little by using the A12 toll road for the first 45km of this route, from just outside La Spezia to Sestri Levante. Few towns of note are skirted by this short cut, though the slower S1 road cuts through coastal foothills and is more scenic if you've the time.

Links: La Spezia, the starting point for this route, is part of the southern Riviera di Levante route (*see page 260*). Genoa, the end point, is the beginning of the Genoa to the French border route (*see page 278*). Both are easily reached by toll roads and trains.

Route: Leave La Spezia ❶, heading north on the S1 (signs and maps will also indicate it as the Via Aurelia), which slices through coastal mountains before rejoining and then hugging the coast through **SESTRI LEVANTE** ❷ on its eventual way to **RAPALLO** ❸, 75km away. Swing south 9km on the S227 (also known as the Strada Panoramica) to visit **SANTA MARGHERITA LIGURE** ❹ and **PORTOFINO** ❺ before backtracking to the coastal S1 via the winding road to San Lorenzo della Costa and then continuing the remaining slow 30km to **GENOA** (Genova) ❻.

Detour: At Portofino, either catch a summertime ferry boat (*tel: 0185 284 670*) or don your walking shoes and hike the 5km through beautiful groves of protected forest to **San Fruttuoso Abbey**, a splendid grey stone structure on the sea with a pleasant beach at its foot. The abbey, founded by Benedictine monks, knew hard times but

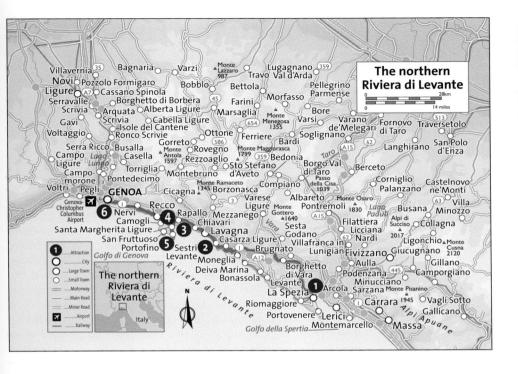

has been restored by locals and opens to the public (*Dec–Oct Tue–Sun*). You can also catch a ferry (*tel: 0185 772 091*) to the abbey's tiny village of San Fruttuoso from **CAMOGLI** as well.

Also worth exploring

The inland drive or train ride from La Spezia to Parma is hardly ever done by anyone but locals, which makes it all the more appealing to the back-road adventurer – be aware that there are few architectural or historical sights along this way, only remote towns perched at angles on the hills and streams. Both the A15 toll road and the slower S62 make this 100km trip a snap; regular trains take a slightly different, mostly parallel route. The first few kilometres are steep as one climbs from sea level into mountains; almost halfway to Parma is **Pontremoli**, useful as a coffee break. More towns follow and then the roads wind back downhill, emerging at little **Fornova di Taro** and its attractive **church**. From here, the land is starkly flat and dull past industry and gigantic fields before reaching the old Etruscan city of **Parma**, one of Italy's greatest dining cities, with an amazing **baptistery**, a **duomo** and plenty of Correggio artwork.

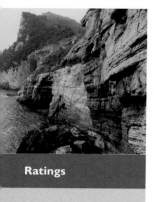

Genoa to the French border: the Riviera di Ponente

Ratings

Beaches	●●●●●
Castles	●●●●●
Geology	●●●●○
Scenery	●●●●○
Architecture	●●●○○
Outdoor activities	●●●○○
Walking	●●●○○
Historical sights	●●○○○

The final long stretch of coast in extreme western Italy, bending from Genoa to the French border, offers very fine scenery, hilltop castles and numerous small fishing towns – mixed in with occasional ugly industrial zones and modern, overbuilt resort areas. As a result, there's really only one choice of route, snug along the coast: worth driving mostly for villages like Noli and Finale Ligure. Once you've pivoted round the shipbuilding business in Savona, you'll be rewarded with yet another long sequence of undiscovered villages. San Remo's a name you might recognise, but continue west and you'll find Italy stubbornly clinging to its character right up to the French border. Ventimiglia finishes off this tour with an unexpected collection of terraced vegetable and flower gardens, Italy's last wave goodbye to travellers headed for Nice and beyond.

ALBENGA

🛈 **TIC** *Pza del Popolo 11; tel: 0182 558 444; fax: 0182 558 740; www.inforiviera.it or www.comune.albenga.sv.it*

🏛 **Museo Navale Romano** € *Pza San Michele 12; tel: 0182 51 215. Open Apr–Sept daily 0930–1230, 1530–1930; Oct–Mar daily 1000–1230, 1430–1800.*

Grotte di Toirano € *Tel: 0182 98 062; www.toiranogrotte.it. Open Jul–Aug daily 0930–1230, 1400–1730; Sept–Jun daily 0930–1230, 1400–1700.*

Quite an old Roman town and no longer on the sea at all, its harbour silted up long ago, board-flat Albenga offers a surprising medieval complex for such a small, nearly forgotten place. From the sea, turn right along the eastern bank of the Centa River to park and find a mini-Pisa of off-kilter towers in the town's central square, Piazza San Michele; an unusual, ten-sided baptistery with an octagonal interior; a cathedral; bell tower; and an amazing number of tall, tilting towers, seven of which are completely intact. Particularly good for history buffs is the **Museo Navale Romano (Marine Museum)**, exploring the town's shipbuilding back to Roman times. **Alassio**, its twin just a few kilometres beyond on the S1, has a better beach and hops with nightlife, well worth the nocturnal jaunt to dance or drink.

Near Albenga, at **Toirano**, are **caves (Grotte di Toirano)** which are not only beautiful, but filled with evidence of prehistoric man – and animals. Huge numbers of bear bones, along with mixed human and bear footprints, have been found here.

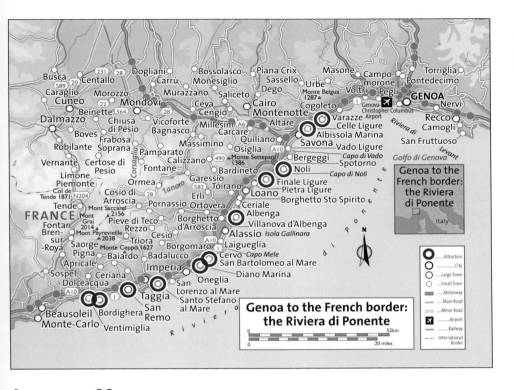

Genoa to the French border: the Riviera di Ponente

ALBISSOLA MARINA

ⓘ *Pza Lam; tel: 019 400 2525; fax: 019 600 5358; www.inforiviera.it*

Ⓜ Casa Museo Giuseppe Mazzotti *€ Vle Matteotti 29; tel: 019 489 872. Open Mon–Sat 0900–1200, 1500–1900.*

Villa Faraggiana *€ V. Salomoni 117; tel: 019 480 622. Open May–Sept Wed–Sun 1500–1900 (last entry 1815).*

Half of one of those 'two-part towns' so common here, Albissola Marina forms the seaside half of its equation. There's the usual collection of boats, beaches and waterside cafés, but also an artistic twist: this town is one of *the* places in northern Italy to buy pottery, owing to a long-established tradition of working the ruddy local clays into pieces of higher-than-functional art. Along with galleries and workshops to visit is the **Casa Museo Giuseppe Mazzotti**. The house is by futurist architect Nicolai Diulgheroff, and it contains a collection of 20th-century ceramic works, from Liberty style to contemporary. Pretty **Villa Faraggiana**, just northeast of the centre in a park, is also worth a look, as are the decorated walkways along the shore.

Accommodation and food in Albissola Marina

Da Mario *€€ Corso Bigliati 70; tel: 019 481 640. Open Oct–Aug Thur–Tue.* Try dishes featuring local fish at this sunny eatery with outdoor seating.

Hotel Garden €€ *Vle Faraggiana 6; tel: 019 485 253; fax: 019 485 255; www.hotelgardenalbissola.com.* Permanent contemporary art exhibits decorate this hotel, which offers exercise facilities, sauna, outdoor pool, Internet access and car park.

BORDIGHERA

ⓘ IAT *V. Vittorio Emanuele 172–174; tel: 0184 262 322; fax: 0184 264 455; www.rivieradeifiori.org*

🏛 Museo Bicknell € *Pza Bicknell 3; tel: 0184 263 601. Open Mon–Fri 0900–1300, 1500–1800.*

🛒 Market day: Thur.

Hemmed in by cliffs and bedecked with flowers and palm trees, Bordighera makes a fine, unhurried stopping point. The place was nothing more than a sailors' town for centuries, until the English discovered its quiet charms and began building a winter resort by word of mouth. The upper town of fortifications and warrens drops to a flat beachside portion with an entirely different character. The **Museo Bicknell**, a museum of natural history and archaeological exhibits, is the chief sight of interest. It's worth noting that Bordighera supplies the Vatican with its palm fronds each Palm Sunday, a plum commission it won more than four centuries ago, when a quick-thinking local sailor averted a disaster in St Peter's Square.

Accommodation and food in Bordighera

Hotel della Punta €€ *V. San Ampelio 27; tel: 0184 262 555; fax: 0184 268 925; www.hoteldellapunta.it.* Attractive, well-located hotel on the shore that can arrange bus tours to the French Riviera, hikes and other activities.

Piemontese €€ *V. Roseto 8; tel: 0184 261 651. Open dinner Wed–Mon.* An unexpected surprise in a seaside town: dishes typical of Italy's Piedmont region such as risotto with Barolo wine, or fondue, plus local fish dishes.

Villa Elisa €€ *V. Romana 70; tel: 0184 261 313; fax: 0184 261 942; www.villaelisa.com.* Another well-appointed villa hotel, this one with a lush garden, pool and sauna.

CERVO

ⓘ IAT *Pza Santa Caterina 21; tel: 0183 408 197; fax: 0183 409 822.*

☾ San Giorgio €€€ *V. Alessandro Volta 19; tel: 0183 400 175. Closed Jan & Nov; no dinner Mon & Tue Oct–Easter.*

🛒 Market day: Thur.

After rounding tough Cape Mele, the coastal S1 road calms down again, passing a number of shallow bays. The Golfo di Diano, one of them, is the beginning of yet another short section of beach resort towns, at whose easternmost end lies exceptionally pretty little Cervo, with a good annual summer classical music festival, and a relatively undisturbed atmosphere. A surprising Baroque church, **San Giovanni** (*tel: 0183 408 095*), tops the small rise which spills houses down to the water. Built by local fishermen, its decoration reflects their gratitude for safe return.

DIANO MARINA

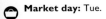 **IAT** *Corso Garibaldi 60; tel: 0183 496 956; fax: 0183 494 365.*

Market day: Tue.

Diano caps the other end of the gulf named after it and is a more self-consciously touristy town than Cervo at the opposite end. It also has a far better beach. Its appearance, different from other towns here, results from rebuilding after an 1887 earthquake levelled it. You can see all the art and altars rescued from the ruined churches now assembled in **Sant'Antonio Abate**. Vineyards dotting the nearby hills deserve exploration and the whites they pour are superb.

Accommodation and food in Diano Marina

Il Caminetto €€ *V. Olanda 1; tel: 0183 494 700; www. ristoranteilcaminetto.it. Closed Nov, Mon (winter).* A trattoria serving typical local specialities.

Gabriella €€–€€€ *V. dei Gerani 9; tel: 0183 403 131; fax: 0183 405 055; www.hotelgabriella.com.* Swim in the heated pool, lounge on the beach, or rest in the garden at this posh *pensione* (*open Jan–Oct*). Parking is available and there's a restaurant.

FINALE LIGURE

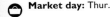 **TIC** *V. Ghiglieri 6; tel: 019 681 6004; www.comunefinaleligure.it. Open Mon & Wed–Thur 0930–1330, Tue & Fri 0930–1330, 1530–1730.*

Market day: Thur.

Pleasant Finale Ligure marks the beginning of yet another scenic little cape, this one known as Caprazoppa. Finale's seaside has one of the better beaches along this stretch of coast, set below rocky cliffs studded with villas and gardens and more, close to the town centre. Behind its tree-lined promenade, narrow streets are filled with cafés, restaurants and shops. The wildly pealing bells of **San Giovanni Battista** summon the faithful through its yellow Baroque exterior into an interior where only a row of plain round columns provide serenity amid the stucco swirls and frills. Accommodation is easy to find here, as is nightlife and good food. A kilometre uphill from the water is an even older, fortified settlement complete with its own crumbling **castle**. This is a good place to stay the night, sampling Ligurian charm and food with just a dash of history.

Accommodation and food in Finale Ligure

Rosita € *V. Mànie 67; tel: 019 602 437; fax: 019 601 762; www.hotelrosita.it.* Small, inexpensive *pensione* with meals on a terrace with splendid views of the water; parking is available.

Ai Torchi €€–€€€ *V. dell'Annunziata 12, Finalborgo; tel: 019 690 531. Open Feb–Jul & Sept–Dec Wed–Mon; Aug daily.* It's advisable to reserve a spot here to sample some of Italy's best pesto a few kilometres outside Finale Ligure.

Punta Est €€€ *V. Aurelia 1; tel: 019 600 611; fax: 019 600 611; www.puntaest.com. Open May–Oct.* Terraced along a garden-draped hillside that drops almost straight to the beach, this villa-turned-hotel sets standards other villas should follow. In summer, the excellent restaurant €€–€€€ moves to the pebbly terrace, under a canopy of trees.

NOLI

ℹ️ *Corso Italia 8; tel: 019 749 9003; fax: 019 749 9300; www. inforivieria.it. Open Mon–Sat 0900–1230, 1500–1830.*

🏛️ **San Paragorio** € *Open Tue–Sun 1000–1200, 1500–1700.*

🛒 **Market day:** Thur.

Drive slowly around beautiful **Cape Noli**, as this round of land protruding into the Mediterranean is more attractive and wilder than most of Liguria – which is saying something. Noli, a little mountain-backed beauty of a town lined with tiny streets, is at its beginning. Take time for a stroll down its amazingly well-preserved main street, **Corso Italia**, imagining, if you can, a grandeur that once rivalled that of port republics like Venice and Genoa. Towers, part of the original loggia, gates and walls remain from those heady medieval days. From the steps of the **duomo**, San Pietro, you can see four of these towers. **San Paragorio Church** rivals many of its better-known cousins for Romanesque splendour and is one of Liguria's best. If you've got the time, hiking the trail to the ruined mountain-top **castle** is an energetic way to spend a few hours. Beyond Noli, the cape road opens up tantalising views of the Mediterranean, then ducks back behind thick trees again.

Accommodation and food in Noli

Bar Torino € *Corso Italia 17.* Serves gigantic bruschetta (try *prosciutto cotto* and Gorgonzola) at amazingly low prices.

Romeo Albergo Ristorante € *V. Colombo 81; tel: 019 748 973; www.albergoromeo.it.* Veal Milanese, fillet of sole and other unadorned typical and tasty dishes. Guest rooms, as well.

Trattoria/Locanda de Massimo € *Pza Militi Ignoto 2; tel: 019 748 5230.* Inexpensive upstairs dining room with simple guest rooms.

Miramare €€ *Corso Italia 2; tel: 019 748 926; fax: 019 748 927; www.hotelmiramarenoli.it.* This 16th-century fortified palazzo with outdoor garden contains 28 rooms, all with sea views.

Lilliput €€€ *Regione Zuglieno 49; tel: 019 748 009. Open Mar–Oct & Dec Tue–Sun.* Award-winning traditional Ligurian cuisine, which serves lunch only at weekends.

SAN REMO

ⓘ *Corso Cavallotti 51; tel: 0184 580 353; fax: 0184 505 611; www. commuedisanremo.it. Open Mon & Wed 0930–1300, 1500–1700, Tue & Thur–Fri 0930–1300.*

ⓟ There's convenient parking at a large garage in the centre of town at Via Asquasciati; this central square is a right turn off the coast road as you enter from the east.

ⓜ **Museo Civico €** *Corso Matteotti 143; tel: 0184 531 942. Open Tue–Sat 0900–1200, 1500–1800.*

Below
Finale Ligure and its beaches

By far the largest true resort on this section of coast, bay-side San Remo is the Italian version of Monte Carlo, at a somewhat more affordable price. The chief attractions are the lush foliage, villa gardens and beach life; a quick walk down the Corso Imperatrice gives a sense of having arrived somewhere important. The famous local **casino** (about half a mile west of the centre via Corso Matteotti) is divided into upmarket and downmarket areas. The downmarket area, limited mostly to coin-gobbling machines, can be played for free in any dress, but the attractive upmarket rooms host games of chance and skill – for well-dressed clientele, at a small admission charge. If you don't fancy a gamble, head uphill for the maze-like **La Pigna** district, which winds in roughly concentric circles through a slightly ragged old quarter of arches and alleys. The most important church in town is **San Siro** on Via Palazzo, with its separate baptistery and oratory, while the nearby **Museo Civico** housed within the **Palazzo Borea d'Olmo** should satisfy history buffs. Equally interesting is the handsomely domed Russian Orthodox church, **Cristo Salvatore**, just beyond the casino at the waterfront Piazza Battisti.

Accommodation and food in San Remo

Casino *Corso Inglese; tel: 0184 5951. Open daily 1430–0300.* It's free to play the casino's slot machines, but there's a cover charge €€ to play the tables.

Antica Trattoria Piccolo Mondo € *V. Piave 7; tel: 0184 509 012. Open Aug–Jun Tue–Sat.* Friendly staff and outstanding local dishes such as octopus stew.

Paradiso €€ *V. Roccasterone 12; tel: 0184 571 211; fax: 0184 578 176; www.paradisohotel.it.* Refined, relaxed hotel where flowers tumble out of boxes and guests enjoy drinks in the garden. Parking in a covered garage, Internet access in rooms and half-board in a convivial restaurant.

ⓘ Early each morning during summer a huge and fragrant flower market dominates the town centre.

ⓘ Market days: Tue, Sat.

Royal €€€ *Corso Imperatrice 80; tel: 0184 5391; fax: 0184 661 445; www.royalhotelsanremo.com.* Lavish hotel in the heart of the action with direct access to both the famed casino and town centre. There's a posh restaurant on the terrace, plus parking, mini-golf, saltwater pool and tennis court.

SANTO STEFANO AL MARE

ⓘ *V. Boselli Arma di Taggia; tel: 0184 43 733.*

ProLoco Santo Stefano al Mare *V. Roma 2; tel: 0184 487 629. Open daily.*

After Imperia, olive groves begin to replace the vineyards and gardens, as things become less frantic and towns further apart. Santo Stefano only jumps to life in summer, when the good local beaches attract holidaymakers. Restaurants here are excellent, perhaps even a cut above the usual high Ligurian standard.

Accommodation and food in Santo Stefano al Mare

La Reserva €€ *V. Roma 51; tel: 0184 484 134. Closed Mon, Sun dinner in Sept–Jul.* Rustic, lovely seaside restaurant.

Lucciola €€€ *Lungomare di Alvertis 69; tel: 0184 484 236; fax: 0184 484 238; www.albergolucciola.com.* Small, family-run hotel of 34 well-appointed rooms and Italian-speaking staff; breakfast is included.

VARAZZE

ⓘ *Corso Matteotti 58; tel: 019 935 043; fax: 019 935 916; www.inforiviera.it*

Celle Ligure *Tel: 019 990 021. Open Mon–Sat 0900–1300, 1530–1800, Sun & hols 1000–1230, 1530–1730.*

ⓘ Market day: Sat.

The first town of real note west of Genoa, Varazze was important long ago as a shipbuilding centre in the pre-Columbian era and was the birthplace of the famously wandering monk Jacopo. Today it's a combination of working docks and beach villas, not bad for a short stop and a bite to eat in one of the good local seafood restaurants. Several interesting churches include a 10th-century ruin and the 12th-century baptistery of **San Vittore** and **Sant'Ambrogio** with a bell tower. The Villa Mirabello houses a set of **museums** (*open Tue–Sat 0930–1230, 1400–1730*) containing local history items and art.

Accommodation and food in Varazze

Hotel Eden €–€€ *V. Villagrande 1; tel: 019 932 888; fax: 019 96 315; www.hoteledenvarazze.it.* Although one of the priciest hotels in town, this is still a bargain, with modern conveniences such as air conditioning, TVs, Internet access points and parking.

Antico Genovese €€€ *Corso Colombo 70; tel: 019 939 388; www.anticogenovese.com.* The Hotel Eden's restaurant, serving local-style foods.

Left
San Remo casino

Ventimiglia

ℹ️ *V. Cavour 61; tel: 0184 351 183; fax: 0184 351 183.*

🅿️ Friday is market day for flower wholesalers in Ventimiglia, but this also mucks up traffic and parking for everyone else; plan carefully to avoid the congestion. There's public parking on either side of the mouth of the Roia River.

Terraced gardens surrounding the town at least hint of Ventimiglia's former glory. The border town is useful mostly as a place to change trains (French and Italian trains mostly operate with different engines). The older portion of town, located just inland from the sea, is definitely the better part of Ventimiglia, with fading palaces lining a main street and a very old **library** of rare books (*V. Garibaldi 10; tel: 0184 351 209. Open Oct–late May Mon & Sat 0930–1330; summer hours vary*).

Suggested tour

Total distance: 155km, with detour 195km.

Time: 3–4 hours' driving. Allow 2 days with or without detour. Those with limited time can take the A10 toll road, shaving substantial time from the stop-and-go of the coastal road. In summer, especially, this is an attractive option although one must often drive several kilometres inland to connect to the A10. Definitely consider at least a short hop on to the toll road to avoid built-up Savona; turn right and head due north from Albissola Marina to find it, getting off about 10km south at Zinola.

Links: Genoa (Genova), the starting point for this route, is the end point of the northern Riviera di Levante route (*see page 268*).

Route: From Genoa (Genova) ❶, drive approximately 10km west on the A10 autostrada, getting off at **Voltri**. Follow the coastal S1, first 17km west to **VARAZZE** ❷ and then through **Celle Ligure** another 8km to **ALBISSOLA MARINA** ❸. Now the road begins to arc southward. Use the autostrada for 10km or so if you wish to skip over bigger **Savona** ❹, then return to the S1 and drive 7km south round lovely Cape Noli to the village of **NOLI** ❺; it's 12km further to **FINALE LIGURE** ❻, another attractive village. From here, continue southwest 20km to **ALBENGA** ❼, then 22km to and round little Capo Mele, which ends at **CERVO** ❽. Continue 8km to **DIANO MARINA** ❾, skirt Imperia, which is hardly worth a look, emerging in a slightly different, rougher landscape on the western side of town. Proceed straight through to **SANTO STEFANO** ❿ (20km beyond), always keeping to the S1, and finish with a delightful 30-km stretch of towns including **SAN REMO** ⓫, **BORDIGHERA** ⓬ and **VENTIMIGLIA** ⓭ before reaching the French border.

Detour: At Ventimiglia, turn right (north) on the SS548 and climb the Nervia Valley towards Camporosso, continuing 8km to **Dolceacqua**, a lovely little medieval place of vineyards, olive groves, a bulky ruined castle and sprawling views. The town's single-arched stone bridge,

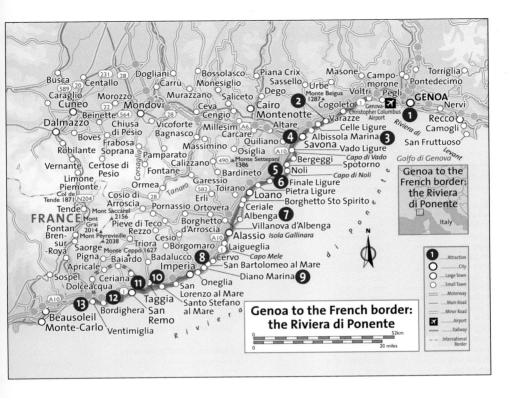

Genoa to the French border:
the Riviera di Ponente

Tip: Note that on signposts, Ventimiglia is abbreviated to 'XXmiglia'.

which gracefully connects the newer town with medieval lanes, is one of the most distinctive in northern Italy. **Gastone** (€ *tel: 0184 206 577*) on Piazza Garibaldi is a good choice for local cuisine. The town might be worth a stay if you enjoy quiet country towns, though the only accommodation hereabouts is in such places as farmhouses and olive-oil mills. Continue north 4km, branching right at Isolabona and then branching again on twisting roads through Apricale to more olive trees and views at **Baiardo**. From Baiardo, **Mount Brignone** can be seen, but not reached directly; descend towards Ceriana and branch right after the bridge to find the mountain. Descend via twisting, unnumbered roads to San Remo to complete the circuit.

Language

Italian shares a common Latin basis with Spanish, Portuguese and French, so a knowledge of any of those will help you recognise words once you become accustomed to the differences in pronunciation. When words fail you, first try the English word, giving it an Italian pronunciation. For example, English words ending in 'ion' will almost always be the same, ending in 'ion-e'. You will be surprised at how often English, spoken slowly and with a smile, can be understood by Italians who speak no English. Be attentive to the lilt and cadence of people talking around you, and it will help you turn everyday English words into functional Italian.

Basics
yes/no	si/no
thank you	grazie
please	per favore
you're welcome	prego
excuse me	scusi
I'm sorry	mi dispiace
I would like	vorrei
I don't understand	non capisco
I don't like that	non mi piace
I would prefer	preferisco
OK	va bene
big/little	grande/piccolo
hot/cold	caldo/freddo
open/closed	aperto/chiuso
right/left	destra/sinistra
good/bad	buono/cattivo
fast/slow	presto/lento
much/little	molto/poco
expensive/cheap	caro/economico
go away!	va via!
at what time?	a che ora?
do you speak English?	parla Inglese?
where is...?	dove...? (pronounced 'doh-veh')

Driving
car	la macchina
petrol station	il distributore
full	pieno
petrol/diesel	la benzina/il gasolio
unleaded	senza piombo
air pressure	la pressione
oil	l'olio
water	l'acqua
breakdown	il guasto
accident	l'incidente
does not work	non funziona
motor	il motore
ignition	l'accensione

Signs and directions
attenzione	watch out
deviazione	detour
divieto di accesso/ senso vietato	no entry
divieto di sosta/ sosta vietata	no parking
gira a destra/sinistra	turn right/left
incrocio	crossroads
limite di velocità	speed limit
parcheggio	parking
pericolo	danger
pronto soccorso	first aid
rallentare	slow down
sempre diritto	straight ahead
senso unico	one-way street
strada chiusa	road closed
strada senza uscita	dead-end, cul-de-sac
tenere la destra	keep right
traffico limitato	restricted access
uscita veicoli	exit
vietato fumare	no smoking
vietato il sorpasso	no overtaking (passing)
vietato il transito	no through traffic
zona rimorchio	tow-away zone

Strong language
sparisci	disappear
smettila	stop it
lasciami in pace	leave me alone

Numbers and measures
1	uno	50	cinquanta
2	due	60	sessanta
3	tre	70	settanta
4	quattro	80	ottanta
5	cinque	90	novanta
6	sei	100	cento
7	sette	101	centuno
8	otto	110	centodieci
9	nove	200	duecento
10	dieci	500	cinquecento
11	undici	1,000	mille
12	dodici	5,000	cinquemila
13	tredici	10,000	diecimila
14	quattordici	50,000	cinquanta mila
15	quindici	1,000,000	un milione
16	sedici	2,000,000	due milione
17	diciassette		
18	diciotto	$1/2$	un mezzo
19	diciannove	$1/4$	un quarto
20	venti	$1/3$	un terzo
21	ventuno	100gm	un etto
22	ventidue	1kg	un chilo
30	trenta	1 litre	un litro
40	quaranta		

Index

Acknowledgements

Project management: Cambridge Publishing Management Limited
Project editor: Tom Lee
Series design: Fox Design
Cover design: Liz Lyons Design
Layout: Cambridge Publishing Management Limited
Repro and image setting: PDQ Digital Media Solutions Limited/Cambridge Publishing Management Limited

Thomas Cook Publishing wish to thank **Barbara Radcliffe Rogers** and **Stillman Rogers,** to whom the copyright belongs, for the photographs in this book (except for the following images):

Dreamstime.com (pages 1A & 60 Robert Caucino, pages 1B & 177 Dan Breckwoldt, page 18 Peter Wey, page 67 Fabio Omes, page 129 Liane Matrisch, page 141 Daniel Prudek, page 203 Martin Zima); **John Heseltine** (pages 40, 44, 46, 49, 226, 237, 270, 276); **Pictures Colour Library** (page 45); **Neil Setchfield** (pages 234, 239, 246, 257); **Edith Summerhayes** (page 241); **World Pictures** (pages 39, 119, 182, 196).

Feedback form

We're committed to providing the very best up-to-date information in our travel guides and constantly strive to make them as useful as they can be. You can help us to improve future editions by letting us have your feedback. Just take a few minutes to complete and return this form to us.

When did you buy this book? ....

....

Where did you buy it? (Please give town/city and, if possible, name of retailer)

....

....

When did you/do you intend to travel to Northern Italy & Italian Lakes?............................

....

For how long (approx.)? ....

How many people in your party? ....

Which cities, towns and resorts did you/do you intend mainly to visit?

....

....

....

....

Did you/will you:

❏ Make all your travel arrangements independently?

❏ Travel on a fly-drive package?

Please give brief details: ....

....

Did you/do you intend to use this book:

❏ For planning your trip?   ❏ Both?

❏ During the trip itself?

Did you/do you intend also to purchase any of the following travel publications for your trip?

A road map/atlas (please specify) ....

Other guidebooks (please specify) ....

....

Have you used any other Thomas Cook guidebooks in the past? If so, which?

....

....

Please rate the following features of *driving guides Northern Italy & Italian Lakes* for their value to you (Circle VU for 'very useful', U for 'useful', NU for 'little or no use'):

The Travel facts section on pages 12–21	VU	U	NU
The Driver's guide section on pages 22–7	VU	U	NU
The touring itineraries on pages 38–9	VU	U	NU
The recommended driving routes throughout the book	VU	U	NU
Information on towns and cities, etc	VU	U	NU
The maps of towns and cities, etc	VU	U	NU

Please use this space to tell us about any features that in your opinion could be changed, improved or added in future editions of the book, or any other comments you would like to make concerning the book:

....

....

....

....

....

....

....

....

Your age category: ❏ 21–30   ❏ 31–40   ❏ 41–50   ❏ over 50

Your name: Mr/Mrs/Miss/Ms ....

(First name or initials) ....

(Last name) ....

Your full address: (Please include postal or zip code)

....

....

....

....

....

Your daytime telephone number: ....

Please detach this page and send it to: driving guides Series Editor, Thomas Cook Publishing, PO Box 227, The Thomas Cook Business Park, 9 Coningsby Road, Peterborough PE3 8SB.

Alternatively, you can email us at: *books@thomascook.com*